D1235420

ZUMA

JEREMY GORDIN

ZUMA

A Biography

SECOND EDITION

JONATHAN BALL PUBLISHERS
JOHANNESBURG & CAPE TOWN

© Jeremy Gordin, 2008
© Photographic copyright holders for the pictures in the photo section
are credited with each caption.

This edition first published in trade paperback in 2008 by
JONATHAN BALL PUBLISHERS (PTY) LTD
PO Box 33977
Jeppestown 2043

Reprinted 2009
This revised and updated edition published in 2010

Front cover and back cover images – Gallo Images, Johannesburg

ISBN 978-1-86842-381-1

Edited and indexed by Frances Perryer, Johannesburg
Cover design by Michiel Botha, Cape Town
Text design by Triple M Design, Johannesburg
Set in 11/15pt Adobe Caslon Pro
Printed and bound by CTP Book Printers, Cape

Contents

David therefore departed thence, and escaped to the cave of Adullam: and when his brethren and all his father's house heard it, they went down thither to him. And every one that was in distress, and every one that was in debt, and every one that was discontented, gathered themselves unto him; and he became captain over them ...

First Samuel xxii.1-2.

The world is what it is; men who are nothing, who allow themselves to become nothing, have no place in it.

A Bend in the River, VS Naipaul.

One thing therefore History will do: pity them all; for it went hard with them all. Not even the Seagreen Incorruptible but shall have some pity, some human love, though it takes an effort. To the eye of equal brotherly pity, innumerable perversions dissipate themselves: exaggerations and execrations fall off, of their own accord.

The French Revolution, Thomas Carlyle.

Don't be so anxious. Don't peep so much into Freud.
Look to the Zulu – and relax.

Letter from Elias Gordin to Jeremy Gordin, 1974.

The new president [Thabo Mbeki] appointed as deputy president Jacob Zuma, a loyal ANC member who had no formal education and posed no challenge to Mbeki's leadership.

A History of South Africa (2001), Leonard Thompson.

'Once upon a time,' [Nikita] Khrushchev said, 'there were three men in a prison: a social democrat, an anarchist and a humble little Jew – a half-educated fellow named Pinya. They decided to elect a cell leader to watch over distribution of food, tea and tobacco. The anarchist, a big burly fellow, was against such a lawful process as electing authority. To show his contempt for law and order, he proposed that the semi-educated Jew, Pinya, be elected. They elected Pinya.

'Things went well, and they decided to escape. But they realized that the first man to go through the tunnel would be shot at by the guard. They all turned to the big brave anarchist, but he was afraid to go. Suddenly poor little Pinya drew himself up and said, "Comrades, you elected me by democratic process as your leader. Therefore, I will go first."

'The moral of the story is that no matter how humble a man's beginning, he achieves the stature of the office to which he is elected.

'That little Pinya – that's me.'

Khrushchev: The Man, His Era, William Taubman.

Preface to the Second Edition

The first edition of this book ended as Judge Chris Nicholson withdrew from Jacob G Zuma's mouth the sharp hook that had been lodged in it for about nine years by the National Prosecuting Authority. However, despite this enormous fillip, in December 2008 life did not look wonderfully rosy for Zuma. Consider: it soon became obvious that the NPA would appeal as quickly as possible against the Nicholson judgment and probably win (this is indeed what happened). Then it would re-charge Zuma. Were this to happen (and it did), what would Zuma and the ANC do? Could a national election – due in April 2009 – be fought with him sitting in court? What if he were found guilty? A conviction and a sentence to a jail term of more than 12 months would have made Zuma ineligible for election to Parliament and therefore ineligible to serve as President of South Africa.

Then there occurred the most remarkable intervention: the decision by the acting National Director of Public Prosecutions to drop charges of racketeering, money laundering, corruption and fraud against Zuma – notwithstanding everything that had gone before.

On 6 May 2009, Parliament voted Zuma fourth president of a democratic South Africa, defeating the Congress of the People's presidential candidate by 277–47 votes. Three days later, he was sworn in. As one of the talking heads on television remarked, it was 'the greatest political comeback ever' (certainly in South African politics).

What's more, though he inherited a country wallowing in the doldrums, Zuma received a very good press, foreign and local – not only for his first 100 days but for the first eight months of his rule. He was featured on the cover of *Time* magazine on 7 December 2009, and the inside article was none too shoddy either. In addition, the political opposition, as much as 'the people', seemed disarmed by his brand of charm, his promises to eradicate corruption and create jobs, and his sweeping aside of former President Thabo Mbeki's HIV/AIDS denialism.

But on a balmy Sunday morning, 31 January 2010, the *Sunday Times* arrived – *thump!* – in the driveway, carrying incendiary matériel. Suddenly, Zuma was in trouble again; in the blink of an eye, he had again become the dirty rascal. Just when Zuma's getting ahead in the game, he … well, he doesn't shoot himself in the foot … but he does often commit a sexual misdemeanour. But more important than the brouhaha precipitated here and overseas by Zuma's peccadilloes was the reaction of his allies in the ANC and the tripartite alliance. It was apparent from their lukewarm response that quite deep fissures existed in the party and the alliance. Zuma's policy of governing by consensus had effectively meant perpetual compromise, and in such a process there can be little bold leadership.[1] By trying to be all things to all people, Zuma has clearly failed to satisfy most, if any, of the competing factions in his government.

This second edition of *Zuma: A Biography* contains three new chapters that incorporate all the new events that I have mentioned above – from October/November 2008 until the first weeks of March 2010 and the pomp and ceremony of his journey to London to see Queen Elizabeth II.

Much of the material in the three new chapters flows from articles I have written on politicsweb.co.za, where I have been a weekly contributor since about June 2009, and articles written for East London's *Daily Dispatch*. My thanks and acknowledgements to James Myburgh and Alec Hogg of Politicsweb, for allowing me the space and giving me encouragement, and to Myburgh in particular for fruitful discussions and for letting me profit from his indefatigable questioning of the status quo and dislike of racist cant and political propaganda; and thanks and acknowledgements to Andrew Trench and Dawn Barkhuizen of the *Dispatch* for giving me an opportunity to write a monthly Zuma column.

In the first edition of this book, there were a number of instances where, without making proper acknowledgment, I used material directly from *The Arms Deal in Your Pocket* (Jonathan Ball Publishers, 2008) by Paul Holden. These omissions of acknowledgement have now been corrected; and I apologise to Holden. Some factual mistakes relating to Zuma's family have also been repaired, and I apologise to Zuma as well.

Journalists David Beresford and Paul Trewhela had two similar 'problems' with this book. The first related to the way in which I dealt with – or, rather, failed to deal with – Zuma's membership of the SA Communist Party, which membership had been clearly mentioned by Zuma himself in an autobiographical piece written on 2 May 1985 under the alias 'Pedro'. The second related to my failure to damn Zuma sufficiently for his alleged complicity or culpability in the death of Thami Zulu. I deal with both these issues and reproduce the 'Pedro' document in a new appendix.

Besides again thanking the long-suffering Jeremy 'where's my copy?' Boraine, publishing director of Jonathan Ball Publishers (JBP), and Frances Perryer, editor extraordinaire, I want also to thank Jonathan Ball for his support, friendship, and superb operatic rendition of *Awelethu mashini wami*, 'Bring me my machine gun', as well as the rest of the JBP staff, especially Anika Ebrahim, JBP's director of publicity. When I needed a proverbial pillar of strength on which to lean a little, Anika was there.

I also want to thank: Michael Hulley, Zuma's attorney, for further assistance and friendship; Ajay Sooklal, formerly Thint's attorney, also for further assistance and friendship; Justin Cartwright, for his unexpected encouragement and praise; my friend Benjamin Trisk for his continual carping about Zuma (if he let up, what would I have to think about?); Anthony Butler, head of Politics at Wits, for reminding me gently that it's not only the economy, stupid – it's also the politics, stupid; Anton Harber, my boss at Wits Journalism School, who didn't look too hard to see where I was, though he knew that I sometimes wasn't where I was supposed to be; and all the people, most of whose names I unfortunately do not know, who in the weeks immediately following publication in December 2008 came up to me in Cape Town, Durban, Johannesburg and East London, or wrote to me, to say they had enjoyed the book.

Finally, thank you to Jacob Zuma – a careful reader of those texts he must, or chooses to, read – who told me he enjoyed the book a great deal, notwithstanding 'a few things that we need to discuss sometime'. I am delighted that Zuma's note thanking me, inscribed on the title page of my copy of *Zuma: A Biography*, was written on 06/04/2009 – the evening on which he was celebrating the dropping of charges against himself.

Jeremy Gordin
PARKVIEW, JOHANNESBURG
MARCH 2010

Preface and Acknowledgements

I once said to Jacob Gedleyihlekisa Zuma, aka 'Msholozi' (his praise name), that his life story seemed so fascinating, I was surprised no one had written about him.

'Why should anyone write about me?' Zuma asked. 'I'm not an important person. I'm not from a politically famous or royal family. I'm not an influential businessman. I'm just an ordinary person.'

It was a vintage Zuma response because it was self-deprecatory, some might even say humble, yet at the same time quietly, almost obliquely, sarcastic about a number of South African leaders whom politically knowledgeable people would find it easy to identify. It was also inaccurate, at least insofar as he claimed to be unimportant, for his name and career are now inextricably parts of the history of South Africa in the late twentieth and early twenty-first centuries.

I need not discuss here why this is so – for the book that follows is about Zuma's remarkable rise and fall and rise again, the consequent sacking of President Thabo Mbeki, as well as the possibility that Zuma's road to presidential inauguration could still be blocked by corruption and racketeering charges. Zuma is also a highly controversial politician and person, and that's putting it mildly. And, since being made president-in-waiting in December 2007, he has become the epicentre of the country's political turmoil.

The aim of this book is to tell Zuma's story in such as way as to offer some insight beyond the daily and weekly reporting in the media and to capture something of the man, his ambitions, and the political roller-coaster he has been on – his travails in his quest to be the next president of South Africa.

It's a 'pull-together', as journalists say, with the necessary background and context; an 'overview' that tries to sew together all the elements of the story. The main focus remains on the last eight or nine years during which Zuma has been accused of corruption and during which he emerged as the spear of the Left in its 'battle' against Mbeki. But I also cover Zuma's early life in rural KwaZulu-Natal, his 10 years on Robben Island, his adult life as a member of the ANC underground, and the transitional years of the 1990s.

It would be silly, however, to pretend that this short book is 'definitive'. Doubtless there are many lines of investigation, facts, and events missing from it. Nor is this a 'thesis' book; I have no over-arching point to prove, or all-encompassing 'explanation' to offer, about Zuma.

The historian Eric Hobsbawm adapted a comment of Karl Marx's as follows: 'Men make their lives, but they do not make them just as they please, they do not make them under circumstances chosen by themselves, but under circumstances directly encountered, given and transmitted from the past, and by the world around them.'[1]

This comment is particularly applicable to a person who was six years old when legal apartheid started being clamped like a vice on society, who spent 10 years jailed on Robben Island, whose life was devoted to political and underground struggle, and who is an ANC man through and through. The party is, literally, his life, and has been so for half a century. I have obviously therefore had to be careful not to 'over-emphasise the role of the individual in shaping and determining events' or to 'ignore or play down the political context' in which Zuma has operated.[2] To put it another way: Zuma's story is also largely inseparable from the story of South African politics of the last decade and longer.

But, though they are *the* major factor when dealing with a politician, external circumstances are not everything. One must also deal with the person. Zuma's actions and choices have not been due solely to environment and external occurrences. His story is also about his character. At the same time – in the same breath, so to speak – I am well aware, as an astute biographer remarked, that 'none of us can enter into another person's mind; to believe so is fiction. We can only know actual persons by observing their behaviour in a variety of different situations and through different perspectives.'[3]

This book, then, does not even try to be a so-called psychobiography. I have tried, rather, to base my interpretations of Zuma the person, such as they are, on observation and palpable evidence.

This book was not authorised by Zuma. I accepted a commission to write it from Jonathan Ball Publishers and then told Zuma about it. He did not, in other words, have any control over its content, nor did he try to have any. I suspect, too, that he was not deliriously overjoyed at the idea. Yet he cooperated graciously and patiently. Zuma is a busy person and became extremely busy once he was elected ANC president. Moreover, he prefers to talk face-to-face, which is time consuming. So I am especially grateful that he afforded me time whenever he could. He also took the trouble to answer questions that must have been annoying to hear. It can't be much fun to have someone asking: 'According to the National Prosecuting Authority, you are corrupt – what do you say to that?'

I can't recall experiencing a failure of Zuma's good humour or the disappearance of that infectious laugh of his, which seems to emanate from the core of his being and lights up his person. It has been an unexpected gift to have been able to meet and write about a person who, despite 10 years in prison, various other tribulations, and more than six decades among humankind, is still apparently enjoying himself. Zuma argued with me, but, significantly, this was mainly when he thought I was being derogatory or misguided about the ANC. The only complaint I am able to dredge up about my dealings with him is the lack of real coffee at his Forest Town home.

Various members of Zuma's family were also kind and helpful: Nompumelelo Ntuli, Zuma's fourth wife (or fifth, depending how one counts these things), who made me and photographer TJ Lemon feel at home at Nkandla; Zuma's sons, Edward and Duduzani; and Zuma's daughter, Duduzile, she of the smile that could launch a thousand ships.

This book is built, firstly, on and around the articles that I have written, sometimes with others, during the last six years or so, about Zuma or related events, and which appeared in the *Sunday Independent*, *The Star*, and other Independent Group newspapers. Unless necessary for reasons of context, I have not provided references to my own work or joint-work; it would have been tiresome for the reader. Nor have I provided references for information that is in the public domain. But I have tried hard to make acknowledgements where acknowledgements are due.

At Independent Newspapers, the following were generous with time, page space, advice, grunts, bellows, or assistance: Dave Hazelhurst and Moegsien Williams of *The Star*; Jovial Rantao, Andrew Walker and Alf Hayter of the *Sunday Independent*; Peter Fabricius, Independent Group foreign editor; Roslyn Kenny, formerly editorial assistant at the Independent News Network (INN); Alan Dunn, Philani Mgwaba, and Bruce 'Shark' Colly of the *Sunday Tribune*, though during the Hefer Commission and Schabir Shaik trial, Dunn was INN editor and Mgwaba editor of the *Pretoria News;* Denis Pather and Deon Delport, then of the *Daily News*; Ivan Fynn, former editor of *The Argus*; Diana Powell, Martine Barker, and Robyn Leary, also of *The Argus*; Brendan Seery, formerly executive editor of the *Saturday Star*; and Kevin Ritchie, now managing editor of the *Saturday Star* and, when I was acting editor of

INN, my irrepressible deputy and the best *shabbes goy* a Jew could ever hope for. TJ Lemon of the *Sunday Independent*, photographer extraordinaire, and I went on some memorable Zuma expeditions. And when I had missed my deadline and was in deep trouble with the publisher, Walker, Rantao, and Williams arranged for me to take leave not due to me and added some extra time to boot.

I'm grateful to Walker, my boss at the *Sunday Independent*, for reminding me at strategic times – in his own, inimitable phraseology – of Lord Northcliffe's words: 'News is what somebody somewhere wants to suppress; all the rest is advertising.' And Walker not only kept me on the straight and narrow in terms of hard news values, steering me away (as best he could) from bias and partisanship, he was also supportive in other ways, above and beyond the call of duty. As Zuma would say: I thank you, my brother.

My thanks also to those with whom I worked at different times on different parts of the story: Estelle Ellis, formerly of *The Star*; Nalisha Kalideen; Karyn Maughan and Gill Gifford of *The Star*; Ingrid Oellerman, formerly of *The Mercury*; Caroline Hooper-Box, formerly of the *Sunday Independent*; Angela Quintal, formerly the group's political editor; and a couple of colleagues from rival publications, who I'm certain would prefer not to be named. I also thank the management of Independent Newspapers; if they had not paid for air tickets and accommodation in various places, I could not have covered much of the story.

The book is based, secondly, on interviews with Zuma and others, whose names are mentioned unless they asked to remain anonymous. As a result of my coverage of Zuma and Zuma-related stories since 2003, I have won a number of awards, including in April 2008 the Mondi Shanduka South African Journalist of 2007. But, though the accolades were pleasing, and the money that went with some of them equally (if not more) so, of greater importance to me were the people whom I came to know and to like, while on the Zuma trail.

They were (and are): Kessie Naidu SC, who was evidence leader at the Hefer Commission, acted at various times for Zuma and Thint, then left the Zuma arena; Ajay Sooklal, Thint's attorney; Michael Hulley, Zuma's attorney; Ranjeni Munusamy, Zuma's sometime *aide-de-camp* and friend; Moe and Yunis Shaik, former members of the ANC underground, brothers of Schabir Shaik, and much more than that; and Mac Maharaj, underground leader and minister in the Nelson Mandela government, and his wife, Zarina, both of whom I had met prior to 2003 but came to know better during and after the Hefer Commission. For me, all these people were, and are, in their different styles, people of warmth and humanity. I value highly the relationships I formed with them and still have with most of them.

I have also profited, personally as well as professionally, and I am not talking about money, from getting more than merely the time of day from Kemp J Kemp SC, Zuma's lead counsel; Jerome Brauns, Kemp's junior during Zuma's rape trial; Anton Steynberg, Deputy Director of Public Prosecutions in KZN; Jeremy Gauntlett SC; Wim Trengove SC, who acted, and continues to act, for the state in various matters; Neil Tuchtin SC, who acted for Zuma from time to time; Gilbert Marcus SC; Judge Denis Davis; Reeves Parsee, Schabir Shaik's attorney; and Pierre Moynot, chief executive of Thint, and his wife, Bijou. My respect for the human intellect and the judiciary was refreshed by listening to and reading the judgments of judges Joos Hefer, Hilary Squires, Willem van der Merwe, Herbert Q Msimang and Chris Nicholson.

Ebrahim Ismail 'Ibie' Ebrahim, ANC stalwart and Robben Island veteran, Blade Nzimande, General Secretary of the Communist Party, and Jeremy Cronin, Deputy General Secretary of the Communist Party, have been generous with their time and thoughts, as have Chippy and Schabir Shaik. Janet 'armed and dangerous' Love, previously a member of Operation Vula, now a member of the ANC's National Executive Committee, and mother of the more famous Thandi, gave me good advice when she had time. Stephen Laufer was a valuable sounding board, as was veteran political journalist Patrick Laurence, ever helpful and a mine of information.

My views are, of course, not necessarily held by any of the people just mentioned.

Thirdly, I have drawn for this book on other people's writings, either in articles or books. All the written material I have used or poked my cerebral nose into is listed in the chapter notes.

As far as South African history and the history of the Zulu people are concerned, I have leaned very heavily on the scholarship of Jeff Guy and Dan Wylie. Their work should be compulsory reading in our schools and universities. I could not have written this book without having at my elbow books by Allister Sparks, Patti Waldmeir, and Luli Callinicos, as well as the majestic *The Dream Deferred: Thabo Mbeki* (2007) by Mark Gevisser, *Shades of Difference: Mac Maharaj and the Struggle for South Africa* (2007) by Padraig O'Malley, and *Cyril Ramaphosa* by Anthony Butler (2007). Despite its daunting title, 'The Rape of a Trial: Jacob Zuma, AIDS, Conspiracy, and Tribalism in Neo-liberal Post-Apartheid South Africa', written in April 2007 by Elizabeth Skeen as a thesis for Princeton University, was a boon. Paul Holden's *The Arms Deal in Your Pocket* (2008) in which he has culled and collected the newspaper and Internet coverage of the Arms Deal and related matters, including stories of mine, was a useful reference tool.

In 1936 an irritable Sigmund Freud threw down the gauntlet to biographers: 'Whoever turns biographer commits himself to lies, to concealment, to hypocrisy, to embellishments, and even to hiding his own lack of understanding, for biographical truth is not to be had, and, even if it were, one could not use it.'[4]

In this book, though not conscious of any hypocrisy, I am aware of some concealment (to avoid identifying certain people) and some embellishment, and I daresay I must be guilty at times of a lack of understanding. A larger problem, however, when it comes to me having 'turned biographer' of Zuma, is determining whether I am capable of dealing with Zuma objectively: without the distortion caused by personal feelings, prejudices, or unfounded interpretations.

This issue requires some unravelling because I have been accused of being a 'Zuma spokesman' or 'Zuma apologist'. In the view of some (perhaps many) people, mainly journalists, I have been unprofessionally biased in favour of Zuma. Here is a small and relatively tame sample. In the 4 February 2008 issue of *Empire*, a Johannesburg-based arts and media magazine, Chris Vick, a professional 'public relations' person one of whose clients is (or was) businessman Tokyo Sexwale, wrote the following about the media fall-out that he foresaw would happen after the Polokwane conference: 'Keep an eye out for Zuma's pre-emptive media missile, journalist Jeremy Gordin, who uses Independent Media's editorial space to ensure strategically timed leaks that advance Zuma's cause and ensure his side of the story is well told.'

That comment would not be too unkind – it could perhaps even be read as a back-handed compliment – were it not for the toxic little barbs, 'who uses Independent Media's editorial space' and 'pre-emptive'. Vick was saying that I have 'an agenda' and that I am or have been part of, or party to, a considered Zuma media strategy (which assumes, errone-ously, that Zuma has a media strategy).

This kind of 'accusation' began with, or picked up real momentum from, the lead story I wrote in the *Sunday Independent* on 13 November 2005, about the woman who accused Zuma of raping her. At the end of Zuma's rape trial, the judge, who had acquitted Zuma, ruled that the woman should not be identified. So I shall call her what she was called during the trial by her supporters: Khwezi.

Khwezi had in fact laid a charge of rape against Zuma, but in my story vehemently denied that she had done so. The story came out on the same morning that the *Sunday Times* wrote unequivocally and correctly that such a charge had been laid. What happened was simple. Khwezi lied to me. In chapter 11, I will deal with the reasons for Khwezi lying: her frame of mind, the behind-the-scenes manoeuvring related to 'compensation' for her, and so on. Suffice it to say for the moment that she lied; that I believed her (I had no reason not to – she was the person who had al-legedly been raped or, according to her then, not raped!); and that, once the *Sunday Times* story and mine came out, each directly contradicting the other, a hullabaloo ensued. I was accused of being a spin doctor, a propagandist, a purveyor of misinformation, of 'putting the Zuma line out there', and the rest.

Following this incident, it also was generally thought and said, at least by some people, that I was 'embedded' in the Zuma camp; that I knew and consorted (horrors!) with some of the people who gathered in Zuma's parlour of an evening, and even had been in his parlour myself.

Notwithstanding Admiral Jackie Fisher's famous dictum – 'never contradict, never explain, never apologise' – let me try to set the record straight: I *was* successfully manipulated by the Zuma camp as far as Khwezi was concerned. At that point it suited Zuma and his advisers, on the one hand, and Khwezi and her mother, on the other, to keep the existence of the rape charge a secret. And I was 'used' to deny its existence. And there have probably been other occasions, though I cannot now pinpoint any particular one, when I have been manipulated by the Zuma camp.

As for being embedded: the reasons I came to enjoy better access at certain times to Zuma and the Zuma camp would seem, like most things in life, to be a mixture. One reason would have been that I was a reasonably credible media voice who was sympathetic to Zuma and therefore to some extent malleable. But there were other reasons. During the months and years when Zuma was mostly demonised by the media (from the end of 2005 until the end of 2007), I simply chose to heed the golden text, handed down from generation to generation to me: You shall not take up a false report nor shall you follow a multitude to do evil. I also took the trouble to form relationships with Zuma and those around him; tried to avoid bias and the usual clichés, of thought as much as of word; and (it seems) worked harder than many others at finding out Zuma's side of the story.

For the record then: I am not a member of the Zuma camp or any allied sect, order or organisation, on earth or anywhere else. I have also never been offered or given a bribe or blandishment of any kind by Zuma or anyone associated with him.

I like Zuma a great deal (if I didn't, there would little point in writing this book), and my approach to him has always, I hope, been one of 'sympathy and understanding that is as free from denunciation as from apologetics'.[5] Trying to stand inside someone else's shoes, as Bob Dylan put it, is not an apology; it's an attempt to understand the other person and to try to feel things the way he does.

This does not necessarily mean that I approve of everything Zuma does, has done, will do, or thinks. When Samuel Johnson agreed that the commissioning publishers would have the right to choose the poets to be written about in what would become his famous *Lives of the Poets*, his biographer James Boswell rounded on him, asking caustically whether he, the great Johnson, would really write about 'any dunce's work'.

'Yes, sir,' replied Johnson, 'and say he was a dunce.'[6]

Of course I also assume that I have the right, as presumably Johnson did, not to call someone a dunce if in my view he is not one. In any case, my approval or disapproval of Zuma is irrelevant, in general and in this book. At issue is what Jacob Zuma thinks or feels about certain issues, legal charges, and events. This book is about him.

This book would have taken even longer to complete than it has, if I had not been assisted by Laura Lopez, an American lychnobite of extraordinary energy. Obviously, errors, misrepresentations, pretentiousness, solecisms, polysyllabic words, and so on, should be blamed on me alone because I alone am responsible for this book.

In August 2006, Jeremy Boraine, the publishing director of Jonathan Ball Publishers, asked me to write a book about Zuma. In retrospect this was perhaps not such a good idea. But – as Eliphaz the Temanite mentioned to my ancestor Job, man is born unto trouble, as surely as the sparks fly upward – and I agreed. I quickly found out, however, that my employers expected me to do some work, other than on the book, if I wanted to be paid; that my children thought they occasionally merited some attention; that typing words according to the rules of grammar while applying one's mind, such as it is, so that the words have some semblance of logical meaning, grows more difficult rather than easier with the passing of time; and that I have never managed to shuck my habit of paying close attention to everything under the sun except the main task.

Still, though I missed my deadline by some 11 months, Boraine remained understanding. I don't know if there's a publishers' award for saintliness. If there is, I nominate him. I also nominate the unflappable Frances Perryer for whatever award there is for editors; she has indeed turned the proverbial sow's ear into something less so.

It is a truth universally acknowledged that I am not the sweetest of human beings and that, when engaged in work that conflicts with my innate laziness, I change into a creature worse than a bear with a cluster headache. Thanks then are also due to my family: Deborah, Jake, and Nina. It could be argued that they don't have much choice about putting up with me. Maybe; but I'd like to thank them anyway.

Despite knowing me for roughly 25 years and being married to me for about 15, Deborah was always supportive. 'Of course you must go,' was, without exception, her response when told that I had to go away to another commission or trial, leaving her with two relatively young children. (Maybe she was simply happy to have me out of the house; as a journalist, one must consider every option.)

Jake (Eli) is named after my niece, Jacqueline Yonat Gordin, who died in Israel in 1989, aged 20, and after my father, Elias, who also died in 1989. Nina is named after my sister, Lenina, who died in Pretoria in the late 1930s. Both Jake and Nina are thus named after my 'significant dead'.[7] But both are very much members of my significant living. Jake helped refine my thinking – and of course succeeded in irritating me – when he occasionally came home from school and said with a twinkle, reminiscent of his grandfather: 'Some of the children at school say that Zuma is a bad man – is this true or not?' On days when the world, or my world, seemed irretrievably stalled, Nina's smile always made it move again.

Jeremy Gordin
PARKVIEW, JOHANNESBURG
OCTOBER 2008

CHAPTER 1

1942–1959

Zulu boy

Kusempondozankomo:
THE MOMENT JUST BEFORE DAWN, WHEN THE HORNS OF THE CATTLE BECOME VISIBLE

On 12 April 1942 Jacob Gedleyihlekisa Zuma was born into the Zuma clan at Nkandla, the first son of Gcinamazwi Zuma and Nokubhekisisa. 'Gedleyihlekisa' is a shortened version of an isiZulu phrase his father constructed – *'Ngeke ngithule umuntu engigedla engihlekisa'* – which translated means 'I can't keep quiet when someone pretends to love me with a deceitful smile.'

With its deep gorges and steep ridges, the rainy Nkandla forest has always been a place of mystery, legend and final refuge.[1] King Cetshwayo, defeated by Zibhebhu, spent his last days there; in Nkandla the people once successfully defended themselves against King Shaka; more recently the rebels of Bhambatha had taken refuge in its depths.

These days the forest is badly denuded. The area around it, and the people who live in it, are deeply impoverished, and were even more so when Zuma was born. For some, there is electricity and water, and there are roads too, though many of them are still not tarred and, if you travel there during the rainy season, it is wise to do so in a four-wheel-drive vehicle. The poverty in those days, however, was also a poverty of spirit – of a once wealthy and powerful kingdom brought to its knees.

Zuma is a Zulu, a member of a tribe – or, more precisely, a federation of clans – which a bare 190 years ago, under Shaka kaSenzangakhona, became what has been called 'Africa's Sparta'. As the historian Leonard Thompson put it:

> [The Zulu kingdom under Shaka] was a militarized state, made and maintained by a conscript army of about 40 000 warriors. Instead of the initiation system, which had integrated young men into the discipline of their particular chiefdoms, men were removed from civil society at about the age of puberty and assigned to age regiments, living in barracks scattered throughout the country. During their period of service they were denied contact with women and subjected to intense discipline.
>
> … To foster loyalty to the state, Shaka and his councillors drew on the customary Nguni festivals. They assembled the entire army at the royal barracks for the annual first-fruits ceremony and before and after major military expeditions, when they used spectacular displays and magical devices to instil a corporate morale. The traditions of the Zulu royal lineage became the traditions of the kingdom; the Zulu dialect became the language of the kingdom; and every inhabitant, whatever his origin, became a Zulu, owing allegiance to Shaka.[2]

But to talk about an African Sparta is to have a skewed picture of the Zulu kingdom. This is because it emphasises what Dan Wylie has called the 'stereotypical imagery of massed warriors – extravagant feathers waving, short stabbing-spears rusted with blood – pouring down grassy hillsides … a specifically Zulu cult and culture of romanticised yet rigorous brutality' at the expense of all the other aspects of Zulu society, as it developed from roughly the 1820s until – under King Cetshwayo – it was destroyed in the 1880s.[3] For destroyed it was. Thompson summed it up succinctly:

The Zulu had been subjected in four stages. First, the kingdom was conquered and its army was broken up. Secondly, the country was split into thirteen separate units. Thirdly, white magistrates supplanted the chiefs as the most powerful men in their districts. And fourthly, the land was partitioned, leaving only about a third of the former kingdom in Zulu hands. Before the war, Theophilus Shepstone had expressed the hope that Cetshwayo's warriors would be 'changed to labourers working for wages'. That process had begun by the end of the nineteenth century.[4]

In 1906, the colonial authorities put down with a great loss of life and cruelty an uprising known as the Bhambatha (or Maphumulo) Rebellion, a popular revolt against the payment of poll tax. One of the major incidents of carnage during the rebellion took place in the Mome Gorge below the Nkandla forest. It was here, on 10 June 1906, that 1 000 men were trapped in the gorge and ripped apart by artillery trained on them from the surrounding high ground. 'The injured and those who had found a cave or crevice in which to hide, had been finished off by the colonial militia and the African levies that had moved in with small arms, bayonets and assegais.'[5]

This happened 36 years before Zuma was born and it is not melodramatic, I believe, to say that the Zulu people remember with powerful feelings demeaning events such as these as well as their former glories.

'When I was a young boy, there were two very old people in the village,' said Zuma. 'One came from the Ndlovu clan, another from the Bhengu, and they had been in their teens when the Bhambatha Rebellion ended. They used to tell of their experiences. And that, more than anything else, is what made me appreciate the sufferings of Africans. It was then, for the first time, when I was little, that I came to understand and to be angry about colonial oppression.'

Zuma makes no claim to gentle birth – he was an impoverished son of the soil, from a family of peasants. Blade Nzimande, the General Secretary of the South African Communist Party, loves to start his speeches at Zuma rallies by singing the Communist Party song that goes:

'My mother was a kitchen girl,/ My father was a garden boy,/ That's why I am a comm-u-nist …' There's a good reason for Nzimande's choice. Zuma's mother was a domestic worker. He remembers nothing of his policeman father, who died when he was about four.

His mother had three sons with his father – Jacob is the eldest – and the 'big mother', his father's first wife, had four daughters and three sons, so there were plenty of siblings about. But, soon after her husband's death, Zuma's mother returned with her children to her parents' home at KwaMaphumulo.

'I was supposed to start school there, I was about seven or eight years old, but my grandfather, whose herdboy had gone off somewhere, asked that I take care of his cattle. He was supposed to find another herdboy, but he never did. So, although I was supposed to go to school, I couldn't. That was it,' said Zuma.

'Later, my mother came to take me back to Nkandla – the family asked us to return – but there was no school at Nkandla. I was told to tend to the cattle and goats. And my mother went off to work as a domestic servant in the Durban area.'

Zuma liked the life.

'Oh yes, besides tending the cattle, we did many things. Nkandla looked much the same then as it does now, though there were more ploughed fields then. We used to hunt birds in the surrounding area and in the forest with a rudimentary catapult. We also used to hunt animals with small knobkerries. We used to kill snakes. Actually, I was terrified of snakes – and I remember being told that the best way to deal with the fear was to kill even more of them. But, well …'

The herdboys would also dig holes so as to get into the ground hives of bees and steal their honey. They were trained in stick fighting, at which Zuma excelled. 'He was a hero among his stick-fighting peers because he used to beat the hell out of them. He had good tactics. Everybody among his peers respected him for that,' said Mncikiselwa Shozi, who knew Zuma as a boy.[6] But he wanted to learn things – he really missed school.

'The media always report that I learned to read and write on Robben

Island. Maybe they think it's romantic. And of course my literacy was improved there and, yes, Ibie Ebrahim who was in my cell used to lend me books, and Judson Kuzwayo, who was arrested with me, also used to assist. But in fact I taught myself as a boy in Nkandla and later in the Cato Manor area of Durban where my mother was working.'

Zuma said that he used to harass the other children who were attending school in the area and would come home at night or at weekends.

'I used to ask if I could look at their books and their slates. I really wanted to know what it was all about. Then I organised a kind of a night school. There was a woman in Nkandla, her name was Maria, and she had done standard four but was staying at home and not doing much of anything. I asked my uncles whether I could go to her for help after I had put the cattle back in the kraal in the evenings.

'I remember the answer still – it came from either my mother or one of my uncles: "If the cattle are at home and well, then, yes, do that." Other boys joined me, even ones who had been to school, and she took us through the work. I arranged it all – we paid her two shillings and sixpence a month, I remember.'

In 1990, Zuma said in an interview with the Helen Suzman Foundation:

Part of the reason I talk about my self-education more these days, is that I am trying to encourage those whose circumstances also did not allow them to go to school. If you are determined to educate yourself, it is possible – I've done it. People without formal education are looked down upon and often feel shy. But I am one of the few exceptions. I have done everything the educated have done. Education is education, whether it is formal or not. I want to use my example as an inspiration to those who did not have the opportunity to go to school. Without education one is like a warrior without weapons. You can't fight the battle to survive in life. You can't defeat things. You get defeated all the time. Once you have an education you remove those obstacles.[7]

As Zuma moved into his teens, he would visit his mother more often. He wasn't allowed to go to the home where she worked in Cato Manor, but he had a cousin living in the Greyville area and he would walk around the city and take whatever odd jobs came his way.

Those days – the early 1950s – were a time when apartheid was gathering momentum, probably not a good time, if there ever was one, to be a black person. Does he feel bitter about whites? Does he, in truth, dislike them?

'I once went into a café in Umgeni Road. I used to wander around in those days in my bare feet. There was a particular sweet that I liked. And it was there on the counter so I picked it up. But the owner thought I was taking it away from the white boy who was in front of me – or maybe he thought I was stealing it, I don't know. He gave me such a *klap* that I was reeling. I was so angry that I cried and cried. And I thought: "One day I'll fix him." But, you know, I came to understand that this attitude was not part of the general oppression. It was just one man's stupidity.

'And so, no, I am not bitter or biased. That stuff is just too petty for words. It's just not my way.'

But what made him – a rural Zulu boy with precious little education, brought up in the patriarchal traditions of the Zulu – turn to the African National Congress? Why give his life to the ANC, which it has turned out that he has? Why go to jail for a decade if he could have gone on with his life, got a job, and, if he wanted to be involved in politics, joined the resurgent Zulu nationalist movement that would become the Inkatha Freedom Party?

Zuma says that the first big influence on his awareness was the stories he heard as a child about Bhambatha's rebellion. But he was especially influenced by his 'father's first son', Muthukabongwa Zuma.

'He had fought in the Second World War and he was a member of the ANC and he was a trade unionist. He preached endlessly about colonial oppression and the working class, and had an enormous influence on me.

'Thirdly, in the Cato Manor township, and in Greyville when I used to stay with my cousin, I used to see the ANC volunteers in their uniforms, and I used to go to ANC public meetings, and I listened and I learned.

'I used to visit my mother in Durban a lot, especially in winter, when there wasn't so much work in Nkandla. But in those days it was not so much apartheid *per se* that worked on my mind – it was the overall and unrelenting oppression that Africans had faced.'

This was a time of great challenges and opportunities for the ANC, which already had a long and proud history. Since 8 January 1912, when it was founded as the South African Native National Congress (SANNC), it had fought – patiently, moderately and modestly, in the words of its first Nobel Peace Prize winning leader[8] – for the rights of black South Africans.

From its inception the ANC (which is what the SANNC became in 1923) represented both traditional and modern elements, from tribal chiefs to church and community bodies and educated black professionals, though women were only admitted as affiliate members from 1931 and as full members in 1943. The conspicuous failure of its gentlemanly approach to win any concessions from the government prompted the formation in 1944 of the ANC Youth League, which expressed the desire of a new generation for non-violent mass action. In 1947, when Zuma was five, the ANC allied with the Natal Indian Congress and Transvaal Indian Congress, broadening the basis of its opposition to the government.

In 1948, when Zuma was six, the National Party won the whites-only election and DF Malan became prime minister. In 1949, the Prohibition of Mixed Marriages Act was passed and then, in 1950, a rash of apartheid legislation appeared on the body politic: the Group Areas Act (people were not allowed to live among people of a different colour), the Suppression of Communism Act (banning the SA Communist Party), the Population Registration Act (people had to be registered according to their colour), and the Immorality Act (people of different colours were forbidden to have sexual intercourse). Significantly, so-called coloureds who had the vote were removed from the electoral rolls.

In June 1952, the ANC joined with other anti-apartheid organisations in a Defiance Campaign against the restriction of political, labour and residential rights, during which protesters deliberately violated oppressive laws, following the example of Gandhi's passive resistance (*Satyagraha*) in Natal and India. More than 8 500 people courted imprisonment for contravening pass laws and curfew regulations, orders segregating whites and non-whites in railway stations and post offices, and other so-called petty apartheid measures. The campaign led to the formation of the Coloured People's Congress, the Congress of Democrats (white) and the Congress Alliance, formed across the race divide. Nelson Mandela, president of the ANC Youth League, was appointed volunteer-in-chief. But the campaign was called off in April 1953 after new laws prohibiting protest meetings were passed.

In 1953, the Bantu Education Act (black and white children had to be educated separately) and the Reservation of Separate Amenities Act (people of different colours were not allowed to enjoy social intercourse with one another) were passed.

In 1955, when Zuma was 13, the Freedom Charter, claiming ownership of the land for all South Africans, was adopted at the Congress of the People in Kliptown, Johannesburg. But the Nationalist government pressed on, and forced removals of black people settled in designated 'white' areas such as Sophiatown caused widespread suffering and discontent.

In 1956, 20 000 women marched to the Union Buildings in Pretoria in a mass demonstration against black people being forced to carry at all times an identification document known as a pass (or 'dompas') to justify their presence in white areas, and which effectively allowed the police to find, almost without fail, that they were in a given area 'illegally'.

Also in 1956, the five-year-long Treason Trial began. The 156 accused, including Nelson Mandela, were charged with high treason. In 1957, the inhabitants of Alexandra Township on the edge of Johannesburg boycotted the buses in protest against an increase in fares. Thousands of residents walked 20 km to work and back. The Pound-a-Day national minimum wage campaign was launched as result of the boycott. Women also held anti-pass demonstrations throughout the country all year, as well as protesting against the beer hall system, in terms of which the home brewing of traditional beer was prohibited so that municipal beer

halls could provide the major source of revenue for township adminis-
trations.[8]

In 1958, Dutch-born Hendrik Frensch Verwoerd, the so-called theo-
retician and one of the 'hard men' of separate development, became
prime minister. In May a number of rural people in Sekhukhuniland re-
volted against the formation of homelands or Bantustans; the revolt was
brutally put down, 16 people were executed, and there was a clampdown
in Pondoland, Tembuland and Zululand. The 'Farm Labour Scandal' received wide publicity after first appearing in *New Age*. Ruth First and
Joe Gqabi conducted an undercover investigation into the kidnapping
and enslaving of workers on farms. Their revelations led to a successful
potato boycott nationwide.

In 1959, after a schism in the ANC, Robert Sobukwe set up the Pan-
Africanist Congress (PAC), an organisation that was more African
nationalist in orientation than the ANC in its aims, and not for whites,
though a few white people belonged to it over the years. The Promotion
of Bantu Self-Government Act (the legislation mandating that black
people would have to live in their own 'homelands' ruled by homeland
leaders) and the Extension of University Education Act (non-whites
should have their own universities) were passed. And as a result of
tensions over the municipal beer hall system, together with looming
forced removals, Cato Manor township, where Zuma's mother worked,
exploded into riots.

In 1959, at the age of 17, Zuma joined the African National Congress.

CHAPTER 2

1960–1963

Working-class warrior

"Kaffir, hierdie is Pretoria. Dis nie Durban nie. Wat dink jy, kaffir? Hier gaan jy praat."

'Then he hit me. I don't know how he hit me or if he hit me with something. I didn't see it coming. He must have chopped the side of my neck because I was out. All I know is that I woke up later, with water dripping down my face. I must have been unconscious and they must have thrown water all over me.

'The thing was that I couldn't speak Afrikaans then. I had just come from Durban. I didn't have the faintest idea of what he was saying. And also, I wasn't watching him, the white policeman. He was the interrogator. But there was an interpreter, a black policeman. And he was the one who seemed to be getting agitated. I mean, I was young then, so I was cheeky. I hadn't learnt yet how to deal with people like that. The interpreter was sort of moving around as though he was about to hit me. So I was watching him.'

Zuma was part of a group of about 50 comrades who in June 1963, under the aegis of Umkhonto weSizwe (MK), were planning to cross the border into Bechuanaland (Botswana) and go to Lobatse. From there they aimed to head for Zambia for military training. But their plan to join the 'Freedom Train' out of South Africa[1] had been revealed to the security police before it even started.

'They nabbed us with ease because they knew about us. Two of our so-called leaders had sold us out. Besides that, serious torture by the police was relatively new then, people weren't prepared for it, it was savage, and many of the people in the group also gave away the game.

'In short, the police didn't need anything from me. They had the case sewn up. They beat us a little. I suppose they did so because that is what they did. But after that they mostly left me alone.'

Zuma's group was caught near Zeerust in the Groot Marico area. They had been travelling in five kombis back to Pretoria 'to deliver some comrades' when the police on the side of the road spotted them and realised they were part of a larger group about which they had been tipped off.

The keen new MK recruits – some of them elderly – were arrested and held under the new 90-day detention law. This effectively kept them incommunicado and allowed the police to do with them as they wished. They were imprisoned in the Marabastad jail, Pretoria Central Prison, Hercules Police Station near Pretoria, and other jails nearby.

Zuma found the 90 days of being held mostly in solitary, in Hercules Police Station, one of the most difficult times of his life – far more trying than his decade on Robben Island.

'I remember being called out of my cell at some point for interrogation. There was something wrong with my eyes; I couldn't focus them; it was strange. I think it was about sitting in that cell in the darkness, doing nothing but thinking, for weeks.'

All of those arrested were charged with conspiring to overthrow the government and sabotage.

'Con … spiracy, con … spiring … to … overthrow … the … government.' Zuma savoured the words in a recent interview.

'I think, if I remember correctly, "conspiring with Russia against South Africa" was also included somewhere. Funny charges. I always get the funny charges in my life … conspiring to overthrow the government, racketeering …'

The trial was held in the Pretoria Old Synagogue, in which a number of major political trials have been held since the 1960s, and the presiding judicial officer was Judge Fritz Steyn.

'I remember that courtroom and that trial. Everyone and everything was hostile. Steyn was notorious. If he put you away, he really put you away. But some of the older people got only five years.'

On 12 August 1963, 21-year-old Zuma was sentenced to 10 years' jail for conspiring to overthrow the government. He was apparently better known than either he or recent history has acknowledged. The headlines on page 6 of the City Late edition of *The Star* read: 'JACOB ZUMA JAILED':

Jacob Zuma, a prominent member of the banned African National Congress and activist in the ANC's military wing Umkhonto weSizwe, has been sentenced to an effective ten years' imprisonment for conspiring to overthrow the government. He was arrested with a group of 45 recruits near Zeerust in the Western Transvaal. The 21-year-old Zuma, the son of a policeman from Nkandla in Natal, became involved in politics at a very early age and joined the ANC in 1959 when he was a mere 17. Zuma was one of the ANC's rising stars when the political party was banned by the government …

Where had Zuma been since joining the ANC, and how did he end up with such a sentence at the tender age of 21? In those four years a great deal had happened.

In 1960, the ANC planned a major campaign against the pass laws. It was set to begin on 31 March 1960, but was pre-empted by the PAC 10 days earlier. Heavily armed police outside a police station in the small southern Transvaal township of Sharpeville apparently panicked and opened fire on a peaceful gathering of protesters. Sixty-nine people were shot dead and 180 injured in what became known as the Sharpeville massacre. Most were shot in the back as they fled.

A state of emergency was declared on 1 April. Nelson Mandela was among about 2 000 political activists detained from all the liberation movements; the ANC and PAC were banned and went underground, and set up offices outside the country.

International opposition to the regime increased throughout the 1960s, fuelled by the growing number of newly independent African nations, the anti-apartheid movement in Britain and the civil rights movement in the United States. But the situation was bleak in South Africa, especially for members of the ANC.

In May 1961, South Africa became a republic and left the Commonwealth. The ANC, in conjunction with the Communist Party, had arranged a nationwide strike to protest the establishment of the Republic of South Africa, and Mandela had written to Hendrik Verwoerd to call for a constitutional convention. Verwoerd ignored this last call for negotiations and the strike was suppressed.

Not without some anguish, knowing that it would be against ANC President-General Albert Luthuli's wishes, the ANC leadership concluded that methods of non-violence were not an appropriate response to the brutality that was being levelled at non-white South Africans. They chose the 16 December state holiday for the debut of their military wing, Umkhonto weSizwe, 'Spear of the Nation', planting homemade bombs to blow up electrical substations and government buildings in all the major centres. The sabotage campaign had begun.

Where was Zuma during these years? He had been a member of the ANC since 1959. Until 1961, however, when he joined MK, most of his activities were related to the South African Congress of Trade Unions (SACTU), the forerunner of Cosatu, run by the influential Moses Mabhida. Besides being influenced by his uncle at Nkandla, Zuma had also met a relation, Obed Zuma, who was known as a fiery trade unionist. SACTU was organising effectively in Durban in the late 1950s, and in 1959, the Cato

Manor riots brought in 13 500 new members. Between 1957 and 1960 SACTU organised major workers' strikes and actions around the country. Zuma and Joseph Mdluli (who was later to die in security police detention in 1975) comprised an underground cell at Bolton Hall in Durban. So far as MK activities went, Zuma does not seem to have been involved in any guerrilla activities besides the burning of sugar cane fields.

Mathews Ngcobo – an MK operative later imprisoned on Robben Island – remembers meeting Zuma at Lakhani Chambers, a non-descript three-storey building in downtown Durban, on the corner of Yusuf Dadoo and Saville streets. Ngcobo was in his early twenties and Zuma 18 when they shared political education classes on the third floor of the building. Ngcobo, Zuma, and about 28 others were tutored by Mabhida and another unionist, Steven Dlamini.[2] Youngsters assembled in the evenings after work and learned about trade unionism. At 10 pm they dispersed to make it home in time for the 11 pm curfew imposed on blacks in the city.

Ngcobo spent three years, from 1960 to 1963, attending classes there with Zuma. Recalling the years at Lakhani Chambers, Ngcobo said: 'Zuma always asked questions and the questions he asked showed he was bright. He was searching then, he was eager to learn about workers' rights around the world.'

Ngcobo says that Zuma's fellow students were struck by his ability to learn. 'He would always excel and go beyond the obvious when we were taught anything. He's a problem solver. He always has time for people.'

Another person who remembered Zuma from Lakhani Chambers was Cletus Mzimela, who trained with Thabo Mbeki, Joe Slovo and Mabhida in the USSR and was on Robben Island for 15 years. In the 1960s he worked at a rope factory and attended evening classes with Zuma. 'He was a thin, handsome fellow.' He recalls that Zuma worked in a kitchen, in a house somewhere off Musgrave Road. 'He used to wear those white shorts and polish the floors and clean the windows.'

Historian Luli Callinicos has written in her biography of Oliver Tambo that 'the carnage of that horrific afternoon in 1960 [at Sharpeville] would forever change the face of the liberation struggle and, indeed, the path it was to follow'.[3] She was referring specifically to the decision by the young ANC leadership to move from non-violence to armed struggle. Simultaneously, however, the apartheid regime was preparing for war. This included an increase in banning and house arrest; the new 'Sabotage Act' carried the death penalty, and by 1963 the General Laws Amendment Act empowered police to enforce a 90-day detention – anyone could be picked up and held without access to lawyers. Consequently, torture became more frequent and eventually routine.[4] In 1963, 'Looksmart' Ngudle, a SACTU member, was tortured and killed in detention. He was said to have 'fallen' from the seventh or tenth floor of The Greys, security police headquarters in Johannesburg.

After Mandela's 1962 trip through Africa, during which he had garnered promises of support from independent African countries, MK told its activists to leave South African secretly to undergo military training. The number of recruits for such training increased steadily. 'The journey was circuitous, arduous, and dangerous. Dozens were arrested, charged and imprisoned before they had even reached the border.'[5]

One of those who had had a look around him, seen what was happening in the country, and decided that military training was the answer was Zuma. He arranged to 'disappear' for six months, hoping to return after a six-month military course. But he was also one who was caught.

In July 1963, while Zuma was being held under the 90-day detention law at Hercules Police Station, disaster struck. The top leaders of the MK High Command – Sisuslu, Motsoaledi, Mhlaba, Mbeki, Mlangeni, Kathrada, Goldberg, Bernstein, Hepple, Goldreich, and Kantor – were arrested in a security police swoop on Liliesleaf Farm in Rivonia, on the outskirts of Johannesburg. Mandela had already been caught and imprisoned. Some of the detainees 'mopped up' in subsidiary security police operations cracked, and soon the police had crushed the ANC leadership. They also learned about Operation Mayibuye ('Operation Restore'), MK's plan to overthrow the government by guerrilla warfare.

CHAPTER 3

1963–1973

The Island

The register of prisoners on Robben Island contains the following listing: Prisoner 1/5268; name: Gedleyihlekisa Zuma; address: c/o Betty Zuma, B363, Cato Manor, Durban; date admitted: 63.12.30; date released: 73.12.29.

For all of his 10 years on the Island, sharing a communal cell with between 30 and 50 men, washing in cold water, cut off from womankind, eating mealie-meal and boiled mealies (maize) three times a day, day in and day out, working in the lime quarries five days a week, and then having to strip to be searched, winter or summer, Jacob Zuma never received one visit.

'My mother was a domestic servant. It would have been very expensive for her to travel from KZN to Cape Town, then to arrange to cross to the island, and she would have seen me for 30 minutes. What was the point? I wrote to her to keep her money for the other children and that I would see her in due course.'

The first time Zuma would see his mother again was in December 1973, in the Pietermaritzburg police cells, where he was held for two weeks before being driven back to Nkandla and released.

How did Zuma cope with not seeing a single face from home? Did he not feel depressed? I asked him these questions recently, as we sat in the dining room of his Forest Town, Johannesburg home, late one evening. Sixty-six-year-old Zuma had just returned from an ANC National Working Committee meeting at Luthuli house and he was so weary that his eyes were sliding back into their sockets, giving him a slightly reptilian look.

'I'm one of those people … well, I make myself feel at home wherever I am,' he said. 'And yes, of course, it was very hard. But I was young and also I don't get depressed very easily. Depression and I are not good friends. What would have been the point, anyway? There was nothing anyone could do. We were there. We had to deal with it.'

After being sentenced to 10 years' imprisonment for conspiring to overthrow the government on 12 August 1963, the 21-year-old Zuma was taken from Pretoria to Leeuwkop Prison on the outskirts of Johannesburg and from there transported to Cape Town.

The prisoners were handcuffed and put in leg irons for the whole of the journey, in a windowless van containing only a sanitary bucket. Each prisoner was shackled to another with leg irons. It was on this journey to Cape Town, during which they slept over at Colesberg prison, that Zuma met Ebrahim 'Ibie' Ebrahim, an MK activist, sentenced to 15 years' imprisonment in the Pietermaritzburg sabotage trial and also sent to Robben Island via Leeuwkop. Ibie still works at Luthuli House, ANC headquarters in Sauer Street, Johannesburg, in the ANC's foreign affairs department.

Robben Island, cut off from the mainland by eight and a half kilometres of cold sea, had been used as an occasional place of banishment from the days when the Dutch arrived at the Cape. Later the place was turned into a leper colony, a lunatic asylum and a naval base. Then, from the early 1960s, the apartheid government decided to use it as a prison again. It was where African, Indian and coloured political prisoners were incarcerated between 1962 and 1991. From 1963 the warders were exclusively white, usually Afrikaans-speaking.[1] The number of inmates fluctuated. From the mid- to late 1960s there were more than 1 000 PAC and ANC men on the island, as well as a sprinkling of others from smaller organisations – and until 1968 a comparable number of common law criminals (murderers, thieves, rapists) as well. The number of prisoners dropped as sentences were completed but expanded again after the 1976 uprisings, by which time Zuma was gone. Until the late 1960s the PAC activists outnumbered the ANC ones.

Zuma's group arrived on Robben Island before the 'famous' ones who had been sentenced to life imprisonment at the end of the Rivonia Trial, though Mandela had been there for a short time before.

'Mandela and that group were given single cells, because they were leaders of the ANC, and the authorities were frightened that they would have a bad influence on the rest of us,' chuckled Ebrahim. 'But the rest of us were put in communal cells – and so I spent the next 10 years with Zuma, Steve Tshwete and Harry Gwala, among others.'

Initially there were roughly 1 000 prisoners divided into insufficient cells. There were supposed to be about fifty prisoners to a cell, but in the early days, when they put their sisal sleeping mats and blankets down at night, there were so many of them per cell that there wasn't space for the number of sleeping mats. Three men would sleep on two mats. This was for about six months. But many of the PAC prisoners, who had been jailed at about the same time, were in for relatively short periods, and after they left and conditions grew better in general, the cells were not as crowded.

The waking bell rang at 5 am; watches were not allowed, so prisoners' lives were controlled by bells, whistles and warders' commands. The prisoners had to wash in communal areas in cold water, clean the cell, fold their blankets, empty the stinking sanitary bucket used overnight by all the men in the cell – and then form up in pairs. The water on Robben Island, besides being cold, was hard and salty. Hot water would only come much later – in 1973. If you washed your hair with soap, it stuck to your head like glue.

The warders counted the prisoners and then, squatting in the open air, which in winter was icy, kitted in the standard clothing for black prisoners – short trousers, a rough khaki shirt, a canvas jacket, rubber sandals, but no underwear – the men had breakfast. This came in a metal drum and was stiff mealie-meal porridge.

The prisoners would then be marched in groups of four to the quarries where they had to dig out limestone with picks and break it up, apparently for a dyke that was being constructed.

'Well, I suppose I do have to thank the work in those quarries for preserving me,' said Zuma when I interviewed him. 'I'm 66 but I'm still going strong.'

Oddly, Zuma smoked while he was in prison, but gave up for ever in his early thirties, when he came out of jail.

Some of the warders pushed the prisoners around, sometimes assaulting them for sport, at least in the early days. If the men didn't meet their quota in the quarry, if they didn't dig and break up enough stone, there was a special punishment – no food for the whole of Sunday.

Lunch was always boiled hard mealies – always cold because it took a while to bring it from the kitchens to the quarries on a cart – and *phuzamandla*, a drink concocted from powdered maize and yeast mixed into water, though it should have been milk. And supper was always mealie-meal porridge, yet again.

I asked Zuma if he still ate mealie-meal.

'Yes,' he said, and hesitated for a second, his mind apparently reverting for a moment to the Island, then he looked at me and said, 'but not with great enthusiasm.'

The worst part of the day was returning from the quarries to the cells at about 4 pm. Everyone had to strip naked. In winter, standing there for 15 or 20 minutes while being searched was agonising. This was the so-called humiliating 'tausa' ritual during which the prisoners, stripped naked, had to jump up and down to loosen any concealed objects, finally bending over to expose their rectums to the warders.

The warders had been instructed to look for food and, above all, for cut-up pieces of newspapers. The chief interest of all of the political prisoners was to find out what was going on in the outside world, especially politically and in terms of the struggle.

The third meal of the day was, yet again, mealie-meal.

But once the prisoners were locked up for the night at about 5 pm, they would read if they had books – these also came later – or argue, sometimes vociferously, about politics. Prisoners were told to go to 'bed' at 8 pm, though the lights in the cell were never turned off. 'When I came out after 15 years, I found it almost bizarre to be able to go to sleep in darkness,' Ebrahim remarked laconically. But prisoners studying for primary and secondary school qualifications were allowed to stay up till 9 pm, and university students till 11 pm.

The men worked in the quarries five days a week. Initially on Saturdays they were locked up all day, but after a few years, they were allowed to play soccer and rugby and other games on Saturdays.

Zuma's face lit up when he talked about his prowess at soccer: 'I was the best defender on Robben Island. I was captain of a team called Rangers – and we were the best team that place ever saw.'

'Oh yes,' said Ebrahim, 'obviously Zuma was much leaner then – well, we didn't get much to eat anyway, we were all thinner – but he did play a very good game of soccer.'

Lizo Sitoto, one of the main protagonists in *More Than Just a Game*, a recent book about the way in which the lives of Robben Island prisoners were enriched by playing soccer, describes how he expected a 'bruising encounter' when he stepped out one day on to the concrete pitch on the Island – because 'the Rangers captain was a tough, no-nonsense ANC activist called Jacob Zuma, known to be as uncompromising on the soccer pitch as he was in the political arena …

'Experience told Lizo that he would have to be on his guard because Zuma would, as ever, be putting himself about in the penalty area, at corners and set pieces. Zuma was a tough soccer player who played as a defender mainly at right back and centre half …'[2]

Zuma also organised a choral group that sang mainly liberation songs, and a traditional dance team: 'I also played table tennis, a bit of chess, and of course *marabaraba*, the game played with stones that you move around in holes on the ground. And I was not too bad an athlete.'

Another thing about Zuma, said Ebrahim, was that he was – and probably still is – a brilliant storyteller: 'He has a remarkable memory – there are advantages to coming from a predominantly oral culture and not being fully literate – and he knew all these stories about Zulu history and so on. And he would start telling a story – say about Shaka and say at night in the cell – and then he would have to stop. But he would carry on the next night where he left off. The other prisoners were spellbound.'

But what really gets Zuma going, when he talks about his years on Robben Island, is the study groups and political discussions. Zuma was on the political committee, responsible for organising political discussion and activities.

'You ask about depression and loneliness on Robben Island. What really kept us together and alive were the activities we organised for ourselves – the sport but mostly our political education,' said Zuma. 'And it was the Durban boys who were at the forefront. There were five of us from Durban, including myself and Harry Gwala and Ibie. We had already in Durban had study groups and we led those discussions on the Island, in the communal cells. And we studied intensely. We really worked hard.'

Ebrahim doesn't want to cross swords with Zuma about just how 'literate' he was in those days – 'of course he could read and write isiZulu' – but he said that it was Gwala and himself who played a major role in expanding Zuma's knowledge of English, and especially his political horizons.

We know from the memoirs of Nelson Mandela and Mac Maharaj that some of the political discussions, often about what might now seem to be inconsequential subjects, became extremely heated, and that Mandela and Govan Mbeki clashed repeatedly to the detriment of their relationship.

Maharaj tells us that Mbeki and Gwala argued that the SACP and ANC were one and the same, while Mandela insisted they were not – and that a solution to the issue had to be found by deferring the question to the ANC in Lusaka (which came down on Mandela's side).[3]

This kind of acrimonious exchange also happened regularly in the general cells. In particular there were often serious manifestations of hostility between ANC and PAC prisoners: 'And then,' remarked Ebrahim, 'when it got really serious, we would send a message to the leadership, Mandela and Govan Mbeki, asking them to make a determination for us. And we would get incredibly lengthy and serious replies.'

Zuma and Ebrahim say that there were two 'absolutely remarkable' aspects about the group of political prisoners on Robben Island. The one was that, due to their efforts, the place was not so much a jail as a high-level school for political education. By the time that study privileges were allowed, largely as the result of the efforts of Mandela and the men in the single cells, those doing university degrees ordered books that often bypassed the censors, or a political prisoner who was passing through the study office would 'borrow' a relevant book, and newspapers were often smuggled to the 'politicals' by the common law prisoners.

The second remarkable aspect of the Robben Island community of political prisoners was the iron discipline of party members. Issues were settled by debate and consensus – and that was how it had to be. The ANC did not allow smuggling of food or the drinking of 'booze', which some of the common law prisoners made by fermenting various things. The party also had a strict rule about sex: it was forbidden between the men. Zuma and Ebrahim concurred that the worst thing that could happen to one of the prisoners was to be 'excommunicated from the structures'– and this happened to those who broke the ANC's rules.

Ebrahim said that Zuma was energetic and the self-appointed morale officer for his block. 'The prison conditions were such that they wanted to break our morale and spirit. Zuma wouldn't be broken.'

Zuma might have come to Robben Island informed only by general political notions learned at trade union meetings in Durban, but he left the island with a clarified and focused political understanding; a resolute belief that only the ANC had the right solutions to the problems bedevilling South Africa; and an unshakable commitment to the ANC and to the discipline and ways of dealing with the struggle to which the party subscribed.

He had indeed graduated from one of the most difficult, yet strangely invigorating and fecund institutions of higher learning that have ever existed. It was not a rite of passage that one would wish on anyone; but, having had to pass through it, it would stand him in good stead for the rest of his days.

Zuma left the Island about two-and-a-half weeks before the official end of his prison sentence, towards the end of 1973, and was trucked back to Pietermaritzburg, where he was held for two weeks in the police cells. Prison rules stated that he had to be delivered home and so, on the day of his release, he and two policemen, one white and one Indian, set out from Pietermaritzburg for Nkandla in a police car. Zuma was hand-cuffed on the back seat.

After hours of driving, they got lost on the winding, muddy roads from the midlands to the heart of Zululand. Zuma tried to give the po-licemen some directions but they told him he was a prisoner and should keep quiet; they knew what they were doing. Then the car got stuck in the mud in a dip in the road. Zuma offered to help the policemen but they told him he was a prisoner and was not permitted to do so. So he sat, like the lord of the manor on the back seat, while the two men grunted and groaned, pushing the car out.

But they were still lost. Finally, they came upon a young woman standing in the sunshine on the side of the road somewhere between Kranskop and Nkandla. Again, Zuma offered to help – by speaking to her. Again, he was told to mind his own business. One of the policemen asked the woman – who, Zuma says, was young and comely – for direc-tions to Nkandla. And she started to explain.

'That young woman's voice was the most beautiful sound I had heard for 10 years,' said Zuma.

'I had not realised till that moment that I had not heard a young woman's voice for all those years. It was like a bird singing. It was beauti-ful. It was the end of Robben Island for me.'

CHAPTER 4

1974–1990

Silence, Exile and Cunning

'Silence, exile, and cunning'[1] – and underground warfare. This seems a fitting sobriquet for the 15 years of Jacob Zuma's life following his release from Robben Island. Why 'silence'? If you look at the Wikipedia entry for Jacob Zuma, you will find – not much:

> After Zuma's release, he was instrumental in the re-establishment of ANC underground structures [a favourite ANC word] in the Natal province. He left South Africa in 1975, based first in Swaziland and then Mozambique, and dealt with the arrival of thousands of exiles in the wake of the Soweto uprising. He became a member of the ANC National Executive Committee in 1977. He also served as Deputy Chief Representative of the ANC in Mozambique, a post he occupied until the signing of the Nkomati Accord between the Mozambican and South African governments in 1984. After ... the Accord, Zuma was appointed as Chief Representative of the ANC. Zuma was forced to leave Mozambique in January 1987 after

considerable pressure on the Mozambican government by the PW Botha regime. He moved to the ANC head office in Lusaka, Zambia, where he was appointed Head of Underground Structures and shortly thereafter Chief of the Intelligence Department. He served on the ANC's political and military council when it was formed in the mid-1980s.

Other than these words, there is very little information to be found, and the name of Jacob Zuma does not appear in books, articles and 'official' documentation (except as one of the ANC's senior office bearers) until 1987, when he was transferred to 'head office' in Lusaka. There he also became one of the select group that took part in the first meetings between the ANC and South African businessmen and political leaders and then, more importantly, between the ANC and the secret representatives of the Nationalist government.

Part of the reason for Zuma's non-appearance is that he never attracted any particular attention – relative to, say, those with a greater 'media appeal', such as Mac Maharaj, Joe Slovo, Chris Hani, and others. A more important part of the reason is that Zuma did not want to be known. Besides being the ANC's official deputy chief representative and then chief representative in Mozambique, Zuma's main task was running its Swaziland/Natal operations. In short, he needed and wanted to keep as low a profile as possible and he still will not talk in detail about the operational events of those days. In his view, these are the 'property' of the ANC, not his.

From 1974 to 1989, Zuma's whereabouts and activities were roughly as follows. From the beginning of 1974, after his release from Robben Island, to December 1975, Zuma was back at Nkandla and in Natal, setting up contacts and groups – re-establishing the underground in Natal. His attorney, Phyllis Naidoo, found him work in a Durban pet shop. At one stage, she is said to have had five ex-Robben Island detainees – Zuma among them – as messengers at her law firm.

Zuma took recruits for MK training and intelligence out of South Africa into Swaziland; and MK fighters, weapons and instructions back in. He also married Sizakele Khumalo, a shy childhood sweetheart, whom he had met in 1959. She, wife number one, still lives at Nkandla, where she prefers to this day to keep as low a profile as any intelligence operative. When the University of Zululand conferred an honorary degree on him in 2002, Zuma described her as an amazing person who had shared the better part of his life as 'a wife, a friend, a sister and a mother to me. As a girlfriend, she waited 10 years and six months for me while I was imprisoned on Robben Island. As a wife she waited for 14 years and a half when I was in exile. She indeed suffered a lot because of her loyalty, love and commitment to me.'

So Sizakele was not with him in Swaziland and, fearing that he was about to be arrested, which seemed very likely, Zuma remained there from the end of December 1975 until he was deported to Mozambique, along with Thabo Mbeki, in April 1976, just before the June 1976 Soweto uprising. From then until 1987, his main base was Maputo, though he often moved in and out of Swaziland and perhaps even Natal, and travelled to London and other places. In 1977 he became a member of the ANC National Executive Committee (NEC). At some unspecified time during his Maputo sojourn, he went to the USSR for military training. In December 1986/January 1987, he moved to Lusaka, where he was made chief of intelligence.

Mark Gevisser, author of the biography of Thabo Mbeki, *The Dream Deferred*, has described Zuma as having the 'stolid, deliberate mien of a rural Zulu man'; 'fearless, loyal and affable'; and 'possessed of a canny wit that made him one of the ANC's most effective operators'.[2] Rare photographs from the 1980s show Zuma to have been anything but stolid and deliberate, with his expressive face and quick smile. Television cameras, however, do have the effect of 'freezing' him. He was doubtless a highly effective operator – not only because he was canny but because he was innately suspicious and, above all, had what we would these days call a high EQ (emotional quotient as opposed to intelligence quotient). Zuma might not have read books with ease, but he read people well and rapidly and instinctively knew how to handle them.

Jacob Zuma likes women a great deal and he likes making babies; he is the proverbial family man. He is also an unabashed polygamist. In 2007, he would tell a television interviewer: 'There are plenty of politicians who have mistresses and children that they hide so as to pretend they're monogamous. I prefer to be open. I love my wives and I'm proud of my children.'

For this book, however, he refused to discuss the details of his marital or romantic life, or lives. 'I will write about my family and my wives in the book that I am going to write myself' – even if he is 'busy' being president from the middle of 2009.

At any rate, on his release from Robben Island, Zuma had, as we have said, married Sizakele Gertrude Khumalo, a childhood sweetheart, whom he had known since he was 17, to be known later as MaKhumalo. She did not go into exile with him but stayed on at Nkandla – remaining 'his woman', as he said many years later, throughout his decade on the Island and during his 15 years of exile. The rondavel at Nkandla in which she stayed was small and poor – nothing like the fancy set of rondavels, comprising the so-called 'traditional homestead' that Zuma built in the mid-1990s. Nonetheless, she kept the home fires burning and has never been heard by anyone say a cross or complaining word about him.

Towards the end of 1976, having moved to Maputo, Zuma married Kate Mantsho, who worked for a Mozambican airline, and with whom he would have five children. And some time in the 1980s – precisely when is not clear – he married Nkosazana Dlamini, who worked as a pediatrician at Swaziland's Mbabane Government Hospital, and with whom he would have four children.

Unfortunately, neither of Zuma's exile marriages ended happily. In June 1998 Zuma and Nkosazana divorced, and Kate committed suicide in December 2000.

In 1977 or thereabouts, Zuma had a liaison with Minah Shongwe, the sister of a man who would, as we will see, become one of the deputy judges president of the Transvaal Provincial Division and reappear in Zuma's life. They had a son called Edward who has spent most of his adult life in Zuma's household.

In 1974, the Portuguese military overthrew dictator Marcello Caetano, partially because the 'wars' in the former Portuguese colonies were dragging on and the army had had enough; and so Mozambique looked set for independence, with Frelimo's Samora Machel, an ANC ally, as the likely president. The ANC immediately saw the opportunity of opening an eastern front.

A perfect launching pad for military operations, given its proximity to South Africa and porous borders, was Swaziland. Thabo Mbeki had been on a reconnaissance mission to the little kingdom with Max Sisulu in January 1975 and reported that Swaziland was indeed ripe with potential for the ANC. A large contingent of young black South Africans were studying there and it was within striking distance of Johannesburg and Natal – which was then the epicentre of resistance inside South Africa.[3] The difficulty was that the reigning monarch, King Sobhuza II, was, for obvious reasons, under the fat white thumb of his large neighbour.

Mbeki, 33 years old and newly elected to the NEC, was therefore sent back to Swaziland in March 1975. His primary task was recruitment. Joe Modise, the head of MK, said he wanted 50 men a month for his army. It was here that Mbeki met Zuma, a month and six days his senior. Zuma ran the South African side of the conduit into Natal that Mbeki and Albert Dhlomo ran on the Swazi side. Since 1974, Zuma had been active behind the scenes of the industrial unrest in Natal, where a series of wildcat strikes had led to there being more than 60 000 workers on strike at 146 companies,[4] recruiting potential information-gatherers and soldiers for the struggle.

There were enormous setbacks to the ANC underground in South Africa in 1974–75, for much the same reason as there would be setbacks for the next decade: the security police seemed to be ahead of the game. The reason above all others for this was, as Mac Maharaj has put it, 'the worms within': informers, *impimpis*, enemy agents.

During this time there were numerous arrests in the Pietermaritzburg/ Durban region, Port Elizabeth, Cape Town and Johannesburg, and many of the people arrested had come off Robben Island relatively recently. Zuma crossed to Swaziland in December 1975 (his first time), evading the police net in which more than 50 activists, including Harry Gwala, had been caught. He had been concerned that his Swaziland counterparts might be being a little cavalier about procedures and he came over the border to talk to them about focusing harder. On his way back, he picked up a newspaper which reported the detention of two of his key people.

Mbeki, the commander, was away, but when he returned, he forbade Zuma to return to South Africa – and Zuma's weekend away turned into a 15-year exile. Zuma wanted to return to Natal – not doing so, he thought, would be to flush away two years of hard work. But Mbeki was adamant that it would be irresponsible for Zuma to do so; all the information about the Natal operations was in his head. So Zuma stayed – though, being Zuma, a little later, when Mbeki was out of Swaziland again, he slipped across the border for two weeks to reactivate his networks.

It was in Swaziland that Mbeki, who had been militarily trained, taught Zuma how to use a gun, and he also taught Zuma and others about arms and underground communication and propaganda, as well as the importance of 'diplomatic' skills, of charm in general; there were different ways of achieving one's goals.[5]

Then, in March 1976, not long before the Soweto uprising, the three leading ANC lights in Swaziland – Mbeki, Zuma and Albert Dhlomo – found themselves in Swaziland's Matsapha maximum security prison, awaiting deportation to South Africa. Mbeki had been picked up by the Swazi police on the roadside, Zuma and Dhlomo at their lodgings. The latter two had been found with ammunition and a drawing by Mbeki showing a bullet's trajectory. Mbeki and Dhlomo were quasi-official representatives of the ANC in the country and were not supposed to be involved in 'military' activities. Zuma in particular not only ran the Natal underground but was illegally in Swaziland.

The three were caught as a result of the activities of six security branch agents who had infiltrated the movement in Durban and been recruited as potential MK soldiers. Zuma had suspected something was not 'right' about them and suggested that they be quickly sent to Mozambique for security vetting. But three of them escaped from the safe house where they were being held and went to a local police station and asked to be returned to South Africa.

The three caused a great deal of damage. As a result of their activities, Joseph Mdluli, a leading underground operative, the man who had recruited them, was arrested and murdered; two other ANC members inside Swaziland were kidnapped, tortured and imprisoned. Worst of all, from Mbeki's and Zuma's point of view, if they were deported to South Africa, which was the idea, they – important people in the organisation – would be tried and imprisoned, a huge coup for the security police. In addition, the South African authorities had demonstrated to the Swazis that the ANC was involved in more than diplomatic work, which is all they were officially supposed to be doing.[6]

Luckily for them, six months before they were arrested, Tambo had made a secret visit to Sobhuza II and the king had declared that he supported the ANC. So Tambo immediately dispatched two ANC senior members, Moses Mabhida and Thomas Nkobi, to see the king. Sobhuza wanted to know why 'young boys' had apparently been allowed to run riot in his kingdom, but he said he would grant official status to the ANC – Mabhida would be the Chief Representative, the United Nations having recognised the ANC in 1973 – and, as for the three young boys, they would have to be deported to another African country.

The three were taken to the airport to be flown to Lusaka. But they noticed that the flight was via South Africa, where they could have been arrested while in transit. The Swazis were probably aiming to please both the ANC and South Africa, but the men protested. Mbeki handled the negotiations with the Swazis very coolly and professionally, Zuma said. A massive tug of war was going on, with the South Africans trying to get their hands on the men and the ANC trying to save them. In the end, in April 1976, a month after their arrest, they were escorted to the border of the newly independent Mozambique.[7]

Not long after this, in June 1976, Soweto erupted. A massive explosion in South African society, the biggest and most significant since Sharpeville, had gone off. Within 10 months, 575 people had died; by

December 1976, more than 10 000 people had been detained, many of them children as young as eight.

This meant that a major part of Zuma's activities – from his new base in Mozambique – was 'receiving' and organising the exiles streaming across the borders. Zuma has estimated, for example, that, before he and Mbeki were deported from Swaziland, they 'processed' more than 100 people from Natal alone, bringing them through Swaziland and then transporting them to Mozambique, where the ANC had relative security in addition to official status, and from where they would be sent for training in Eastern Europe or North Africa. And this was a trickle compared to the flood of young people who came across the borders after June 1976. It has been estimated that some 4 000 young black South Africans went into exile in the 18 months following Soweto and that most joined the ANC. MK's operational force tripled during the course of 1976.[8]

For the ANC the Soweto uprising was also highly significant in another, negative way. The movement had had precious little to do with the uprising; was in fact caught almost completely unawares by it; there were certainly no units on hand to take advantage of the situation. The 'war of liberation' had moved inside South Africa and from then onwards would be fought there, as well as by the ANC in exile.

The hard truth – though Zuma refuses to put it as bluntly as this – was that the ANC underground had not been, and was not going to be, potent or successful until the very late 1980s, if at all; nor, unfortunately, would its cross-border military operations. This was not necessarily because the ANC was inefficient or weak. It was facing difficult odds: trying to mobilise meaningful political and underground military operations from a distance, and via other people's countries, against a well-equipped, well-trained and exceptionally brutal security force.[9]

From the late 1970s, the South African Police's notorious counter-insurgency Vlakplaas unit, and other units, were crossing South Africa's borders with impunity and launching the equivalent of military ambushes and attacks on MK personnel. The list of 'successful' killings, abductions and torture inflicted on ANC or MK members by the security forces, especially in Swaziland and Natal, is frighteningly long.[10]

One person who could testify that the ANC was inefficient, disorganised and far too porous was Satyandranath Ragunanan 'Mac' Maharaj, a former Robben Islander and favourite of Nelson Mandela, who had not met Zuma on the Island (he would meet him in Maputo in 1978). Mac went into exile in Lusaka in 1977, and was mandated by the ANC high command to re-establish the kind of political underground that had not been there for the Sowetan students.

One of the revelations that he makes in his biography by Padraig O'Malley, *Shades of Difference*,[11] and in an earlier interview with journalist Howard Barrell,[12] was that he was told by Thabo Mbeki in December 1978 that many underground 'actions' had been initiated when he was in Swaziland, but for some reason nothing had come of any of them.

Maharaj requested the detailed records of those operations but was given nothing. Mbeki said the records were in the safekeeping of Stanley Mabizela, in Swaziland. When Mac asked, early in 1979, for the trunk in which the records were kept, Mabizela fobbed him off: he had to have permission from Mbeki to hand them over. But Mbeki was travelling a great deal – and Maharaj never saw any records. It was Maharaj's view, about which he was quite open in front of the ANC high command, that Mbeki had been a poor front-line commander and that not much, by Maharaj's standards, had been achieved in Swaziland. It is not surprising that Maharaj and Mbeki never became close comrades and that events of the late 1970s – or, at any rate, old animosities dating from then – would rear their ugly heads again in 2003 at the Hefer Commission.

Maharaj would say that there was another major reason for the continuing failure of the underground, one alluded to already: the ANC was infiltrated from the bottom to the top; it was toxic with informers. And Zuma agreed with him.

This was why the Mandla Judson Kuzwayo (MJK) unit, which fell under Zuma's command in 1986 when he was still in Mozambique, came to play an important role in his life. Put together by Yunis Shaik (codenamed Mandla), and with two other members – Moe Shaik (Judson) and Jayendra Naidoo (Kuzwayo), the unit had infiltrated the security branch's 'system' and had a finger on the full gamut of informers. A senior SB officer, disgusted by the extreme torture that he witnessed being inflicted on Yunis Shaik in 1985, 'turned' and became an ANC mole (code name Nightingale), and his sole handler was Moe Shaik. This ongoing project was known as Operation Bible (because Tambo had said that, when it came to spies or informers, the information 'had to be as true as the Bible' or horrible, irreversible mistakes might be made).

At the beginning of 1987, Maharaj was nominated by Tambo and Joe Slovo, head of MK operations, to prepare for the launch of the top secret Operation Vula (for *Vulindlela*, meaning 'Open the Way'), which was so secret that many members of the ANC high command were unaware of it – and which would have enormous ramifications later, because it would not be closed down even when the negotiations for a 'new South Africa' were taking place in 1990 and later. According to Zuma, Tambo wanted him to return to South Africa as part of the Vula team, but he was made chief of intelligence at about that time and had to remain in Lusaka.[13]

So Zuma's main focus, from operating as a diplomat and trying to execute secret missions into Natal and to get people out, turned increasingly to intelligence and counter-intelligence. Yunis Shaik recalls Zuma as having been a 'good commander' – protecting his sources impeccably, making sure there were no leakages and helping to reorganise the underground inside South Africa, as best he could from a distance.

'Zuma was fast, active and strong,' said Yunis. 'Don't mistake the man you see now, wearing a suit and smiling and perhaps reacting thoughtfully, with the man who was our commander.'

Going back a couple of years, to a time before the MJK unit was formed, we come to the Nkomati Accord of March 1984. This was the non-aggression treaty signed by the Mozambican government and the apartheid government on 16 March at Komatipoort, and its focus was on preventing Mozambique from supporting the ANC and South Africa from supplying the Mozambican National Resistance Movement (Renamo) with weapons and training.

Mozambican president Samora Machel never fully honoured his

commitments (nor did South Africa), but the ANC was effectively banished and it was a huge blow to the organisation in terms of organising military actions. ANC leaders, including chief representative Lennox Zuma, Joe Slovo, Ronnie Kasrils, and Chris Hani, all had to pack their bags. Zuma stayed behind, becoming the ANC's chief diplomat.

In June 1986, Vlakplaas' Eugene de Kock kidnapped Sidney Msibi, a former bodyguard of Oliver Tambo and a leading MK intelligence official. Msibi, in conjunction with Glory Sedibe, Joe Modise's brother-in-law and the MK intelligence chief for the Transvaal, had recruited a Warrant Officer Malaza of the Nelspruit security branch, who sold them out.

In August, De Kock kidnapped Sedibe from a Swazi jail – and he was 'turned'. The information given to the police by Sedibe enabled them 'virtually to wipe out' MK in Swaziland.[14] Among those captured by the security police was Ibie Ebrahim, Zuma's former cellmate, who was chairman of the ANC's Swaziland Regional Political-Military Council (RPMC). He was abducted in December 1986, tortured and sentenced to 20 years for high treason – but was released when it was found, on appeal, that his abduction had been 'illegal'. In July 1987, the security police ambushed and killed Cassius Make, chief of ordnance for the MK high command, and Paul Dikeledi, a senior Transvaal commander.

The destruction of the Swazi networks was accompanied by 'diplomatic' attacks on the ANC in Mozambique. In December 1986, the Mozambican authorities expelled Zuma, Sue Rabkin (now married to Pallo Jordan), Bobby Pillay, Indris Naidoo and Keith Mokoape, deputy head of ANC military intelligence.

So thoroughly were ANC structures undermined that in 1988, virtually all the commanders of the Natal underground were withdrawn to Lusaka for investigation by the ANC's security department. Maharaj's anguish about the state of toxicity of ANC underground structures is understandable, as is the ANC's extreme reaction to suspected traitors. Militarily speaking, the ANC – and people such as Zuma in particular – was having an extremely tough time.

In its 1998 report, the Truth and Reconciliation Commission (TRC) found that:

> [T]he ANC, particularly its military structures which were responsible for the treatment and welfare of those in the camps, were guilty of gross violations of human rights in certain circumstances and against two categories of individuals – suspected 'enemy agents' and mutineers … [T]here were cases where such individuals were charged and convicted by tribunals without proper attention to due process being afforded them, sentenced to death and executed … With regard to allegations of torture, the commission finds that, although it was not ANC policy to use torture, the security department of the ANC routinely used torture to extract information and confessions from those being held in camps, particularly in the period 1979–89 … The commission finds further that adequate steps were not taken in good time against those responsible for such violations.[15]

The TRC was reacting to the fact that between 1979 and 1989, the ANC had indeed been responsible for 'various human rights abuses' of its own members in exile, many of which were committed by the ANC's security department, established in the mid-1970s and known by the acronym NAT (for National Security) or Mbokodo/Mbokotho ('crushing boulder').

One of the places where 'significant abuses' took place was a detention camp known as Quatro in Angola. In 1991 the ANC set up the Skweyiya Commission of Enquiry which, though it had no statutory or subpoena powers and no witness protection facilities, nonetheless found that Quatro had been a persistently brutal place where torture was rife. The commission was criticised for not dealing with camps besides Quatro and for not finding specific individuals responsible for abuses, and in 1993 Nelson Mandela set up the Motsuenyane Commission of Enquiry.

This found that there was a lack of accountability for any of the excesses and that the 'leadership' had not dealt at all adequately with human rights violations. In response to the Motsuenyane Commission, the ANC NEC apologised for the 'excesses' that had taken place and acknowledged that 'there had been a drift in accountability and control away from established norms, resulting in situations in which some individuals within the NAT began to behave as a law unto themselves.'

Zuma was one of those 'leaders' censured by the Motsuenyane Commission – for failing to supervise properly the investigation into David Mbatha, an elderly ANC member and father of nine children.

Mbatha and his wife had travelled to Zambia in 1988 to visit their children. Shortly after his arrival, Mbatha was detained – on the authority of Zuma, a security department official told the commission. He was held for 10 months in Quatro, and when in Lusaka was beaten repeatedly on his bare feet.

Zuma told the commission that he had not even been in Lusaka when Mbatha was arrested. But, in condemning Zuma for not exercising proper supervision, the commission seems not to have been at all happy with this explanation.

Another better known case in which Zuma was implicated – because he was then head of counter-intelligence – was the death of Muziwakhe Ngwenya, better known as Thami Zulu or 'TZ'. From the 1976 generation of recruits, TZ had been commander of the Natal 'structures' in the mid-1980s and was very close to Chris Hani. He had apparently been implicated by a self-confessed spy known as 'Comrade Cyril' or 'Fear' (real name Ralph Mgcina), and he had been the commanding officer of the turncoat Sedibe. TZ was said to have been disliked by his comrades because he behaved 'like a little Napoleon', but also because he was a Sowetan and not a Zulu.

TZ was arrested by NAT and held for 17 months. He was released on 11 November 1989, and five days later he was dead. TZ had entered detention, in the words of the 1989 (Albie) Sachs Commission Report on the Death of Thami Zulu,[16] a 'large, well-built slightly overweight person, and come out gaunt, frail and almost unrecognisable'.

On his release, he was taken to stay at a house of a friend, Dr Ralph Ngijima. He told Ngijima that his condition had deteriorated drastically while he was in an isolation cell. Having developed diarrhoea, mouth sores (thrush) and a spiking fever, he had been taken to hospital in Lusaka where a blood test showed he was HIV-positive. Although he was furious at his treatment, he never alleged that any violence had been used against him.

Ngijima himself fell seriously ill and had to be taken to hospital for an emergency operation, so he was not there when TZ died four days later of heart and lung failure. Medical opinion in Lusaka – and London, where specimens of blood and stomach contents were taken for analysis – was that he had died of AIDS, which had destroyed his immune system, allowing for the rapid advance of TB (from which he had suffered previously). The problem was that his blood and stomach contents showed traces of diazinon, an organic phosphorus pesticide, and also the equivalent of three pints of beer. Alcohol is one of the few liquids in which diazinon is soluble and which could hide the taste of the pesticide.

It seems – and the Sachs Commission agreed – that TZ was poisoned at some point during the few days that he was at Ngijima's house. The question was: by whom? The commission's view was that it was security agents from South Africa. Press reports written (by David Beresford of *The Guardian* and Phillip van Niekerk of the *Weekly Mail*) in September 1991 – based on interviews with Hani – said that, when Hani saw TZ on 14 November, two days before he died – TZ was worried that 'the Security Department' was going to 'finish me off'. He had pointed a finger directly at the ANC security department, headed by the late Joe Nhlanhla, Jacob Zuma, and Sizakele Sigxashe. The newspaper reports suggested strongly that Hani was actually pointing a finger at Zuma.

In his testimony to the TRC, TZ's father, Philemon Ngwenya, a retired Soweto headmaster, said he had gone to Lusaka to see Zuma about TZ after he was arrested – but had been fobbed off with false assurances or 'lies', and that Zuma had then refused to see him, even though he, Ngwenya, had 'waited and waited for 18 days' in Lusaka.

Complicating matters is that it has never been clear whether TZ was a spy or not. At a later TRC hearing, Christo Nel, a former Civil Cooperation Bureau (CCB) intelligence agent, testified that it seemed that there had been a 'project' to make TZ look like an agent and that 'MK had killed him'. According to Maharaj's biographer, Padraig O'Malley, security branch officer Hentie Botha told him that the Security Branch (SB) fed the ANC misinformation about TZ 'in the knowledge that Zulu would be recalled to Lusaka and arrested by NAT'.[17] The view among some ANC members who were connected with the incident is that TZ was probably not a spy – though there were so many spies and informers on both sides, and so many damaging counter-intelligence initiatives, that no one really seems to know for certain.

At a TRC hearing in May 1997, Mbeki responded to the incident on behalf of the ANC. 'Thami Zulu died of poisoning after his release,' Mbeki stated, 'and to this day it is a matter of conjecture as to who administered the poison and why this was done. Our own security department has reason to believe that an agent or agents of the regime was responsible.'

Someone who at the time worked very closely with Zuma in counter-intelligence, and prefers to remain anonymous, told me that 'there was credible information, which Zuma knew about, for suspecting that TZ had been involved in, shall we say, some dubious enterprises'. In his view, however, there is little doubt that TZ was poisoned by enemy agents. 'We had had him in detention for 17 months and could have killed him then if that is what we wanted to do. Why would we kill him when we had just released him? Secondly, Lusaka was full of enemy agents, operating with a great deal of impunity, and we were infiltrated. Thirdly, the choice of poison seems a security branch sort of thing to me. I think TZ was killed because the SB feared he was sooner or later going to divulge a network. Certainly, JZ didn't order his death.'

One of the most bizarre, horrifying and illuminating series of events that ever occurred during the struggle against apartheid – the one that would prise open apartheid's foulest barrel of worms – kicked off in Pretoria Central Prison's death row on the evening of 19 October 1989.[18]

Constable Butana Almond Nofemela, due to be hanged on 20 October for murdering a farmer from Brits – a non-political murder – asked Lawyers for Human Rights (LHR) to send someone to take a statement from him because he had something important to say. LHR sent Steve Katzew, a young lawyer, to whom Nofemela gave an affidavit, stating that he had been a member of the security branch's 'assassination squad' – no one, except those involved, knew of any such squad at the time – and that he had been one of those who had murdered Griffiths Mxenge, a well-known attorney and ANC activist.

Nofemela apparently believed – or so Eugene de Kock, the commander of Vlakplaas, told me[19] – that the least the police should have done for him was to see to it that his housing subsidy continued to be paid to his family. According to De Kock, he recommended to Brigadier Willem Schoon, overall commanding officer of the police's counter-intelligence units, that this should be done. But Schoon said no, and De Kock sent a message to Nofemela that he 'needed to take the pain'.

Nofemela won a temporary reprieve and the Independent Board of Inquiry into Informal Repression, founded by the Reverend Frank Chikane after he had survived an assassination attempt (his clothing had been poisoned by the security police), started investigating Nofemela's claims.[20]

On the morning of 17 November 1989, the Afrikaans-language *Vrye Weekblad*, edited by Max du Preez, came out with one of the greatest journalistic coups of all time. Journalist Jacques Pauw revealed the brutal story of Dirk Coetzee, one of the previous commanders of the police's Vlakplaas death squad. He corroborated Nofemela's stories, confirmed that he had been in charge of the squad that murdered Mxenge, 'outed' De Kock, and much more besides: he had knowledge about the deaths of Ruth First in 1982, Jeanette and Katryn Schoon in 1984, the bombing of the ANC's London offices in 1982, and the death by thallium poisoning of Siphiwo Mtimkulu.

Pauw and Du Preez had been privy to Coetzee's story for some time. But Nofemela's statement meant that they needed to publish it as quickly as possible. It also meant that Coetzee needed to be hidden or to leave the country before *Vrye Weekblad* published. De Kock disliked him in any case, and would certainly have become obsessed with killing the traitor.

Prior to Nofemela's confession being made public, Du Preez, Pauw and Coetzee decided that Du Preez would contact André Zaaiman, a director of the Institute for a Democratic Alternative in South Africa (Idasa), asking him to ask the ANC if it would protect Coetzee 'if he came out'. What better propaganda tool against the apartheid regime?

Zaaiman had done so – and one Jacob Zuma, the ANC's chief of intelligence, had agreed to take charge of the project. On 5 November 1989, Pauw and Coetzee flew to Mauritius and then to London, Lusaka, and Jacob Zuma.

In early January 1990, lawyer Peter Harris was asked by the ANC to come to Lusaka, along with Max Coleman, a political activist, to take a detailed statement from Coetzee. They were met by Zuma, who explained to them that Coetzee had 'gone through a lot' and that they needed to be patient with him. Coetzee had been resistant to talking to people from South Africa, Zuma explained, 'but I told him that we all come from South Africa. It's just that some of us have been outside for longer. And one thing's for certain: we're all going back.'

Harris notes that Zuma spoke about Coetzee without recrimination and that he seemed to be a true '[intelligence] professional, chewing the information from his charge like cud, extracting the nutrients.'[21]

After Coetzee had fled South Africa, his wife, Karen, had an affair with a security police plant and this drove Coetzee, trapped in Lusaka, almost literally mad. Zuma arranged to have Coetzee's wife flown to Lusaka and apparently helped patch up the rift. Harris wrote: 'The next few days [spent by the Coetzees] were blissful, and Coetzee is particularly grateful to Zuma, whom he credits with saving his marriage. This is a turning point for Coetzee; he is now Zuma's man.'[22]

According to historian and biographer Luli Callinicos, Oliver Tambo was plagued for many years by a recurring nightmare. A day would come when the apartheid regime would send a signal to the ANC that it wanted to talk – but the ANC would be 'unable to understand' the message.[23]

From as early as 1981, remarkably, a variety of signals presaging a *toenadering* ('coming together') – or, at any rate, a kind of jab in the general direction of sanity – emanated from South Africa. In 1985, Zambia's Kenneth Kaunda suggested an informal meeting between South African corporate businessmen and the ANC, and he contacted Gavin Relly, then a director of Anglo American. President Botha's finger-wagging intransigence was making big business edgy, as were highly organised strikes and stayaways and financial sanctions. The huge mining companies, such as Anglo, had been around for a century – and besides, in 1985, had a 54 per cent stake in the Johannesburg Stock Exchange. Talking to 'the enemy' was preferable to seeing more general industrial unrest or bloodshed.

Relly organised a trip, although some of the Afrikaner businessmen withdrew. However, in the company of two high-profile editors, *Die Vaderland*'s Harald Pakendorf and the *Sunday Times*'s Tertius Myburgh, plus Hugh Murray, the irrepressible editor of *Leadership* magazine, a number of important executives (including Tony Bloom, the chief executive of Premier Milling, for whom this book's author then worked) met the ANC leadership on 13 September 1985. It was accounted a success and was certainly a huge eye-opener for both sides. A few months later some of the same business leaders were joined in London by a few major British businessmen in a meeting with Tambo in the Connaught Rooms.

In the same year, Kobie Coetsee, the Minister of Justice, visited Nelson Mandela in hospital – and it may safely be assumed that it was not the famous prisoner's prostate operation that he was interested in.

There was a discreetly successful meeting in the US between Thabo Mbeki, Mac Maharaj and Seretse Choabe and some influential Afrikaners, including Pieter de Lange, head of the secret Broederbond. In 1987 Frederik van Zyl Slabbert, who had recently resigned as leader of the Progressive Federal Party, led a 50-strong delegation to meet the ANC in Dakar, Senegal.

Then came the first big one. In November 1987, Professor Willie Esterhuyse brought a few colleagues to a meeting arranged with the ANC by Consolidated Gold, the holding company for Goldfields. Niël Barnard, the head of the National Intelligence Service (NIS), had asked for a report on the discussions, and Esterhuyse had agreed, provided he could tell Mbeki and the colleague who would accompany him, Jacob

Zuma, about this.

Several meetings followed over the next few months between Mbeki and Zuma and Esterhuyse and other prominent Afrikaner academics. After the first meeting, the rest (12 in all, between November 1987 and May 1990) were held at Mells Park, a secluded English manor house outside Bath in Somersetshire, owned by ConsGold. And throughout Esterhuyse would convey to Mbeki and Zuma what was on Barnard's mind and then tell Barnard what was on Mbeki's and Zuma's minds.

Mbeki told journalist Allister Sparks that he remembered a discussion with one of the Afrikaner participants, 'still very much in the apartheid mould', who kept returning to the issue of 'group rights', which he said was fundamental to any agreement.

'I remember Jacob Zuma saying to him, "Look, I'm a Zulu and so is Chief Buthelezi, and if we got together we could speak Zulu to one another, we could do the traditional dances, we could do all sorts of things, but there's no way you are going to find Chief Buthelezi and me in the same party. The fact of our Zuluness doesn't result in our sharing common political perspectives and aspirations, so you can't say that negotiations must be between Zulus and Afrikaners and so on." And this Afrikaner chap says to him, "I've never thought about it like that. Of course, you're right. I can eat boerewors with Andries Treurnicht [the Conservative Party leader at the time] but you won't find us in the same party."'[24]

On 31 May 1989, Esterhuyse gave Mbeki a code name and a telephone number. When given the go-ahead by Tambo, Mbeki called Esterhuyse, thus giving the professor permission to set up a meeting between the ANC and the NIS. Mbeki was told to expect a call from an agent named Maritz Spaarwater, who would call himself John Campbell, and who would set up a meeting in Switzerland.

There were three months of covert phone calls as John Campbell set up the meeting with John and Jack Simelane (Mbeki and Zuma). NIS chiefs Spaarwater (now calling himself Jacobus Maritz) and Mike Louw (Michael James) finally met John and Jack Simelane at the Palace Hotel, Lucerne, on the evening of 12 September.

Mbeki walked into room 338 first and said: 'Well, here we are, bloody terrorists and for all you know fucking communists as well.' He was clearly nervous. Zuma recalls that, once they were seated, Mbeki whispered to him in isiZulu, 'Sitting here with the enemy, I feel my stomach churning.' They talked until three in the morning, covering issues such as Mandela's continued imprisonment, the continued banning of the liberation movements, the ANC's alliance with the Communist Party, and much else besides.

On 2 February 1990, the bans on the ANC, SACP, PAC and 31 other political organisations were lifted and on 11 February Mandela was released from prison. After 15 years in exile, Nkandla – and home – beckoned to Zuma at last.

CHAPTER 5

1990–1994

The talking times

Late one morning during the first Convention for a Democratic South Africa (Codesa 1) negotiations, Moe Shaik exited the vast warehouse-like structure for a smoke.

Packing tobacco into his large, gleaming pipe, he strolled over to where the cars were parked. There he found Jacob Zuma sitting alone inside a car, with the radio turned on at a deafening volume. The music playing was Indian and Zuma was bobbing his head up and down and sideways 'in that special way that is particular to people who listen to Indian music,' says Shaik.

Moe knocked on the window and asked: 'Comrade JZ, what in heaven's name are you doing?'

'When I was a teenager and used to visit my cousin, who lived as a tenant in a shack in the back yard of someone's house in Greyville, all the houses and shacks in the area would have the same Indian music on at the same time – all the radios switched to full volume – and all the doors and windows would be open … and this was the music that was always playing. I find it comforting,' said Zuma.

The tableau still amuses Shaik all these years later, even though there is not a lot happening that he finds funny, least of all that his brother Schabir is in jail and ill.

'There he was, man, listening to that *charra* music and bobbing away in that special way. Remarkable,' says Shaik, chuckling.

Perhaps, given the sidelining of Zuma (and Thabo Mbeki) by an axis of their comrades just before Codesa 1, Zuma needed some comforting. More likely, as an already seasoned negotiator, he was merely taking 'time out' from the tedium of the process.

In the middle of 1989, Nelson Mandela had been taken to meet President PW Botha and told him that it was 'in the national interest' for the ANC and the government to meet urgently to negotiate a settlement. A month later the ANC prevailed on the Organisation of African Unity and the United Nations to adopt its Harare Declaration, which set out the basis for the transition to democracy and demanded that a representative and elected body draft a South African constitution.

In September 1989 FW de Klerk became president. Meanwhile, Mbeki, Zuma and others had been meeting with representatives of the NIS, who were effectively PW Botha's and then De Klerk's emissaries. On 15 October several ANC leaders, including Walter Sisulu and the remaining Rivonia trialists, were freed and on 8 December the Conference for a Democratic Future took place, at which 6 000 representatives of the Mass Democratic Movement (MDM) passed a resolution in favour of negotiation.

Also in December, Mandela, after meeting top National Party Cabinet ministers, wrote to De Klerk warning again of an urgent need for negotiations. Meanwhile, the ANC's NEC met in Lusaka and resolved to consider a negotiated settlement.

Then came the opening of Parliament on 2 February when De Klerk announced the unbanning of the ANC, the South African Communist Party and other liberation movements. Two weeks later, on 11 February,

Nelson Mandela walked free, and many other political prisoners and detainees were also released and unbanned.

In short, it was clear to everyone that the time had come for constitutional negotiations and everyone in power was doing his best to get these going. But there had to be a series of preliminary meetings to set things up – 'meetings about meetings', as everyone, including Zuma, called them.

The kick-off one would be held on 2–4 May at Groote Schuur, the mansion at the foot of Table Mountain bequeathed by Cecil John Rhodes as the official residence of the country's prime ministers. Before that one could happen, however, Jacob Zuma and Penuell Maduna, the head of the ANC's legal department, were smuggled into South Africa on 21 March 1990 for a meeting about that meeting.

The ANC might have been unbanned, but many individuals, including Zuma, were still criminals in terms of the law and could be arrested for past acts of 'terrorism'. Before anyone could do anything, indemnities had to be sorted out. Moreover, neither side yet had the full support of its constituents. De Klerk certainly was walking a knife's edge; and not everyone in the ANC believed that a negotiated revolution was the answer.

'In those early days of contact,' Patti Waldmeir wrote in *Anatomy of a Miracle*, 'the rank and file of the opposing sides were radically polarized; only the elites were beginning to edge along the tightrope toward a meeting in the middle.'[1]

So the Zuma party had to be secret. As part of the disinformation smoke blown out at the time, the police actually put out a warrant for Zuma's arrest. This amused him mightily, since when the news broadcast about the warrant went on air, he was spending time with General Basie Smit, chief of the security police. Having touched down from Lusaka in the home of the boers, Zuma found himself settled in the back seat of a government vehicle next to the grand inquisitor himself.

Smit had been very intent on sitting next to Zuma and had been especially friendly to him and his party, as had everyone else, during the braai to which they had been treated that evening and on the tour of

Pretoria they were given under cover of night. The short tour included the Voortrekker Monument, the massive shrine built to celebrate the triumph of Afrikaners over the Zulu nation at the Battle of Blood River (or, as Zuma knew it, the Ncome Battle). Smit, however, would have to resign in 1994 after being accused of helping arm Chief Mangosuthu Buthelezi's Inkatha Freedom Party (IFP) to fight Zuma and the ANC.

'The world is full of people with their own strange agendas, but I already knew that,' said Zuma.

The ANC party was initially taken to an NIS safe house in Pretoria's eastern suburbs; then they were transferred to the Hertford Hotel, about 25 km north of Johannesburg. There they were joined by two 'internal' members of the ANC, Mathews Phosa and Curnick Ndlovu. Members of the South African steering committee, including Roelf Meyer, later to play a significant role in the 'negotiated revolution', as journalist Allister Sparks would call it,[2] met them there.

It is difficult now, even for Zuma, to recall what Patti Waldmeir referred to as 'the tension that permeated the dealings between the two sides in those days,' as well as 'the mutual suspicions which were the dynamic that drove and undermined the negotiations process.'

Resistance within the National Party delayed the Indemnity Bill in Parliament three times. Operation Vula, by then a major network, continued operating; though when the security police uncovered Vula and arrested Siphiwe 'Gebuza' Nyanda, Mac Maharaj and others, the ANC leadership – notably Mbeki – let them swing in the wind. Yet some of the leaders, the important 'external' ones, knew about Vula and that it was the ANC's 'insurance policy' lest negotiations went awry. According to Maharaj, Zuma at the time also 'questioned the [ongoing] operation' of Vula (within the NEC, not publicly) – and of course Maharaj never forgot the attitude of Zuma, Mbeki and others.[3] What was significant about Zuma's attitude to Vula – which he does not deny – is that there was no doubt about the identity of the person to whom he had tied himself: Mbeki.

FW de Klerk was appalled that Joe Slovo, the communist devil incarnate, would be part of the mooted ANC team for Groote Schuur. After a discussion with Niël Barnard of NIS, however, he dropped his objection. Mandela himself forced the postponement of the meetings between the sides, scheduled for 11 April, after police shot dead 11 demonstrators in Sebokeng near Johannesburg.

For security reasons – serious trouble could have come from either the left or the right – or, at that delicate point, from anywhere – two alternative venues were set up: if Groote Schuur proved unviable, the Ysterplaat air base near Cape Town would be used, or even a ship in the Simonstown naval base.

The ANC delegation was accommodated at the Lord Charles Somerset Hotel in Somerset West. Security had to be tight, but of course members of the ANC delegation – this was the larger delegation for the Groote Schuur talks, not Zuma's scouting party – spent part of their time disappearing into Cape Town and the environs to see internal leaders and comrades. Without so much as a 'by your leave', motorcades would zip in and out of the Lord Charles, driving the local security folk frantic.

In the end, the meeting was held for three days from 2 to 4 May, and, though there were disagreements about important issues, Zuma's efforts at organisation had clearly paid off. The talks were exploratory and dealt with obstacles to negotiation. But the main thing was that the participants found that after decades of hostility they actually got on with one another and could talk openly and directly.

By the end of the third day they had reached an agreement. The ANC would 'review' its armed struggle and the government would 'review' security legislation and the end of the state of emergency. A working group was appointed to consider amnesty for political offences and the release of political prisoners. The main achievement of the Groote Schuur meeting, however, besides creating a decent relationship between the main protagonists, was that it generated hope in South Africa and in the international community: it looked as though a 'solution' was indeed possible. The only detractors came from the far-right-wing Conservative Party, which said the National Party was selling out the whites, and from the PAC and Azapo, which said the ANC was selling out blacks.

The text of the Groote Schuur Minute agreement read as follows:

The government and the African National Congress agree on a common commitment towards the resolution of the existing climate of violence and intimidation from whatever quarter as well as a commitment to stability and to a peaceful process of negotiations.

Flowing from this commitment, the following was agreed upon:

The establishment of a working group to make recommendations on a definition of political offences in the South African situation; to discuss, in this regard, time scales; and to advise on norms and mechanisms for dealing with the release of political prisoners and the granting of immunity in respect of political offences to those inside and outside South Africa. All persons who may be affected will be considered. The working group will bear in mind experiences in Namibia and elsewhere. The working group will aim to complete its work before 21st May 1990. It is understood that the South African government, in its discretion, may consider other political parties and movements and other relevant bodies. The proceedings of the working group will be confidential. In the meantime the following offences will receive attention immediately:

    a. The leaving of the country without a valid travel document.

    b. Any offences related merely to organisations which were previously prohibited.

1. In addition to the arrangements mentioned in paragraph 1, temporary immunity from prosecution of political offences committed before today, will be considered on an urgent basis for members of the National Executive Committee and selected other members of the ANC from outside the country, to enable them to return and help with the establishment and management of political activities, to assist in bringing violence to an end and to take part in peaceful political negotiations.

2. The government undertakes to review existing security legislation

to bring it into line with the new dynamic situation developing in South Africa in order to ensure normal and free political activities.

3. The government reiterates its commitment to work towards the lifting of the state of emergency. In this context, the ANC will exert itself to fulfill the objectives contained in the preamble.

4. Efficient channels of communication between the government and the ANC will be established in order to curb violence and intimidation from whatever quarter effectively.

The government and the ANC agree that the objectives contained in this minute should be achieved as early as possible.

Cape Town, 4th May 1990

Within weeks, however, the new hope that had been ignited at Groote Schuur was badly doused by a number of events. One was the uncovering of Vula. Mandela, who had not known about it, was furious, notwithstanding his affection for Maharaj. In his view, the ANC could not afford, at that point, to have a secret agenda to overthrow the state.

On 7 August 1990, Mandela, in an attempt to re-ignite negotiations, which had foundered since May, and in exchange for very little except the moral high ground, did the unthinkable: the ANC unilaterally suspended the armed struggle. He was advised to take this step by, of all people, Joe Slovo. After Mandela had gone through the new 'agreement' with De Klerk and his government – which had to agree in turn to pull troops out of the townships and cease hostilities against the ANC – it became known as the Pretoria Minute.

FAX FROM SECURITY BRANCH, 23 OCTOBER 1990

1. In accordance with paragraph 5 of the Groote Schuur Minute, the Minister of Law and Order, Mr Adriaan Vlok and Mr Jacob Zuma, information chief of the anc, met to discuss the creation of efficient channels of communication between the government and the anc. After an in-depth discussion it was agreed that:

a. Liaison committees be established on a regional level and also on a district or local level depending on the needs that are identified. The objective of the committees is to maintain regular contact between the SA Police and the anc.

b. Both the SA Police and the anc will, as soon as possible, provide one another with the names and addresses and telephone numbers of persons they appointed as liaison officers on the different levels so that the system can become operative by 30 October 1990.

1. The object of the exchange of names of liaison persons is to ensure a line of two-way communication. Up to date the SA Police has received only 29 names of anc liaison persons.

2. Please furnish the SA Police with the rest of the names of your liaison persons so as to ensure the efficient functioning of the channels of communication.

Signed: Brigadier RP McIntyre

A very tough journey had only just started. Murderous violence immediately began to escalate throughout the country, spreading from Natal to the Witwatersrand. Most of it was perpetrated by Inkatha, renamed the Inkatha Freedom Party (ifp), or by a mysterious 'third force' made up, it turned out, of former (or not-so-former) South African security personnel. Often the two operated in tandem.

The uncovering of the third force, whose actions almost derailed the train travelling laboriously to the station called the 'new South Africa', was undertaken by the Goldstone Commission in 1992–94. The revelations had started with Almond Nofemela's death-row statement and Dirk Coetzee's revelations in *Vrye Weekblad* – with which Zuma had been involved – and would be further revealed later in various books[4] and countless testimonies given at the Truth and Reconciliation Commission. Among the activities of the Third Force was giving paramilitary training to ifp vigilantes and gun-running to them, either in Witwatersrand hostels or in Natal. For example, in June 1991, the 'Inkathagate' scandal emerged: the IFP's trade union arm had been receiving covert funding from the government and the South African Defence Force had been training IFP members.

How much De Klerk knew about the existence of the Third Force would be the subject of debate for years to come. Judge Goldstone said later that the president had been like a man whose wife was having an affair, and who discovers the other man's keys in her pocket, but simply doesn't want to acknowledge to himself what they signify.[5]

The original Inkatha 'Yakazulu' was founded in 1922 by King Solomon Dinizulu. 'Inkatha' means 'traditional headband'. It was a cultural movement aiming to preserve the Zulu heritage and mobilise support for the king. In March 1975, Chief Mangosuthu Buthelezi revived Inkatha and the organisation adopted the ANC flag and uniform; Buthelezi would often refer to the time when he was a member of the ANC Youth League. He claimed in the organisation's early days that the Zulu foundation of Inkatha merely served as an expedient foundation for the 'national liberation' movement. By 1985 it had become common for township residents to be confronted by large groups of assegai-bearing men rallying to the traditional Zulu battle-cry of 'Usuthu' – the signal of the 'Amabutho' (warriors), who in reality were vigilante mobs.[6]

There had in fact been political violence in Natal since 1985, claiming thousands of lives. Much of Natal, including inside the borders of the KwaZulu homeland, had been gripped by a low-intensity civil war between Inkatha and the ANC. Both sides had committed atrocities in support of their respective causes.

Inkatha's position as the ruling party of KwaZulu, with access to government resources, meant that it had enormous advantages. Buthelezi had fiercely promoted an ideology in which the 'Zulu nation' was described as the inheritor of a warrior tradition, and had repeatedly defended the carrying of so-called 'traditional' weapons, such as assegais (spears), knobkerries (club-like sticks) or pangas (machetes) by Inkatha supporters, claiming that their prohibition would be 'cultural castration' designed 'to destroy the Zulu ethnic identity and awareness'. In

November 1990, the KwaZulu legislative assembly repealed three sections of the Natal Code of Zulu Law that outlawed the carrying of any 'assegai, swordstick, battle axe, stick shod with iron, staff or sharp-pointed stick or any other dangerous weapon'. This prohibition had been in place since the Natal Code of 1891. The KwaZulu government and Inkatha also failed to take any action against their own members when they were accused or convicted of involvement in violent incidents. Certain MPs or Inkatha officials acquired a reputation as 'warlords', but no action was taken by anyone against them either.

The problem was that no one had been paying sufficient attention to Buthelezi, a descendant of King Cetshwayo, who had indeed been a member of the Youth League and had been encouraged in his formation of Inkatha by Tambo himself. 'Inkatha was to have been the ANC's Trojan Horse in South Africa. It was even referred to as the "internal wing of the ANC".'[7]

As Zuma says, 'The formation of Inkatha was the ANC's idea. The idea was to have a political organisation undermining apartheid from inside.' And for a long time Buthelezi had been a thorn in the flesh of the apartheid regime, refusing to accept 'independence' for KwaZulu and campaigning for Mandela's release from jail. But then in 1979, in London, Tambo and Buthelezi had argued viciously and never made peace with one another.

After that, in Zuma's view, the ANC played the Zulu leader very badly. He was laughed at as a stooge of Pretoria and generally vilified in ways hateful to a proud Zulu: the legitimacy of his birth was questioned; he was described as a 'snake', and depicted in ANC posters as an oversized baby in nappies.[8]

When the United Democratic Front (UDF) became powerful in Natal in the mid-1980s, ANC leaders thought Buthelezi's power would be weakened. But they underestimated the reverence that most Zulus had for the prince, who played the 'ethnic' card brilliantly; he knew that his people admired strength, authoritarianism and militarism and thought of the ANC as a Xhosa organisation whose leaders in any case wore suits and ties instead of leopard skins, as befitted a true warrior. It was not clever behaviour on the part of the ANC; the Zulu people comprise the country's largest ethnic group.

By 1990, the IFP had violently consolidated its power in Natal and, within days of his release, Mandela thought that he and Buthelezi should meet. But the ANC national executive told him that it was out of the question. Mandela therefore urged that Walter Sisulu take up an invitation to see King Goodwill Zwelithini kaBhekuzulu, Buthelezi's nephew. But Sisulu did not want to go to Ulundi, the capital of KwaZulu, because it would have meant recognising the homeland. So he offered to meet the king at Nongoma, the royal kraal. But the plan was aborted, and it would be a year before Mandela met Buthelezi – and, in the meantime, another 1 600 people died in Natal and 2 000 throughout the country. The violence that had been unleashed by the tension between the ANC and Inkatha had become a way of life and no one seemed able to end it.

Through 1990, Buthelezi had watched Pretoria and the ANC apparently cementing an alliance that excluded him, and he was furious. In addition, the ANC misguidedly launched a nationwide campaign against him; in July 1990, anti-Buthelezi protests were held calling for the dissolution of the KwaZulu police and the abolition of the KwaZulu government. In Natal, Cosatu organised for three million people to stay home from work as a protest against Buthelezi.

Buthelezi fought back, sending word to the roughly two million Zulus living outside Zululand in migrant workers' hostels, desolate, barrack-like buildings, under the quasi-militaristic control of their indunas or headmen, that it was time for battle.

Zuma did not defend Buthelezi then, and does not now – I have seen him privately irritated with things the prince has done or said – but he believed that the deathly battles that broke out until the mid-1990s were the result of Mandela not having been allowed to see Buthelezi immediately on his release.

'Of course it was vital that Buthelezi was made to feel part of what was happening,' said Zuma. 'If Mandela had embraced him in the beginning, what happened might not have. And it wasn't even so much the national leadership that stopped Mandela – it was the Natal leadership, people like Harry Gwala. It was a giant mistake.'

It was into the maelstrom of Natal that Zuma went during 1990 and again in 1991 – and throughout the next few years. In November 1990, at the first regional congress of the ANC in KwaZulu-Natal, he was elected chairperson of the ANC's southern Natal region and became a leader of the fight against the bloody violence in the area, talking repeatedly to the IFP about quelling it. This resulted in a number of peace accords between the ANC and the IFP, which, though not very effective at the time, were better than none.

One of the Zulu leaders with whom Zuma could deal was Frank Mdlalose, who in 1990 had become national chairman of the IFP. In 1991, they would set up the Peace and Reconstruction Foundation to rebuild the devastation wrought in Natal.

At the same time, Zuma was effectively tugging at the rug under Buthelezi's feet, charming his way into the heart of the 'ordinary' Zulu. He went to great lengths to repair the damage done by the likes of Natal ANC leader Sbu Ndebele, who treated Zulu royalty with disdain. Some people – journalist Fred Khumalo for one – say that if anyone should be credited with destroying Inkatha, it was Zuma; and his efforts to do so dated from this period.

Using his charm and exploiting the Zulu deference to royalty, Zuma started winning over ordinary rural folk to the ANC. In him, they saw a person who not only respected their king but had also fought the apartheid regime. The IFP, as journalist and political analyst William Mervin Gumede wrote,[9] had worked hard to portray the ANC as a party that wanted to destroy Zulu tradition, culture and institutions. But Zuma matched Buthelezi's use of the symbols of Zulu culture for political ends. He was a 'natural' when it came to appearing at traditional ceremonies in leopard skins, brandishing a shield and spear.

In the meantime, there was also party business to be attended to, and the business of helping to propel South Africa towards majority rule. In July 1991, Zuma was elected deputy secretary-general of the ANC during the ANC's 48th national conference, at which Mandela was elected president; Walter Sisulu deputy president; and Cyril Ramaphosa secretary-general (SG).

Ramaphosa? Where had he come from? Why wasn't Zuma the SG?

The simple, though indirect, answer to these questions is this: Zuma and Mbeki were almost joined at the hip; they operated as a team and had for a long time; and in early 1991 they were unceremoniously sidelined by those who did not favour them and who had the upper hand in the party.

It was Chris Hani who moved against Mbeki and therefore Zuma.[10] In the lead-up to the national conference it had been agreed that Mandela would replace Tambo as ANC president and Tambo would be given the new position of national chairman. That meant that the position of deputy president – specially created for Mandela when he was released in 1990 – was up for grabs. Two candidates emerged: Sisulu and Mbeki. Sisulu said he was too old, so it looked as though Mbeki had it. But Hani declared that he would not serve under Mbeki; if Mbeki stood for DP, Hani would stand against him. The ANC likes to pretend that it is a unified organisation and does not like to hang out its dirty washing (certainly not in those days); so Sisulu was persuaded to come back into the contest.

There was also agreement that Alfred Nzo, the incumbent SG, needed to be replaced by someone younger and more dynamic. Zuma said he would stand against Nzo. But Zuma was effectively Mbeki's 'deputy' and he had quit the Communist Party with Mbeki and others in 1990. (Ostensibly, they had decided that they could no longer effectively serve two masters, but the truth was probably simpler: Mbeki could not abide Joe Slovo and vice-versa.) So Slovo and the fellows looked around for someone they preferred to oppose Zuma (who, some 15 years later, would be styled as 'the Left's man'). They came up with Ramaphosa – the most successful trade unionist the country had ever seen; a man who had shot to prominence as the head of the Release Mandela Committee; the darling of the 'in-ziles' as opposed to the exiles.

Ramaphosa trounced both Zuma and Nzo at the conference held at the University of Durban-Westville – and Mbeki was not one of the ANC's big six, though he scored well on the NEC vote (second only to Hani) and came first in the selection for the ANC's National Working Committee (NWC).

Things grew worse for Zuma and Mbeki. In a famous incident – during the first week of August 1990, while Mandela was in Cuba and Mbeki and Zuma were attending a conference in England – Ramaphosa convened the NWC and sidelined both of them. Zuma lost his position as head of intelligence to Mosiuoa 'Terror' Lekota, who had no previous intelligence experience, and Mbeki was replaced as head of negotiations with the apartheid government by Ramaphosa himself. The Slovo–Hani axis had struck. Mandela was furious with Ramaphosa & co, but the man was the secretary-general and the priority was negotiations with the De Klerk government. The caravan moved on.

But the matter of the Ramaphosa–Slovo–Hani power grab was not completely over.[11] Shortly before Codesa was due to begin at the end of 1991, Mandela and Tambo summoned the ANC's negotiations commission to an emergency meeting at headquarters – Shell House in Johannesburg. The commission consisted of Mbeki's 'old' negotiating team and Ramaphosa's new appointees. Still concerned about the decision to replace Mbeki with Ramaphosa, Mandela pulled a classic 'Mandela'; he said no one would leave the room until each had indicated who in his opinion should lead the negotiations. When Tambo's turn came he was too frail to speak properly. But he lifted his cane, and, remarkably, pointed at Zuma. No one wanted to disagree with Tambo.

So, Zuma, rather than anyone else, was chosen to chair the ANC negotiations commission. But this was a position that exercised power from behind only; it was Ramaphosa who was in charge on the front line. Still, Mbeki and Zuma played major roles at Codesa, even if Zuma occasionally had to pop outside to listen to a little music.

Under the chairmanship of Judges Michael Corbett, Petrus Shabort and Ismail Mahomed, Codesa began with a plenary session on 20 December 1991. The first session, Codesa 1, lasted a few days, and working groups were appointed to deal with specific issues. These working groups continued their negotiations over the next month.

Nineteen groups were represented at Codesa, including the South African government, the National Party (NP), the ANC, the IFP, the

Democratic Party, the SACP, the South African Indian Congress, the Coloured Labour Party, the Indian National People's Party and Solidarity Party, and the leaders of the nominally independent bantustans of Transkei, Ciskei, Bophuthatswana, and Venda. The right-wing white Conservative Party and the PAC boycotted Codesa. Buthelezi didn't participate because his demands for additional delegations for the KwaZulu homeland and the Zulu king were declined. The IFP was represented by Mdlalose.

In the period between Codesa I and II in early 1992, the National Party lost three by-elections to the Conservative Party. De Klerk therefore announced that a 'whites only' referendum would be held on the issue of reform and negotiation. The result was a landslide victory of more than 68 per cent for the 'yes' side.

The second plenary session took place in May 1992. But, in June 1992, the Boipatong massacre took place. Forty-six residents were butchered mainly by Zulu hostel dwellers, aided and abetted by Third Force operatives. Mandela accused De Klerk's government of complicity in the attack and withdrew the ANC from the negotiations, leading to the end of Codesa II.

The ANC instead took to the streets with a programme of 'rolling mass action'. This ended in tragedy with the Bisho massacre in September 1992, when the army of the nominally independent 'homeland' of Ciskei opened fire on protest marchers, led by Ronnie Kasrils (fresh from Operation Vula). He led the marchers across a boundary that a local magistrate had ruled should not be crossed. Twenty-eight marchers died.

During the negotiations, De Klerk's government pushed for a two-phase transition with an appointed transitional government with a rotating presidency. The ANC pushed instead for transition in a single stage to majority rule. Other sticking points included minority rights, decisions on a unitary or federal state, property rights, and indemnity from prosecution for politically motivated crimes.

Following the collapse of Codesa II, bilateral negotiations between the ANC and the NP became the main negotiation channel. The two key negotiators were Ramaphosa and Roelf Meyer, one of the government men who had met Zuma and Maduna in Pretoria in March 1990. They formed a close friendship. In one incident, they went trout-fishing together and Ramaphosa's wife famously removed a fly hooked in Meyer's hand.

It was Slovo who in 1992 proposed the breakthrough 'sunset clause' for a coalition government for the five years following a democratic election, including guarantees and concessions to all sides. On 26 September the government and the ANC agreed on a Record of Understanding. This dealt with a constitutional assembly, an interim government, political prisoners, hostels, dangerous weapons and mass action – and restarted the negotiation process.

On 1 April 1993 the Multiparty Negotiating Forum (MPNF) gathered for the first time. Participants now drawn into the process included the white right (the Conservative Party and the Afrikaner Volksunie), the PAC, the KwaZulu homeland government and delegations of traditional leaders.

Following the Record of Understanding, the two main negotiating parties, the ANC and the NP, agreed to reach bilateral consensus on issues before taking them to the other parties in the forum. This put considerable pressure on the other parties to agree with the consensus or be left behind. In protest at the perceived sidelining of the IFP, Buthelezi withdrew the party from the MPNF and formed the Concerned South Africans Group (Cosag, later renamed the 'Freedom Alliance') together with traditional leaders, homeland leaders and white right-wing groups.

A period of brinkmanship followed, with the IFP remaining out of the negotiations until within days of the election. Buthelezi was finally convinced to give up his boycott when Mandela offered King Goodwill Zwelithini a guarantee of special status of the Zulu monarchy, and promised Buthelezi that foreign mediators would examine Inkatha's claims to more autonomy in the Zulu area.

On 10 April 1993, Chris Hani was shot down in the driveway of his

Boksburg home by a white right-winger – and the country was brought to the brink of disaster. In fact, if Mandela had not handled the situation so calmly and wisely, the country might have gone over the brink.

The negotiations were dramatically interrupted in June 1993 when the right-wing Afrikaner Weerstandsbeweging stormed the World Trade Centre, breaking through the glass front of the building with an armoured car and briefly taking over the negotiations chamber. But this turned out to be more of an attempt at gaining attention than a serious threat.

On 7 August 1993, Mbeki and Zuma were taken to a secret rendezvous at a pigeon racing club in Lynnwood, east of Pretoria, by a man called Jürgen Kögl, a businessman and 'player'. The meeting was with the former head of the army, General Constand Viljoen, who had mustered a large force of men – some said as many as 50 000 – who wanted Afrikaner self-determination. They were allied with Buthelezi's Cosag and called themselves the Afrikaner Vryheidsfront (AVF). Their aim: a *volkstaat*.

Mbeki and Zuma talked it out with Viljoen and two of his fellow leaders – Zuma offering the reassurance that the ANC would not repeat the white regime's mistake of excluding others – and five days later Viljoen and his 'Committee of Generals' went to meet Mandela in Johannesburg. It had been the debate at the pigeon club – at which Mbeki and Zuma argued out the impossibility of a separate state – that had shifted Viljoen's attitude.

Between August and December, there were six more meetings. Eventually the parties agreed that a joint working group would be set up to investigate the viability of a *volkstaat*, and the AVF would participate in the general elections set for April 1994. But then, at the eleventh hour, one of Viljoen's co-leaders reneged on the deal: Viljoen could not sign, Mandela became angry and declared there would never be a *volkstaat*, and communications between the two parties died.

In late January 1994, they met again. Viljoen argued that if they did not have some sort of agreement, the defence force would split, and there would be no way the ANC could rule the country. But Zuma prevailed on Viljoen to consider the unsigned agreement that they already had as binding, and Mbeki suggested the April elections be used as a referendum for a *volkstaat*. The 'Accord on Afrikaner Self-Determination' was ratified just four days before the elections.

Meanwhile, the MPNF ratified the interim constitution in the early hours of the morning of 18 November 1993, and a Transitional Executive Council oversaw the run-up to a democratic election.

The election was held on 27 April 1994 and resulted in the ANC winning 62 per cent of the vote. Mandela became president, with De Klerk and Mbeki as deputies. The National Party, with 20 per cent of the vote, joined the ANC in a Government of National Unity. Transitional politics continued after the election, with a new constitution finally agreed upon in 1995, and the Truth and Reconciliation Commission appointed to deal with the crimes committed during the apartheid era.

CHAPTER 6

1993–2003

The greasy levers of power

When Jacob Zuma knows you reasonably well, he will walk forward to greet you and, grasping your hand firmly, will say sonorously: 'My brother, how are you?'

I occasionally have a picture of him in my head doing precisely that, but saying to me slowly: 'My brother, it is all about politics.' For, in observing the years of Zuma's life from about 1975 onwards, it becomes clear that his life – and his life *was* the ANC – was about 'politics', not the art or science of government, but competing for position, hitching yourself to the right person, sticking a knife in, and all the rest.

Two other obvious realisations flow from this. Zuma was a Thabo Mbeki man through and through; they were a double act. Secondly, journalists, including me, are fond of referring to the ANC's 'quaint pseudo-Stalinist habits' of pretending that all is well in the party, that they never compete against one another in party elections, and that they are actually all loving comrades. But this is more than a charming habit. It actually often amounts to a conspiracy of silence. Not even the Mac Maharajs of this world, not even the Moe Shaiks, will say a bad word about the ANC to an outsider. The attitude is that the ANC is family – Moe Shaik calls it a tribe – and that everything must stay inside the family circle.

In short, most of what was going on inside the ANC's leadership circles during Codesa and following the election victory of 1994 was kept under wraps, and much of it wasn't particularly loving. At any rate, Thabo Mbeki, and therefore Zuma, had been pushed out of the limelight by Cyril Ramaphosa and his supporters, though not entirely. But he and Mbeki did not weep into their whiskey (Zuma does not drink anyway). Instead, their struggle continued.

According to Mark Gevisser,[1] Mbeki resolved that he should aim for the chairmanship soon after Oliver Tambo, the national chairman of the ANC and Mbeki's mentor, died in April 1993. One person who had a problem with this was Mandela. He wanted the position to go to Professor Kader Asmal, not least because he was conscious of the accusation that the ANC leadership was Xhosa-heavy.

Mandela and Sisulu decided to appoint Asmal by acclamation. But they were challenged by Peter Mokaba, president of the Youth League, whose support – along with Winnie Mandela's – Mbeki had cleverly harnessed. Mokaba argued that there should be a secret ballot.

It might have been the first time – but it was not the last – that a Youth League president was used as a stalking horse by someone intent on gaining power in the organisation. Zuma would do much the same with Fikile Mbalula in 2006 and 2007 and with Julius Malema in 2008. (We will look later at the strange story of Mokaba and why he supported Mbeki, when we analyse Zuma's character and consider simultaneously the 'strange' attitude of ANC leaders towards alleged spies and informers.)

There was a secret ballot and Mbeki whacked Asmal 56-13. He had the chairmanship.

Then came the country's first democratic national elections. Mandela would be president, but the question was: who – as mandated by the interim constitution – would be the deputy presidents? FW de Klerk, the former president of South Africa and leader of the National Party, would be one in the Government of National Unity (GNU). What about the other?

Mandela wanted Cyril Ramaphosa. But his senior colleagues – deputy-president Walter Sisulu, deputy SG Zuma, and treasurer Thomas Nkobi – suggested Mbeki. Mandela apparently continued consulting and played his cards very close to his chest. Even Mr Cool, Joe Slovo, for example, a senior and influential colleague and friend of Mandela's, was deeply nervous about the choices that Mandela would make in those fateful days.[2] And in his cabinet choices, Mandela, it should be noted, put members of the left axis of the party into graveyard portfolios – Slovo into housing and Maharaj into transport – while many mediocre exiles secured the plum jobs such as defence, foreign affairs and intelligence.[3]

Interestingly, Ramaphosa's biographer, Anthony Butler, writes that one of the reasons Mandela might have decided against Ramaphosa as DP was that he seemed to have 'difficulty engaging' with the Zulus – not so much Buthelezi as the royal court, especially King Goodwill, and especially with one Zulu prince who allegedly proclaimed that 'We are not prepared to be ruled by the Venda dog Ramaphosa'.[4]

So Mbeki was appointed deputy president. But DP of the country was one thing. More important – as Mbeki knew then but apparently would forget in 2007 – was to have the backing of the ANC.

The party's next national conference was held in December 1994 in Bloemfontein. And Ramaphosa blinked. He did not challenge Mbeki for the ANC deputy presidency but chose instead to accept an unopposed nomination to remain SG. So Mbeki was also DP of the ANC, while Zuma was elected chairman of the party.

Meanwhile, Zuma had, in May 1994, following the national and provincial elections, been appointed as Member of the Executive Committee (MEC) for Economic Affairs and Tourism in KwaZulu-Natal, and would remain in this post until June 1999. Zuma had been nominated as the ANC candidate for the premiership of KZN. But the KZN ANC – of which

Zuma was re-elected chairman in December as well – lost the provincial elections in April.

Zuma believed that the gaping wound dividing the Zulu people had to be healed and that Inkatha had to come back into the ANC, which had been its mother-movement, and he had been talking to Mandela.

Zuma was a commoner but he was a traditionalist and he understood – as so many others apparently did not – the Zulu ethos. He believed that Buthelezi, a genius at brinkmanship (not unlike Zuma), should be 'engaged with', not 'neutralised'. It was largely as a result of Zuma's requests that in March 1994 Mandela had finally met Buthelezi – with the result that finally, after many shenanigans, the IFP had taken part in the elections.

'I asked Madiba whether I could go to KwaZulu-Natal in 1994. I thought I could do positive things there,' said Zuma.

Politically, as always, life was not straightforward. For one thing, Zuma did not get on with the local ANC strongman, S'bu Ndebele, and in fact, because Ndebele wanted Zuma out of his hair, he nominated Zuma for the deputy presidency of the ANC in December 1994, so that he (Ndebele) could become the provincial ANC chairman and therefore candidate premier.

Zuma was obviously correct in thinking that KZN was a bomb waiting to explode. The conflict between the IFP and the ANC had spiralled out of control between 1990 and 1994 and had become a virtual civil war in the months before the national elections of April 1994. And, although the first year of democratic government led to a decrease in the monthly death toll, the figures remained high enough to threaten the process of national reconstruction. In particular, the violence could have prevented the establishment of democratic local government structures – as ANC politicians like to refer to them – following the further local elections that were held on 1 November 1995.

The basis of this violence remained the conflict between the ANC and the IFP, the majority party in KZN. Although the IFP had participated in the April 1994 poll, neither this decision nor the election itself had resolved much. While the ANC had argued during the year since the election that the final constitutional arrangements for South Africa should have included a relatively centralised government and the introduction of elected government structures at all levels, the IFP continued to maintain instead that South Africa's regions should form a federal system, and that the colonial tribal government structures should remain in place in the former homelands.

Of course, the violence was more than the result of two political parties competing, albeit violently, on equal terms. The context of the violence was the control exerted by the IFP over local and regional government. Both sides had committed atrocities in the conflict in which more than ten thousand people had died over ten years, and both sides maintained 'no-go' areas which individuals identified with the other party could not visit without risking their lives; but, despite the change of government at national level, the IFP was able to continue enforcing its regional dominance.

ANC and Inkatha did, however, lay down their weapons in the mid-1990s, and many people credit Zuma for bringing the warring factions together. In radio and TV advertisements, Zuma urged rivals to stop fighting; he met with rival political leaders, and went into the former no-go areas.

'Zuma's role was basically being decent to the IFP, to engage in some sort of diplomacy with the IFP,' said Mary de Haas, who has been monitoring the violence in the province since the 1980s.

'In my book Zuma deserves more credit than any other individual for helping to end the bloody conflict in KwaZulu-Natal in the years after 1990. That was a prerequisite for a successful election in 1994,' wrote Max du Preez in *The Star* on 14 August 2006.

Another political analyst said to me (during one of Zuma's later court cases), 'His biggest achievement in my view was stopping the violence in KZN – and how he pulled it off. His charm offensive really worked on the warlords of the IFP.'

'I don't know about charm,' said Zuma. 'And actually the problem in my view was not the IFP warlords. It was our own on whom I had to use my "charm". You ask me what I did in KZN. I spent most of my time talking to our own people. They were the ones who had to be settled down. It was our own warlord, Harry Gwala, who …' Ever loyal to the ANC, Zuma will not say more about Gwala publicly. But Mac Maharaj, not one to mince his words, has said that Gwala had turned the heartland of Natal 'into the scene of some of the fiercest fighting between the UDF/ANC and Inkatha … Gwala declared a scorched-earth policy on Inkatha. Among all ANC leaders, Gwala came closest to being a warlord in his own right.'[5]

Back in KZN, Zuma wanted to make something of his home at Nkandla. He had been away for close to 20 years, and in truth he wanted to make a home because there was not really anything there. He too wanted to have the trappings of a patriarch. 'I didn't fight in the struggle to be poor,' as Smuts Ngonyama, head of the ANC president's office during Mbeki's years, once said. It was a thought that many had had, even if they had not articulated it. And, although Zuma was not as inclined towards conspicuous consumption as some of the other returned exiles, it was difficult not to be infected. A kind of *nouveau riche* mentality did grip many of the returned exiles. Who were you if you didn't have a new BMW and the latest cell phone, not to mention a spiffy suit? Wasn't even Mandela something of a fashion plate – and what about Mbeki's beautifully-tailored suits and shirts?

Zuma's finances in general were in a bit of a shambles and, in terms of family, he had large expenses. He had three wives in the late 1990s and although only his first wife, Sizakele, lived at Nkandla, he nonetheless supported his wife Kate Mantsho, who lived in Durban before they went together to Pretoria, as well as Nkosazana Dlamini-Zuma, and all his children – none with Sizakele, four with Kate, and four with Nkosazana.

In June 1998, Zuma and Nkosazana, then Minister of Foreign Affairs, divorced due to 'irreconcilable differences'. Every time I have been to Zuma's Johannesburg house, one or two of their four daughters have been there. They are Msholozi, 24, Gugu, 22, Thuli, 21, and Thuthu, 19.

On 8 December 2000, Kate committed suicide in the deputy president's residence in Pretoria. She took an overdose of sleeping pills and malaria drugs. She said in her suicide note that: 'Strictly my dear children, my maternal family to attend. From the Zumas only Bro Mike [Zuma's brother Michael] and all the Mzobe family … I wish you success with new Makoti and would advise her that the seat she is going to occupy is very, very, very Hot.'

Zuma and Kate had five children: Saady, 29, twins Duduzile and Duduzane, both 25, Phumzile, 21, and Vusi, 15.

The 'new Makoti' to whom Kate referred might have been Nompumelelo 'MaNtuli' Ntuli-Zuma, with whom Zuma has two children – a seven-year-old daughter and three-year-old son – and whom he married 'properly' in January 2008.

When, on his return from exile, Zuma had discussed his financial situation with Schabir Shaik and his brothers – those stalwarts of the Natal operation and still stalwarts of the struggle (Moe had been in Vula, Yunis in the trade union movement) – they had told him to stay with politics, while Schabir would take care of the money side. Almost every document later produced at Shaik's trial that dealt with money lent to Zuma mentioned interest-free loans with no specified date of repayment. In 1999, Shaik wrote all the loans off without any explanation.

Shaik, who handled Zuma's money at the time, knew that Zuma could never afford to repay the sum of the loans on his salary. He also knew, since he had access to all of Zuma's financial records, about unpaid home loans, an overdraft of about R70 000 in a Nedbank account; another debt owed to Wesbank; that Zuma spent more money than he earned, and that he was writing bad cheques and failing to meet credit card payments.

Shaik did not expect to be paid back, however. According to him, he was lending the money to Zuma because that was the way it was between comrades. According to the state, however, in Shaik's later trial for corruption, it was because Shaik was buying influence with Zuma, which was used to win government contracts for his company, Nkobi Holdings.

The ANC's 50th conference was held in December 1997 in Mafikeng. Mandela stood down as president and Mbeki was elected in his stead. Zuma was elected deputy president. Ramaphosa stood down as secretary-general and Kgalema Motlanthe was elected to the job unopposed; Mosiuoa 'Terror' Lekota was elected national chairman.

Consequently, it was no surprise that in June 1999, following the next national elections, in which the ANC obtained more than 66 per cent of the vote and Mandela retired, Mbeki became president of South Africa, and Zuma, deputy president. Zuma also served as Leader of Government Business in the House of Assembly.

It had not been as simple as it appeared. In those days, it did not necessarily follow that the deputy president of the ANC should be the DP of the country – and, when, following the 1999 provincial elections, it became clear that the ANC was not going to win KZN, Mbeki offered the deputy presidency to Mangosuthu Buthelezi. The condition was that, in return, the ANC would get the premiership in KZN. In any case, Mbeki knew he was going to strip all power from the DP's office and take it with him, leaving the deputy president with a largely ceremonial role. The DP could take care of the country's moral regeneration, HIV-AIDS, perhaps some peace-making in Africa, and other matters that Mbeki considered secondary.

Analyst William Mervin Gumede has suggested that there were additional motives on Mbeki's part: that he wanted to build a 'new [national] consensus' by bringing the Zulu monarchists into the larger fold; that they would give him 'numbers' that would make up for the shortfall if Cosatu and the SACP, already irritated and estranged by his attitudes and economic policies, broke away from the alliance to form a left-wing party; and, thirdly, that it would dampen tensions in KZN that continued to simmer.[6] S'bu Ndebele, an Mbeki loyalist, would presumably have been given the premiership.

Because Zuma never squawked about Mbeki's offer to Buthelezi, we must presume that Zuma had been told by Mbeki about his thinking and more or less agreed with it. But did he?

The ANC leadership in the province – some members of Mbeki's inner circle blame Zuma[7] – scuppered the plan by leaking a distorted version of the deal to the IFP leadership, who urged Buthelezi to refuse the offer until the office of the deputy president was upgraded to that of a full-fledged prime minister. As it turned out, Mbeki rejected Buthelezi's counter-offer and Buthelezi rejected Mbeki's original one.

Zuma became deputy president – thus remaining in line for succession to the presidency – while Mbeki eventually gave Buthelezi the home affairs ministry, which turned out not to be a great success for anyone concerned.

Of course, the real version of events – in so far as it is possible to know what it was – was not the one presented to the public. On 20 June 1999, the following report appeared from Sapa (the South African Press Association):

> Deputy President Jacob Zuma on Sunday applauded Inkatha Freedom Party and African National Congress leaders in KwaZulu-Natal for reaching a political settlement on the composition of the province's government.
>
> Without the agreement, Zuma said, the province could have returned to the political violence which claimed 20 000 lives in the pre-1994 era.
>
> KwaZulu-Natal was left with a hung parliament after the June 2 election because neither party obtained a simple majority on the provincial ballot. The ANC and IFP had nominated S'bu Ndebele and Lionel Mtshali respectively for the premiership in that province.
>
> For a week after the election results were announced, the parties were deadlocked on who should lead the once-troubled province, despite high-level discussions between the two parties.
>
> The ANC's offer to give the national deputy presidency to IFP leader Mangosuthu Buthelezi in exchange for the premiership of KwaZulu-Natal fell through.
>
> The IFP leader said he declined the offer of the deputy presidency because of the premiership condition.
>
> On Thursday last week, the ANC withdrew Ndebele's nomination,

paving the way for Mtshali to be premier and an IFP-led coalition government to be formed.

Zuma told Sapa both parties had realised the need to work together if there was to be progress, peace and stability in that province.

'I think our colleagues, both the IFP and ANC, are cautious of this fact, and guided by that. I think that's why they managed to agree.

'You couldn't risk reaching a deadlock because in that province ... any heated confrontation could have resulted in the province slipping back into the violent situation.'

Zuma and the IFP's Celani Mthethwa were instrumental in discussions between the two parties, which led to the signing of a peace-pact in May in Durban. He said the agreement paved the way for the ANC and IFP to work together for the benefit of KwaZulu-Natal's more than seven million people, the majority of whom supported either the ANC or IFP.

Zuma said the ANC pulled Ndebele out of the premiership race because 'there are bigger issues ... the interest of the country ... of the people that have always guided the ANC.'

He said there had been a risk in a hung parliament of the peace process 'going astray'.

'I think it became important to show maturity,' he said.

He described the coalition agreement as 'the meeting of minds' between the provincial leadership of both parties, who agreed the interests of their people were more important than their own or those of their organisations.

'I think there has been a very responsible appreciation of this and therefore responsible decisions that the two parties took, and we are very happy about it,' the former KwaZulu-Natal economic affairs MEC said. – SAPA

It was classic Zuma-speak.

Mark Gevisser believes that the almost-deal with Buthelezi could have been the beginning of the end of a beautiful relationship.[8] Certainly, Zuma and his staff got the impression that they were mostly not part of the inner circle; and the folk clustered around

Mbeki thought Zuma was some sort of dinosaur. Also, Mbeki had been fiddling in Zuma's bailiwick, KZN, where the politics are even more Byzantine than anywhere else, and he seemed keener on Ndebele than Zuma anyway. A Zuma aide, who prefers not to be identified, said the two men soon retreated to different parts of one wing of the Union Buildings. 'Zuma felt like a misfit there. He hated all the restrictions and security and formality. Plus he had no relationship with his boss. Somehow Zuma got transformed from backer-in-chief to he-who-must-be-dumped.'

Then there was the strange story of the plot against Mbeki. In April 2001, Steve Tshwete, the Minister of Safety and Security, confirmed on national television that the state was seriously investigating a coup plot against Mbeki and that the president might even be in physical danger. He said the plotters were Cyril Ramaphosa, Tokyo Sexwale and Mathews Phosa. All three had gone into business, and the first was the former darling of the Codesa negotiations and a former secretary-general, while the latter two had been the premiers of Gauteng and Mpumalanga respectively.

The allegations were made by a man called James Nkambule, a discredited Mpumalanga Youth League official, who said – on videotape – that the plotters would get rid of Mbeki by proving that he had been behind the murder of Chris Hani.

It was bizarre stuff and there was a howl of outrage from the alliance partners, the media and from the men themselves. Mbeki said that his advisers recommended that he take the matter seriously, but some of the people he spoke to – including the Minister for Intelligence, Lindiwe Sisulu – said they had told Mbeki to ignore the allegations. In the end, Mbeki cleared the alleged conspirators and conceded their names should never have been made public.[9]

But contained in the Nkambule allegations was 'evidence' that Phosa had some confidential information about the restructuring of the Presidency, including plans to downgrade the deputy presidency. Mbeki seemed to have reached the conclusion that Zuma was Phosa's source. And, after he and Zuma viewed the Nkambule video, Mbeki confronted

Zuma and even suggested that his deputy president might have been part of the plot.

Zuma then issued a press release saying that he had never been involved in a plot against Mbeki and that, what's more, he had no ambitions to be president.

It was really the end of a beautiful friendship.

From late in 2002 Zuma took over from Nelson Mandela in trying to broker peace in Burundi. More than 300 000 people had died in Burundi since rebels from the Hutu majority took up arms in 1993 against the Tutsi-led government and army. In October, his spokeswoman Lakela Kaunda said the talks would focus on outstanding issues between the Burundi transitional government and the two major wings of the two Hutu rebel groups.

In December 2003, Zuma reported to the United Nations that the 20th Summit of the Great Lakes Regional Peace Initiative on Burundi, held on 16 November, had mandated him to request 'urgent direct assistance' for the peace process. It would help to consolidate gains, prepare the ground for successful democratic elections within 11 months, and firmly root Burundi on the road to lasting peace and stability.

In 2004, a power-sharing deal aimed at paving the way to elections in Burundi was signed by a majority of its parties. 'This is a decision taken by the majority of parties and therefore a decision taken for the Burundian people,' Zuma said after the parties signed the deal in Pretoria. The pact, he said, 'allows the parties in Burundi to begin the process of drawing up a constitution, electoral law, communal law and establishing an independent electoral commission. That commission will say whether we are ready or not to hold an election ... We will make a report to the regional summit headed by Ugandan President Yoweri Museveni, given that we have very little time left until the Arusha process runs out and we must have elections.'

Roger Southall, a research fellow at the Human Sciences Research Council who studied the Burundi settlement, rated Zuma's role after the 2 000 Arusha Agreement as 'absolutely critical'. Zuma, he said, had been 'enormously vigorous', making more than 20 trips to Burundi to deal with the final vital details of the peace settlement.

Jan Van Eck, a conflict analyst who has specialised in the Great Lakes regional conflict, has said Zuma was a first-rate negotiator and facilitator.

CHAPTER 7

1999 – 2004

Bring us our machine guns

The Department of Defence's Strategic Arms Acquisition programme, better known as the Arms Deal, is a Byzantine saga in which the devil truly lives in the details. Full and first-rate coverage of the Arms Deal is to be found in Paul Holden's *The Arms Deal in Your Pocket* and this chapter is based on his timeline.[1] In brief, soon after it came to power the first democratically elected government decided that the country needed to beef up the Defence Force's capability by purchasing a range of sophisticated military hardware: corvettes, submarines, light utility helicopters, maritime helicopters, fighter trainers and advanced light fighter aircraft. Why this decision was made has been the subject of intense speculation. The government said the country needed a modern defence force and that the offset projects connected with the Arms Deal – the promise by foreign arms manufacturers to invest locally and create employment – made the project worthwhile.

Some said that the first ANC leaders who came back to the country in the early 1990s and encountered the chiefs of the then security establishment had been overly impressed by them and the power they commanded. One of the reasons Nelson Mandela and his advisers opted for a Truth and Reconciliation Commission, for example, and not a set of Nuremberg-type trials, was to avoid finding the Union Buildings ringed by tanks. Still others said that the impetus for the Arms Deal was provided by those who realised that the process – the putting out of tenders and the awarding of contracts – was an easy way to make money. As some wit once remarked, two investment sectors that will always give a good return are contraception and arms.

At any rate, the Arms Deal contracts (worth some R30-billion) were finally signed in December 1999. This was the same year in which Patricia de Lille, then a PAC member of Parliament, told Parliament that the Arms Deal process had been riddled with corruption.

Enter the Shaik family – businessman Schabir, and Zuma's comrades from the struggle in KZN, Moe and Yunis, who had operated underground for the ANC, reporting directly to Zuma in his capacity as MK chief of intelligence. A younger brother, Shamin, known as 'Chippy', was, as it happened, the chief of acquisitions for the Arms Deal in the defence department.

Zuma had told the Shaik brothers in the early 1990s that he was under severe financial pressure. He had returned to South Africa with nothing; had not had the opportunity to cash in, as many others in the movement had; had numerous wives and children to take care of; and had to start upgrading his 'life style' in all ways – it had become *de rigueur* for the new leaders to do so in the new South Africa. But he had no money, and was thinking seriously of opting out of politics and going into private enterprise, as others had.

No, no, said the Shaik brothers to Zuma. Stay where you are. You are vital to the political health of leadership of this country – look at what you've achieved in KZN. And Schabir also probably thought, though he might not have said it openly, that Zuma could be helpful to him. He was starting up businesses and needed all the assistance he could get. It was, after all, in the heady days of the new South Africa, more so than ever, not about what you knew but who you knew.

So the Shaiks told Zuma to stay in politics. Moe worked for the government, Yunis was a labour lawyer, Chippy worked for the Department of Defence, but Schabir was an entrepreneur – and he would take care of business. As it turned out, much of Shaik's business had to do with the Arms Deal.

From 1989 to 1992 the 'old' South African Defence Force languished under budget and staff cuts. In 1993, however, it was announced that the navy was in the market for four new warships – or in fact corvettes, which are small, manoeuvrable strike craft. By the end of the year foreign arms companies were flooding the Defence Force with enquiries. In 1994, after the first democratic elections, Joe Modise, the newly appointed Minister of Defence, ordered the navy to allow tendering to begin for the corvettes.

At the end of January 1995, Schabir Shaik registered Nkobi Holdings as a holding company. But then, due to a public outcry, the corvette deal was scrapped and it was announced in June that new arms purchases would only be made after the new SA National Defence Force's needs had been reassessed.

In October 1995 Zuma received the first of his 'loans' from Shaik.

From May to August 1996, the French company Thomson-CSF (to be known later as Thales internationally and Thint in South Africa) made an agreement with Shaik in terms of which Nkobi became Thomson's joint venture partner in all of its South African business.

These were the early days of the new South Africa and it was obvious that foreign investors would need partners whose owners were kosher: 'previously disadvantaged' (black, so-called coloured or Indian) and with good 'struggle credentials'. As the brother of Moe and Yunis, with Chippy chief of acquisitions for the defence department, Shaik was well set up. Above all, he let it be known that he was close to Zuma, a man clearly headed for bigger and better things.

On 18 June 1997 the Cabinet of Nelson Mandela's government approved a defence review which found that South Africa needed to 'undertake extensive arms purchases to maintain the SANDF's capability'. In August, Parliament gave its approval and in October Deputy President Mbeki announced that tenders for the purchase of arms would be re-opened.

In April 1998 Thomson-CSF (Thales) bought shares in Altech Defence Systems (renamed African Defence Systems, ADS), the company that would win the tender to supply the 'information management system' (the computer systems) in the corvette combat suites. The French had heard rumours that Mbeki and others were not so keen on Shaik, and they had excluded Nkobi from the Thomson/ADS contract. In May Shaik wrote for the second time to Jean-Paul Perrier, the head of Thomson-CSF, asking what the hell was going on.

In November 1998, Zuma (then MEC for Economic Affairs and tourism in the KZN provincial government) went to a meeting with Shaik and representatives of Thomson-CSF in Durban — and, whatever happened there, Nkobi was given a share in ADS.

In June 1999 the ANC won a landslide election victory; Mbeki became president and Zuma, now enormously more influential, was his deputy and Leader of Government Business in Parliament. And then along came 9 September when De Lille alleged that skullduggery had taken place in the Arms Deal process. According to Leonard McCarthy, director of the Investigating Directorate: Serious Economic Offences (later known as the Directorate of Special Operations, or Scorpions), Shaik, Nkobi, Zuma and the Thomson companies were merely some of the people and companies alleged to be party to a range of possible irregularities and offences.

On 21 September Mosiuoa Lekota, the new Minister of Defence, gave the Auditor-General the go-ahead to make a special review audit of the Arms Deal process. In November, an audit steering committee, including Chippy Shaik, was formed to facilitate the investigation. On 3 December the government closed the Arms Deal (estimated to cost about R30-billion) by signing the loan and purchase agreements.

Meanwhile, however, by February 2000, McCarthy's outfit had started its own investigation, at just about the time Zuma started building his new, rather sprawling home, budgeted to cost about R1-million, at Nkandla.

On 10 or 11 March, according to Judge Hilary Squires, who would preside at Shaik's trial in 2004/5, Zuma, Shaik and Alain Thétard, then the local director of Thomson (Thint), met in Durban and agreed that Zuma would receive R500 000 a year in return for 'protecting' Thomson from any investigation into Thomson's activities related to getting its Arms Deal contract. On 17 March this was followed, also according to the findings in the Shaik trial, by Thétard sending an encrypted fax to his bosses giving details of the arrangement.

On 15 September 2000 the Auditor-General signed his review of the Arms Deal, suggesting that certain irregularities might have taken place. And, in October, Parliament's Standing Committee on Public Accounts (Scopa) conducted a public hearing into the Arms Deal, at which Chippy Shaik was questioned. He claimed to have recused himself from meetings involving discussions about ADS, the company in which his brother had a shareholding. He still claims this was the case, but the Joint Investigating Team (JIT), which we will come to in a moment, would beg to differ.

On 30 October, Scopa released its '14th Report' into the Arms Deal. Scopa recommended that 'further independent and forensic investigation' of Arms Deal corruption be discussed by the Auditor-General, the Public Protector, the National Prosecuting Authority (NPA), and the Special Investigation Unit (SIU), known then as the Heath Special Investigating Unit, headed by Judge Willem Heath.

On 6 November McCarthy decided to hold a preparatory investigation, in terms of the NPA Act, into corruption and/or fraud in connection with the Arms Deal, and on 13 November the Auditor-General, the Public Protector, and representatives of the NPA and the SIU met and decided to form the Joint Investigating Team (JIT) to conduct a joint investigation.

On 19 January 2001, Mbeki had the first of the strange attacks of anger (though they are controlled ones) that he would have while president, and said that he would not let Heath anywhere near the Arms

Deal. It has never been clear why Mbeki did not want the Heath Unit to be involved in the investigation. Perhaps he was indeed aware of some Arms Deal corruption, or perhaps Heath, who made a habit of talking a great deal to the media, had simply got up the president's nose.

Interestingly, also on this day, Zuma sent a letter to Gavin Woods of Scopa decrying the investigation as a 'fishing expedition'. During the Shaik trial, Judge Squires found that the letter had seemed to take a special delight in rubbing the collective nose of Scopa (and Woods) in the rejection of its recommendations. But it turned out that, though Zuma had signed the letter in his capacity as Leader of Government Business, Mbeki had orchestrated its composition.

Between January and November 2001, the JIT conducted a wide-ranging investigation into the Arms Deal, and on 14 November 2001 it submitted its report, which was accepted and approved by Parliament. The key finding was that, although improprieties may have existed, and although Chippy Shaik was suspected of 'irregular activities', none of the irregularities could be laid at the door of the president and the ministers involved. There were therefore no grounds for suggesting that the government's 'contracting position' in the Arms Deal had been flawed. However, the report added that investigations into possible criminal conduct were continuing and that, due to the nature of the investigations, the JIT had decided not to make public the details of its investigations.

By the time of the report, the NPA had issued more than 100 summonses, obtained 57 statements from witnesses as well as numerous documents, and searched various premises in France, Mauritius and South Africa, including raids by the Scorpions on Shaik's Durban home and offices.

One of the 'areas' that the DSO examined, McCarthy would later testify, was the records of the Thomson-CSF (Thint) companies. One of the reasons for this was the probability that Chippy Shaik had indeed influenced the process that led to the awarding of contracts to the companies with which his brother was involved. A company in the Thomson-CSF group was part of the consortium (the German Frigate Consortium) awarded the contract for the supply of corvettes, and ADS was the subcontractor to the German Frigate Consortium for the supply of the corvette combat suite.

On 15 September 1999, Schabir Shaik's Nkobi Investments had acquired an effective shareholding of 20 per cent in ADS through a 25 per cent shareholding in Thint, which on the same date acquired 80 per cent of the shares in ADS from Thomson-CSF (International), a wholly owned subsidiary of Thomson-CSF (France). In the Thomson-CSF audit working papers obtained by the Scorpions, McCarthy said, the Scorpions discovered a reference to a report of bribery related to the corvettes and involving a senior government minister.

The Scorpions summoned members of the auditing firm Arthur Andersen, which had conducted the annual Thomson-CSF audit. The auditors said that during the audit, conducted in the first quarter of 2000, they had received a report concerning the involvement in possible bribery of Alain Thétard, the executive chairman of the board of directors and chief executive officer of Thomson Holdings. They added that they had been told that the possible bribery involved a senior government official by the name of Jacob Zuma.

When the Scorpions questioned Thétard, he denied having been approached to pay a bribe. But, since the DSO had no reason to doubt the honesty of the auditors and since the details of Thétard's denials differed at different times, the Scorpions decided to investigate Thomson Holdings, Thétard and Zuma further.

In mid-2001, the DSO's investigations led them to Thétard's secretary, Sue Delique. She told them that, after the publication during February 2000 of an article alleging corruption in the award of the corvette combat suite contract to ADS, there had been a flurry of faxes between Thétard and his superiors in Paris. Delique said that during that period Schabir Shaik, who like Thétard was a director of ADS, requested a meeting of the ADS board in Durban. When Thétard returned from Durban in March 2000, he had given her a letter, handwritten by him in French, to type and then fax in encrypted form to Yann de Jomaron of Thales International in Mauritius and to Jean-Paul Perrier of Thomson-CSF (International) in Paris.

Although when first interviewed Delique could not find the letter (she discovered it later, among her papers), she recalled the contents clearly. They were to the effect that Thétard, Shaik and Zuma had met in Durban and that during that meeting it had been agreed that in exchange for a payment to Zuma of R500 000 a year until ADS started paying dividends, Zuma would protect Thomson-CSF against the investigation into the Arms Deal and would support and lobby for Thomson-CSF in future projects.

When, in about June or July 2001, Delique gave the DSO Thétard's handwritten letter, in the Scorpions' view it confirmed what she had claimed earlier. Delique's evidence, especially about Shaik's presence at the meeting with Thétard and Zuma, and the agreement that the annual payments of R500 000 would stop when ADS started paying dividends, as well as the fact that Shaik had an effective shareholding of 20 per cent in ADS, prompted the DSO to investigate the Shaik-Zuma relationship even more closely.

The investigations led the DSO to Shaik's personal assistant, Bianca Singh, who said that Shaik and Zuma had a close and long-standing friendship and that various payments had been made by Shaik on Zuma's behalf.

According to McCarthy, the next major step in the investigation into Zuma, Shaik, the Nkobi companies, Thétard, and the Thomson companies was to apply for warrants for Thétard's arrest and to conduct the local and international searches and seizures. A difficulty, however, he said, 'resulted from the fact that one of persons under investigation – Zuma – was the incumbent Deputy President of South Africa'.

Meanwhile, in November 2001, Schabir Shaik was charged with the theft of state documents: he had been found to be in possession of Cabinet minutes during the raids on his home and office. Chippy was then suspended from the Department of Defence for leaking classified information related to the Arms Deal. He would later be issued with a written warning, after which he resigned (in March 2002).

With the information it had discovered about Zuma, the NPA proceeded as discreetly as possible. By 2002 a picture had emerged of a 'financial relationship' between Shaik and Zuma that was far more extensive than the investigators initially thought.

'It now appeared,' McCarthy said, 'that Zuma was connected to some of Shaik's private business dealings, not all related to the Arms Deal. The DSO investigators inferred from the wider financial relationship between Shaik and Zuma, and from Zuma's suspected involvement in some of Shaik's private business dealings, that Shaik's payments to Zuma might constitute corruption unrelated to the Arms Deal. As a result, the DSO investigators decided to recommend that the terms of reference for the investigation be expanded to cover this new aspect.'

On 9 July 2003 the NPA sent Zuma a list of 35 questions related to all these matters. On 29 July Zuma issued a media statement about the 35 questions, saying that although he regarded many as insulting, invasive of his privacy, and unrelated to any conceivable investigation into the Arms Deal, he had decided to answer them. On 13 August 2003, he sent the DSO a reply which included a detailed refutation of the case against him and answers to only those of the 35 questions which, Zuma said, he had been advised were relevant to the investigation.

According to McCarthy, the DSO investigation team concluded that despite Zuma's protestations of innocence, the evidence gathered during investigations tended to confirm that the contents of the encrypted fax were true. The evidence also showed, in their view, that Zuma and Shaik had a corrupt relationship and that Shaik's payments to or on behalf of Zuma had been made corruptly. The investigation team accordingly recommended that a criminal prosecution be instituted against Zuma.

But, McCarthy said, he and Bulelani Ngcuka, the then National Director of Public Prosecutions (NDPP), did not accept the investigation team's recommendation. After receiving a detailed briefing, Ngcuka said that while there seemed to be a *prima facie* case of corruption against Zuma, the NPA's 'prospects of success are not strong enough. That means that we are not sure if we have a winnable case.'

After reaching this decision, Ngcuka told Zuma about the results of the investigations and also reported on these to Penuell Maduna, then Minister of Justice. On 23 August 2003, Ngcuka and Maduna held a media conference at which Ngcuka announced the NPA's decision not to prosecute Zuma – and also noted that the NPA would charge Schabir Shaik for fraud and corruption.

On 30 October 2003, Zuma complained to Lawrence Mushwana, the Public Protector, about the manner in which the NPA had investigated him. This culminated in a report by the Public Protector (in May 2004) which found that Ngcuka had unjustifiably infringed Zuma's right to dignity and acted unfairly and improperly in making the media statement. Much fun was made of Mushwana over this report – especially by Maduna and Ngcuka – and yet, ironically, a judge's findings five years later would be pretty much in tune with Mushwana's.

In November 2003, Shaik, and nine companies in the Nkobi group represented by Shaik, were indicted on charges of corruption and fraud. Shaik was accused number 1 and the Nkobi group companies accused numbers 2 to 10. A company in the Thomson-CSF group – Thomson (Thint) – was indicted as accused number 11 on charges of corruption.

In the second half of 2003 an intermediary acting for the Thomson-CSF group contacted Maduna saying that Thomson-CSF wanted to meet him and Ngcuka because they were ready to furnish the NPA with information for which it was looking. This is McCarthy's version: Thint has claimed that it was contacted by the NPA via an emissary, Tony Georgiades (former husband of Elita, who married former president FW de Klerk). Whoever made the approach, it was made against the backdrop of the request by the South African authorities to the French authorities to interrogate employees of companies in the Thomson-CSF group, including Thétard and Perrier.

Ngcuka and McCarthy travelled to Paris for an off-the-record meeting with Thomson-CSF executives in about July 2003, which was followed by a second trip by Ngcuka to France in about September 2003. Nothing came of those discussions, according to McCarthy.

In early 2004 Maduna was contacted by Robert Driman, a South African attorney acting for Thomson-CSF. Driman requested another meeting between the authorities and representatives of Thomson-CSF, saying that Thomson-CSF was now ready to co-operate. After discussing the matter with Ngcuka, Maduna agreed and the meeting was held at his house in April. The Thomson-csf delegation included Driman, Pierre Moynot, the 'new' local managing director of Thomson/Thint, Ajay Sooklal, Thint's attorney, and Christine Guerrier, a lawyer from Thomson-csf in France.

During the meeting the Thomson-csf delegation said that they were willing to co-operate and, as Ngcuka and Maduna accepted their *bona fides*, it was agreed – according to McCarthy; again, the French have suggested otherwise – that they would contact Ngcuka's office to discuss this co-operation.

On 19 April 2004 Ngcuka and McCarthy met Kessie Naidu sc, who was then acting for Thomson-csf/Thint, Driman, and Guerrier. The meeting resulted in an agreement, which was recorded in a letter from Ngcuka to Naidu. Ngcuka confirmed that if Thétard made an affidavit that he was the author of the encrypted fax, the npa would retract the subpoena and two warrants of arrest against Thétard and withdraw the prosecution against accused 11, Thint, in the Shaik trial.

On 20 April 2004 Thétard made an affidavit confirming that he was the author of the encrypted fax, which Naidu then forwarded to Ngcuka. On 4 May 2004 Ngcuka wrote to Naidu thanking him for the copy of the affidavit and confirming that as a result, the state would withdraw the charges against Thint.

On 10 May 2004, however, Thétard made a further affidavit, which, according to McCarthy, had not been solicited by the South African authorities, and which the npa received only on 22 May 2004. In this affidavit Thétard said that the encrypted fax was 'a rough draft of a document in which I intended to record my thoughts on separate issues in a manner which was not only disjointed but also lacked circumspection'; that he had never faxed the document or directed that it be faxed, but rather crumpled it up and thrown it in a waste paper basket from where it was possibly retrieved and handed to the state; and that he refused to be interviewed or to testify in any country outside France.

CHAPTER 8

2003-2004

Hefer or: Hamlet without the prince

In August 2007, about four years after the official October 2003 start of the Hefer Commission of Inquiry into whether Bulelani Ngcuka, the National Director of Public Prosecutions (NDPP), had been a spy for the apartheid regime, Yunis Shaik and I were drinking coffee at his favourite restaurant in Greenside, Johannesburg.

I was, as usual, smoking Shaik's cigarettes and he, as is sometimes the case, was philosophising or, at any rate, delivering a short discourse on a particular subject. On this particular day, the subject was the Hefer Commission. I had raised the issue, saying something along the lines of 'what a horrible and embarrassing mess that was for you guys'.

'I don't think so,' Shaik responded. 'I think we pretty much achieved our goals – and that's the point of doing anything, isn't it?'

What had been these goals? I asked.

Shaik said that one aim obviously had been to counter-attack on behalf of his brother, Schabir, who was being investigated by the National

Prosecuting Authority's Scorpions and who Ngcuka had said would be charged with corruption and fraud. But the main goal had been 'to show' that Schabir and by extension all the Shaiks were loyal to and protective of Zuma.

'The thing is,' Yunis said, 'when Ngcuka gave that notorious briefing to which only African editors were invited, in July 2003, he made comments about Mac [Maharaj] and Zuma. But he also made a racist comment about Indians, and we didn't want people to start saying: "You see, the Deputy President is surrounded by grasping Indians. They've got their hooks into him, they're running the show, they're dragging him down, and they're sullying the struggle." That had to be nipped in the bud, fast.'

When the Hefer Commission was long past, Ranjeni Munusamy, who played a major part in precipitating the commission, and as a result lost her job and was shunned by her colleagues and many others for years to come, said something similar to me. Soon after Ngcuka's briefing, she had visited a relative who had just had a baby.

'I don't know exactly how to put it,' said Munusamy, 'but when I saw that baby, I thought to myself: :What kind of South Africa is this child going to grow up in? Is she going to be discriminated against because she's Indian? Is this what the struggle was all about? Why should Ngcuka get away with saying those things?"'

Yunis Shaik continued: 'We had to demonstrate publicly who the Shaiks really are, and we also had to intervene on Zuma's behalf. After all, he'd been dragged into everything because of Schabir.'

Rationalising the past is something we all do, and Yunis tends to look for the bigger (and more abstract) picture more than most, so there was nothing 'wrong' with what he said. But it did occur to me that there existed a chasm between his retrospective analysis of the commission and the reality. For, though the commission was often bizarre and therefore often quite funny, it had been a very ugly business indeed for everyone involved, including Yunis, who during parts of the commission had acted as legal representative for his brother Moe and for Mac Maharaj, the accusers. I could recall numerous occasions when he had been beside himself with anger and frustration.

Most of all, the Hefer Commission was a horrific experience for Bulelani Ngcuka and his family. His wife, Phumzile Mlambo-Ngcuka, was then the Minister of Minerals and Energy Affairs and, when Zuma was fired about 18 months later, was appointed deputy president by Mbeki. Ngcuka was put in the dock for a crime he had not committed and accused of one of the worst things of which someone who had been through the struggle and gone to jail could be accused. He was publicly accused of having been a spy for the apartheid regime; an *impimpi*; a sell-out. And he had to explain to everyone – or have it explained through the commission – that he was not an *impimpi*. It's hard to think of anything more humiliating.

In November 2002, as a result of one of the infamous leaks from the NDPP's office that infuriated Zuma and Maharaj during that period, the *Mail & Guardian* reported that Zuma had allegedly solicited a R500 000-a-year bribe from France's Thomson-CSF, the company that had won the contract to supply the combat suites for the newly purchased corvettes and of which Schabir Shaik's company, Nkobi, was its black empowerment partner.

Then, in July 2003, the Scorpions interviewed Shaik for seven hours and the next day it was reported that Mac Maharaj, the transport minister in Nelson Mandela's government, was being investigated for corruption. A series of payments had allegedly been paid into Maharaj's account by one of Shaik's firms. The suggestion was that Maharaj had helped Shaik's Nkobi Holdings to secure part of the R265-million contract to supply bar-coded driver's licences. That the driver's licence contract had been awarded by the State Tender Board and that neither Maharaj nor the Ministry of Transport had anything to do with the contract seemed to have been overlooked by the media.

A month later, Maharaj provisionally resigned from First Rand Bank, of which he was a director. On 14 August 2003, First Rand officially cleared Maharaj, though it never released the full text of its internal report. The NPA, however, refused to issue a statement clearing Maharaj. According to Maharaj,[1] Ngcuka refused to exonerate him unless he intervened to get Zuma to answer 35 questions that had been faxed to him in connection with the documents seized from Shaik's office and unless he got Shaik to agree to a plea bargain. Maharaj agreed to resign from First Rand and received a healthy payout of R1-million, but it was pretty clear that the bank hadn't left him with much of a choice in the matter.

Then, on 23 August, a Saturday, Ngcuka, in the company of Penuell Maduna, the Minister of Justice, made his famous statement – one of the most famous legal statements of the last 14 years. He said that the NPA had investigated Zuma and his financial advisor and that the NPA would charge 'Shaik for various counts of corruption, fraud, theft of company assets, tax evasion and reckless trading. We have decided to prosecute the Nkobi group of companies and Thomson-CSF' as well, said Ngcuka. Zuma, however, would not be charged. Ngcuka said that, although there was a *prima facie* case of corruption against the deputy president, the NPA was not certain that it had 'a winnable case'.

Five years later, in the Pietermaritzburg High Court, Judge Chris Nicholson would say that the decision not to charge Zuma with Shaik had been 'bizarre to say the least' because bribery was clearly a 'bilateral' matter.

What was happening, of course, was that Maduna and apparently Mbeki had decided to protect Zuma; he was still, then, their comrade and he was, after all, the deputy president.

Two weeks later, on 7 September 2003, *City Press* ran an article by a journalist called Elias Maluleke in which he wrote that Ngcuka had been investigated as an apartheid spy by the ANC, which had believed him to be a security police spy with the codename RS452. This was based on a set of 'documents leaked to City Press ... by a senior investigative journalist, which are said to have been sourced from the National Intelligence Agency database.'

Judge Josephus 'Joos' Hefer, the chairman of the commission and former acting chief justice of South Africa, put it well in his final report:

Considering the role of the ANC in the struggle for democracy, it must have come as a rude shock to those who were acquainted with Mr Ngcuka's impressive career in the organisation to learn from a Sunday newspaper that he was once suspected of spying for the apartheid government. The story which appeared on 7 September 2003 in *City Press* under the heading 'Was Ngcuka a spy?' read

- that the ANC had investigated Mr Ngcuka during the 1980's to establish whether he was an 'apartheid spy';
- that documents leaked to *City Press* 'by a senior investigative journalist, which are said to have been sourced from the National Intelligence Agency (NIA) database, identify the head of the DPP as possibly, but not conclusively, an apartheid police spy nicknamed 'Agent RS452'; and
- that, according to Mr Moe Shaik, a special advisor to the Minister of External Affairs [sic], an intelligence unit of the ANC had come to the conclusion by late 1989 'that there was a basis for suspecting Bulelani Ngcuka as being RS452'.
- On 8 September 2003 Mr Mac Maharaj, a senior member of the ANC and former Minister of Transport, confirmed the contents of [the newspaper] paragraph in a radio interview and added that he still supported the conclusion arrived at in 1989.

Moe had given the story to Munusamy, who was then a leading and well-connected political writer on the Johannesburg *Sunday Times*. She was fired soon after the story was published because her editor, Mathata Tsedu, knew all about it. She had initially approached him with it, but he had thought it was clearly defamatory and untrue. That, at any rate, was his version. Hers was that Tsedu did not check it out in any way or seriously consider it but had merely discussed it with Ngcuka and that, because he knew Ngcuka, who had obviously said it was untrue, Tsedu had promised the NDPP the story would not see the light of day.

Munusamy then did, from a journalist's point of view, the 'unthinkable' and gave the story to the editor of another newspaper, Vusi Mona of *City Press*. Mona had one of his reporters 'take over' Munusamy's story and then he published it – and was damned.

Munusamy's story was built around documents that Moe Shaik had put together during Operation Bible, the ANC intelligence operation to try and discover who the apartheid spies were in the 1980s and the 1990s. The project had been under the direct command of Zuma. Moe remained insistent during the Hefer Commission that – in Hefer's own words – the intelligence unit 'had come to the conclusion by late 1989 that there was a basis for suspecting Bulelani Ngcuka as being RS542'.

The response to the allegations was one of shock and disbelief. Mbeki lost no time in ordering a commission to determine whether Ngcuka had been an agent for the apartheid state at any stage prior to 1994. But then he started fiddling with the Commission's terms of reference and extended them on 7 October to include an examination of whether Ngcuka, 'due to past obligations to the apartheid regime', had abused his powers of office as NDPP. Then he changed the terms again on 11 November so that the Commission had to report on the 'allegations by Messrs Maharaj and Shaik' that Ngcuka was spy RS452. In other words, if Ngcuka wasn't RS452, then his 'abuse of office' – Maharaj's bugbear – wouldn't have to be dealt with.

In short, Mbeki was loading the deck. Suddenly Maharaj and Shaik had to prove not that Ngcuka had been a spy, or had been investigated as a spy (which is all they were really claiming and had claimed – the purple journalism of *City Press* had effectively changed this claim into 'We say Ngcuka was definitely a spy'); they had to prove that Ngcuka had definitely been RS452, which they had never claimed.

On 15 October 2003, the Hefer Commission of Inquiry started proceedings with a series of public hearings. The evidence leader was Kessie Naidu SC, a shrewd advocate who had in fact done work for Zuma. But only a few minutes of business took place. Given the changes to the terms of reference, Maharaj and Shaik asked for time to gather more evidence.

Five days later, Vanessa Brereton, a former Eastern Cape human rights lawyer, living in England, admitted that she, in fact, was Agent RS452. She confessed that she had begun working for the apartheid security forces in 1985 as an informer.

There were all sorts of fun and games when proceedings re-opened. Munusamy refused to testify; Hefer insisted that she should, and his decision was taken on review by her lawyers. But in the end the judge came to realise that her newspaper story had emanated from Moe Shaik and that she wasn't going to add much anyway. So he opted not to pursue the issue.

In Hefer's view, however, the situation was 'insufferable'. The state intelligence security agencies refused to cooperate on the grounds that all intelligence files were classified. The ANC as an organisation apparently took a similar stance. Zuma, the former head of intelligence, wrote saying he was 'not at liberty to disclose information without the express mandate and direction of my organisation'.

Then, on 11 November, Frank Chikane, the director-general of the presidency, wrote to Hefer that his boss had access to all the records of the intelligence and security 'structures' and that there was no need for anyone from the state security services to give testimony. In other words, there was no indication in the state files that Ngcuka had been a police spy: the whole issue could have been resolved by Mbeki, who needed only to put the security services together with Shaik and Maharaj to get to the bottom of the matter. There had been no need for the Commission, as Maharaj's biographer, Padraig O'Malley, has pointed out.[2] It seems that Mbeki had been intent on calling Maharaj's bluff and embarrassing him.

So Hefer moved on and considered the evidence against Ngcuka presented to the Commission by Shaik and Maharaj, which in his final report he divided into six sections. The first related to ANC operations in Durban in the early 1980s; the second to Ngcuka's detention in jail; the third to the activities of ANC supporters in the then Eastern Province; the fourth to Ngcuka's identification documents and passport; the fifth to Shaik's investigation in 1989; and the sixth to the alleged abuse of power by Ngcuka as NDPP.

In connection with ANC operations in Durban, Hefer found that Ngcuka had not been responsible for the betrayal of ANC operatives Ntobeko Patrick Maqubela, Mboniso Maqutyana and Mpumelelo

Gaba. They had all been sentenced to 20 years on Robben Island.

This saga emerged during the Commission in the evidence given by Litha Jolobe, who had been sent to Durban to operate underground with Maqubela's unit. Jolobe had been told by his handler in exile to collect documents from a dead-letter box at the University of Natal.

'I was instructed in Swaziland, by my commissar in the underground, the late [Mr X] to pick up a parcel (understood to be passports, manufactured by ANC operatives in South Africa).' The parcel was not there at the designated time, so Jolobe 'called [Mr X] from a phone booth, whereupon he reinstructed me to collect the parcel at about 5pm.'

Jolobe returned to the dead-letter box, where he was arrested and taken to the 14th floor of the security police headquarters in Durban, known as the 'panelbeating shop'. There, he said, he was so severely 'panelbeaten by police officers' that he finally 'succumbed' and revealed that the local commander was Maqubela.

The suggestion by Ngcuka's accusers was that Ngcuka had sold out Maqubela's unit. But Maqubela told the Commission that this could not have been so. He said the informer had been a man known as Mr X and that Mac Maharaj and Moe Shaik knew perfectly well who he had been and what he had done. He said Mr X was now dead, but that for the sake of the man's family he did not want to reveal his identity.

Maqubela also said that Ngcuka had not even known about his unit's operation, and had only found out about the unit when he, Ngcuka, was finally arrested and tortured for refusing to give evidence about Maqubela.

There was also no evidence that Ngcuka was treated any differently from any other prisoner or received any special favours during his time in jail.

Regarding the third category, Ngcuka's activities in the Eastern Province, it seemed clear that Shaik had located Ngcuka in the wrong place and that it had been Brereton and not Ngcuka at a meeting of the National Association of Democratic Lawyers (NADEL).

As far as Shaik's suspicions about Ngcuka's identity documents and passports were concerned, Hefer said that he had been convinced that

Shaik's sinister inferences had not been justified. 'I do not intend dealing with all the points and merely mention two of them by way of example,' he said.

> First, there is the fact that a passport was issued to Mr Ngcuka during December 1981 with apparently unseemly haste. According to Mr Vorster [a witness from the Department of Home Affairs], this was by no means unusual. Then there is the fact that the Security Branch wrote a letter advising the Department of the Interior that there was no objection from a security point of view to the issue of a passport to Mr Ngcuka. But there is conclusive evidence showing that the letter was written before Mr Ngcuka's arrest, and no suggestion that the authorities were aware of his activities in the ANC underground at the time.

Regarding Shaik's special investigation into Ngcuka, Hefer said that it had been flawed. Because Shaik had no real evidence of any duplicity on Ngcuka's part, he had relied on 'inferences which he drew from documents stolen from Security Branch files and from peculiarities pertaining to Mr Ngcuka's passport and identity documents. He repeatedly stressed in his evidence that, in the event of one of his inferences or assumptions being shown to have been fallacious, he was prepared to concede the fallacy of his conclusion too.'

Hefer said that for a number of reasons, which he laid out in detail in his report, he had reached the conclusion that Shaik's 1989 investigation into Ngcuka had been fatally flawed 'by unwarranted assumptions and unjustifiable inferences and by the blatant failure to examine available avenues of inquiry.

> I have not found anything showing, as a matter of probability, that [Ngcuka] was a pre-1994 government agent. On the contrary, the probabilities heavily favour the opposite conclusion. I need only remind the reader that Mr Ngcuka was detained without trial on no less than three occasions (on one of which he went on a hunger strike) and thereafter restricted to Gugulethu. This is certainly not the kind of treatment meted

out to government agents ... I have accordingly come to the conclusion that he probably never at any time before 1994 acted as an agent for a state security service. As I have shown, the suspicion which a small number of distrustful individuals harboured against him fourteen years ago was the unfortunate result of ill-founded inferences and groundless assumptions.

Maharaj told the Commission that Ngcuka had abused his position as National Director of Public Prosecutions and damaged Maharaj's name by leaking stories to the press. The *Sunday Times* knew about a Scorpions' investigation into Maharaj's activities before he knew about it himself. 'The *Sunday Times* story was a fundamental attack on my integrity, which is the only thing I have in my life ... I had no way to clear my name. I offered to resign,' he said.

Hefer later lambasted the Scorpions for the number of leaks emanating from them, which he referred to as 'most disturbing'. Maharaj, Hefer found, had been the subject of unfair media leaks and his family had been vilified.

> Months have elapsed since Mr Maharaj had been questioned by members of the directorate [but] no charges have yet been preferred against Mr Maharaj or against his wife. In the meantime, press reports about allegations against them kept appearing ... In a country such as ours where human dignity is a basic constitutional value and every person is presumed to be innocent until he or she is found guilty, this is wholly unacceptable. ... One cannot be assured that the Prosecuting Authority is being used for the purposes for which it was intended.

These comments were not dissimilar to the finding by Judge Chris Nicholson four and three-quarter years later in Pietermaritzburg.

Precipitating the Hefer Commission (though they did not know that Mbeki would appoint a commission) was the first attempt by the Zuma camp to stymie the NPA. Although it was aimed at hitting back at the NPA for its investigations into Schabir and Maharaj, it was also aimed at protecting Zuma by neutralising Ngcuka.

In some respects it might seem as though it failed, but actually, as Yunis said that day to me over coffee, it didn't: Ngcuka would resign in July 2004. Doubtless, therefore, it was worthwhile, even though this was the comment Moe had to read in Hefer's final report of January 2004:

> Mr Moe Shaik revealed in his evidence that, after many years, his interest in Mr Ngcuka was rekindled when he came to know of the investigation against Mr Zuma. His renewed interest, he says, stemmed from his complete faith in and undying loyalty to the latter. For this reason he re-examined the information about the 1989 investigation, proceeded to make further inquiries and eventually confided in Ms Munusamy in order to make the public aware of the 1989 investigation and findings. What he could not understand initially, was why Mr Ngcuka's office was investigating Mr Zuma at all. But later, when Mr Maharaj was also investigated, it dawned on him that Mr Ngcuka might have become aware of the 1989 investigation and might have resolved to investigate the persons who had investigated him. This notion is so implausible that it deserves no serious consideration. Apart from anything else, if Mr Ngcuka were acting against those who had investigated him, one wonders why he has investigated Mr Maharaj who really had nothing to do with the 1989 investigation, and has left Mr Shaik alone. This supposition is in any event quite insufficient to bring Mr Shaik's complaint about the investigation against Mr Zuma within my terms of reference.

But what about Zuma? What was his role in the commission – 'An Omission of Inquiry' *The Star* of 26 November 2003 called it – and the events leading up to it?

At first glance, his role seems to have been remarkably small. In fact, there were aspects of the evidence on which Zuma could have thrown some light, so much so that in this final report, Judge Hefer remarked with irritation on Zuma's apparent unwillingness to appear before the commission.

But Zuma was being told by his lawyers that he should be very wary of leading with his chin. No one knew what was going to come out of the Scorpions' investigation of Shaik; and Ngcuka, who did not see himself as Zuma's enemy, whatever Zuma might have thought then and would think later, would tell Zuma in mid-August that things didn't look too good for him. Besides, the Shaiks were following a policy, one that would continue to be the bedrock of their behaviour until and during Schabir's trial a year later, of 'keeping Zuma out of things' – for his own protection.

Although Zuma was absent, his spirit hovered over the Commission in many ways and, especially when you consider the Shaiks' motivation for setting it in motion, the Commission is an important part of Zuma's story.

Moe Shaik wanted to shut Ngcuka down to protect his brother. But, as importantly, as expressed by Yunis at the beginning of this chapter, and by Moe himself during the Commission, Moe was there 'to fly Zuma's flag', especially as it had been Schabir and all the family who had drawn Zuma into trouble by telling him that Schabir would take care of business for him.

The Shaiks are a close, loving, loyal and, one has to say, emotional family. Above all – and this is a very important thing to bear in mind – Moe and Yunis spend much of their thinking time cogitating on 'political strategy'. They are also conspiracy theorists par excellence – as is Maharaj. And Moe, once he has an idea in his head, is possessed of a tenacity that would make the average bull terrier seem like an amateur.

So what, in the proverbial nutshell, was the Hefer Commission really about? It was an attempt by Moe Shaik and Mac Maharaj to spike the guns of Ngcuka and thereby the National Prosecuting Authority as well.

Maharaj wanted to do this because he was angry beyond words that he, of all people, had been investigated and publicly humiliated by the NPA – and had therefore lost the company directorships that were his nest egg. Maharaj had paid a high price during his struggle – in terms of his family life, not to mention physical pain and damage due to torture by the security police – and he simply couldn't believe that an organ of the state he had helped create would treat him as it had.

One of the issues that especially incensed Maharaj flowed from a telephone call from Jovial Rantao, then the political writer on *The Star*, and now editor of the *Sunday Independent*. Rantao divulged that the information about which he wanted to ask Maharaj had come from the Scorpions. Maharaj got Rantao to call him back and then tape-recorded the conversation. It appeared that the information came from Ngcuka's infamous briefing to seven 'editors' (only Africans need apply) of 24 July.

At the briefing, Maharaj would find out later, Ngcuka had allegedly called him a liar, said that the way to get at Mac was through his wife (one thing you do not do with Maharaj is threaten his wife), and added that he was going to charge Zarina Maharaj with tax evasion. He had also allegedly made disparaging remarks about Indians and said that he would let Zuma dangle in the unpleasant winds of public opinion.

Wasn't it as obvious to Moe as it is to us that the Scorpions were investigating Schabir, and consequently Maharaj and Zuma, because of what they had uncovered in their raids on Schabir's office? Yes, it was; and yet Moe, Zuma, and the Shaik brothers were strategists and conspiracy theorists. Not for nothing had Moe been an intelligence operative and not for nothing was he someone who put one and one together when some people would not even have been able to locate either of the 'ones'.

There they were; Maharaj was a former minister and a struggle icon; Moe was a senior civil servant; Zuma was the deputy president. In 2001, following a political gelding by Mbeki of potential rivals, Cyril Ramaphosa and Tokyo Sexwale, Zuma had been happy enough to state publicly that he harboured no ambitions for Mbeki's job. Maharaj and Mbeki disliked one another, but Maharaj had told Mbeki that he was not available to serve in Mbeki's government, so he was history politically. Why then – Zuma and the Shaiks wondered – was the NPA looking to devour its own? It had to be, they calculated, a move against Zuma as well as Maharaj, with Ngcuka happy to lead the charge because he knew that the Shaik cell had investigated him in the bad old days.

If the Hefer Commission itself was ugly, the events that led up to it were even uglier. Vicious attacks had been made on various people, mostly Ngcuka, by e-mail to various newspapers and others. I do not say there was warfare waged between 'the Shaik and the Ngcuka camps' because it was never clear from where the worst excesses came.

It was because of this disinformation war – though disinformation is too tame a word – that Ngcuka called newspaper editors together on 24 July to explain what was going on and why there were those sorts of rumours flying around. Why he omitted to invite any non-African journalists, why he picked the leading black journalists to come to his briefing, which immediately raised hackles as well as the level of curiosity, and why he made disparaging remarks about Zuma and Maharaj (though he would deny this at the Commission), one cannot say.

Another result of the disinformation war was that many journalists split into camps and became suspicious of everything they were told. And this state of journalistic affairs continued long past the Hefer Commission. So, for example, two years later, when a strong rumour circulated that a woman had laid charges of rape against Zuma, some news desks or political bureaus ignored it, or treated it so cautiously that they didn't even tell other sections of their own newspapers.

CHAPTER 9

2004-2005

Shaik goes down

The trial of Schabir Shaik started on 11 October 2004 and ran for about 75 court days. The transcript of what was said during the proceedings ran to almost 6 700 pages and the documentary exhibits filled more than 25 lever arch files. The judgment was so long, it took two days for Judge Hilary Squires to read it.

On 2 June 2005, Squires convicted Shaik on two counts of corruption and one count of fraud, and on 8 June he sentenced him to 15 years' imprisonment on two counts of corruption and three years' imprisonment on the count of fraud, to run concurrently. Several of Shaik's Nkobi companies were also convicted and sentenced to pay substantial or suspended fines.

According to Squires and two assessors, the nub of Shaik's corruption was that he gave Zuma more than a million rand in the expectation of being helped out in various ventures. Second, Squires ruled that Shaik negotiated a bribe of R1,5-million from French arms manufacturer Thint for Zuma, in exchange for Zuma providing future protection from the governmental probe into Shaik/Thint's role in the Arms Deal.

In his judgment, Squires said the following about Zuma and his relationship with Shaik: 'From the full result of all this additional information, it emerges that the state case is not the usual corruption charge of one payment for one act or omission … It is that the payments made by the accused effectively constituted a type of retainer by which accused [Shaik] agreed, expressly or impliedly, to pay these many expenses over this period to Zuma or for his benefit, or to make cash payments to him as and when he needed such financial help, while [Zuma], in return, would render such assistance as he could to further [Shaik's] interests, as and when asked.'

Shaik wasn't guilty of corruption involving just anybody, as Paul Holden has said in his book on the Arms Deal:[1] he was found guilty of corruptly attempting to influence the decisions made by Jacob Zuma, the deputy president. In finding Shaik guilty, Squires set in train a series of events that are still playing their way out, that had a devastating effect on Zuma's life (he would be fired), and that, as this book was being completed in September 2008, have resulted in the toppling of Mbeki, the president of the republic.

The trial was also the last panel in a triptych of major legal or investigatory events – first the Arms Deal investigations, then the Hefer Commission, and finally Shaik's trial – in which Zuma was involved but not involved. He had been emulating Brer Rabbit – layin' low and sayin' nuffin' – for about three years. But after Shaik's trial, he could run but he couldn't hide.

Why wasn't Zuma tried with Shaik? How did this 'bizarre' situation, as Judge Chris Nicholson would call it four years later, arise?

Zuma wasn't tried with Shaik because the National Director of Public Prosecutions Bulelani Ngcuka had said that, though Zuma was clearly involved, the NPA did not believe it had a winnable case against him. Ngcuka and Penuell Maduna, the Minister of Justice, wanted to shield Zuma because he was the deputy president and their comrade and they thought he had been led into evil by Shaik and his wily brothers.

The state was in fact quite nervous about its case against Shaik, and it wasn't until Squires gave his judgment eight months after the trial began, that the NPA realised what a 'winner' it had on his hands.

As the trial progressed, as it went from bad to worse for Shaik, did Zuma offer to give evidence on Shaik's behalf? The answer to the question depends on which particular stage the trial had reached. Zuma says that, had he been asked to do so, he would have been willing to testify; the Shaik brothers say that he offered to do so. However, one of Zuma's legal advisers, who does not want to be named, clearly remembers suggesting to Zuma, as the trial turned sour for Shaik, that he ought to testify – because, if he did not, Shaik would be convicted and he, Zuma, would be charged. But the lawyer recalls that Zuma did not want to do so; he was not on trial, why should he? Zuma also had other advisers, legal and otherwise, who recommended that he should not testify. The lawyer who thought that he should have given evidence says now: 'Look, maybe Zuma was right. Maybe he would have incriminated himself badly. I just thought that he would have been a good witness – because he is always a good witness – and that he could have scotched many issues there and then.'

However, when the issue of the letter signed by Zuma to Scopa came up – the letter which the judge would find had shown that he was helping shield Thint from investigation – Zuma and the Shaik brothers discussed in detail whether he should be called. After all, Zuma knew that though he, as Leader of Government Business, had signed the letter, Mbeki had been its architect. But, given that evidence about the letter's true authorship was not, it seemed then, going to have a major influence on the main issues of the trial, and that it would make Zuma out to be someone who blindly signed what was put before him, the Shaiks and Zuma decided together that he should not give evidence.

One must remember that, until the end of the trial, in fact until the day of Squires' verdict, no one, least of all the Shaik brothers, realised how severely Schabir Shaik would be penalised. So the Shaik brothers suggested Zuma hold his peace and let Schabir run the hard yards, not fully realising just how hard those yards would become.

During the early days of the trial, Schabir came to court in his special model BMW, with his beefy driver at the wheel, and his family surrounding him, beautifully dressed and full of bravado. He clearly enjoyed being the centre of attention. But, at the end, though his accoutrement remained the same, Shaik was clearly deflated.

Judge Squires, especially recalled from retirement for the case by KZN Judge-President Vuka Tshabalala, was a courteous, precise, elderly, ex-Rhodesian (he had actually served for a while in Ian Smith's government as Minister of Justice) and he was at pains to point out at the beginning of the proceedings that Shaik was on trial, not Zuma.

A thin, almost cadaverous man, he also demonstrated from the bench in the wood-panelled, cramped courtroom of the colonial Durban High Court, that it was his court and that he was little interested in anything approaching histrionics. For example, before the state led one of its star witnesses, KPMG forensic auditor Johan van der Walt, through his lengthy forensic report, I was given a copy of the report and wrote a story based on it for the *Sunday Tribune*. Billy Downer SC, the lead prosecutor, was livid and in court said to Squires that the behaviour of one of the journalists was bordering on contempt.

Squires said quietly that he recommended that all the journalists present abide by the proper rules of reporting, but, he continued, 'the only way that could be bordering on contempt is if I were influenced – but, Mr Downer, I regret that I do not even read the newspaper you have mentioned'.

Shaik's trial started amid an intense media circus. He pleaded not guilty to charges of corruption and fraud, insisting that the state had misunderstood his dealings with Zuma. Shaik admitted, upfront, through his lead advocate Francois van Zyl, that he had made payments to Zuma, which were used to pay school fees for Zuma's children, clothing bills, the repair of cars, air fares, a number of attorneys, and settling debt obligations that Zuma had with Standard Bank where Zuma had a home loan and chequing account. But, Shaik argued, these payments were not inappropriate or corrupt at all: they were made purely out of friendship, as Zuma and Shaik shared a deep and close bond. In particular, Shaik noted how his relationship with Zuma stretched back into the mists of exile: 'My association with Zuma began in the 1980s during the struggle against apartheid. I went to London where I met Zuma and Aziz Pahad.

Zuma recruited me for the ANC and sent me for training ... I was often in charge of carrying information from my brother, Mo, to Zuma.' Shaik began paying Zuma money when he realised that 'between 1996 and 1997, Zuma had dire financial problems and he wanted to leave politics'. Shaik, deeply concerned by the possible loss to politics of Zuma and solicitous of his friend's wellbeing, took it upon himself to support Zuma, which was an attempt, Shaik noted, to 'help in an effort to keep him in politics'.

These payments, Shaik argued, were never conceived of as donations, but, rather, as forming part of a loan agreement. According to Shaik, Zuma insisted that he would repay Shaik, and they entered into a loan agreement to this effect. Importantly, this loan agreement did not include any interest charges, Shaik claimed, 'because of my religious beliefs' as a Muslim, which provided clear condemnation of the institutions of interest and usury.

As to the other charges Shaik faced, he issued flat denials. On the charge of fraud, he acknowledged that he had written off the R1.2m from the books of Kobifin, but that this was a mistake of which he was not at first aware. When he learnt of the mistake, he argued, he instructed the matter to be rectified in the books. On the charge of soliciting a bribe, he argued that he had never done so.[2]

Downer said his case would be based on facts and patterns and that 'we will principally be talking of the Arms Deal'. The first charge against Shaik was one of general corruption. In their efforts to prove this charge, the state led a number of witnesses to show, as explained by Downer, that Zuma was 'on retainer for Shaik'.

As regards the first charge of corruption, Downer argued that Shaik had paid Zuma R1 340 078.01 from 1 October 1995 to 30 September 2005. To prove this charge, the state gave evidence of all the financial transactions between Shaik and Zuma.

The state's first witness for this charge was Shaik's former secretary, Bianca Singh, who gave testimony while accompanied by three bodyguards. She said, 'Zuma was quite close to Shaik. They would speak on the phone and he would come to visit.' She also testified that Shaik arranged financial affairs for Zuma, managed his bank accounts and discussed his financial situation with him. She concluded by saying that she knew that Shaik mentioned Zuma's name often because she overheard him while he was on the phone.

Singh mentioned that Shaik had once ridiculed the type of relationship he had with 'various ministers'. 'He said he has to carry a jar of Vaseline because he gets fucked all the time but that's okay because he gets what he wants and they get what they want.'

The state's next major witness was KPMG forensic auditor Johan van der Walt, who testified for several hours that the payments made by Shaik to Zuma 'sometimes threatened the financial existence of [Shaik's] whole group.' He continued that the payments were not sensible for any other purpose than to buy influence with Zuma.

Shaik's lawyers argued in cross-examination that their own forensic auditor showed that payments to Zuma were only a small percentage of the group's turnover. Van der Walt replied that 'one can have a billion rand turnover and still have an overdraft. If you don't have the money, you can't operate.' Van der Walt also stated that Zuma lived well beyond his means, but seemed to accept that other people would pay his debts.

Van Zyl said Shaik would testify that as far as he knew, Zuma had by now paid all his creditors and should have no problem paying him back. Van der Walt replied that whether the money paid to Zuma was a loan or a donation, Zuma benefited: 'My review indicated that Zuma had no access to major funds to repay his debts. The repayments must have taken place outside the period of review.'

Van Zyl produced a written revolving credit agreement between Shaik and Zuma of which, he said, Parliament had been told. The state said it would dispute its authenticity.

Van der Walt would take the court through all the financial details included in his report. As summarised by Paul Holden:

Two key points established by the KPMG report stood out. The first was that, between July 1996 and December 2003, Zuma's salary amounted to R3.86m. Unfortunately, Zuma spent R4.29m, leaving Shaik's businesses to settle the R1.2m shortfall (which included a number of debts). If, as

Shaik's defence argued, Zuma had intended to pay back Shaik with his pension money, Zuma would have owed Shaik half of the pension he was due. This reflected the fact that, at almost all times, Zuma's style of living extensively outstripped his income. Only a few examples of these financial difficulties included the following:

1. In 1995, Zuma took out a bond for a home in Killarney worth R400 000. However, by 1997, the bond was R30 000 in arrears. Shaik and one of his companies paid in R40 000, but it was too late. Later in the year, Standard Bank sued Zuma for R443 000 plus interest. This was resolved when the debt was paid by a number of third parties.

2. In June 1997, Standard Bank informed Zuma that his current account was in arrears. In October of the same year, they sued him for R118 842, the amount outstanding on the overdraft account. It seemed that the amount was never really settled as, by the time of the Shaik trial, Zuma still owed Standard Bank R128 301.

3. In 1997, Zuma bought a Mercedes-Benz, but wasn't able to pay even the first instalment on the car.

4. In 1998, Zuma bought yet another Mercedes-Benz for roughly R250 000. Almost from the start, debit orders to settle the car financing failed. Mercedes-Benz threatened action, but the amounts were settled by Shaik's Kobitech company.

5. In May 2001, Zuma financed a Mitsubishi Pajero for R275 000. By December 2003, he still owed a huge R350 000 on the car, of which about R129 000 was in arrears. This even though Shaik had made a payment of R47 000 towards the financing of the car in 2002.

The second was that Shaik's Nkobi companies were almost always in financial difficulty. Although it secured some key contracts, Nkobi was always in a 'cash-starved' position. This meant that, in order for Shaik and his companies to pay R1.2m to Zuma, Nkobi had to finance the transfers by using its bank overdrafts. [3]

Ian McLeod, credit manager at Absa Group Limited, said that neither Shaik nor Zuma mentioned a loan agreement when they were asked to make a list of their assets and liabilities. From what he saw, he said that he doubted very much if Zuma could repay Shaik. Tracy O'Brian told the court that she sublet a flat to Shaik. Shaik told her that it was for his financial director. She later discovered, however, when there were complaints about bodyguards with guns, that Zuma lived there. Although Shaik or one of his companies paid the rent, it was always late. She terminated the lease.

Professor John Lennon of Caledonian University in Glasgow told the court that Zuma advised him to use Nkobi as the South African partner for a proposed eco-tourism school. When Lennon seemed hesitant, Shaik threatened to derail the proposal and tell Zuma.

Zuma had intervened, said the state, when Thomson was hesitant to take Nkobi on as its BEE partner because Mbeki allegedly said that he had reservations about Shaik and his business ventures. Van der Walt said Zuma intervened in sorting out Nkobi's shareholding in ADS, a company strategically placed to get a multimillion-rand contract in the Arms Deal. Van Zyl countered that both Mbeki and Mandela were involved in attempts to negotiate a BEE settlement for ADS.

When the Malaysian Renong Group wanted local partners for a Durban development, Zuma proposed Shaik's involvement. Another Absa official testified that Shaik and Zuma were considered a 'package deal' when the bank invited Zuma to become a private banking client.

At the end of the testimonies related to the first charge, Downer pointed out that the state didn't need to prove that Zuma did anything out of the ordinary to help Shaik – 'you can corrupt a politician by paying him to do something he is paid to do every day'.

On the second major charge, fraud, the state alleged that Shaik had written off more than R1 million that he owed to his own companies in the Nkobi group, and the amount included payments made to Zuma. The write-off meant that it disappeared from Nkobi's books. Shaik said that it was a mistake and that he had his auditors fix it in subsequent financial years. Van der Walt said that it did not matter that it was fixed, as it was still a crime, asserting that 'you can fix the amounts, but not the irregularity'. He said Shaik stood to benefit most from the write-off. He also added that the fact that an auditor was advising him did not reduce his liability as director.

Shaik told the court that the company's auditors and financial director Colin Isaacs took full responsibility for the financial side of operations, that he was sure that the accounting books were in order, and that when he became aware of the problem he had it corrected. He had no intention to commit fraud.

Auditing clerk Anthony Reed said he was instructed by Ahmed Paruk to effect the write-off. Paruk said he was following instructions from Shaik. Former Nkobi accountant Celia Bester said that the money written off was cash bribes paid to 'various ministers' by Shaik. The writing-off, she said, was the main trigger for her final resignation. She told Judge Squires that she 'saw it purely as bribe money'.

In the third charge, the second one of corruption, as summarised by Paul Holden:

> Shaik had, according to the State, solicited a R500 000-a-year bribe from Thomson to be paid to Zuma. This was done in order to influence Zuma to protect Thomson against any problems arising from the investigations into the arms deal. This bribe, the State claimed, was to be disguised by means of a service provider agreement between Nkobi and Thomson that exactly matched the amount of the bribe to be received by Zuma. Further, the State alleged that the payments did end up as part of Zuma's assets as the payments were channelled to Development Africa, which, at the time, was one of the companies belonging to the businessman, Reddy, who was paying for Zuma's Nkandla rural village. And, lastly, Zuma had acted on the bribe agreement by writing a stinging letter to Gavin Woods of Scopa attempting to prevent Scopa from leading a full-fledged investigation into arms deal corruption.[4]

Squires accepted this evidence because Shaik never contested it, but it was common knowledge that Mbeki had organised that letter.

As evidence for the charge, Van der Walt said there were clear signs that an 'informal corrupt' process was followed during the Arms Deal, apart from the formal process. A government auditor James Edward van

Heerden, who did a special review of the arms acquisition process, told the court that there had been deviations from the accepted arms acquisition practices, with no plausible explanation.

The most controversial document produced by the state was a fax ostensibly setting out a bribe agreement between Shaik, Zuma, and Alain Thétard regarding the March 2000 meeting at which the bribe for Zuma had been set up. Both the handwritten fax and a disk with a typed copy were handed to the Scorpions by Thétard's former secretary, Sue Delique.

Delique told the court that she was asked to type the note and fax it in encrypted form to Paris. After she resigned she told Thomson's auditors at the time, Gary Parker and David Read, about it, but refused to give them the documents. She told the court that she did not fax the agreement to Shaik.

Parker and Read concluded at the end that she was a disgruntled employee. They found no proof of what she told them in Thomson's financial statements, and then dropped the matter. Shaik admitted that there was a meeting between himself, Thétard, and Zuma. But he said it was about a donation for the Jacob Zuma Education Trust.

The encrypted fax was headed FAX CRYPTE, 'Subject: JZ/S. Shaik', and read:

> Dear Yann: following our interview held on 30/9/1999 with S. Shaik in Durban and my conversation held on 10/11/1999 with Mr J.P. Perrier in Paris I have been able (at last) to meet JZ in Durban on the 11th of this month, during a private interview in the presence of S.S. I had asked for S.S. to obtain from J.Z. a clear confirmation or, at least, an encoded declaration (in a code defined by me), in order to validate the request by S.S at the end of September 1999. This was done by JZ, (in an encoded form). May I remind you of the two main objectives of the 'effort' requested of Thompson-CSF are:
>
> •   Thompson-CSF's protection during the current investigations
> •   (SITRON)
> •   JZ's permanent support for the future projects
> •   Amount: 500k ZAR per annum (until the first payment of the dividends by ADS).

Squires decided that the fax copy was admissible evidence, and that it did show that Shaik had facilitated a bribe for Zuma, although Thétard had written conflicting affidavits about it.

Singh had told the court that an agitated Shaik had phoned her from the golf course to tell her to tape hearings by Scopa when Chippy Shaik was being questioned about the Arms Deal. She said he told her the next day that they were 'focusing on the wrong person'. Singh also said that she overheard Shaik calling Zuma the next day. According to her he said: 'Hello my brother, hello JZ. Chippy is under pressure. We really need your help to land this deal.'

Later, when Singh went to Mauritius with Shaik, ostensibly to do secretarial work, she said that Shaik said he and Thétard had to discuss 'damage control'. If the Heath investigating unit continued to probe the Arms Deal, and if a certain ANC member opened his mouth, 'they would be in big trouble'. Shortly afterwards the alleged bribe agreement was concluded. Van der Walt said he found a great deal of correspondence about the payment of the money and a service provider agreement. Only one payment was made, of R250 000.

Shaik denied any attempt to bribe Zuma for protection and told the court that he did not know why Thétard wrote the note setting out the bribe agreement. He also testified that what the state thought was correspondence about the bribe was really about the donation to an education trust. Shaik said that the trust was in financial difficulty in 2000 and the donation was urgently required for them to be in a position to give bursaries for the next year. But Gerhardus Pretorius, who managed the Jacob Zuma Education Trust at the time, told the court that nobody ever told him of a significant donation expected from Thomson. Theunis Benemere, involved in the day-to-day administration of the trust, said that 'there was always enough money'.

The defence rested its case on 7 April 2005, which was followed by the state's final arguments on 28 April. Judge Squires reconvened the court at the end of May to deliver his sentence. Describing corruption as a 'pervasive and insidious evil,' he found that Shaik's actions had been aimed at advancing his business interests through an association with Zuma:

'His corporate empire's progress and prosperity was plainly linked to the possibility that Jacob Zuma would finally ascend to the highest political office. What was important to him was the achievement of a large multi-corporate business group ... And the power that goes with that and close association with the greatest in the land. It is precisely in such circumstances that corruption works.'

Squires also said that he was convinced that Shaik gave Zuma 'a sustained level of support' designed to maintain a lifestyle the politician could never have afforded otherwise, and that this was an investment in Zuma's political profile from which Shaik expected to benefit. Judge Squires continued that the payments 'were not ... to a low-salaried bureaucrat seduced into temptation', and that the higher the status of the beneficiary, the more serious the offence.

Squires found Shaik guilty of being in a corrupt relationship with Zuma and of soliciting a bribe for Zuma from Thomson-CSF. He also found him guilty of fraud for irregularly writing off loans from the books of Nkobi Group. Squires dismissed Shaik's anti-apartheid 'struggle credentials', saying what he had sought to achieve was exactly the same as the apartheid regime's 'command of the economy' by a privileged few, which is exactly what the struggle had sought to replace.

Shaik irritated Squires with his 'irrelevant and long-winded answers; the fact that Shaik contradicted himself during his testimony; the fact that he contradicted his original plea of defence during the testimony (which suggested that he was 'extemporising' responses as he needed to); and the fact that he often made claims about other witnesses that his counsel had not thought to ask them during their cross-examination.'[5] As Squires said: 'In the result, we were not impressed by his performance as a witness, either in content of evidence, or the manner in which he gave it. That, of course, does not make him guilty of any offence. It does not even mean he is never to be believed in anything he says. Some of his evidence was plainly truthful. But measured against an otherwise convincing State witness, it may be something of a disadvantage.'

As Paul Holden recounts, 'After assessing Shaik's credibility, Squires moved on to assess the case against Shaik on the first count of corruption (of having a corrupt relationship with Zuma). Starting at the beginning, he traced the various instances in which Shaik turned to Zuma for help before Zuma became Deputy President. ... Squires found that Shaik could always turn to Zuma, and Zuma was almost always willing to help ... The next thing for Squires to assess was whether or not these interventions were motivated by anything other than friendship. Squires described, first, the way in which Shaik had helped Zuma with his finances, noting that Shaik had almost total access to Zuma's finances by means of "computer contact with and control of Zuma's account with ABSA", and that Shaik was, at almost all times, there to help Zuma out of any financial difficulty.'[6]

Squires noted: 'The evidence showed that notwithstanding the regular ongoing payments to institutions of secondary and tertiary learning and the lengthy period of time over which the post-dated cheques [were] issued by accused No 9 ... every now and then some sudden and unexpected expenditure incurred by Zuma or occasionally by his wife, would cause a temporary crisis in the management of his finances, until other arrangements could be made by Shaik to accommodate the immediate emergency and stabilise matters once more.'

Squires described Shaik as a man with commendable vision, ambition, and energy, but one who appeared to have lost his moral compass and scruples. Concluding the sentencing proceedings, he said: 'I do not think I am overstating anything when I say that this phenomenon [of corruption] can truly be likened to a cancer eating away remorselessly at the fabric of corporate privacy and extending its baleful effect into all aspects of administrative functions, whether state official or private sector manager. If it is not checked, it becomes systemic. And the after-effects of systemic corruption can quite readily extend to the corrosion of any confidence in the integrity of anyone who has a duty to discharge, especially a duty to discharge to the public.

'One can hopefully discount the prospect of it happening in this country, but it is that sort of increasing disaffection which leads and has led on other parts of our continent and elsewhere to coups d'état or the rise of popular leaders who in turn manipulate politics for even greater private benefit ... This is the last step in a thousand mile journey.'

CHAPTER 10

2005

Annus miserabilis

For Zuma, Schabir Shaik's conviction was the start of a new 'thousand mile journey' – and his *annus miserabilis*, even if 2005 was already six months old. No sooner had Squires found on 2 June that there was 'overwhelming' evidence of a 'corrupt relationship', than Zuma's trouble started in earnest.

Shaik immediately asked for leave to appeal, which Squires granted on 29 July, except for the first count of corruption, the roughly R1,2-million paid to Zuma for 'assistance'. Six days later, on 14 June, Mbeki fired Zuma at a special session of both houses of Parliament.

Mbeki's speech on that occasion has been quoted extensively, or rather the nub paragraph has: '… as President of the Republic I have come to the conclusion that the circumstances dictate that in the interests of the Honourable Deputy President, the government, our young democratic system, and our country, it would be best to release the Honourable Jacob Zuma from his responsibilities as Deputy President of the Republic and member of the Cabinet.'

Given that it was largely as a result of this decision that South Africans witnessed Mbeki being 'recalled' (fired, that is) by Zuma's ANC in September 2008, perhaps it would be a good idea to look again at his speech.

Mbeki found the root of Shaik's and Zuma's woes to have been the Arms Deal. In one obvious way, he was correct: Shaik's prosecution flowed from the Scorpions' investigation into the Arms Deal. But I agree with Professor Shadrack Gutto, Director of the Centre for African Renaissance Studies at Unisa, who, in the wake of Judge Nicholson's judgment and Mbeki's recall, questioned the prominence given to the Arms Deal (*The Star*, 24 September 2008) in relation to the crimes of Shaik and the alleged crimes of Zuma. Be this as it may, in June 2005, Mbeki's speech went as follows:

> Some three and half years ago, the Joint Investigation Team of the Auditor-General, the Public Protector and the National Directorate of Public Prosecutions completed its work and released to Parliament a report on the Defence Procurement Process. This team came to the conclusion that:
>
> 'No evidence was found of any improper or unlawful conduct by the Government. The irregularities and improprieties ... point to the conduct of certain officials of the government departments involved and cannot ... be ascribed to the President or the Ministers involved in their capacity as members of the Ministers' Committee or Cabinet. There are therefore no grounds to suggest that the Government's contracting position is flawed.'
>
> With regard to matters of the cost of the Procurement, the Investigation Team concluded that:
>
> 'What was achieved by the Affordability Team and the International Offers Negotiating Team ... is unprecedented in the international credit market.'
>
> On each of the allegations of impropriety with regard to the primary contracts, in which government played a pivotal role, the investigators found that there were cogent technical and/or strategic reasons behind the decisions taken.
>
> The team identified some weaknesses in the procurement process, and

made recommendations which are being followed up, the better in this regard continually to improve our work as government.

It also called for investigations on matters pertaining to secondary contracts, in which, though government may have formally played a role to ensure reliability and cost-effectiveness, the arrangements were essentially between the companies chosen as primary contractors and third party corporate sub-contractors.

We refer to this matter in some detail because we believe that it behoves [*sic*] all of us to recognise that the investigations that resulted in the court case that has just been concluded were not only recommended in that Joint Investigation Team Report, but were also supported by the whole of government, including the Hon Deputy President.

These further investigations do not contradict the fundamental conclusion about the integrity of the decisions of the government with regard to the Defence Procurement.

No facts were adduced during the trial in question and no findings were made that are inconsistent with the Report that the Joint Investigation Team submitted to Parliament, a report whose recommendations the government accepted.

Then, having pointed out that there would doubtless be an appeal in the Shaik matter, Mbeki added that JZ should be regarded as innocent until proven guilty:

In this regard, I would like to emphasise two basic pillars of our jurisprudence, namely, equality before the law and the right to be presumed innocent until proven otherwise.

We are of the firm view that this principle applies to the Deputy President not merely as a matter of principle and common decency, but also in deference to the individual occupying such office and the service that he has rendered to the Republic and its people before and after the attainment of our liberation. Unambiguous as the judgment may be about an assumed unsavoury relationship, the Deputy President has yet to have his day in court.

But then Mbeki said that Zuma should go anyway! '... as President of the Republic I have come to the conclusion that the circumstances dictate that in the interests of the Honourable Deputy President, the government, our young democratic system, and our country, it would be best to release the Honourable Jacob Zuma from his responsibilities as Deputy President of the Republic and member of the Cabinet.' And he added:

> Personally, I continue to hold the Hon Jacob Zuma in high regard, and I am convinced that this applies to most Members of Parliament. We have worked together under difficult and challenging conditions for thirty years. In this regard, I wish to thank him for the service that he has rendered as part of the Executive, at national and provincial levels, sparing neither strength nor effort to ensure that, with each passing day, we build a better life for all South Africans. I am certain that I speak on behalf of all who have served with him in Cabinet when I say that we shall remain friends, colleagues and comrades in the service of the people. And, as government, we shall continue to draw on his experience and expertise where the need arises.

It is difficult not to agree with Judge Nicholson, three-and-a-quarter years later, that something appears to have been awry, for there is no discernible logic in Mbeki's pronouncement. On the government side, he said, the Arms Deal process had been hunky-dory. There would doubtless be an appeal by Shaik, the outcome of which was obviously unknown at that point; he might be found not guilty. Zuma would remain innocent until proven guilty. Therefore, he was firing Zuma.

There are two things that need to be borne in mind. The less important one is that the ANC still retains some charming, though deeply irritating and silly, neo-Stalinist habits that it just cannot shake. So, for example, when its leaders are vying for an important position, lobbying here and lobbying there, making all kinds of pacts with this interest group and that one, the public is told that it is contrary to ANC tradition for its leaders to compete for positions – so it simply cannot be happening. (This Orwellian approach reached its nadir in the run-up to the December 2007 Polokwane conference.) Or, when irreparable and cruel hurt is inflicted on one of its leaders, this is the moment at which he or she is lauded to the skies. When Zuma's ANC gave Mbeki the boot in September 2008, one would have thought – from what was said by the ANC leaders, who had just put the knife into Mbeki's back – that the messiah had been toppled. This is why Mbeki said he still held Zuma in the highest regard, and so on.

More importantly, we need to consider what had been happening during those momentous days between 2 and 14 June 2005.

On the weekend immediately after Squires' judgment, both Mbeki and Zuma were in residence at their official homes in Pretoria, each a short stroll across the park from the other. Zuma had just returned from Zambia. But they managed not to meet even once. Mbeki held a meeting with Mendi Msimang, the ANC treasurer-general, and Kgalema Motlanthe, the secretary-general.

Msimang and Zuma had been good friends in exile; they shared a room at one stage in Lusaka. (Zuma tells some amusing anecdotes about the genesis of the relationship between Mendi and his future wife, Manto Tshabalala – apparently Manto was quite a 'hottie', or so Mendi thought.) Despite his low public profile, Msimang was an influential person in the ANC, which was one of the reasons why Mbeki was so supportive of his deeply unpopular Minister of Health. At any rate, it was Msimang and Motlanthe who went to see Zuma. This was one of the biggest of Mbeki's many blunders in the sphere of human relations. Zuma's roots are truly peasant ones; where he comes from, you talk things out – or you try to do so, anyway – and above all, you do this face-to-face. A man talks to another man, looking into his eyes. But Mbeki sent go-betweens who told Zuma that Mbeki thought Zuma should, given the Shaik verdict, resign.

'But I can't do that,' Zuma told Motlanthe and Msimang. 'I'm not guilty of anything. My conscience is clear. I never did anything that would hurt the country or was illegal.'

The emissaries returned to Mbeki – and were dispatched again to see Zuma. But the damage was done. Zuma was affronted and angry. If there ever had been a possibility that he might have been talked into stepping down from the deputy presidency in 'the interests of the country and the party', it was lost.

Then Mbeki deigned to spend two hours talking to Zuma, one on one. But it was all over. Zuma, who had been happily prepared to play second fiddle and had supported Mbeki for the party leadership in 1999; who, in 2001 when the president's paranoia started surfacing, had gone on record that he was an Mbeki man – Zuma, the smiling and easygoing Zulu boy, apparently only interested in the easy life, set like steel. He refused to resign from the deputy presidency. Mbeki could do his worst. So Mbeki did.

As Mbeki left for Chile on a two-day official visit, he asked Joel Netshitenzhe, the government spokesman, to issue a statement: 'The President has indicated that as soon as practicable after his return from a state visit to Chile, he will communicate to the public any decisions that he will have taken on the [Shaik judgment] matter.' Mbeki cancelled the second leg of his South American trip, a planned visit to Argentina, and came back to South Africa on Thursday, 9 June.

Among those on the trip to Chile was Vusi Pikoli, the new head of the NPA following Ngcuka's resignation. Pikoli and Mbeki apparently flew separately and had their own respective matters to attend to: Mbeki aides were adamant that the two never discussed Zuma and later Pikoli would swear an affidavit to this effect. But Zuma never believed this.

Mbeki quoted a Pablo Neruda poem at a special sitting of the Chilean Senate on the Wednesday afternoon: 'For my part and yours, we comply/ We share our hopes and winters/ We go on loving love and in our blunt way/ We bury the liars and live among the truth-tellers.' (Two years later, with just the smallest hint of a twinkle behind the thick lenses of his spectacles, and saying not a word, Mac Maharaj signed my copy of his biography, *Shades of Difference*, as follows: 'Jeremy Gordin – there are no comfort zones for those who seek "to live among the truth-tellers". With deep respect, Mac Maharaj.')

Mbeki returned from Chile and discussed the Zuma matter with Mojanku Gumbi, his legal counsel – and, alas, the apparent author of many disastrous legal moves on Mbeki's part over the years – and with Motlanthe, Msimang and Netshitenzhe. On Friday 10 June, he presided at a ceremony to mark the retirement of Chief Justice Arthur Chaskalson and the swearing-in of his successor, Chief Justice Pius Langa. Mbeki quoted Canadian Appeal Court Justice Rosalie Silberman Abella: 'The occasional judgment will collide with some public expectations, which will, inevitably, create controversy. But judgments that are controversial are not thereby illegitimate or undemocratic; they are, in fact, democracy at work.' One wonders if he remembered these words in September 2008 after Judge Chris Nicholson had delivered his judgment in Pietermaritzburg.

On Monday morning, 13 June 2005, Mbeki conveyed his decision to Zuma, Msimang, Motlanthe, Mosiuoa Lekota, the ANC chairman, and Deputy Secretary-General Sankie Mthembi-Mahanyele. Zuma was present, but let it go, saying little. On Tuesday morning, Mbeki met the party leadership at a special 'extended' National Working Committee meeting of the ANC and its allies in Cape Town. An extended meeting meant that, besides the 22 elected ANC officials and a further three ex-officio members, it included the party's provincial party chairmen and the secretaries-general of Cosatu and the SACP. The presence of Cosatu's Zwelinzima Vavi and the SACP's Blade Nzimande was significant. Both had already gone on the record that Zuma should not be penalised for the Shaik conviction. But on that morning, facing Mbeki perched on the moral high ground and the realisation that it was his prerogative to fire the deputy president, they apparently said little – or decided that the battle had to be fought elsewhere.

By the time of Squires' judgment, the question of who the next ANC president would be was already an issue in the ANC and among its tripartite allies. Even before Mbeki sacked Zuma, there had obviously been serious political rumblings. Cosatu was already annoyed with Mbeki's economic policies and attitude and wanted him out and Zuma in – and suddenly Zuma had presented the labour federation with a rallying point.

The day after Shaik's conviction, Netshitenzhe said that the government 'accepted the outcome of the trial' and that Mbeki was the 'custodian' of the rule of law in the country. This was considered a rebuke to Zuma's supporters in Cosatu and the SACP, the SACP's youth wing and the ANC Youth League, which had cast aspersions on Squires and questioned the legitimacy of his judgment.

The government's statement came hours after Cosatu had upped the ante in the battle over Zuma's political future, challenging Mbeki and the ANC to come to Zuma's defence. The federation had warned of 'devastating consequences' for the ANC-led tripartite alliance if the ANC failed to protect Zuma. Cosatu's statement came three weeks ahead of the ANC's national general council, at which Mbeki would be looking for buy-ins from his allies for his plans to reorient the party's economic policy (the ANC was proposing a range of measures, such as a dual labour market, and would need Cosatu's support for the reforms to pass).

Vavi had already thrown his weight behind a presidential bid by Zuma. Earlier in 2005 he had said that Zuma's bid for the ANC presidency was an 'unstoppable tsunami'. And he said: 'The manner in which the whole [Shaik] trial was run for years [*sic*], and not just for the official duration, indicates a systematic campaign to assassinate the character of the Deputy President.'

The Cosatu leader said state resources had been misused to target a political opponent in the organisation's increasingly messy leadership tussle: 'Zuma would not have received the same kind of attention if his name was not top of the list [of succession candidates].' Shaik's trial was 'nothing but a political trial of the Deputy President in absentia'.

Flanked by the federation's leaders, Vavi said: 'It would create a dangerous precedent in the future that individuals' constitutionally guaranteed rights to a fair trial would be denied in pursuance of clear political agendas and vendettas.'

Why did Mbeki make the decision to fire Zuma? And why did he act without waiting for Shaik's appeal? One does not rightly know. Mbeki was increasingly touchy about corruption. He was about to leave for the 2005 G8 summit at Gleneagles and probably felt that he could not boast of South Africa as a shining beacon of probity – and therefore also garner aid and support for the country and Africa in general – if he still had a deputy president who had been clearly implicated in corruption. Some of his advisers also apparently said that he could not afford to have his authority challenged or to allow for the 'security' risk of having the deputy president in the pocket of a foreign arms company. And perhaps Mbeki was as Machiavellian as he has been alleged to be, and thought that maybe it was as good a time as any to spike one Jacob Zuma.

Zuma, giving away nothing publicly, issued a statement after he was fired, responding in mostly ANC-speak:

President Thabo Mbeki has taken a decision regarding my presence in Government and Cabinet. It is the President's prerogative to take such a decision, in the context of, and within his authority as the President of the Republic. I accept and respect his pronouncement.

I believe he has taken this decision not because he believes I am guilty of any crime, but because of considerations relating to the constraints within which government operates.

In light of this decision, I have also offered to resign my seat in Parliament, not as an admission of guilt of any kind, but in order to make it easier for the ANC and government to function in Parliament.

As stated before, let me reiterate that my conscience is clear. I have not committed any crime against the state or the people of South Africa. I however still maintain that I have been treated extremely unfairly through-out the entire debacle for about half a decade. Throughout this period, I did not use my position in government in any way to interfere with the due process of law, because I believe in, and cherish our democracy and Constitution. I believed that organs of state and other role players would be guided by the principles in our Constitution.

But contrary to this, I have been tried by the media and in effect found guilty by a court in absentia. I have not been given an opportunity in an appropriate forum to defend myself against the allegations made. Yet our Constitution states that everyone is innocent until proven guilty.

I sincerely trust and hope that those authorised to take decisions – at whatever level – will act within a reasonable period with regard to the conclusion of this matter. I need to be given an opportunity to tell my side of the story, and bring finality to these accusations and speculations.

Zuma also resigned his parliamentary seat, hardly an hour after he was sacked from the Cabinet, although he was entitled to retain it because it was an elected position. He was still the deputy president of the ANC, of course, and he knew he was not going to be removed from that position (as would be officially confirmed by the party on 1 July).

Less than an hour after he was sacked, Zuma said to journalists at Tuynhuys, the presidential home in Cape Town, 'Let me reiterate that my conscience is clear: I have not committed any crime against the state or the people of South Africa.'

The trial of Shaik had been a political one, he said to the *Mail & Guardian*: 'In 1963, I was sentenced to 10 years in prison by Justice Steyn. It was a political trial. I listened to Judge Squires and there was nothing different to what I heard 42 years ago in terms of the political judgment.'

Was this an overstatement? What happened next persuaded Zuma that it was not. He had also said in his 'farewell' statement that he hoped 'those authorised to take decisions – at whatever level – will act within a reasonable period with regard to the conclusion of this matter.' Note the barbed 'at whatever level' – he was already suggesting that the real decisions were coming from the president's office. At any rate, Zuma did not have to wait long for those in authority to act.

On 20 June, six days after Zuma was fired, Vusi Pikoli, the National Director of Public Prosecutions who had succeeded Ngcuka, announced via his spokesman that Zuma would be charged with corruption:

In his judgment Justice Squires, assisted by two assessors, convicted Mr Shaik and some of his companies on all three counts, namely two counts of corruption and one of fraud. Furthermore, Justice Squires made adverse remarks on the nature of the relationship between Mr Shaik and the then

Deputy President of the Republic, Mr Jacob Gedleyihlekisa Zuma.

After judgment was passed we informed the nation that the National Director of Public Prosecutions and Head of the National Prosecuting Authority of South Africa (NPA), Advocate Vusi Pikoli, would study the judgment of Justice Squires and where necessary make certain pronouncements.

Adv. Pikoli has concluded his study of the judgment and taken into consideration aspects of it that relate to former Deputy President Zuma. An application for leave to appeal by Mr Shaik and others, and its likely impact on the merits of the case against Mr Zuma, were also taken into consideration.

Adv. Pikoli also took into account evidence at the NPA's disposal, allegedly linking former Deputy President Zuma to specified crimes. Such evidence was reviewed in order to determine whether there was a reasonable prospect of a successful prosecution.

Some time last week Adv. Pikoli invited the team that investigated and prosecuted Mr Shaik and others to his offices in Pretoria. During the meeting Adv. Pikoli was apprised of the facts of the case, from the perspective of the team, and also canvassed their own views on the matter.

Over the past weekend Adv. Pikoli applied his mind to this matter, taking into account the interest of the public, the interest of former Deputy President Zuma, the interest of justice and the integrity of our criminal justice system. Consequently, he arrived at a decision that he felt positively addressed all these considerations.

This afternoon Adv. Pikoli has informed former Deputy President Zuma that he has decided to bring criminal charges against his person. Such charges will be constituted by, amongst others, two counts of Corruption.

Mr Zuma will in due course be informed of the date, time and place where he will have to avail himself at court to face these charges.

Responding to media questions, Makhosini Nkosi, the NPA spokesman, said that the prosecution was 'not through pressure from anyone' and that Mbeki had urged the country to allow the law to take its course.

Presidential spokesperson Bheki Khumalo said: 'Vusi Pikoli, today, June 20, informed President Thabo Mbeki that the National Prosecuting Authority will advise former Deputy President Jacob Zuma of its decision to prefer charges against him. President Mbeki was informed as a matter of courtesy and was not asked for any comment. The President hopes that all South Africans will allow the law to take its course.'

The next year, 2006, Scorpions head Leonard McCarthy would say in an affidavit that a number of findings in the Shaik trial had contributed to a reappraisal of the admissible evidence against Zuma and led to the decision that he should be prosecuted. These included that, on count 1, the court accepted that the state had proved that there was a corrupt relationship between Shaik and Zuma and that, on count 3, the court accepted that the contents of the encrypted fax reflected the truth of the matter.

But Zuma was now convinced that the decision to charge him was a clearly directed and concerted onslaught. Pikoli said he had made a decision based on the views of his colleagues and had not talked to Mbeki, and he would go on saying this, later under oath. But simple common sense suggested otherwise.

On 29 June 2005, Zuma appeared for the first time in the Durban Magistrates' Court and was charged with two counts of corruption, including one of accepting a bribe to use his influence to stop an investigation into a 1999 arms deal to buy aircraft, ships and submarines. He was released on R1 000 bail and his next court appearance was set for 11 October. The case was postponed 'for further investigation, including a forensic investigation and report'.

On 8 August, Aubrey Thanda Mngwengwe, the acting investigating director of the DSO, decided to extend the Zuma investigation to include the suspected commission of fraud by Zuma in connection wiith his declarations to the Registrar of Parliamentary Members' Interests, the secretary for the Cabinet of the government of South Africa, and the South African Revenue Service, 'in respect of benefits received from Shaik and/or companies associated with Shaik, as well as contraventions of the Income Tax Act 58 of 1962 in respect of those declarations'.

The postponement of Zuma's trial 'for further investigation', as well as its extension to include fraud in his declarations to Parliament, led Zuma's legal team to realise that Pikoli had charged Zuma prematurely. He had gone off half-cocked – because, Zuma believed, of the 'pressure' exerted by Mbeki's decision. Clearly the NPA believed that other material existed that could be used against Zuma. But the Scorpions obviously did not have this material; they were proceeding against Zuma with a mirror image of the Shaik indictment, with which they were obviously not satisfied.

Kessie Naidu SC, who was handling Zuma's defence, realised that the faster he could get a trial date settled in the High Court, the better, because the Scorpions were clearly not ready. October 11 could not come fast enough for him.

Meanwhile, Cosatu, and Vavi in particular, as well as other friends of Zuma's, grew increasingly hot under the collar. On 16 August, Cosatu demanded that Zuma be reinstated as deputy president of South Africa and that the charges of corruption be dropped. '[We have resolved] to call on the president of South Africa to review the decision to relieve Comrade Zuma of his responsibilities as the deputy president,' said Vavi. 'It is clear that he would not get a fair trial. In this context, Cosatu will start a petition campaign to call on the president to ensure withdrawal of charges.'

Vavi said that if the case went on despite the federation's call, Cosatu would demand that a full bench hear it. In one of his finer flights of oratory, he told reporters that Zuma was politically targeted because the capitalist elements of society wanted to impose a succession plan on the democratic movement. For this reason, Zuma had been tried by the media and in absentia, and the NPA had actively leaked information to selected media.

'The trial of Comrade Zuma is a classic attempt to drag the working class into a war whose terrain and outcome have been predetermined by neo-liberals using their control over key components of the state machinery, in this case in particular the judiciary.'

It was also announced that a trust, The Friends of Jacob Zuma, which would administer a fund, would be launched to help Zuma. The chairperson would be businessman Don Mkhwanazi; it would be a collaboration between Cosatu, business and civil society groups, and Ranjeni Munusamy would run a website.

Netshitenzhe came back punching. He said that Mbeki's hand would not be forced. 'We hope no one is calling on the president to break the law, trash the constitution, and undermine our young democracy, because that is something the president will never do. Among other things, the constitution enjoins us to a separation of powers and decisions of that kind are not taken by the president,' he said.

On 18 August, the Scorpions struck. Judge Bernard Ngoepe, the Judge President of the Transvaal, had given them a series of 22 search warrants for Zuma's various residences, including Nkandla; Zuma's office and those of his former secretaries and assistants at the Union Buildings in Pretoria and Tuynhuys in Cape Town; the offices of the KwaZulu-Natal Department of Economic Development and Tourism in Durban, where Zuma had served as MEC for Economic Affairs and Tourism; the office of Zuma's attorney Michael Hulley in Durban; the office and residence of Zuma's former attorney Julekha Mahomed in Johannesburg; and the Pretoria business premises of Thint Holdings and the residence of Pierre Moynot, the chief executive of Thint in South Africa.

Computers, a very large quantity of documents (allegedly 93 000), and other materials were seized. The reasons for the searches, according to Leonard McCarthy, included the fact that searches performed in October 2001 had, for reasons of discretion, deliberately excluded Zuma's offices and residences. Another reason, said McCarthy, was that Shaik's attorney had told the NPA that all Zuma's documents held by Shaik or the Nkobi group of companies had been forwarded to Zuma's new attorney, Hulley. There was also evidence, McCarthy said, that Mahomed had liaised with the Thomson-CSF group on Zuma's behalf.

Then there was 'the fact', McCarthy said, that the investigations into the alleged corrupt payments by Shaik to Zuma had only covered the period up to November 2002. During his trial in 2005, however, Shaik testified that the payments, which he claimed (falsely, in the opinion of the trial court) to be in the nature of loans, had continued long after November 2002 and indeed were still continuing.

The Scorpions, including armed men and investigators, arrived at Zuma's Forest Town, Johannesburg home at about 7 am and blocked off the street. Flourishing their warrants, they proceeded to search the house. Zuma was there and summoned members of the police's special presidential protection unit, who arrived brandishing R-4 rifles, the tyres of their vehicles squealing. There was an unpleasant and potentially dangerous stand-off until the Scorpions agreed to leave the premises and disarm – at which point they were allowed back in.

Hulley, who was relatively new to the wonderful world of Zuma, and consequently a little bewildered at the turn that events had suddenly taken, rushed up to Johannesburg from Durban to be with his client. 'Charge and investigate later' were the tactics being used by the state, he said that morning. 'One is puzzled and concerned by the search and seizure on the homes of Mr Zuma. We are convinced that the state has embarked on a tactic of charge and investigate later. It seems that the state is engaging in a fishing expedition,' he said.

Hulley said he was concerned that searches of the offices of Zuma's lawyers in Johannesburg and Durban were contrary to the principle of lawyer–client privilege. 'For the past five years, the state has had the opportunity to investigate this case. These matters ought to have been dealt with long ago.'

'This was a normal raid for more evidence. As far as the evidence at our disposal is concerned, we already have enough to make out a case,' responded Scorpions spokesman Nkosi, uncharacteristically stretching the truth a little. (Nkosi, a gentlemanly type of person, later resigned from the NPA, citing the 'pressures' that had been placed on members of his family who lived in KZN as a result of his high-profile job.)

Essentially, the Scorpions wanted to lay their hands on proof of all Shaik's post-2002 payments to Zuma and whatever else they could find – and clearly they succeeded in their endeavour because in the indictment that would be served on Zuma on 28 December 2007, the charge sheet was no longer a mirror image of Shaik's: racketeering and tax evasion had been added to an expanded and different set of charges.

The Scorpions had opened a whole new can of worms for themselves, and the August raids would have far-reaching consequences. To begin with, Zuma had already been charged. And so the question that would hover over all of his forthcoming court actions was: why had he been charged if the case against him had clearly been incomplete? The fact that it was incomplete (the forensic 'processing' of 93 000 documents takes a long time), and that the warrants would be legally challenged by Zuma, would mean that his trial would be struck off the roll in 2006.

The legal challenges to the warrants would end up going to the Supreme Court of Appeal and then to the Constitutional Court, where they were only finalised on 31 July 2008, when the Court ruled that the search and seizure operations were legal and did not infringe on privilege. Matters turned uglier in May 2008, when the Constitutional Court judges accused Judge John Hlophe, the Judge President of the Western Cape, of interfering with some of them by trying to get a pro-Zuma verdict on the search warrant appeals. The political climate of South Africa in 2008 – Zuma having been elected president of the ANC in December 2007 – was different from that of August 2005, and the finding against Zuma regarding the 2005 warrants, in tandem with the events surrounding Judge Hlophe, would precipitate a period during August 2008 when the ANC would launch a series of ugly verbal attacks on the judiciary.

Meanwhile, back in August 2005, Cosatu condemned the swoops as 'apartheid-style' and as 'a direct, challenging attack on the revolution itself'. The raids on the homes of Zuma and the properties of confidants were causing a split in the ruling alliance and could lead to unrest in South Africa, Cosatu said: 'These raids also showed that the prosecuting authority and the government system could be manipulated and influenced to take biased political decisions and act accordingly.' Cosatu alleged that the sudden action was more proof that the prosecuting authority, after five years of investigation, still did not have any evidence against Zuma.

Seemingly lost in the events of those weeks was that on 26 August, Mbeki proposed a tripartite alliance commission of inquiry into rumours that he was behind a political plot to block Zuma's path to the presidency. Buoyed perhaps by the 'success' of the Hefer Commission in 2004, he said the alliance should establish the commission to establish whether 'members of the ANC and the broad democratic movement, including the president of the ANC, have been and are involved in a conspiracy targeted at marginalising or destroying [ANC] deputy president Zuma'.

The letter was submitted by Motlanthe to an alliance meeting and posted on the ANC's website. 'I would like to assure you that I would be ready to appear before the commission, if so requested, and truthfully and to the best of my ability, to answer any questions relevant to the scope of its inquiry,' Mbeki wrote. 'Specifically, our movement must act urgently and in unity to protect the ANC deputy president, and therefore our movement as a whole, from any hostile factional offensive, if it is established that such an offensive exists.'

Both the SACP and Cosatu rejected the commission. Cosatu president Willie Madisha (who would later fall out spectacularly with Vavi and Nzimande and be expelled from Cosatu in 2008) said that if a commission were established, it should look at the entire operation of the tripartite alliance and not just one person. Madisha said there were several reasons why the commission would not work. Some witnesses might not want to give evidence for fear they might not be promoted. He said that, unlike a judicial commission, an internal commission was seriously limited in its ability to gather information. The SACP said it was not convinced the commission would adequately deal with the problems that had arisen regarding Zuma's treatment.

There was an occasional glimmer of light, at least legally. Julekha Mahomed, who had done legal work for Zuma, moved fast and applied urgently on 26 August in the Johannesburg High Court to have the search warrants related to her office and residence set aside. On 9 September, the Johannesburg court found in Mahomed's favour, though the state immediately appealed this judgment.

Judge Ismail Hussein found the search warrants were obtained and executed unlawfully. They were set aside; all documents, files and other objects seized from Mahomed's home and office on 18 August had to be returned; and the NPA had to pay the costs of the application. Judge Hussein said it was imperative attorney-client privilege be kept in mind when applying for a search warrant of that nature. Privilege was a right and an important principle that had not been breached by the police even during the dark days of apartheid.

Zuma's trial had been postponed until 11 October. On 29 September, the NPA wrote to Hulley saying that the state had no option but to apply for a further adjournment because it needed to investigate, among other things, Zuma's financial relationship with Shaik after September 2002. It also needed to examine the more than 93 000 documents and other computer information recently seized. Hulley rejected Downer's proposal and gave notice that he would fight it in court.

In the meantime, on 10 October, Zuma and Hulley applied for the setting aside of the seven search warrants for the residences and offices of Zuma and Hulley, and for the return of all the items seized.

On 11 October, Zuma appeared for the second time in the Durban Magistrates' Court. The state applied for the matter to be transferred to the High Court before the indictment was served, but this was opposed by the defence. An agreement was eventually reached that entailed postponing the case to 12 November for the state to serve a provisional indictment. The state said it would need to amend the provisional indictment but would try to deliver this by March 2006.

The NPA also decided to indict Thint, which had been let off the hook in Shaik's trial in exchange for the Thétard affidavit; this was done on 4 November. And on 9 December, the state applied for the issuing of a letter of request to the Attorney-General of Mauritius for further assistance – namely the release to the South African High Commissioner in Mauritius of the documents seized from the premises of Thomson

Holdings in Mauritius on 9 October 2001. This was so that the state could get originals of some of the copied documents it had used in the Shaik trial; it was concerned that Zuma's team would argue that copies were inadmissible.

As if things weren't bad enough for Zuma, on 13 November the *Sunday Times* had reported that a 31-year-old woman had laid a charge of rape against him.

CHAPTER 11

November 2005

Interlude in Zuma-land

A large electronic sign at Durban's airport proclaims the city to be the gateway to the Zulu kingdom. It is also therefore the entrance to Zuma-land. It was Saturday, 12 November 2005, and I was on my way to cover the latest of the ex-deputy president's tribulations at the Durban Magistrates' Court. The NPA's indictment against him was due to be handed over by Billy Downer SC, and he was applying for his trial to be referred to the High Court.

The application was the idea of Kessie Naidu SC, Zuma's counsel. Naidu wanted the referral because it meant that a trial date had to be set in the High Court. This meant in turn that the state would have to get on with the trial; it seemed to be avoiding doing so and Naidu sensed this.

As it would turn out, the decision by Vusi Pikoli to charge Zuma in June had been over-hasty. The NPA's rush to charge Zuma, in the wake of the successful conviction of Shaik and Zuma's sacking, would have enormous repercussions.

Zuma's appearance had been scheduled for a Saturday, when the courts are usually closed, because Durban's chief magistrate did not want the other courts to be disrupted by Zuma's supporters, as happened previously when Zuma appeared on a normal working day.

For me, the significance of it being a Saturday was that the Independent group's Sunday newspapers would be going to press that evening and I needed to file a story by late afternoon.

Ten days previously, on the late night of Wednesday 2 October, and including perhaps the very early hours of Thursday, Zuma had been having the proverbial good time at his Forest Town home. At any rate, we can assume that that's what he thought at the time.

Unfortunately, the woman who would be known in court as Khwezi ('morning star') – because it is illegal to publish the name of a rape complainant – did not see it that way at all. Or, at any rate, she had changed her mind by Thursday morning, or very soon after that, about what had happened with her '*malume*' (uncle), as she claimed she always referred to Zuma because of their close father–daughter relationship. Zuma would deny during his trial that such a relationship existed, claiming that all the ANC children in exile referred to the older males in their parents' circle as 'uncle'. Indeed, he could have pointed out that it is common among (urban) black people to refer to people who are not their siblings as 'sis', sister, or 'bra', brother, or someone who is not their mother as 'ma' or 'mama', mother, out of friendship or respect. Similarly, respectful young Afrikaans-speakers will address an older person on whom they have not clapped eyes before as '*oom*', uncle, or '*tannie*', auntie.

On 4 November Khwezi had laid a charge of rape against Zuma at the Hillbrow police station. A mutual acquaintance soon alerted Zuma to the charge. Zuma found that Khwezi would not take his telephone calls and quickly realised, or was advised, that he had better not call her lest he be accused of intimidation or interference, which he later was anyway.

A few days later, Zuma met Khwezi's mother, whom he knew pretty well. Her husband had not only been a friend of Zuma's but had spent 10 years on Robben Island with him.

Zuma apologised to Khwezi's mother, not for raping but for 'taking advantage' of her daughter, and their conversation dealt not with indignation or recrimination. In keeping with African mores (and those of other cultures), they talked about compensation. A person's child is his or her 'property' and, if 'used', must be paid for. One ANC 'auntie', who had become embroiled in the matter through the grapevine, spoke of marriage, the right and proper thing to do, which meant that *ilobolo*, the down-payment for marriage, would have to be paid.

Khwezi's mother did not discuss marriage, however, but other sorts of compensation. Khwezi apparently wanted to study homeopathy in the UK, an expensive undertaking if you have no money, and a security fence was needed for the family home in KZN. The trouble was that Khwezi's mother, like many others who continued seeking an audience with Zuma then, as now, obviously did not read the newspapers, or did not believe what they read. During Schabir Shaik's trial, seven months earlier, it had been made painfully clear that financially speaking Zuma was on the bones of his posterior and had been so for a long time. (Zuma does, however, own a herd of cows, of which he is very proud, at Nkandla; during his trial he would say that his cows had been 'ready' for *ilobolo*.)

Khwezi's mother needed to confer further with her daughter and Zuma obviously needed to do so as well. But the family lived in KZN and Zuma could not talk directly to Khwezi, lest he be accused of intimidation. So Zweli Mkhize, a medical doctor friend of Zuma's, and KZN MEC for finance, became Zuma's emissary in KZN. Ranjeni Munusamy, operating as Zuma's informal aide-de-camp, became responsible for handling the communication with an attorney, Yusuf Docrat, who managed the Johannesburg end of the negotiations.

What Zuma and his friends were not initially certain about, however, was whether Khwezi had in fact laid a formal rape charge or whether her claim that she had done so was merely a bargaining chip. If it existed, they wanted to 'pull it' – presumably not too difficult a thing to do if Khwezi also wanted it to disappear and if one has the right connections. Zuma summoned his attorney, Michael Hulley, from Durban and, during the week beginning 7 November, Hulley trawled the police stations

...test against apartheid laws - the disciplined and the unruly. *Top:* 20 000 women marched to ...toria in 1956 to deliver a petition against the pass laws to the Prime Minister. (PICTURENET) ...*ve:* Cato Manor riots in 1959. (GALLO IMAGES)

Clockwise from top left:
Public Protector Lawrence Mushwana
(GALLO IMAGES); National Director of
Public Prosecutions Bulelani Ngcuka
and Minister of Justice Penuell Maduna
(*SUNDAY TIMES*); Gavin Woods (GALLO IMAGES)
and Andrew Feinstein of Scopa, the
parliamentary committee that investigated
the Arms Deal. (*SUNDAY TIMES*)

: Judge Hilary Squires reads his judgement on
abir Shaik. (GALLO IMAGES)

ve: The Shaik brothers (*left to right*) Chippy,
abir, Yunis and Moe. (SUNDAY TIMES)

The rape trial. *Top:* Judge Willem van der Merwe. (GALLO IMAGES)
Above: Khwezi arriving at court. (ALON SKUY)

rape trial. *Top:* Not guilty! (GALLO IMAGES)

ve: With daughter Duduzile after the verdict. (GALLO IMAGES)

Home at Nkandla. *Top*: Zuma is proud of his herd of cattle. (SIMPHIWE NKWALE, *SUNDAY TIMES*)
Above: Zuma's first love, wife Sizakele. (MHLABA MEMELA)

The wedding ceremony: Zuma married his fourth wife, Nompumelelo Ntuli, according to Zulu custom in full traditional regalia. (GALLO IMAGES)

Top: Relaxing at home in Forest Town after the rape trial. (TJ LEMON)
Above from left: Cosatu President Zwelinzima Vavi, ANC Youth League President Fikile Mbalula and JZ at the 23rd National Congress of the ANC Youth League. (GALLO IMAGES)

opular man – JZ at the ANC's 96th birthday celebrations. (TJ LEMON)
ve: At the 52nd National Conference, at the University of Limpopo, Polokwane.
LO IMAGES)

The winner and the loser: Jacob Zuma, the new President of the
African National Congress, and Thabo Mbeki at Polokwane. (GALLO IMAGES)

Top: Zuma at Polokwane with Chairman of the ANC Baleka Mbete.
Left: ANC Deputy President Kgalema Motlanthe.
Above: A stressful moment at the Pietermaritzburg trial.
(GALLO IMAGES)

Celebrating Judge Nicholson's verdict with Blade Nzimande and Zwelinzima Vavi in front of a large and supportive crowd in Pietermaritzburg. (GALLO IMAGES)

closest to Zuma's home – Rosebank, Parkview, and others – looking for the docket. But he couldn't find it. No one thought of Hillbrow Police Station; and no one wanted to ask Khwezi.

In any case, the negotiations came to naught because of what happened on Saturday night, 12 November, and Sunday morning.

On the Saturday morning, I knew none of this. I was standing outside the heavily guarded court precinct, feeling the intense heat of Durban, and watching Zuma's supporters milling around, accompanied by the usual human flotsam and jetsam of a South African city. A few minutes after I quit one particular spot, some of them set on fire a T-shirt with Mbeki's face on it. This would lead to a major rebuke for 'Zuma supporters' from ANC headquarters – the first of a long series of such complaints about the behaviour of Zuma 'followers'. It must be admitted that Zuma, crowd-pleaser *extraordinaire*, could usually be prevailed on to sing his trademark *Lethu mshini wami* – Bring me my machine gun – on public occasions.

The only other whitey in sight outside the fence of the court precinct – Allister Sparks, the former editor of the *Rand Daily Mail* – stalked through the unkempt grass, past vendors selling braaied meat and T-shirts, to the wrong gate (a locked one), as I had done, and also had to walk all the way around. Inside the court precinct, the kiosk was closed so there was nowhere to buy a drink, and the toilets were filthy beyond description.

Israelis talk of someone being a *rosh katan*, a 'little head'. This is a person whose mentality is that of the bureaucrat or *apparatchik*: a person incapable of thinking outside the proverbial box because his mind is straitjacketed by a small head.

In my little journalist's head was only one thing. I had a big story because I knew something that other journalists did not yet know: that Kessie Naidu, who everyone thought headed Zuma's legal team, was about to jump ship. This was the story, interwoven with Zuma's application, which I had to file for the next day's paper.

We met Naidu – a prominent and enjoyably flamboyant Durban advocate, dubbed 'the silver fox' by Estelle Ellis of *The Star* because of his mane of grey hair and street smarts – during the Hefer commission. Naidu had been involved with Zuma and Zuma matters for some time; was well connected to the governmental and ANC grapevine, where the *real news* is carried; believed in the old legal adage that a bad settlement is nearly always better than a good case; and was, above all, politically savvy.

Political smarts were important. Many involved directly or indirectly with the Shaik trial thought that Francois van Zyl SC, Shaik's counsel, erred badly by insisting that Shaik's case should be dealt with as a purely criminal/commercial matter and that the political background and ramifications should be played down. In fairness to Van Zyl, he would say that his 'boundaries' during the trial had been heavily policed by Schabir and his brothers, and that some – most – of the strategic choices made were not his at all.

Now, three years later, Naidu's decision to quit the Zuma team and take over the reins of the defence team of Thint, the French arms manufacturer and Zuma's co-accused, does not seem to matter much, though I believe that if Naidu had continued acting for Zuma, there would have been more negotiation with the NPA than there has been.

In November 2005, however, Naidu's decision to represent Thint seemed an indication that the wheels were falling off the Zuma legal vehicle. It was not, after all, a good time for Zuma legally and otherwise. He was still picking up the pieces after being fired and charged; still learning to cope with being suddenly cut off from his whole infrastructure; no more office, telephones, secretaries, spokespeople. More importantly, he was still trying to assimilate what had happened. On one level, it was plain: Mbeki was trying to neutralise him politically; had in fact politically castrated him pretty effectively. But what underlay Mbeki's apparent malignity? Why was he, Zuma, perceived as such a threat to the great man?

Secondly, it remained unclear what exactly Zuma was supposed to deal with. Even the indictment that would be handed over that Saturday morning was 'a mirror image' of the Shaik charge sheet, and it was only provisional, said the NPA. Therefore, there was apparently more to come. It had to be something culled during the Scorpions' August raids, two months earlier. But what was it specifically?

Thirdly, Shaik's conviction also needed a little taking in. It had shocked everyone connected with the matter, and 'shocked' is not too strong a word. Shaik had been an appalling witness in many respects, successfully managing to get up Judge Squires' nose in more ways than two. But few people had expected the judge to find Shaik guilty on every count, to be so icily disparaging of him, and to be so clear that he had been involved in a corrupt relationship with Zuma.

Why was Naidu leaving the team? Part of the reason, presumably, was money. It was unclear in those days how Zuma would pay legal bills. Naidu had attended the Shaik trial on behalf of Thint and, as I have said, anyone who had been there knew that Zuma was desperately short of money.

As it turned out, Naidu chose to leave the Zuma team not only because Thint was a more secure financial option. It also transpired that, true to form, Zuma had simply failed to appoint a top dog among his legal team and this had obviously stuck in Naidu's craw. He would have to be a team player, yet he had 'scant patience' for some on the mooted team and would certainly be uncomfortable being second-guessed on how to play certain issues.

By late morning, Naidu had won his application; Downer handed over a mirror image of the Shaik charge sheet; and 31 July 2006 was set as the date for Zuma's trial in the Pietermaritzburg High Court.

I was on my way out of the court building when I came across a journalist from a rival publication. I had known him for some years; we had worked together, and he was a highly competent, no-nonsense journalist. It was affectionately said about him that, if he ever were to introduce blood into his alcohol stream, he would probably feel quite ill.

'Have you heard the story that's been going around?' he asked me tentatively.

'Well, I'm not sure, though I do know that there's some strange stuff going on,' I replied equally tentatively, wondering whether he had wind of my Naidu 'scoop'.

'Well,' he said, clearly wondering what my strange stuff was, and whether he could trust me with his scoop, 'someone has apparently been phoning news desks all over the country to say that some woman has laid a complaint of rape against Zuma with the police.

'But I must say,' he added, 'that I don't like this sort of shit. I think it's probably the sort of disinformation that's going to come up all the time now about Zuma. But it's not what the Zuma story is really about, in my view.'

'Hmm,' I replied sagely, and off I went, only to find that the photographer who had accompanied me wanted to stay at the courts. So I left him our vehicle and set off to walk to the hotel where we were staying. On the way, I reported by mobile to the editors of the *Sunday Independent*, *Sunday Tribune* and *Weekend Argus* about the rape rumour.

I didn't set great store by it, I said, but I was bothered that, if someone had indeed been 'phoning news desks all over the country', we had heard nothing. Nevertheless, I said, I would check the rumour as best I could. I walked on to the hotel to file my story about Naidu. Then I telephoned Zuma's lawyer.

At that time I had met the Durban-based Hulley in the flesh only once. The meeting had been cordial. But it was clear that Hulley – 40 years old, my height (read: short), balding, bespectacled, and polite – obviously agreed with Mother Teresa that the only thing 'more difficult than bathing a leper' was dealing with a member of the press.

That Saturday afternoon, we spoke briefly. Hulley said that he had heard about the rape charge – from a reporter on another newspaper, not from Zuma; but, as far as he knew, there was no truth in the rumour that a charge had been laid.

Hulley was being somewhat economical with the truth. Strictly speaking, he could say that, as far as he knew, there was no truth to the claim that a rape charge had been made against his client, because, as he told me, he had been in Johannesburg earlier that week looking for the docket, but had not found one. But he did not tell me that two days previously, on Thursday, 10 November, he had been at Nkandla preparing with Zuma for today's application, when Commissioner Norman Taioe and Supt Bafana Peter Linda, the investigating officers from Johannesburg, had arrived to talk to Zuma about the charge. Hulley had in fact helped Zuma prepare a statement, in response to the rape charge, for the two policemen.

Having spoken to Hulley, who had reassured me that the story of a rape charge was part of the gigantic disinformation war surrounding Zuma, I ordered a café latte from room service. I was wondering whether I should watch rugby on television or go in search of the Ultimate Curry when, at about 6.30 pm, I was telephoned by a colleague at the Durban offices of Independent Newspapers, where the printing presses are shared by the KZN edition of the *Sunday Times*.

My colleague had just seen that edition – and you could have blown him down with the proverbial feather. On page one was a story that a charge of rape had been laid against Zuma by a 31-year-old woman.

Alan Dunn, the editor of the *Sunday Tribune*, arranged for me to be picked up and allowed me to use his office for the evening. I was, as they say, incandescent with rage: Zuma was largely 'my beat' and the *Sunday Times* story had come out on my watch. I telephoned Hulley again.

'Listen,' I said, 'this is not the way to treat someone who has so far dealt with you fairly.'

Actually, I did not say that: I was less articulate and more splenetic. Hulley was, I believe, genuinely surprised. He was taken aback, I realise now, not so much because he had not found the docket and the *Sunday Times* apparently had, but because, as far as he knew, the Zuma camp had everything under control: it was negotiating with Khwezi and her mother and, even though the police were sniffing around, everything was going to be all right. It is quite possible that Zuma had told Hulley that, notwithstanding the arrival of the police, it was all a misunderstanding – a young woman's rush of blood to her head – and would be sorted out.

And in fact Hulley then conceded that Zuma had told him that well, yes, he had made the beast with two backs with someone, but that as far as he knew, it had been a mutually enjoyable experience. So Zuma – Hulley claimed – couldn't really understand what the queries from journalists had been about, other than yet another attempt to try to sully his good name. Though, yet again, Hulley did not tell me about the police having been at Nkandla.

Hulley then called me back and said: 'Okay, if you don't believe me that this woman has not made a complaint, how would you like to talk to her directly? Ask her yourself.'

The woman telephoned me on my mobile within five minutes.

With her permission – she was more than happy to be named and quoted – I published her name the next morning. She seemed charming and was well-spoken – clearly she had not been locally educated – and she sounded as though she was thoroughly enjoying herself. This ought to have set off an alarm in my head: who would enjoy being at the centre of a rape furore involving the former deputy president? But obviously I did not know then that Khwezi was always a person of joy and happiness – until someone started delving. In other words, her manner was a misleading patina. Nor did I suspect that she was enjoying herself because she desperately needed to be the centre of attention, and now was.

All I was interested in – the journalist's little head taking over again – was whether she had laid a complaint of rape against Zuma. She insisted that she had not. But how, I asked, did she explain the *Sunday Times* article? Whatever she might think of journalists, I said, the *Sunday Times* crew were a competent bunch who would never print an article like that without being sure of its accuracy.

Khwezi said a *Sunday Times* reporter had phoned her and she had also spoken to the editor, Mondli Makhanya. She claimed that she had 'forbidden' them to publish their story because it was not true. She said she would SMS me the SMS that she had sent Makhanya.

Sent (to me) at 22h38 on 12 November 2005, it reads: 'if u go ahead & publish after me telling u in 2 conversations that it never happened, I will make a public statement tmro saying u insisted on runnin story despite what I said. this is apart from taking legal action.'

Initially I had asked Khwezi for her mobile number so that I could phone her back if we got cut off. Other than asking a variety of questions about herself, her family and Zuma, it was about the only check I could make that she was not a prankster. And, as it happened, we were cut off a number of times, and therefore I called her back a few times. She was always there and she remained adamant that she had not charged Zuma with rape.

'He has never sexually assaulted me. I have no idea where these stories came from. My family has long been friends with Zuma and I often stay at his home,' Khwezi said.

Occasionally, when we were talking – and, altogether, we talked for a long time – I could hear someone prompting Khwezi and assumed this was either a parent or friend. At one point during the evening, I could not get through to her, so I stood down, as they say in military circles, for a while. Suddenly someone from the Zuma camp called me, asking what was happening. It was then that I realised that, remarkably, the link to Khwezi was not Hulley but someone in the Zuma camp.

My story came out on Sunday morning in the *Sunday Independent*; the *Sunday Times* story came out as well (it had already been published the previous night); and the proverbial hit the fan. Khwezi went underground; but it wasn't too long before a newspaper located the actual docket (Hillbrow: 312/11/2005); and I was unofficially appointed by everyone as Zuma's official spin doctor.

A few questions and answers by way of shedding some light on the apparently strange events of Saturday. Why, besides the glaringly obvious reason (it would sully Zuma's reputation), did the Zuma camp want so badly to cut a deal with Khwezi and her mother so as to hide the fact that Khwezi had charged Zuma with rape?

There are many around Zuma who are hardcore conspiracy theorists – it is the meat and drink of their lives – and Zuma is no slouch himself. Not for nothing was he MK intelligence chief; and not for nothing did he emerge as one of the top dogs from the often ugly internecine warfare that was (and is) the ANC.

Khwezi's best friend, known as Kimi, worked in the office of Ronnie

Kasrils, the Minister for Intelligence Services. Zuma knew this and was convinced that Kasrils had helped push Khwezi into laying a charge. He was also certain, after Sunday, that it was Kasrils who told the *Sunday Times* that a charge had been laid and gave the newspaper the details, so much so that during the later rape trial it was touch and go whether Zuma's defence team would subpoena the minister.

Kasrils strenuously denied then, and has always denied, that he had played a role in Khwezi's decision to press charges. Kimi (in court) confirmed this. It is certain, however, that Khwezi spoke to Kasrils on the telephone *before* she laid the rape charge.

Though he does not talk about it any more, for Zuma a question mark hangs over Kasrils' head, and will for ever.

The important point here is that Kasrils' alleged role was proof to Zuma that those around Mbeki were seriously gunning for him; that there was a conspiracy against him; that it was hoped, given his sacking and the corruption charges he was facing, that the rape charges would be the final nail in the Zuma coffin. It was imperative therefore that the public never know about the incident.

Why did Khwezi cooperate, so apparently easily, with Zuma and her mother about making a deal? Why was she still in contact 10 days later with the helpers of the man who had allegedly raped her? Why was she prepared to lie for him?

There are a number of possible and obvious reasons. It would come out at the trial that lying – in particular about sexual encounters and their aftermath – was part of the way Khwezi dealt with life. Or she might have been greedy. Or she might have realised – as some of the aunties told her – that she was causing trouble for an important person and struggle hero, and that this was not the way to behave.

But the reason that I want to highlight is this. Though Khwezi had been back in South Africa from exile for over a decade she remained – like many exiles, and especially their children – locked inside the closed, incestuous world in which she had spent most of her years. Despite what he had allegedly done to her, Zuma was 'still family' and an important member of that family too. This was why the matter could be dealt with 'in the family'; why Khwezi was not horrified, why she did not spit blood and venom, when she knew her mother and others were negotiating with Zuma.

Why was it so easy for Hulley to put me in touch with Khwezi? Why did she later, during the rape trial – in a rather shocking piece of evidence ('shocking' for me anyway) – tell the court off-handedly that yes, she had told one Jeremy Gordin that she had not laid a rape charge and that she did so because she had been instructed to do it by her police minders (whom she named)?

I did not know until the night Khwezi left the country for The Netherlands, soon after the rape trial, that someone in the Zuma camp – not Zuma, let me stress – had a direct line to a very senior police officer. I am not going to name either the person or the officer, because, as this book was being completed, he was still an active senior officer and it is not my business anyway to 'out' other people's contacts.

This officer was in constant touch with policemen in whose 'protection' Khwezi was on the night of 12 November, and Khwezi knew it then or realised it later. So it was easy for the person from the Zuma camp to keep tabs on Khwezi and to ensure she was abiding by her side of the bargain – which, at that point, while negotiations were still going on, was to deny that Zuma had done anything to her and that she had laid a charge. It was also easy later on for Khwezi to blame her police guards for her lie. Doubtless their instructions had been that she could telephone me but that she had to deny that she had laid a charge.

What's a good story without a punch line?

On Sunday morning, 13 November, Zweli Mkhize went to see Zuma in the hotel in which Zuma was staying in Durban. He pointed at the two newspapers and asked, with a puzzled look on his face: 'What is going on? This newspaper says that she laid a charge and this one says that she didn't.'

And JZ laughed like a drain – and went on laughing for a long time.

CHAPTER 12

2006

Rape trial

Zuma's trial for rape, which began on 13 February 2006, introduced South Africans to a world that even gonzo journalist Hunter S Thompson might have struggled to invent, with elements of horror – in the shape of rowdy Zuma supporters outside the court – jostling the pathos of Khwezi's real story.

Bernard Ngoepe, Judge President of the Transvaal Provincial Division – the antediluvian name of the division under whose jurisdiction the case fell – came into court late to announce that he had resolved to recuse himself from the trial. He had been told in chambers by Zuma's legal team, Kemp J Kemp sc, Jerome Brauns, Thandanani Mbongwa, and Michael Hulley, that they would apply for his recusal because he had signed the August 2005 warrants used by the Scorpions to search Zuma's home, the offices of his attorneys past (Julekha Mahomed) and present (Hulley), and the offices of Thint and of Thint MD Pierre Moynot.

In his explanation to the court about his recusal, Ngoepe did not mention this reason. He said that the defence had told him that Zuma had doubts about his impartiality; for this reason, which was sufficient in the Judge President's view, he would recuse himself. Some columnists criticised Ngoepe for his decision; they said it was a bad precedent and implied that Zuma could 'control' the judiciary. But what was remarkable about Ngoepe's statement was that it was the first time in a year that anyone, let alone a judge president, had treated Zuma respectfully and seriously. Zuma was the deputy leader of the country's ruling political party, he had been deputy president, said Ngoepe, and if Zuma had doubts, then he, Ngoepe, would recuse himself.

Ngoepe knew already that the senior of his two deputies, Judge Phineas Mojapelo, did not want to hear the case because he had worked with Zuma during the struggle. Ngoepe therefore indicated that his other deputy, Judge Jeremiah 'Jerry' Shongwe, would, from the next morning, handle the case. Shongwe had apparently indicated to Ngoepe that he would be happy to do so.

When Ngoepe had finished speaking, Zuma's legal team, though they had just had their way, looked uncomfortable. Unbeknown to Ngoepe (and most people), Shongwe's sister, Minah, was the mother of one of Zuma's children, Edward, 29; and Zuma's legal team was not looking forward to breaking this news to the Judge President.

The following morning, before court, Ngoepe was told about the parentage of Judge Shongwe's nephew. He instructed another High Court judge to stand the trial down until 6 March while a suitable judge was found and appointed. Shongwe never even came to court.

Once the story for the postponement came out, Zuma's reputation rocketed to a new high – or low – depending on one's viewpoint. Certainly it added fuel to the anti-Zuma fire that had started raging when the alleged rape became public knowledge, at which point rumours that Zuma was a 'well-known womaniser, didn't you know?' also inevitably emerged. It became difficult from the end of 2005 and in 2006 to find a female reporter willing to interview him.

The chain of events – Ngoepe recusing himself, Mojapelo not being available, Shongwe being the uncle of Zuma's 'love child' – also underlined, for those who did not know, that anyone who was anyone in the new South Africa was somehow connected with the other notables from his or her generation (even if in Ngoepe's case the only connection with Zuma was having signed a search warrant). Before the Shaik trial at the end of 2004, Zuma might not have featured at the front of many people's minds, but clearly the country's decision makers in most fields knew him, and many knew him personally.

A slew of cartoons appeared in all the newspapers. These ranged from the well-known Zapiro's depiction of the door of a house being opened by an obviously female hand. Outside, stretching into the distance, are scores of little Zumas in carry-cots. The woman says 'Jacob!!' A voice inside the house responds: 'Uh oh!'

Another Zapiro cartoon showed American vice-president Dick Cheney – implicated at the time in having mistakenly shot a friend while they were out hunting – and Zuma, with the following words: 'Two vice presidents, two Dicks: Shoot first, ask questions later.' Cheney is shown firing his shotgun; Zuma, unzipping his trousers.

My personal favourite was a 'Madam & Eve' cartoon (by Stephen Francis & Rico) in which a child is asked as part of a biology test where babies come from. She thinks for a moment and then responds: 'Jacob Zuma.'

Much less humorously, when the trial recommenced, there were scenes eerily reminiscent of medieval pogroms against so-called witches: photographs of Khwezi were burnt while the crowd screamed 'burn the bitch' and asked how much she had been paid to lay the charge. It had been a long time since there had been such scenes in the centre of a South African city and the television images scared the living daylights out of people. Zuma himself frightened the body politic quite often by singing 'Bring me my machine gun'. But, though Zuma said that the crowd came of their own volition, it was noticeable that their antics were toned down very rapidly once the media had squawked about them – somebody had issued an order somewhere – and that for most of the trial, until the day of the verdict, there were not more than 100 spectators outside the court, if that many.

On 6 March the trial re-started. The presiding judge was Willem van der Merwe, a late-middle-aged Afrikaner, who had not been active during the struggle and who apparently had no connection with Zuma. Van der Merwe was known, among other judgments, for having 10 years earlier sentenced Eugene de Kock, known as Prime Evil, to life plus 212 years for his crimes as the head of apartheid's so-called counter-insurgency unit at Vlakplaas. (De Kock spoke out from Pretoria Central prison, saying that Van der Merwe had been a 'very fair' judge.)

Elizabeth Skeen, an American whose parents appear to have been South African, submitted a 150-page thesis 'in partial fulfilment of the requirements' for her BA degree, to the department of anthropology at Princeton University in 2007. Titled 'The Rape of a Trial: Jacob Zuma, AIDS, Conspiracy, and Tribalism in Neo-liberal Post-Apartheid South Africa',[1] its basic thesis is that Zuma's trial for rape was turned into something that was not a rape trial ('The rape of a trial'): '… the Zuma rape trial un-became itself as a rape trial and became the nation's trial'. Skeen argued that it became 'the nation's trial' because outside the court, and even at times inside, the focus shifted away from whether Zuma had raped Khwezi or not – instead the trial became a battleground for different 'agendas': rape in South Africa, HIV/AIDS, political dismay, and 'ethnic' issues.

It is a persuasive and intriguing piece of work and, though her main thesis is not my focus, her reporting is very thorough indeed. She seems to be one of the few people who have actually read the transcript of the trial. The following summary of the events at the trial (which I attended every day) is lifted from chapter one of her thesis, though I have abridged, edited and added to what she wrote.

When Zuma was charged with rape on 6 December 2006, his indictment included a 'summary of the substantial facts', the basis of the state's charges against him:

1. The accused is a family friend of the 31-year-old complainant.

2. On Wednesday afternoon, 2 November 2005, and following on an

invitation by the accused, the complainant went to visit him at his residence in Forest Town.

3. During the course of the evening he invited her to stay over for the night and indicated a room to her where she could sleep.

4. Later that evening she retired to the bedroom to sleep.

5. After some time, and whilst the complainant was sleeping, the accused came to her room and offered her a massage.

6. After she declined the offer, he removed the duvet that covered her and proceeded to have sexual intercourse with her against her will and without her consent.

Zuma pleaded not guilty and read out the following:

1. The complainant visited my home in Forest Town, Johannesburg on 2 November 2005 and stayed over for the night. This was of her own volition.

2. Late on that evening of November 2005, we had sexual intercourse which lasted for some time. This was consensual. At no stage did the complainant say no to any of the actions we performed.

3. At no stage did I believe that the sexual intercourse was against the will of the complainant. She was at all times at liberty to say so and voice her disapproval.

4. My daughter Duduzile, who is in her mid-twenties, was in the house and a policeman was on the premises outside at all relevant times during the incident.

5. The complainant had a cellular phone on her and could leave the premises at any time.

6. Enquiries have revealed that the complainant has made similar false allegations of rape against a number of persons, some of which had been alluded to in a statement of a witness provided by the prosecution.

The last point would become critical in the defence's argument as they tried not only to destroy Khwezi's credibility as a witness to her own rape but also to show that lying about having been raped was a tried-and-tested way of life for her.

The two statements also revealed the key differences between the state's version and the defence's. The state maintained that Zuma raped Khwezi; Zuma said that sexual intercourse had been consensual.

Zuma and Khwezi also both told very different stories in terms of their respective intentions. Khwezi would say that she never had nor would ever consider Zuma in any way sexually; Zuma maintained that Khwezi hinted about her sexual attraction to him and was the one who made the advances.

Khwezi would say that Zuma invited her to his home on 2 November, invited her to spend the night, and then came to the guest room where she was sleeping and raped her. Zuma would say that Khwezi invited herself to his home, invited herself to spend the night there, told him to come to her guest room when he finished working in his study, and went with him to his bedroom where she had consensual sex with him.

Khwezi testified that on the day of the alleged rape, she learned that the son of Nokoloza, her sister's daughter (though Khwezi referred to her as her own daughter) had been bitten by a snake in Swaziland. She sent SMS messages to various friends and relations, including Zuma. Khwezi tried to call Zuma repeatedly throughout the day, and finally having got in touch with him, she claimed that he encouraged her to stay overnight at his Johannesburg home before leaving for Swaziland. She said that when she arrived at his home, Zuma greeted her as his 'daughter' and following the evening meal, told her to stay overnight.

Khwezi said that they had a conversation, which he initiated, about why she did not have a boyfriend. She said that there 'were no good ones left', and Zuma said that she must lower her standards and that, despite her HIV-positive status, she deserved to have a companion. Khwezi said that Zuma led her to the guest room and said he would return when he finished his work to 'tuck her in'.

She showered and put on a kanga: an African sarong or 'wrap', also known as a 'kikoi', a colourful, rectangular piece of cotton. One of the most poignant moments of the trial occurred on the first day when Khwezi was asked to show the court how such a garment was worn. The lead prosecutor, Charin de Beer, then asked Khwezi to hand the kanga back because it was part of the state's evidence.

'But can I have it when this is over?' asked Khwezi anxiously.

Van der Merwe said she could – and made it part of his final order at the end of the trial that Khwezi be returned her kanga.

Having put on her kanga, Khwezi went to Zuma's daughter Duduzile's room when she heard noises, thinking that Duduzile had returned home for the evening. Together Khwezi and Duduzile went to Zuma's office to say goodnight to him. Khwezi recounted that she stayed longer than Duduzile in Zuma's office and that he said that as soon as he was finished with his night's work, he wanted to tuck her into bed. She asked him what he meant, and he laughed.

Khwezi returned to the guest bedroom, and Zuma arrived shortly after, asking if she were already asleep. She said that she was not, but would fall asleep soon. He said that he would return later. Khwezi fell asleep and awoke to Zuma telling her that he wanted to 'tuck her in and massage her' – she said no; she wanted to sleep.

Zuma said he could massage her in her sleep, and Khwezi said no again. Khwezi said that he climbed into the bed, began to massage her, and she said no again. She saw that he was naked, became very confused, realised he was about to rape her, and froze in fear. Zuma removed her kanga, began to have intercourse with her, and 'held her hands with his hands'. When Zuma finished, he left, and Khwezi stayed on the bed motionless. In his summing up, Van der Merwe said: 'The complainant did not scream or try to attract anybody's attention before or during the rape. She explained that by saying she was shocked, in a total daze and could not move or do anything.' Zuma did not use a condom.

Khwezi left early the next morning and went to work. She talked to a friend on the phone, told her that she had been raped, and went to see a doctor who examined her. She laid the rape charges on 4 November.

Two women whom Khwezi knew from when she lived in exile came to visit her later that week. They suggested that she should drop the charges because of the damaging effect it would have on the ANC. It appeared to Khwezi that they were 'pro-Zuma and anti-Mbeki supporters'.

Khwezi's mother met Zuma and though 'there was talk of compensation for the alleged rape', Khwezi pursued the rape charge against Zuma.

Zuma's lawyers began cross-examination of Khwezi on 7 March. Kemp disputed that a father–daughter relationship existed with Zuma. He said that after 1985, she had no contact with Zuma for 14 years, and she had not spoken to him at all when she was abroad in London.

Khwezi said that she spoke to Ronnie Kasrils, the Minister of Intelligence Services, on 3 November, the day before she filed charges, out of concern for her safety. Kemp asked Khwezi why she had called Kasrils before reporting Zuma to the police, implying that her decision was politically motivated. But he did not pursue this line then, or later in the trial, having decided, probably correctly, that the issues requiring focus were whether Zuma had had the intention ('*mens rea*') to have intercourse with her come what may, and whether he had indeed done so against Khwezi's will.

Kemp also questioned Khwezi about some inconsistencies between the statement that she made to the police and the statement that she gave in court, in particular the position in which she had allegedly lain on the bed in the guest room. Khwezi conceded, during this cross-examination, that she had had easy access to a telephone or cell phone; she could have left Zuma's house at any point; Zuma 'could not have foreseen that she would freeze if he attempted to have sexual intercourse with her' (in other words, if it had been rape, how could Zuma have known that she would not resist? – Khwezi, as Kemp pointed out later, was not much lighter than Zuma); she could have removed Zuma's hands from her and pushed him away; and she could have told Duduzile or the policemen guarding Zuma's home about his sexual advances toward her.

Kemp produced a copy of 16 pages of Khwezi's written memoirs, a document that she had kept hidden and did not expect to be brought out in court. She referred in the document to three different rapes and one attempted rape that occurred during her childhood and adolescence while living in exile. These began with one at age five that she denied being true, but said that she was raped when she was five in a different incident. The attempted rape, which Khwezi testified was a true account, involved a man named Mashaya who testified later for the defence.

Khwezi said that the other two incidents referred to in the document, with men named Godfrey and Charles, were rapes that did happen to her as described. She said an investigation that was led by two female ANC party members also living in exile found both these men guilty, and she denied telling the investigators that Godfrey and Charles were her boyfriends. Kemp said that one of these women was present in court and was prepared to testify that both the men had been her boyfriends.

Khwezi recanted on her testimony and said that Godfrey was found guilty but that Charles was not. When Kemp said that Charles would tell the court he did not have sex with her, she insisted that he did.

This concluded the cross-examination of Khwezi on her memoirs, but Kemp still had much to ask about her sexual behaviour after returning to South Africa. Khwezi denied being raped by or even knowing a man named Sandile Sithole, a man whom the defence said was involved with her in the Council of Churches. The defence would later bring forward a witness who testified that she indeed made a false accusation of rape against Sithole. Khwezi did say she was raped once since returning from exile, in 1995, by a fellow theology student. She admitted that following this incident, she suffered from attacks (during which she passed out) and psychological problems. She described herself as 'being really disturbed'. In 1994, Khwezi accused a man named Nestor of attempted rape, but another man, a Pastor Mbambo, had walked in on the rape and stopped it. Mbambo would testify this had not happened, and that he saw Khwezi sleeping together on a bed with Nestor naked and Khwezi fully clothed.

Khwezi also denied that she had ever accused Mbambo of rape, and as in the case of Sithole, the defence would bring forward a witness who testified that she had made a false accusation of rape against him. Khwezi finally denied that she had ever been raped at theology college, and the same witness who said she accused Sithole and Mbambo of rape would say also that she accused another man of raping her at the college. The cross-examination of Khwezi set her up against four defence witnesses who would seriously question her credibility.

Khwezi's mother testified next. She told the court about her meeting with Zuma after the charge was laid, how he seemed 'sombre', and that, at a meeting arranged by Zweli Mkhize, they discussed the 'financial implications' of her daughter's further education and a fence she needed around her house.

She was followed by Merle Friedman, a clinical psychologist with expertise in trauma, especially rape trauma. She had examined Khwezi twice and said that her behaviour during and after the rape was consistent with her experience and the literature on rape. She concluded that Khwezi had likely 'frozen' during the rape, explaining her lack of resistance to Zuma, and was suffering from post-traumatic stress disorder.

The prosecution's next witness was Dr ML Likibi, who had examined Khwezi on 3 November, the day after the alleged rape. He said that he found a small tear along her vaginal opening that was not necessarily indicative of rape; it could have been caused by the fact that, as Khwezi said, she had not had penetrative intercourse for seven months before the alleged rape; or by lack of lubrication during intercourse; or from 'passionate intercourse'.

Two friends of Khwezi, known as Pinkie and Kimi, testified next. Khwezi had contacted both in the days after her alleged rape. They said that they understood Khwezi and Zuma to have a familial relationship. Both remarked on the strangeness of her behaviour in the days after she slept at Zuma's home, unaware of its cause until Khwezi told them that she had been raped.

Commissioner Norman Taioe, who investigated Zuma's home after the rape, said that Zuma had clearly indicated to him that nothing happened in his bedroom; that intercourse had occurred in the guest bedroom – thus contradicting his own version of the events. Kemp's cross-examination of Taioe homed in on two problems with his investigation and resulting testimony. The first was that Taioe had not properly read Zuma his rights – he had read them when he went to see Zuma at Nkandla but not when they re-met about five days later at the alleged crime scene (the Forest Town home). The second was that in his written report, Taioe made no mention of Zuma's alleged statement that intercourse occurred in the guest bedroom.

A virology professor specialising in HIV/AIDS testified on the virus, placing the risk for a male contracting HIV from 'a single case of [vaginal] unprotected sex at 0,03 percent to 0,01 percent'. He testified about the dangers of 'super infection' – what happens 'if a HIV-positive person has unprotected sex with another HIV-positive person'. He confirmed that a circumcised man's risk of contracting HIV is less than that of an uncircumcised man, but also said that having sex without lubrication or with someone who has a vaginal tear will increase the risk of contracting the virus.

Superintendent Bafana Peter Linda, another police officer, who was the last witness called by the state, also testified about the initial investigation. There would be differences in the testimonies of Linda and Taioe, and Van der Merwe ultimately ruled that the evidence of the two policemen was inadmissible.

Van der Merwe then considered two applications before the defence called its witnesses. Three non-governmental organisations filed a joint application to lead evidence on the state's behalf as *amici curiae* ('friends of the court'), saying that they could shed light on rape issues. The defence filed an application to have the case dismissed. Van der Merwe denied both.

The defence began its case on 3 April, with Zuma in the witness stand, where he stayed for just over four days and where he insisted, as was his right, on speaking isiZulu, though he occasionally helped the interpreter out. Van der Merwe, it turned out, spoke a credible isiZulu, though he hid this until the last day of the trial.

Despite his acquittal, Zuma's testimony still reverberates (negatively for him) today. He said much in those four days, but as Elizabeth Skeen has pointed out,[2] only a handful of statements and concepts were heavily reported. Journalists wrote, for example, that Zuma placed heavy emphasis on his Zulu identity. The *New York Times* reported:

Taking the stand for the first time this week in the rape trial, Mr Zuma cast himself as the embodiment of a traditional Zulu male, with all the privileges that patriarchal Zulu traditions bestow on men. […] That he is making a political appeal as well as a legal one seems indisputable. […] During the trial last week, he pointedly testified entirely in Zulu, although he speaks fluent English, the usual courtroom language. His remarks had to be translated for the English-speaking prosecutors.

Indeed, there was a heavy 'cultural' content to Zuma's testimony. Charin de Beer, the lead prosecutor, also made use of 'Zulu culture' to forward the state's version of what had happened on the night of the alleged rape, however. De Beer is not Zulu, but she stated understandings that she had about Zulu culture and then asked Zuma questions based on these understandings. Zuma often criticised suppositions that De Beer derived from Zulu culture – and then she would criticise Zuma's reliance on Zulu culture to explain certain actions. Both thus often shifted from logical explanations of events to cultural explanations.

The first questions Kemp asked Zuma were about the role that he played in the struggle, and Van der Merwe interrupted to ask how he knew the complainant's father. Zuma said that they had known each other as members of Umkhonto we Sizwe; both were arrested in 1963 and served 10-year sentences at Robben Island. On their release, they returned to MK. While Zuma began training recruits in Mozambique, Khwezi's father was arrested and detained in Natal, then left South Africa for exile in Swaziland. From Mozambique, Zuma helped direct his work.

Zuma had first met Khwezi when he travelled to Swaziland during the 1980s (she would have been about 11) to oversee MK operations. Her father died in 1985, and Zuma saw Khwezi in Zambia a few times thereafter. Khwezi, during her testimony, had used the Zulu word '*malume*' to refer to Zuma – and the prosecution had emphasised that it was improper and unusual to have sex with one's '*malume*' because it signified a familial relationship. Zuma said that even though '*malume*' literally translates as 'the brother to your mother', among families in exile, children called the older 'comrades' *malume*.

Khwezi had testified that she had a conversation the night of the alleged rape, during which Zuma suggested she find a boyfriend to fulfil her sexual desires. Kemp asked if Zuma had ever had similar conversations with his own daughters: Zuma said he had not because 'Zulu tradition does not prescribe it' – females discuss sexual issues among themselves.

Zuma explained how it was that Khwezi came to see him and stay at his home. She had called him during the day, distressed about her relative, and said she wished to visit him at his Johannesburg home to tell him something. Zuma said he neither asked Khwezi to his home in the first place, nor invited or even expected her to stay the evening. Zuma testified that when he talked to her at his home in the evening, she brought up the issue of not having a boyfriend and concern about her relative. During this conversation, he asked if she had the number for a taxi to take her home, and she replied that she planned to stay the evening. Zuma went to his study, and Khwezi bathed and changed into a kanga – Zuma observed that she had never dressed that way before in front of him. He suggested that a kanga was a sexually provocative outfit.

Khwezi said that she had more to talk about with him. When he said that he had more work to do, she said that she was going to bed, but to wake her when he had finished his work. When he woke her later, she came to his room still in the kanga, climbed under his duvet covers, and talked further about the Swaziland incident. Zuma changed into his pajamas in front of her – he got the sense 'that she did not have any problem if [he] took off [his] clothes'. She did not express disapproval and subsequently asked him if he would give her a massage.

While he was massaging her, Zuma said, Khwezi exposed herself. Then after this massage, she touched him suggestively while she still remained partially naked. He took his clothing off, kissed her, and asked her if she had a condom. She said she did not, and Zuma 'hesitated a bit' and considered the risks. Khwezi responded negatively to his hesitation, Zuma said, encouraging him to proceed: 'She then said you see you cannot just leave a woman if she is already at that state [...] and I said to myself I know as we grew up in the Zulu culture you do not just leave a woman in that situation because she may even have you arrested and say that you are a rapist.' After Khwezi said this, Zuma had sex with her. Afterwards he got up and took a shower, and seeing that she was no longer in his room, he went to the guest room and said goodnight.

Kemp asked Zuma to elaborate on his HIV/AIDS background and why he had chosen to have sex with someone he knew was HIV-positive. Zuma explained that he had headed a government initiative on AIDS and that he had a relatively high level of knowledge about the disease. 'I had knowledge that as a male person the chances were very slim one would contract the disease, just because you had intercourse with a woman you would [not] automatically be infected.' He added that he did not have HIV or any other sexually transmitted infections so would not have put Khwezi at further risk.

Kemp finished questioning Zuma early on the second day with a series of questions that emphasised how Khwezi's behaviour was different on the night of 2 November 2005 compared to the past – she was more sexual in how she dressed and what she said.

De Beer began her cross-examination asking, 'When you had sex with the complainant you did not use a condom, is that correct?' which Zuma affirmed. She asked several more questions, focusing on why Zuma had taken the risk of having unprotected sex with someone whom he knew to be HIV-positive. He restated that he knew there was a risk, although he thought it was very small, and said that he had tested negative a month prior to his testimony.

De Beer observed that regardless of his status one month ago, Zuma still endangered his wives (with whom he does not use condoms). De Beer added that Khwezi, as an AIDS activist, which she had said she was, would never have sex without a condom, and that therefore the sexual intercourse must have *not* been consensual. De Beer also asked Zuma about his role in the government-sponsored Moral Regeneration Movement; he agreed that 'the movement was about bringing back the morals, the values, [and] the traditions', with a particular emphasis on HIV/AIDS and condom use, and that he 'many times said that the leaders must take responsibility in that regard'. De Beer moved from Zuma's leadership position on HIV/AIDS to the relationship he had with Khwezi and her father. Zuma agreed that he and Khwezi's father had been best friends, but resisted the prosecution's efforts to say that they were 'figuratively speaking […] twin brothers'.

De Beer returned to the question of the meaning of *malume* and asked why Khwezi called Zuma *malume* – not by his first name Jacob. Zuma said that 'according to Zulu tradition a child will never call you by [your] name' and repeated that Khwezi called him *malume* because she knew him from exile. Khwezi had testified that Zuma had called her *ndodakazi*, the Zulu word for daughter, which Zuma denied; he did admit that he did call her *nthombi*, *nthunkulu*, and *nthombizana*, Zulu words that he used with his own daughters that loosely translate to girl. De Beer closed this line of inquiry emphasising the 'massive power imbalance' between Khwezi and Zuma; that as a much older man who was the former deputy president of South Africa, sexual intercourse with Khwezi was necessarily coercive.

Khwezi had said in her testimony that she considered herself a lesbian. De Beer asked Zuma if he had been aware of her lesbian status. He said that, prior to hearing her testify, he was not. De Beer raised the issue of Zuma's conversation with Khwezi about her 'man' troubles. De Beer posited that Zuma had brought up the boyfriend discussion to see if Khwezi were available; that he invited her to the home, wanted her to sleep over there, and most importantly, wanted her to sleep with him. 'And I put it to you specifically that she was not interested in you because number one you are this father *malume* figure to her and she is also of a lesbian orientation,' asserted De Beer.

De Beer also queried the nature of Khwezi's sleeping arrangements. De Beer insisted that Zuma had taken Khwezi to the guest room personally, which he denied, to be sure that she did not sleep in the same room as his daughter Duduzile, which, according to De Beer, was the correct place for her to have slept in terms of Zulu custom.

De Beer cross-examined Zuma on his belief that Khwezi's behaviour in the months prior to the rape and specifically on the night of 2 November had changed, and that she had shown increasing sexual

interest in him. Zuma's responses here would prove particularly controversial.

DE BEER: And if you say she acted that way what do you mean by that?
ZUMA: Milord, […] she used to come to my place dressed in pants but
on this occasion she came dressed in a skirt. And the way she was sitting
in the lounge was not the usual way that I know her to be sitting. That
was not usual of her, that is why I say the way she acted was not similar to
the way that she used to be. And at the stage when she came to me in the
study dressed only in a kanga that also indicated to me, because she has
never done that in the past.

De Beer asked Zuma for greater specificity, first whether the skirt was a
'mini skirt', and how Khwezi was sitting that was so unusual. Zuma said
no, that it was a normal knee-length skirt and that wearing it, Khwezi
had not kept her legs crossed together but they were open.

Zuma's choice to proceed with sex with Khwezi despite not having
a condom – the point on which De Beer began her first day of cross-
examination – concerned much of the early part of her second day of
cross-examination. She asked: 'You have explained that the way you grew
up or in the Zulu culture you do not leave a woman in that situation. She
will have you arrested as a rapist?' Zuma agreed and explained, as on the
first day, that 'in my tradition', were he to get to 'that stage with a woman'
and not have intercourse, she might press false charges of rape.

'I want to put it to you,' said De Beer, 'that I cannot imagine that it is
in any culture a rule that you have to continue with sex for that reason,
and I want to put it to you that it can never be the reason to proceed
with condomless sex with an HIV-positive person.'

Zuma responded that if two people wanted to proceed in doing something and both were aware of the risks involved, then it was their own
decision to make. He said that he did it because he did it.

Zuma had testified that after having intercourse, he took a shower.
De Beer inquired about this, leading to what, of all of Zuma's testimony,
would cause him the most ridicule. De Beer asked Zuma, 'Why did you

take a shower then?' Zuma explained, 'I wished to take a shower because it is one of the reasons that would minimise the risk of contracting the disease.' No laughter or disruption from the people in court audience is noted in the court records; neither De Beer nor Van der Merwe responded immediately to his statement.

De Beer began her cross-examination on the third day looking at the sequence of events that led to the rape itself. Zuma had testified on the first day that Khwezi told him to wake her up when he finished his work, and came with him to his bedroom where they had sex. She asked why it was so necessary for Zuma to take Khwezi back to his room; could he not discuss with Khwezi whatever it was she needed to discuss in the guest bedroom? De Beer posited throughout that Zuma had a particular agenda – the rape was not a crime of passion but was a sexual encounter that he deliberately planned and executed against the complainant's wishes.

De Beer moved on to the events following the alleged rape, and how it was that Zuma tried to keep Khwezi from pressing charges against him. Zuma said he was immediately suspicious when he heard of the rape allegations, thinking someone had convinced Khwezi to make false charges, but he was loath to contact her directly. He made contact with her friends and relatives to see if the situation could be settled amicably. De Beer implied that Zuma's attempts to prevent Khwezi from pressing rape charges demonstrated Zuma's cognisance of his wrongdoing. But Zuma said that attempting to contact her family and friends to resolve the issue was a matter of Zulu custom.

Zuma explained to the court that he was prepared to negotiate lobola, paying Khwezi's family for the right to marry her, but that attempts to negotiate failed. Zuma did not give any reason why negotiations had not progressed.

De Beer said that Khwezi did not want lobola negotiations. Zuma had claimed that Khwezi's friends and family related that she was angered with him, not because he raped her, but because he had not called her following their sexual encounter. De Beer asserted that Khwezi never was interested in lobola because she had no interest in marrying

Zuma, reminding him of Khwezi's lesbian orientation. Zuma acknow-ledged the prosecution's argument that Khwezi's sexual status precluded romantic or sexual interest in him, but said that what the complain-ant had told him about wanting a boyfriend contradicted that. He had heard nothing of Khwezi's lesbian orientation until she had said so dur-ing her evidence.

The remainder of the day's cross-examination focused on Zuma's be-haviour during the investigation of the rape allegations. Why had he called Khwezi and her mother repeatedly after hearing she had pressed charges with the police? De Beer said that Zuma wanted to persuade Khwezi not to pursue the rape charges, and Zuma disagreed, saying that he called to see why she made the charges in the first place. De Beer's cross-examination concluded on the morning of 6 April 2006, the fourth day of Zuma's testimony.

Duduzile, Zuma's daughter, testified next. She denied the father-daughter relationship between her father and Khwezi and said she hardly even knew Khwezi. When Duduzile saw Khwezi at her home on 2 November, she said that she felt 'irritated' because she thought Khwezi's visit was just to get money from her father. Duduzile thought that it was 'inap-propriate' for Khwezi to dress in a kanga and was 'convinced that the complainant was trying to entice her father'.

The next series of witnesses testified about Khwezi's past sexual his-tory. The first was Ntswaki, a woman who had investigated and headed a tribunal addressing the allegations of rape that Khwezi made against Godfrey and Charles when she was 13. One was found guilty of rape, the other not, but Ntswaki's testimony indicated that there was a lot of ambiguity about their relationship to Khwezi and their guilt or inno-cence. 'Rape', in this instance, had not been unwanted sexual intercourse but an unwanted sexual act – because Ntswaki said that Khwezi was examined after both accusations, and it was clear that she had never been penetrated. Ntswaki was also aware of Khwezi's situation with Mashaya, whom Khwezi had accused of unsuccessfully trying to rape her, and Ntswaki said that seemed very unlikely. Mashaya testified next, denied any attempted rape, but said they were in a relationship and had consensual sex.

What emerged from these testimonies was that it seemed that Khwezi had sexual experiences at a young age; though unclear if and how these had been coercive, it seemed that her accusations had not been entirely truthful.

After Mashaya, four witnesses testified regarding the three rape accusations Khwezi made while a student at a theological college in South Africa. This testimony was much less ambiguous – each portrayed Khwezi as a liar who made up rape accusations that either never happened or were consensual sex. One witness even remarked: 'I pity the poor complainant. She is sick, and she needs urgent attention, medical attention otherwise many families will be destroyed by her.' Cumulatively, these testimonies suggested that Khwezi had some serious problems in relation to sexual activity and men. The final two witnesses about her sexual history testified about the consensual sexual relations she had with men during the late 1990s.

Van der Merwe, in his judgment, had difficulty in establishing the plausibility of the state's case. Emphasising the long periods with no contact between Khwezi and Zuma, he rejected the state's claim of a father–daughter relationship. The term *malume*, he said, was not proof in itself of such a relationship. The prosecution argued that since Khwezi was lesbian, she would not want to have consensual sex with Zuma. As with the term *malume*, Van der Merwe found that the term lesbian was inconsistent with the reality. Two witnesses had testified to her past sexual behavior with men in the 1990s, and for Van der Merwe, she was at the very least bisexual. Van der Merwe largely dismissed the testimony of Khwezi's mother and her two friends, Pinkie and Kimi.

Khwezi's mother was an elderly woman and Van der Merwe called her testimony incoherent. Though Pinkie and Kimi supported the state's version, their testimony contributed nothing to the rape event.

Van der Merwe said the strength and weaknesses of both the state's case and the defence's case had to be taken into consideration. They were not separate cases, but rather a conglomerate of evidential material.

'The court must not be blinded by where the components come from,' Van der Merwe said. There was no onus on the accused to convince the court of the evidence he gave. If there was any reasonable possibility that his explanation was true, he was entitled to an acquittal.

Van der Merwe had difficulty accepting Khwezi's story. She weighed five kilograms less than Zuma – why had she not fought back? Why had Zuma chosen to rape a woman with a policeman nearby and not far from his own daughter? Why had Khwezi let her clothing be removed and not said no – not once – during ten minutes of intercourse? Conversely, Van der Merwe had no reason to doubt the witnesses who testified to Khwezi's past sexual history. They had convincingly demonstrated her history of making false accusations of rape or attempted rape.

The state's case, Van der Merwe said, rested largely on the credibility of the complainant's testimony, and the defence witnesses gave evidence that suggested she was not credible. The state did not have convincing evidence and arguments to support a guilty verdict. With these points in mind, Van der Merwe found Jacob Zuma not guilty of the crime of rape.

Van der Merwe did tell Zuma, however, that it was 'totally unacceptable' for a man to have unprotected sex with a woman who was not his regular partner, especially knowing that she was HIV-positive. 'Had Rudyard Kipling known of this case at the time he wrote his poem *If*, he might have added the following: "And if you can control your body and your sexual urges, then you are a man, my son".'

Van der Merwe said 'he would not even comment' on Zuma's evidence that he had a shower after the intercourse to lessen his chances of contracting HIV.

Large crowds of Zuma supporters were ecstatic outside the court when the verdict was announced. Punching their fists into the air, they shouted 'Zuma, Zuma'. The crowd had been gathering all day, singing, dancing and waving placards. One section of the crowd was standing on a police armoured vehicle and was ordered off, so they climbed on to the roof of the Innes Chambers building. People cheered, waved their shirts from the roofs of buildings and climbed on to police cars. Dancers in traditional Zulu dress performed in Pritchard Street as well as behind palisade fencing at the entrance to the court. The crowd slowly spilled beyond a police barrier that had confined people to Kruis Street.

Inside the court, hugs, cheers of joy and ululation marked Zuma's not-guilty verdict. People in the court jumped on to the high court benches, sang '"uZuma" for president' and shrieked and ululated. Zuma embraced Kemp, and then moved down the line to thank his other lawyers. De Beer picked up her bag and quickly walked out of court without commenting. Zuma left the court soon afterwards. Asked by some members of the press how he felt after being found not guilty, he smiled and saluted.

Later, he was mobbed when got outside – and the country was introduced to a new 'star', Zuma's 23-year-old daughter Duduzile, whose evidence, said Van der Merwe, had shown that Khwezi had lied.

The most controversial legal issue during the trial was Van der Merwe's decision to allow the defence, in terms of section 227 of the Criminal Procedure Act (CPA), to cross-examine Khwezi about her sexual history (based largely on her own memoir). Section 227 states that a rape complainant's sexual history can only be introduced into a trial with the permission of the court and if it is deemed relevant. When Van der Merwe decided to allow the defence to tell the court why it thought Khwezi's sexual history was relevant – which of course it proved to be – he heard them *in camera*, with no one except the accused, the complainant, the state and the defence present. He also reserved the right to later rule the evidence inadmissible if it proved to be irrelevant.

But his decision, though it was perfectly correct, fuelled the anger of women's groups and journalists, most of whom seemed ignorant of the CPA, and this was part of the reason that the three NGOs, the Tshwaranang Legal Advocacy Centre, the Centre for the Study of Violence and Reconciliation, and the Centre for Applied Legal Studies, had applied to be friends of the court. Parliament was also pilloried by the media about the long-delayed Sexual Offences Bill, which was supposed to have 'dealt with' section 227.

Van der Merwe, irritated by the criticism levelled at him on the air waves and in print, responded extensively in his verdict. He chided organisations and individuals 'who commented on the [227] ruling without having been in court or knowing anything about the contents of the application of the provisions of section 227 of the act'.

What most people remember about the trial are the things that Zuma said – and has never been allowed to forget. One was that he was unable to desist from having intercourse with the complainant, notwithstanding her HIV status, because to leave her primed but unfulfilled was contrary to the strictures of his Zulu 'culture'. Another was that he had dealt with her HIV status, there not having been a condom available at the critical moment, by having a shower immediately afterwards.

Kemp responded to the hullabaloo about the shower by saying in court that, 'If there were a bucket filled with HIV fluid and a Kruger rand at the bottom … no one except a complete moron would not go and wash his hands afterwards.'

A third Zuma utterance (echoed by his daughter, Duduzile) was that Khwezi's sitting with her legs splayed and wearing a kanga sans underwear as pyjamas, was tantamount to an invitation to hanky-panky.

On the last day of argument, Kemp had urged the court to reject the prosecution line that Zuma had relied on Zulu culture to justify some of his actions, including his claim that it would be 'un-Zulu' not to satisfy a sexually aroused woman. Kemp cited Nikos Kazantzakis's work *Zorba the Greek*, in which Zorba said that it would have been a crime to turn away a woman who was 'seeking his bed'.

Van der Merwe might not have been following Kemp at that point because he responded: 'I don't want to refer to the Greek people at the moment. We are talking about Zulus.'

I have not gone into detail about the picture painted by Khwezi's memoirs and by the testimony of the defence witnesses who came to talk about her. But someone should write a book about what life was really like for those exiled by apartheid, especially the children. We, or some of us, tend to romanticise exile – the life in Zambia, Tanzania, Mozambique, Swaziland and Botswana, where the gallant anti-apartheid warriors did what they could, and their families hung on, waiting for the day when they would return home.

But Khwezi's story presented a picture of a woman, a girl actually, who was continually, and with scant or no chance of protection, at the mercy of male predators. Perhaps they were not predators, merely boys, and boys will be boys, and girls will be girls, and Khwezi was Khwezi. Clearly, however, Khwezi had been abused by people around her while in exile. Clearly, too, exile was a destabilising, gut-wrenching experience in which there was much sorrow and difficulty. It wasn't all honey and almonds and heroism.

People still ask me: But didn't Zuma really rape her?

If I asked Zuma, he would reply that he did not. And if I asked Khwezi, she would say that Zuma did rape her. Which is it?

Judge Van der Merwe found that Zuma did not rape Khwezi. Why then, as Van der Merwe asked, would a 31-year-old woman have gone through the trauma of the trial if she had not been raped?

Was Khwezi really so mercenary or so disturbed that she would go through the whole ordeal just to save face? By the time she came to court, had she, like Macbeth, 'stepped in so far' that 'returning' would be as tedious as carrying on? Is it possible that what she imagined had happened became reality for her, or even that she was so desperately in need of attention that any attention would do?

Van der Merwe's response to his own question was that one had to look at Khwezi's history, which included a history of falsely accusing men of rape. When she was confronted with these allegations, she denied knowing the men, or in some instances denied the accusations. This, Van der Merwe said, was because she could not admit that she had previously made false rape claims because then she would be found out. He said it was clear she had experienced previous trauma. After having sex she might have felt guilty and ashamed, and that was why she accused

Zuma of rape. Evidence, he added, had been given that the woman was mentally ill. (This was an exaggeration on the judge's part; her mother had said that she received 'psychological' treatment in Zambia.)

Perhaps that is the answer, or the answers, to the question. Khwezi was not raped; she had sex with Zuma; and then, perhaps because she felt 'used' for the umpteenth time in her life, responded in the way she had responded since she was a child. Yet Khwezi continued to insist that Zuma had raped her and her story, as regards Zuma and the evening of 2 November, was not incredible. And why did she claim that they had sex in the guest bedroom (though she might have worked out that admitting that she had gone to Zuma's bedroom would not put her in a very good light)? Why was Commissioner Taioe so adamant that Zuma had told him that the guest bedroom was 'where it happened'? Taioe might have screwed things up – he did; his evidence was found inadmissible for bureaucratic reasons – but he actually went on record as saying that he was a 'Zuma supporter'. He had, in other words, no reason to lie.

I believe that what happened to Zuma and Khwezi is what I rather lamely call 'real life'. I think that, partially because she comes from a different generation to Zuma, she did not (consciously) understand the implications of her behaviour – loving SMSs, affection, kanga sans underwear. And Zuma, because he comes from a different generation, did not understand that what he read as sexual provocation was merely the way some young people behave. (Khwezi was 31 years old, but some 31-year-olds have the emotional age and social awareness of a 12-year-old.)

So Zuma proceeded to execute the mandate that, as far as he knew, she had given him. And she, in my reading, was taken aback: it was not something that she expected. He was, in her mind, whether it was 'factually' true or not, a kind of father figure and she was unaware of the signals she had (in his view) been giving. She was so taken aback that she didn't fight or scream.

Besides, Zuma didn't attack her or hurt her; he merely went ahead and had his way with her, as countless men do every night of the week with countless women. It's the way of the world. But I don't think sexual intercourse was something Khwezi was especially interested in.

Was that rape? According to the law, if she had in any way indicated that she did not want to have sex, and he went ahead, it was rape. But Khwezi conceded that she had not said anything; she said she 'had frozen'. I believe it was what happens in real life all the time – the only problem having been that Khwezi simply couldn't or didn't want to deal with the way of the world any more, and her friends told her that she didn't have to do so.

A few days after Van der Merwe delivered his verdict, Zuma apologised to the nation for aspects of his behaviour; Khwezi and her mother left the country to live in Holland.

CHAPTER 13

2006

Days of dirty laundry

Here is a diary note written by Kevin Ritchie, managing editor of the *Saturday Star*, on the Friday before the verdict in Zuma's rape trial, outlining the story that he wanted written for that weekend's edition:

Zuma: Once upon a time he was a heartbeat from the throne, officially the next in line to become president. Today, as South Africa celebrates its 10th anniversary of democracy, he has not only been publicly disgraced – fired from his job with all its perks and influence – he stands the very real risk of jail either on Monday or in Durban in a few months' time. First emerging as a byword for cheaply peddled influence, he has become the bogeyman and personification of all that is wrong in our society from gender violence to HIV disinformation, patriarchy, tribalism and populist politics, pandering to prejudice and fears – and yet he remains unbowed, at times rushing headlong into adversity and turning it to his advantage. Have we seen the last of the man they call Msholozi? Or is this just another chapter in his Teflon-like career?

Notwithstanding the breathless prose, the note does sum up how life looked for Zuma early in May 2006. He had just been through his trial for rape, the verdict was looming, and this, whichever way it went, was to be followed by his trial in Pietermaritzburg on charges of corruption.

As we know, Zuma was acquitted on 8 May 2006 of the rape charge, following which the ANC voted to reinstate him in his party duties. But what did the rest of the year hold?

It held mainly legal action – and a trial that would seem to show that Zuma was indeed a species of Teflon man. It was also a trial of accusations and counter-accusations, at which a great deal of everyone's dirty washing was hung out for the public to inspect.

In February, while Zuma's rape trial was standing down so that a suitable judge – one not related to him in any shape or form – could be found, Judge Noel Hurt ruled in the Durban High Court that the search warrants used to search his homes and the office of Hulley were invalid because their parameters were too wide, and that the documents seized had to be returned. This meant that the NPA was restricted to building its corruption case against Zuma solely on evidence gathered before the August 2005 raids. The NPA had wanted to add perjury and tax evasion charges to the corruption ones, but suddenly it was stymied. It immediately gave notice of its intention to appeal against Hurt's decision.

On 5 January, Thint, Pierre Moynot, the MD of the company, and his wife, Bijou, had applied in the Pretoria High Court for the setting aside of the search warrants related to their premises. Their application was more interesting than the others because one aspect of the searches to which the Moynots objected was the Scorpions going through Bijou's underwear drawer. Ham-handed investigators probing the underwear of an elegant and fine-looking French woman indeed conjured up a more exciting picture than Scorpions going through boxes of files in Hulley's office. Unfortunately for them, the Pretoria High Court would dismiss this application on 4 July, though they too would appeal.

So, on the matter of the infamous search warrants, Zuma and Hulley had won their Lower Court application, as had Julekha Mahomed, but

Thint and the Moynots had lost theirs. It was 2–1 for the Zuma team, with the state appealing against the findings in favour of Zuma/Hulley and Mahomed, and Thint against the finding in favour of the state.

Thint also applied, on 12 May, for an order compelling the state to provide a substantive answer to its request for further particulars on the provisional indictment in terms of which it was charged alongside Zuma. This was turned down; the presiding judge said that the trial judge had to deal with the issue.

On 26 June, Billy Downer sc, the lead prosecutor, wrote to all the parties saying that the prosecution could not start on 31 July 2006 and that a realistic date would be February 2007. He said that the state was being hindered in its efforts to produce a final forensic report by the search warrant cases; that the state intended to apply in Mauritius for the release of the documents seized there from the local Thomson-csf company; that the prosecution team was involved in the Shaik appeal at the Supreme Court of Appeal, set down for 21–25 August 2006; that the Shaik appeal judgment would resolve many legal issues that would be contentious in Zuma's trial; and that therefore the Zuma trial should start after the Shaik appeal judgment had been handed down.

Of course neither the Zuma team nor the Thint team was cooperative.

On 18 July, not having received a favourable answer to Downer's letter, the state filed an application requesting that the trial not be held on 31 July because it could not finalise the indictment. And so, on 31 July, just before the trial started, both defence teams filed papers opposing a postponement and also applying for a permanent stay of prosecution.

On 31 July, Zuma and Moynot, representing Thint, appeared before Judge Herbert Q Msimang to face charges of corruption and fraud (corruption only for Thint). The state team – led by Billy Downer sc and Anton Steynberg, with Wim Trengove sc appearing with them from time to time – asked for an adjournment of the trial until some time next year.

The state's reasons for an adjournment were that the full indictment and forensic report were not ready and that it would take the defence a 'long time' to study them when they were completed; Appeal Court judgments related to last year's search and seizure raids on the premises of Zuma, Thint and Zuma's attorneys had not been heard, so the state did not know which material might be legally 'admitted'; and the Shaik appeal had not been heard.

The defence teams, led by Kemp J Kemp sc for Zuma and Kessie Naidu sc for Thint, asked the court to strike the case off the roll completely or temporarily, because justice delayed is justice denied. Zuma had been investigated for five years, after all. They argued too that the case against Zuma was lodged as part of a political conspiracy against him, and that the delays in coming to trial had prejudiced him in his personal and political life.

Msimang told both parties to go away until 5 September, when they could argue their applications before him. In the interim they were to send in affidavits and heads of argument. By 14 August the state was to respond to the defence application and affidavits. By the 21st the defence was to reply to the state's response. By the 28th the defence was to submit its heads of argument. The state put in a supplementary affidavit on the 29th, taking issue with the 2004 Public Protector's report on Zuma that said ex-director of public prosecutions Bulelani Ngcuka had violated Zuma's rights in 2003. On the 31st, the state put in its heads of argument.

It was from these papers and affidavits that all the dirty washing tumbled.

In general, the tenor of the state's argument was that it had proceeded as fast and responsibly as it could in such a highly complex and fluid matter and that the successful prosecution of Shaik had more of an influence than envisaged.

Zuma argued that he was the victim of a strategy aimed at kicking him into touch politically, a major part of that strategy having been to malign and investigate him for years – such as, for example, by declaring in 2003 that there existed a *prima facie* case against him – while inexplicably the state was not ready to bring a case against him to court.

What Zuma was saying, in layman's terms, to the prosecuting authorities was: Either do it right now, which you admit you cannot do, or get off the potty, because you have forced *my* life into a state of excruciating constipation.

As for Thint, it argued that both Penuell Maduna, the former Minister of Justice, and Ngcuka had cut a deal with Thint in terms of which the arms company would never be charged. Why then had they been re-charged?

On 14 August, the state filed six affidavits rejecting the claims made by Zuma, including ones written by Maduna, Ngcuka, Scorpions chief Leonard McCarthy, and Vusi Pikoli, the new NDPP.

Pikoli unequivocally rejected Zuma's claims that the charges against Zuma had been fuelled by a political conspiracy; that he had in some way colluded with the president about charging Zuma; and that Zuma had been dismissed from the deputy presidency because of the charges brought against him by Pikoli. Pikoli said he had decided to charge Zuma following the findings in the trial of Shaik. Among the reasons for his decision to charge Zuma was that certain new information had emerged during this trial. 'The decision to prosecute was based solely on my assessment of the admissible evidence and the prospects of a successful conviction and nothing else.'

Pikoli said he had considered the possibility of delaying charging Zuma until further investigations had been completed. However, some important considerations had taxed his mind, including the huge degree of public interest and the intense speculation about Zuma's political future. He said he was aware that the decision he was about to make was one of national interest, which 'might affect the perception of foreign governments [regarding] South Africa and could even impact on the economy', adding, nastily, that he was aware that Zuma had made repeated calls to have 'his day in court'.

Pikoli had told President Mbeki that he had decided to charge Zuma on 20 June 2005, as a matter of courtesy, given that Zuma had been deputy president until 14 June. He had also informed Zuma in person, which had not been an easy task for him. He had had no discussions with Mbeki about Zuma during a trip to Chile. Zuma had 'effectively branded President Thabo Mbeki a liar', he said: by accusing Mbeki of having fired him because Pikoli wanted to prosecute him, and not because of the Shaik trial finding, Zuma was saying that Mbeki had lied to the nation when he dismissed Zuma.

'I challenge Zuma,' said Pikoli, 'to pertinently state that the president lied to Parliament and to spell out whether or not he asserts that the president is also a party to the alleged political conspiracy against him.'

Maduna said that he wanted to deal firstly with a 'theme that resonates throughout [Zuma's] affidavit' – that he had been targeted to destroy his reputation and 'political role-playing ability'. This was not true: Zuma had offered no facts to bolster his allegation but had relied instead on 'rumours, press reports, speculation and innuendo'.

Maduna said that initially Zuma had blamed him and Ngcuka for being responsible for a plot against him, but later, during his rape trial, had blamed Ngcuka and Ronnie Kasrils. 'This serves,' said Maduna, 'to demonstrate the opportunistic and squalid nature of [Zuma's] allegations.'

Regarding Thint, and the claims by its managing director, Pierre Moynot, that he believed that following a meeting with Maduna and Ngcuka in April 2004, Thint would not be prosecuted in connection with the Arms Deal, Maduna said that the approach for a meeting had come from Thint. He was amazed that Thint had chosen to detail confidential and privileged discussions in its affidavit, and had held confidential discussions with Thint's present counsel, Kessie Naidu SC, about the infamous encrypted fax and its author, Alain Thétard.

'The contents of the discussion [with Naidu] … were to be strictly confidential and I have to date respected this confidentiality. I am advised that I would be within my rights to divulge the contents of this conversation in the light of the selective disclosure [by Thint]. I have decided not to descend to that level.'

Maduna said that in his view Alain Thétard's second statement regarding the encrypted fax (that it was only his 'loose' thoughts about separate issues) had been a 'cynical attempt to sabotage the state's case' – and that if the state had known that this was what Thétard was going to dish up, it would never have agreed to drop charges against Thint in the Shaik trial.

Ngcuka said that Zuma's claim that he was the victim of a political conspiracy was a ploy 'to deflect from the seriousness of the charges which (Zuma) is facing'. 'The irony,' he said, 'is that, far from abusing my powers in order to harm Zuma's reputation, I did everything within my powers to protect it.'

Ngcuka said that, when he had heard that the team investigating Shaik had uncovered evidence implicating the deputy president in corruption, it had come as an 'unpleasant revelation' to him.

McCarthy said Zuma's insults and slurs about how the state had conducted the investigation and prosecution of the case were 'scurrilous and utterly unfounded'. On 17 June 2005, he said, the prosecution and members of the investigation team in the Shaik case had briefed Pikoli and McCarthy on the prospects of a successful prosecution of Zuma on charges of corruption. They had told the two men that, given the findings in the Shaik trial, such a prosecution could be successful.

On 22 August Zuma responded with a second affidavit calling for a stay of prosecution. Once again, he questioned Mbeki's motives in sacking him, and attacked the decision to charge him with corruption and fraud. Zuma said that the Pikoli version of what happened in June last year, when he was both fired and charged, was 'untenable and calls to be rejected'.

'The judgment in Shaik's case was delivered on 2 June 2005,' said Zuma. 'The judgment was delivered on national free-to-air television. I believe it is fair to say that the broadcasting of the judgment gripped the country's attention and dominated the media. The speculation and debate concerning my position as deputy president reached fever pitch. At the height of these events and for a period of four days between 6 and 9 June 2005, [Pikoli] states that he stayed at the same hotel in Chile with [Mbeki] but that he did not discuss with the president the question of whether I would be charged. I respectfully submit that Pikoli's version is untenable.

'To make matters worse,' continued Zuma, 'Pikoli has told the court that Mbeki, having returned to South Africa from Chile, had convened a joint sitting of the houses of Parliament on 14 June 2005, so as to sack me – without so much as having discussed with the NDPP whether I would be charged.' Mbeki would hardly have done this if there had existed the slightest possibility that the NDPP would decide not to charge Zuma after all. 'I find the assertion [by Pikoli] of no discussions [between Mbeki and Pikoli] rather improbable,' he said.

Zuma said that, overall, his right to a fair trial had been irretrievably infringed by the conduct of the state, especially in its publication in papers and elsewhere of unproven allegations, from which unproven and damaging inferences could be drawn. Specifically, he said, the state had not dealt in its affidavits with six crucial issues, which led Zuma to believe that the case should be struck off the roll.

These were: the state's inordinate delay in coming to trial; the impact on him of the investigation on him since mid-2001 and, especially since November 2002, when he first read about it 'in the press'; the impact on him of the media release of August 2003 by Ngcuka, who said that a *prima facie* case existed against Zuma but that he would not be charged; the impact on Zuma of the decision to prosecute him in June last year; the 'purpose' of the investigation and charges ('political conspiracy'); and the impact on him of further postponements, which the state seemed to be trying to be engineer.

Zuma said the NPA had not fulfilled its mandate to investigate fairly and impartially, but had been deeply 'cynical' in its approach to him. To illustrate this, he cited: the 'cynical' extension in October 2002 of an investigation, which had commenced and been conducted since mid-2001, so as to ostensibly legitimise what had gone before and what was to follow; the 'cynical' abuse of power in further extending the investigation in August 2005 to include allegations of Zuma's defrauding of Parliament and tax evasion; the 'cynical abuse' of state power in executing the search warrants of August 2005; and the apparent total reliance on the Shaik judgment, which Zuma argued was in law irrelevant to his matter.

Moynot of Thint also came back punching, making a number of unexpected and remarkable claims: that Maduna, despite submitting an affidavit critical of Thint's bona fides the previous week, worked for the French company in September the previous year and that Thales/Thint never approached the NPA to try to cut a deal before the Shaik trial – the NPA had approached Thales/Thint via a man called Tony Georgiades.

Following the search of Thint's premises and his home on 18 August last year, Moynot said, he asked Ajay Sooklal, his attorney, to approach Maduna to contact Pikoli to find out what was going on, because Maduna had in April 2004 recommended that charges against Thint be withdrawn. Maduna – in August 2005 an attorney at the Johannesburg firm of Bowman, Gilfillan – agreed to meet Jean-Paul Perrier, the chief executive of Thales, to discuss the matter. Maduna asked if he could bring his wife with him and on 11 September 2005 met Perrier, Sooklal and Moynot in London.

At the meeting, Moynot alleged, Maduna confirmed remembering the discussions of 2004, said he was surprised to learn about the search warrants and that he would discuss the agreement of 2004 with Pikoli. He also expressed an interest in purchasing shares in ADS – shares of which Shaik was being forced to divest himself through a curator!

Maduna requested that he be paid for his professional services, said Moynot, and Thint also covered his travel expenses to London. (Moynot told me privately that one of the things that had really annoyed him about Maduna's *volte-face* was that in London, when he had been bought an expensive Cuban cigar by Thint, he had taken another two from the box and stuffed them in his pocket 'for later'.)

'I therefore have great difficulty in understanding the attitude of Maduna' towards especially Thint, but also Zuma, said Moynot. 'Given that Maduna had acted for Thint last year, how could he have stated, as he did in his affidavit on Tuesday, that he had been suspicious of Thint and its legal representatives as early as May 2004?'

Moynot also asserted that Thales/Thint had not first approached Maduna and Ngcuka, then National Director of Public Prosecutions, regarding the NPA's investigation of Shaik, but that Thales had been approached by an NPA intermediary. Some months prior to Shaik's trial, he said, Perrier had been approached in Paris by Georgiades. This man, subsequently identified as the ex-husband of FW de Klerk's second wife Elita, asked Perrier if they could meet. Georgiades introduced himself as a good friend of both Maduna and Ngcuka and asked whether Perrier would agree to meet Ngcuka in connection with the NPA investigations.

When Perrier expressed misgivings about Georgiades' claim of a connection with Ngcuka and Maduna, Georgiades immediately called Ngcuka on his cell phone and passed it to Perrier. Ngcuka confirmed that Georgiades was his emissary and said he wanted to meet Perrier to ask about the 'relationship between Thales and Shaik' and that Thales/Thint was 'not implicated' in the case under investigation. Perrier met Ngcuka, both of them accompanied by other people.

Given these events, Moynot said he could not understand why Maduna and Ngcuka had not mentioned Georgiades in their papers earlier that month. It would be the last time that Maduna became involved in any Zuma court matter.

In its 141-page heads of argument prepared by Wim Trengove SC and put in to the Pietermaritzburg High Court at the end of August, the state said that Zuma's claim that his prospects of becoming a leader of the ANC and the country might be thwarted if the current charges were still pending in 2007 was, at best, speculative. There was no evidence to suggest the criminal trial would not have been concluded by the December 2007 ANC elections, and the state took issue with Zuma's claim that certain individuals would try to 'exclude [him] from any meaningful political role' if the trial were pending, saying Zuma had not identified these 'shadowy' individuals, and that the 'prosecuting authorities cannot be held hostage to the accused's hopes to stand for high office at the end of 2007'.

Trengove argued that if Zuma 'will indeed at the end of next year be a candidate for high public office, then it is all the more important that his prosecution should not be stifled. 'If he is innocent, then it is of vital importance that his innocence be established. If he is guilty, on the other hand, then it is vitally important that his guilt be exposed.'

The state also hit back at what it termed 'gratuitous insults', referring to comments that the state had been 'misleading', 'disingenuous', 'less than frank' and 'acted scandalously'. Arguing that its postponement bid was not unreasonable, the state said Zuma became an accused on 20 June 2005, and arms firm Thint and Thint representative Pierre Moynot on 4 November 2005, so a delay of about 13 months in respect of Zuma and nine months in respect of his co-accused 'is modest compared to the typical systemic delays in High Court trials'.

The state suggested that the prosecution was not to blame for the delays, 'while the accused elected to pursue a strategy of litigation arising from search and seizure raids at 22 premises on August 18 last year, when about 93 000 documents were seized'.

The state detailed the scale and complexity of the investigation, which it said was illustrated by the length of the forensic accountant's report. In the Shaik trial, the report was 250 pages long, with 25 files of annexures. The Zuma report was expected to be 'much longer'. The forensic accountant report was 'near completion'; it would be delivered by 5 September, while the defence would be provided with a revised indictment by 15 October.

On 5 September 2006, Judge Msimang decided to hear the state's application for postponement first. The state wheeled seven boxes of forensic audit documents into the Pietermaritzburg High Court. The new KPMG report covering Zuma's financial affairs up until August 2005 was expected to show that Zuma received payments totalling R3,7-million from Shaik. To support its application for the case to be postponed, the state produced the documents to show that it had completed one of the most significant aspects of its corruption case against Zuma.

Trengove said that the long-awaited forensic audit into Zuma's affairs had been completed. The report, which filled 54 lever arch files, was 'most comprehensive and daunting'. He also continued to argue that Shaik's appeal against his fraud and corruption conviction 'could have profound implications' for Zuma's trial.

On 6 and 7 September, the defence teams opposed the state's application for postponement and again asked Judge Msimang to strike the case off the roll. Trengove continued to argue that this was not in the public interest or the interests of a 'fair and speedy' trial for the accused. But Msimang seemed to have made up his mind from reading the documents – and it seemed not be in the state's favour. Trengove was repeatedly interrupted by the judge as he argued that the trial should be postponed until next year, and asked to 'give your reasons in brief form'.

Trengove then reiterated that the 'main reason' for the state's delay in prosecuting Zuma had been the legal wrangling that followed the search and seizure operations but that the prosecution was 'reasonably confident' about reaching settlements with certain of the parties involved in the litigation (Trengove was referring to Mahomed, with whom the state had decided not to fight, and to material taken from Moynot's home, which was of no use to the state anyway).

But the judge was not impressed: 'I find it a bit strange … I've been hearing about these expectations since your papers were filed [in May]. Surely at some point your expectations become unreasonable,' he complained.

'Imagine,' Kemp said to Judge Msimang, 'if we [Zuma] came to court and said we were just not ready to plead for 15 months. Yet the state believes it has the right to ask continually for postponements because it is simply "not ready". This is not the way a constitutional democracy works. It is destructive of [Zuma's] constitutional right to be tried as fast as is reasonably possible.'

Kemp said that it was remarkable that Downer could list issues that would have a bearing on the trial 'and yet more than a year after Zuma has been charged, we cannot defend ourselves because we still know nothing about the charges'. There was still no final indictment and his client still did not know the particulars of the charges against him – another two contraventions of his rights.

'In any case,' interjected Judge Msimang, 'I do not understand the relevance of the Shaik appeal. It may be months before a verdict in the appeal is delivered. Besides, who knows whether the appeal is going to end in Bloemfontein [where the Supreme Court of Appeal is situated] or Braamfontein [where the Constitutional Court is].'

'Why then was Zuma charged?' asked Kemp. 'These charges should be struck off the roll, the state should get its house in order, complete all outstanding business and then decide whether it wants to lay charges against Zuma.' All he had received from the state by way of particulars was a virus-riddled computer hard drive with some 4-million 'images' on it. 'I plead *mea culpa* to not being technologically literate,' Kemp said, 'but all I can do is read specific documents, which the state must specify as evidence. I cannot grapple with four million unspecified images.'

The best line of the day, however, was Naidu's. Referring to the state's delivery of the voluminous forensic auditor's report to the court, Naidu said: 'This is not a case of the cart before the horse but the trailer before a bus.'

On 20 September, Judge Msimang struck the corruption case against Jacob Zuma off the roll, saying that the state's case had limped from 'one disaster to another'. In his view, it was clear and simple. The NPA's biggest balls-up in relation to Zuma was that the state had charged the former deputy president before it had properly prepared the case against him. This was Msimang's main reason for not allowing the state a postponement of the trial. And it was why, since the state said that it was not ready to proceed with the trial there and then, Msimang there and then said he had no choice but to strike the case off the roll. And the Zulu kingdom (and the Cosatu conference in Johannesburg) erupted in a spasm of joy.

'If a person has been charged very early in [a] complex case that has been inadequately prepared,' quoted Msimang from a judgment by Judge Johann Kriegler, 'and there is no compelling reason for this [early charging of the person], a court should not allow the complexity of the case to justify an over-lengthy delay.'

Msimang continued: 'It is now history that these words of wisdom were jettisoned by the state [in the case of Zuma] in favour of some non-procedural policy and a precipitate decision was taken to prosecute [Zuma] a mere 12 days after what the prosecution perceived to be their success in the Shaik trial.'

A 'non-procedural policy' is one that excludes good or valid legal reasons for doing something, from the judge's point of view. In short, the NPA charged Zuma, before being adequately prepared, for reasons unrelated to the law.

Zuma was charged because the NPA, flushed by its success in the Shaik trial, believed it could easily nail him. Msimang's basic question was: if you were not ready to nail Zuma legally, why did you charge him before you were? What was the hurry? What was the non-procedural imperative?

The correct answer may be that the NPA investigators simply became too ambitious. Titillated by Shaik's admission that payments to Zuma had continued after the period for which he was being tried, they wanted to find more to bring against Zuma than they had, or had from their investigations into Shaik. This led the NPA into a series of events that left the state woefully unprepared – summed up by Msimang as follows:

> [By the middle of 2006] there were legal challenges to the warrants [related to the August 2005 raids on the premises of Zuma, his attorneys, and on Thint] which were far from being resolved, a lengthy forensic report [held up by the challenges to the warrants] to be compiled, an indictment to be formulated, an application for an amendment to the indictment to be attended to and the requests for further particulars to the indictment to be responded to.
>
> It had dawned on us that it was inevitable that the state's efforts to prosecute in this matter would flounder. From the very outset, when a decision was taken to prosecute, those efforts were anchored on an unsound foundation.

According to Pikoli, the state had had a number of reasons for charging Zuma just 12 days after Shaik was convicted. These were, among others: Judge Hilary Squires' ruling that there was a corrupt relationship between Shaik and Zuma; Zuma's public declarations that he wanted the opportunity to clear his name in court; and the enormous public and media interest in the Shaik trial and its repercussions for Zuma. But, according to Judge Msimang, the state's reasons and approach to prosecuting the ANC deputy president had 'jettisoned' standard legal practice 'in favour of some non-procedural policy' and 'ill-advised decision-making'. Essentially, the judge suggested, the state had hurtled into prosecuting a highly complex case with little or no regard for its ability to do so successfully.

Throughout the state's application to postpone Zuma's trial, the judge questioned whether there had been any 'procedural advantage' to be gained by charging Zuma so soon after Shaik's conviction. It is now apparent that he failed to find a satisfactory answer. From the time that the state elected to prosecute Zuma, its case 'limped from one disaster to another', he said.

Msimang's list of disasters for which he criticised the state: Failing to ask for a postponement of Zuma's case for further investigation in October 2005, when the matter was still in the Magistrates' Court; agreeing to provide the defence with an indictment based on the charges for which Shaik was convicted – which, according to the judge, the state 'knew very well' they would not use when Zuma eventually went on trial and which was 'another false foundation for which the state was bound to pay'; failing to 'factor the inherent delays into their headstrong decision to prosecute' – a reference to the legally contested August 2005 search and seizure operations by the Scorpions; reacting to the pressure it felt as Zuma's proposed 31 July trial date drew near by handing 'unlawfully' seized documents over to auditors KPMG and instructing them to proceed with a report into Zuma's financial affairs; taking their chances that the trial court would come to their rescue and admit such evidence, 'overlooking the fact that, even for that purpose, for them to be granted a postponement in the matter, they needed to show that such evidence would be available on the adjourned date – 'a task, we have found, they were not equal to'; ignoring judicial guidelines about the use of disputed documentation; and falsely claiming under oath that the state had given KPMG the contested documents after reaching 'agreements in principle' with Zuma and his attorneys about the seized documents.

In his August affidavit, McCarthy had noted that investigators into the Arms Deal had been taken aback to discover that one of the people implicated was the incumbent deputy president of the country, and that the NPA realised that this posed, and would pose, all kinds of problems. An understatement of note!

CHAPTER 14

2006–2007

The Floating Opera

That moment when Judge Herbert Msimang struck the state's case of corruption and fraud against Jacob Zuma off the roll was a golden one for the 64-year-old warrior. It began about three-quarters of the way through the judge's 40-minute judgment on whether he would grant the state a postponement. Following a synopsis of the case's background, Msimang noted: 'We are ... enjoined by the constitution to treat [Zuma] in exactly the same manner as we would treat any other person ... [but] equally important is that ... [he] should be treated no worse.'

Zuma and his co-accused, Pierre Moynot of Thint Holdings, suddenly strained forward in the dock, following every syllable the judge uttered. And practically every word that Msimang spoke from that moment was critical of the National Prosecuting Authority, especially his comment that the state had taken a 'precipitate decision' to charge Zuma a mere 12 days after what 'they perceived to be their success in the Shaik trial'.

Following that remark, it seemed almost inevitable that, a few minutes later, Msimang would dismiss the state application for a postponement. Zuma's crowd of supporters in court erupted and was reprimanded by the judge. Zuma remained stony-faced, yet he perceptibly flushed, just as he had done during his rape trial when the not guilty verdict was pronounced.

A minute later, having been told by state advocate Anton Steynberg that the state was not ready to continue with the case now, the judge unceremoniously struck the case off the roll and the crowd erupted again. This time, though, they quickly controlled themselves.

Zuma emerged from the court grinning from ear to ear. I asked him how he felt about what had just happened, if he was feeling 'over the moon'. He replied: 'I am very, very pleased.'

Outside the court, on the main Pietermaritzburg taxi-rank, Zuma spoke to the crowd, looking happier than he had for months. He performed a full and robust version of *Awuleth' umshini wami*, and he and his aides were not going to allow anything to tarnish the golden moment. As he launched into the third verse of his song, a group walked towards the stage carrying a replica of a small coffin. At the top was a picture of President Thabo Mbeki. The master of ceremonies immediately told them that they were not at Zuma's celebration to be 'provocative'. The coffin was immediately dismantled and Zuma went on dancing.

Within an hour of Msimang's judgment, the Scorpions were on the job again, collecting more evidence. And the day after the judgment, Thint's attorney Ajay Sooklal discovered that the Scorpions had, while everyone had been in court in Pietermaritzburg, made a request to the French justice ministry for 'mutual legal assistance' – the establishment in Paris of a special tribunal, known as a '*commission rogatoire*', so that more questions could be put to Thint/Thales.

At a press conference, two days after the judgment, Zuma repeatedly answered questions about the possibility that he might be re-charged by saying that it was not his concern and that he refused to spend his time justifying himself. 'All I know,' he said, 'was that I went to court on 31 July to answer the charges against me. The state was not ready then and was not ready on Wednesday, and the judge threw the state's case out. What else is there to say?'

The NPA had immediately issued a statement saying that Vusi Pikoli would study the judgment over the next few days. In addition, Makhosini Nkosi, the NPA spokesperson, indicated that Pikoli and his investigators would clarify 'in due course' whether the NPA would re-charge Zuma and Thint, which it was entitled to do in law.

Yet, by roughly midday on that very Wednesday, Johan du Plooy and Izak du Plooy, two senior special investigators in the Scorpions, known as 'the Du Plooy twins', though they are not related, and who had been present in court earlier for the judgment, had arrived at the Umhlanga office of Davis, Strachan and Taylor (DST), a financial services company.

DST had previously done work for Schabir Shaik, whose appeal was due to start at the Supreme Court of Appeal (SCA). Paul Gering of DST confirmed that the investigators had collected documents from him on the Wednesday morning. The documents related to certain legal fees incurred by Zuma that were allegedly paid for by Shaik.

As for the application for a *commission rogatoire*, the Scorpions had applied quietly to a magistrate and then forwarded it via the Department of Foreign Affairs and the South African embassy in France to the French Ministry of Foreign Affairs which, in turn forwarded it to the French Ministry of Justice. The NPA wanted to put further questions to Thales about the role of Alain Thétard as regards the notorious encrypted fax and Thétard's relationship with Zuma.

To cut a long story (a little) shorter, Vusi Pikoli's NPA had pretty much decided that, despite Msimang's judgment, it was going to bring Zuma to trial. For the rest of 2006 and throughout 2007, there were court skirmishes between Zuma's team and the NPA or skirmishes very much related to Zuma, such as Shaik's appeals.

Zuma's court travails might not have been South Africa's favourite soap opera – not that they qualified as fiction, being all too excruciatingly Zuma's reality and South Africa's as well – but the saga was clearly leading to a conclusion in the ANC's 52nd conference at Polokwane, at which the leadership would stand for re-election. A soapie must also, by definition, be presented in a continuing, regular narrative. We should be able to watch it every working day. But the Zuma story only surfaced from time to time. So a better name for the Zuma story would be 'The Floating Opera' – to borrow the title used by American author John Barth for his first novel.[1]

Barth suggested that life was like a showboat with an open deck, on which a play is performed as the boat drifts up and down the river on the tide, and the audience sits along both banks. The audience catches only that part of the plot that unfolds as the boat floats past them. They have to wait until the tide runs back again to catch another part of it. The audience is left not knowing what is going on. 'I needn't explain,' Barth wrote, 'that that's how much of life works.'

Before the opera floated past again, and within days of Msimang's judgment, Zuma put his foot in his mouth. At the Shaka's Day celebrations in Stanger, he said that same-sex marriages were 'a disgrace to the nation and to God' and he mentioned that when he was growing up, 'an *ungqingili* [homosexual] would not have stood in front of me. I would have knocked him out.' The country's gay lobby grew very angry indeed.

I was at Zuma's Johannesburg house to interview him some months after this incident and after he had publicly apologised for his comments – saying that he 'respected' and 'acknowledged' the 'sterling contribution of many gay and lesbian compatriots in the struggle' – when he explained the incident to two women, isiZulu speakers, who had come to see him. He did so in English; obviously it was for my benefit as well.

'All I was doing – it was Shaka's Day, after all – was explaining the kind of values, for better or worse, I had been brought with up as a Zulu boy. I didn't say that I went around knocking out gays. I meant that, when we were young, gays were not acceptable to most people and anyone suspected of being one, or was somewhat effeminate during our stick-fighting training, would get knocked down. I was merely describing how it was, what Zulu culture was like – because I was talking about Zulu culture at the Shaka's Day celebrations. Why are people always twisting my words to attack me?'

But Zuma was not deeply exercised by the incident – he was more bemused than anything else. Parts of the South African constitution and its non-racial, non-discriminatory bill of rights have taken many of his generation slightly aback when they have been suddenly forced to confront what it actually says.

On 6 November 2006, the Supreme Court of Appeal in Bloemfontein unanimously rejected Shaik's attempts to have his one fraud and two corruption convictions and sentences overturned. Three days later, he went to Westville prison to start his sentence of 15 years.

'I can't believe it,' Shaik said. 'Boom, boom, boom. One, two, three. They didn't uphold anything. All the lawyers were wrong about what was going to happen.' Before the ruling, he had been upbeat, claiming to have slept 'like a baby' the night before, and deciding not to listen – on a hastily borrowed radio – to the judgment summary delivered in Bloemfontein by Judge Craig Howie, President of the Supreme Court of Appeal. He went instead for a walk in the gardens of the Vineyard Hotel in Cape Town, where he and his brothers had gone together to be in close proximity to his senior counsel, Francois van Zyl sc and Jeremy Gauntlett sc.

Schabir's two brothers, Moe and Yunis, listened to the judgment for him and then went to call him from the garden where he was walking with his prayer beads.

Before Howie started reading, Reeves Parsee, Shaik's attorney, had scribbled a quick list on a piece of paper – 'count one, appeal upheld/dismissed, count two, appeal upheld/dismissed', and so on. As Howie read, each tick that Parsee made next to each 'dismissed' seemed like another blow of an axe to a condemned man's neck.

Howie dismissed all Shaik's appeals, except a minor one related to one aspect of the asset forfeiture case against him and his 10 companies. He also upheld the 15-year sentence given by Judge Hilary Squires in the Durban High Court.

'Well, a whole new chapter in my life is just about to start,' said Shaik on the stoep of the hotel. 'Anyway,' he said, 'if they want to lock me up for helping a friend, well, to hell with it, I will help my friend again, any time.'

Shaik flew home to his wife Zuleika and infant son Yasir in Durban for his last days of freedom. What was especially worrying for him, besides the prospect of jail, was the court's denial of leave to appeal on the finding of his 'corrupt' relationship with Zuma, which would make a Constitutional Court appeal more difficult.

Explaining why the SCA was refusing to reduce Shaik's 15-year sentence for corruption, Judge President Craig Howie said 'the very high level of corruption that this case involved … attacks the moral fibre of the people and inhibits [the nation's] development'.

Not only did the five SCA judges reject Shaik's legal challenges, they also potentially bolstered the state's proposed case against Zuma. The judges agreed with Judge Hilary Squires' finding that Shaik had made 238 payments to Zuma totalling R1,2-million. 'There is in our view, only one reasonable inference to be drawn. It is that, in making the payments in issue, whether as inducement or reward, Shaik intended to influence Zuma, in furtherance of the business interests of Shaik and his companies, to act in conflict with the duties imposed upon Zuma … in terms of the constitution.'

'The seriousness of the offence of corruption cannot be overemphasised. We must make every effort to ensure that corruption, with its putrefying effects, is halted,' Judge Howie said.

One of the most damaging rulings made by the court, from Zuma's point of view, concerned the notorious encrypted fax. Though acknowledging that the author, Thétard, seemed to be 'an unreliable and dishonest person', the court noted that it 'did not follow that he was also unreliable or dishonest in respect of what he recorded in the fax'.

The court's difficulty in admitting the fax as evidence revolved around the so-called 'hearsay' provisions in the Criminal Procedure Act and the fact that neither Thétard nor Zuma was ever cross-examined about it.

In deciding to uphold Judge Squires's admissibility ruling on the fax, despite initially expressing certain reservations, the SCA effectively kept both Zuma and Thint on the prosecutorial hook. The court dismissed argument by Shaik's counsel that the payments Shaik made to Zuma were made out of friendship.

Meanwhile, notwithstanding the Msimang judgment, the state was trundling on with its case. On 6 December, the NPA gave notice to Zuma and Thint that it would apply for the release of documents, including Thétard's diary, by the Mauritian High Court, which was currently holding them under seal.

In an affidavit filed with the Durban High Court that week, Isak Du Plooy said the investigation remained current. 'There is a reasonable prospect that charges could in future be reinstituted against one or more of the erstwhile accused and/or others, more particularly since the Supreme Court of Appeal has in the interim comprehensively confirmed the findings of the trial court [in the Shaik appeal]. However, the National Director has not yet decided whether to do so and, if so, on what charges. The indictment may differ in certain respects [from the original] but is likely to contain at least the charges set out [in the original].'

'Yeah,' Michael Hulley, Zuma's attorney, said in December 2006, 'there is a funny sort of game going on. The state said in its affidavit in this most recent matter that the National Director of Public Prosecutions has not yet decided whether to re-charge Zuma and/or Thint. That is the NPA's official stance. It bears as much resemblance to reality as the official ANC line that there is no presidential race going on in this country.

'The state is clearly taking all the steps necessary for re-charging Zuma. This latest move to try to have the Mauritian documents unsealed is just one of those steps,' he said.

The other matter with which the state had to deal before it would be able to feel free to re-charge Zuma and Thint formally was the three search and seizure appeals, scheduled to be heard at the SCA during the last week of May 2007.

Hulley said the state's case against Zuma appeared to consist of the corruption charges on which Shaik was found guilty in the Durban High Court relating to the use of Zuma's name and influence to achieve certain business goals; the corruption charge on which Shaik was found guilty related to a Thint bribe for Zuma; and other charges, which would infer that Zuma allegedly received money from people other than Shaik.

The year turned from 2006 to 2007 – and it was time to start preparing for the 52nd ANC conference at Polokwane. Electioneering is always a strange business with the ANC and difficult for the media to report because the ANC's senior members always insist that electioneering is the last thing on their minds.

Zuma would soon be busy putting together his 'campaign' (which of course did not exist) for Polokwane – and more especially for the pre-Polokwane provincial and regional conferences – with the help of the likes of Blade Nzimande of the SACP, Zwelinzima Vavi of Cosatu, and Fikile Mbalula of the ANC Youth League. But of course he kept these talks and strategy sessions very firmly under his non-existent hat.

Meanwhile, the taxman got in on the act with the NPA. In February 2007, Hulley was spotted emerging from the Durban Magistrate's Court where he had dealt with a summons served by the South African Revenue Service (SARS) on Zuma.

The summons had been served because SARS had sent Hulley questions about the 'completeness' of Zuma's disclosure of his income and because he had failed to submit a tax return. Hulley had told the court that an agreement had in fact been struck with SARS that the information it was looking for would be furnished by early April.

Zuma (and Hulley) suspected that there was a clear connection between the SARS queries and the NPA's continuing investigation into Zuma's relationship with Schabir Shaik.

'I said we are not going to comment, and I am certainly not going to comment on the motivations of SARS,' Hulley said. 'You cannot fairly ask me whether I, or we, think that SARS is harassing Mr Zuma. Some people would say that SARS harasses everyone. That's their job,' Hulley said.

In September the previous year, during Zuma's trial in Pietermaritzburg on corruption charges, Kemp J Kemp said the state had applied for a postponement because it wanted to make 'a different case with different evidence' against Zuma and needed time to do so. He was referring to the possibility that Zuma would have additional charges of tax evasion brought against him in the wake of the massive KPMG forensic audit into his financial affairs.

Clearly the NPA was going to re-charge Zuma, but it was having to juggle a number of balls: the state of Zuma's taxes, the outcome of Shaik's Constitutional Court appeal (which had gone to the highest court in the land in December 2006), the Scorpions' success in getting hold of the Mauritian documents, and the outcome of the NPA's appeal regarding the search and seizure warrants ratified by Judge Bernard Ngoepe at the end of 2005.

In connection with the documents in Mauritius, one of the more Kafkaesque, though minor, moments in the Zuma legal saga took place in the Pietermaritzburg High Court in March. Zuma and Thint, each represented by a senior and a junior counsel, and by an attorney, spent one-and-a-half days trying to persuade Phillip Levinsohn, the Deputy Judge President of KwaZulu-Natal, that he should not comply with the request by the NPA that he write to the Mauritian authorities asking them to release the originals of 13 purportedly incriminating documents.

What was Kafkaesque about it was that the NPA, represented in court by a senior counsel and two juniors, and by two senior investigators, already had copies of the documents, one of which was a page from the diary kept by Thétard. Copies of the documents had been used in the prosecution of Shaik. But, as Billy Downer SC, for the state, explained to Levinsohn, when the state's case against Zuma and Thint was struck off the roll in the same court by Judge Herbert Msimang, the judge told the state it needed to do its homework properly. Getting hold of the originals of the documents was part of that homework, Downer said. If Zuma and Thint were recharged, they would obviously argue that copies of the Mauritius documents were inadmissible as evidence.

Aha, said Kemp – though he said it in legalese – it was obvious then that the state was preparing to recharge Zuma and Thint. If it were not, asking Levinsohn to write to the Mauritian authorities would be a waste of the court's time. And, if the state was preparing to recharge Zuma and Thint, why not say so.

Downer, however, would not be drawn. The NPA had been stung by Msimang – and it was going to play matters close to the chest from then onwards.

Then the Scorpions moved against Zuma in another venue: in April in the Pretoria High Court. The Scorpions had apparently discovered one of the conduits by which Zuma was paid the R500 000-a-year bribe money that they alleged he was given by Thint. This emerged from the letter of request for international assistance that Leonard McCarthy, the Scorpions chief, submitted to the Pretoria High Court. The request was ratified by Judge Ben du Plessis, who asked the 'competent authority' in Britain to assist the Scorpions to get their hands on the document or documents specified in the request.

McCarthy requested details of a payment that would be found at the offices of the London solicitors Berwin Leighton Paisner and/or at the firm's bank, the address of which was given as Barclays Bank, London. The details related, McCarthy testified, to a payment or payments made in August 2001 to an entity named Cay Nominees (Pty) Ltd, which made a payment to Zuma.

The sole shareholder of Cay Nominees was businessman Jürgen Kögl – who, we will remember, was one of the people who took Mbeki and Zuma to a secret meeting with General Constand Viljoen prior to the first democratic elections.

According to McCarthy, earlier explanations from Kögl regarding the source of the funds to Cay Nominees, and from Cay Nominees to Zuma, were very unsatisfactory. McCarthy continued: 'Apart from [these considerations], there are some indications that the payments may in fact be linked to Thomson/Thales [Thint] and their undertaking to pay Zuma R500 000 per annum as a bribe. If so, it appears that Berwin Leighton Paisner's account was used to launder the payment of money from Thomson/Thales to Zuma in accordance with the bribe agreement in the encrypted fax.'

McCarthy said that, according to a document obtained at the Thint offices in South Africa, dated 17 May 1999, Kögl was apparently 'authorised to handle matters at that stage' on behalf of one of the forerunner companies of Thint. In addition, one of the payments that Kögl had admitted to paying to Zuma in August 2001 was related to a bond for his flat in Killarney, Johannesburg.

'At about the same time and on 23 August 2001, Shaik was meeting Thétard and De Jomaron [Thales representative and Thétard's superior in Mauritius] at the Thales office in Mauritius. The evidence … reveals, and Shaik confirmed in his evidence, that Shaik created two documents in Mauritius on that day … [the purpose being] to cause Thomson/Thales to make further payments to Shaik pursuant to this ostensible service provider agreement … The trial court found that the ultimate purpose of the service-provider agreement was to disguise the payment of the bribe money to Zuma …'

McCarthy said the payment to Zuma from Cay Nominees had previously been investigated in connection with the investigation into Shaik, the Nkobi group, the Thales group, Thint and Zuma's wielding of influence on behalf of Shaik and the other companies. In 2005, the investigation had been extended to include fraud and tax offences suspected to have been committed by Zuma. And in 2006, said McCarthy, the investigation was extended even further to include racketeering and money laundering in contravention of the Prevention of Organised Crime Act (POCA), committed by Zuma, Thint and persons associated with Nkobi.

McCarthy said that R1 075 090,80 had been paid to Zuma by Cay Nominees and a total of R1 191 390,12 had been transferred to Cay Nominees by Berwin Leighton Paisner. Before the Shaik trial, the Scorpions had tried to find out what the million rands had been for but affidavits from Kögl had been incomplete and unsatisfactory.

The first affidavit had said that certain amounts had gone to a Michigan Investments CC and were apparently for the purchase of the flat in Killarney. But the second affidavit appeared to have contradictory information, while the forensic analysis of all the transactions showed that R183 000 had gone into an FNB account of DaimlerChrysler Finance for the account of Zuma.

'It appears that there are numerous contradictions between the affidavits, bank information, accounting records and financial statements – and Kögl's affidavits do not adequately address the source of the R1 191 390,12,' said McCarthy.

Although the charges against Zuma and Thint had been struck off the roll, McCarthy said he remained 'firmly of the view that there exists no legal bar to the reinstitution of the prosecution against Thint or any of other accused'.

Jürgen Kögl had clearly been busy, and his relationship with Mbeki *et al* had apparently continued beyond 1993. It also emerged from the Scorpions' court application, though they tried to play it down, that Penuell Maduna and Barbara Masekela, South Africa's ambassador in the US, had received money from Kögl. The details of the payments were listed in a KPMG draft report, 'The State versus Jacob Zuma and others: Forensic investigation', dated 2 September 2006. But Maduna, who was Minister of Justice when he received R145 000 from Cay Nominees, told me the money was a lawful payout for a legitimate investment. He added that, as far as he knew, the same situation applied to Masekela.

Regarding four other payments of R115 000 each, made in September 2004 by a Kögl-controlled company to four people identified only as TM, AP, MM and JZ (Jacob Zuma), Maduna said that he would 'not be at all surprised' if TM stood for Thabo Mbeki, the President; AP for Aziz Pahad, the Deputy Minister for Foreign Affairs; and MM for Mendi Msimang, the Treasurer-General of the ANC.

'The thing is,' said Maduna, 'many senior ANC people were present at an initial meeting with Kögl in 1993 or 1994 at which he offered us excellent investment opportunities, and many of us invested. Later, when some of us, like me, became members of government and could not hold those investments, they were shifted into a blind trust by Kögl. None of it was illegal and none of it is surprising to hear about. I can't understand what the fuss is about.'

Mbeki did not respond when I sent him questions on the matter. Pahad said via Ronnie Mamoepa, the spokesperson for foreign affairs, that he had 'never received a cent in any way, shape or form from Jurgen'. The KPMG report also noted that Cay Nominees was also listed as a shareholder of African Renaissance Holdings (ARH), incorporated in 1994 as an empowerment investment holding company. Both Kögl and Masekela were founder shareholders of ARH which, according to documentation in the possession of KPMG, was incorporated in response to a 1993 'request by returning ANC leaders' to '… create a commercial vehicle with the singular objective – to be at the vanguard of the economic transformation and empowerment of black South Africans'.

Maduna said he would find it 'very difficult to believe' that Kögl had ever been involved in the 'commission of a crime' because 'quite simply, Kögl had no need to. He had plenty of money of his own. Let me tell you too,' Maduna said, 'that Kögl was a great friend of ours in the early days. Those were times when we in the ANC needed people who were discreet and could get things done. He was one of those. During those days of early negotiations, he was also able to facilitate meetings with certain people – let's say certain Afrikaner elements. Without him, we would never have got to them.'

Asked what he thought of the linking by the Scorpions of Kögl to the alleged laundering of money for Thint and Zuma, Maduna said: 'Well, if you suspect there has been the commission of a crime, you have to investigate, but still …'

A very senior ANC leader, who asked not to be named, said: 'The irony of this whole business is that I'm pretty sure that Zuma never knew Kögl initially. We knew that JZ, who was our comrade and was doing important work in KwaZulu-Natal, was in big financial trouble. So we asked Kögl to assist him. If we had not asked, Kögl would not have helped him.' He was wrong, of course: Zuma, as we recall, met Kögl in 1993 with Mbeki.

At the end of May, Schabir Shaik told the 10 judges of the Constitutional Court that he had been convicted and jailed because he was the sacrificial lamb in the state's attempt to nab Zuma. 'If anyone believes that my client was the ultimate fish that was sought to be landed [by the state], they obviously haven't been reading the newspapers,' Martin Brassey SC, Shaik's advocate, told the court.

Shaik and the 10 companies in his Nkobi Group had applied for leave to appeal against the Supreme Court of Appeal's upholding of their conviction and sentences, and the related confiscation of their assets.

Shaik's claim that he was a scapegoat was not stated directly in the heads of argument because it is not usual legal practice to write 'the state is a bully and made me the fall guy' or 'I was a dummy run, a test specimen, used by the state to see whether it could later go after its real target, Jacob Zuma'.

It is also difficult to make such an argument when you have been convicted in the High Court of corruption and fraud (June 2005) and sentenced to 15 years' jail; the conviction and sentence have been upheld by a full bench of the Supreme Court of Appeal (November 2006), and the state has painstakingly demonstrated that you made more than 230 payments of various kinds to the man on his way to becoming the deputy president.

It is even more difficult to make such an argument when you have previously failed to raise it in the other two courts in which you have spent a great deal of time arguing your case. Still, it was an ingenious argument that Brassey delivered, verbally, and he certainly won the attention of the court.

The nub of Shaik's argument was that he had been unfairly tried, thus violating his constitutional rights, because he had been charged with being in a conspiratorial relationship with Zuma and with Thint. And yet his co-conspirators were not charged alongside him. This, Brassey argued, was unfair because no one could say what might have happened if Zuma had been charged alongside Shaik.

The issue of Zuma's exclusion from the trial became even more vexed, Brassey said, when one took into account the affidavit of Leonard McCarthy, the Scorpions boss, which was presented to the court during Zuma's aborted trial in September. This was because the affidavit allegedly made it clear that the Scorpions were merely waiting to see what happened to Shaik before proceeding against Zuma. This brought one back to the statement made in 2004 by Bulelani Ngcuka, then National Director of Public Prosecutions. Ngcuka said then that there was a *prima facie* case against Zuma, but he would not be charged because it seemed that the case was not winnable. Brassey argued that, in terms of the law, it was never a prosecutor's job to decide whether a case was winnable or not. He was supposed to prosecute without fear, favour or prejudice. It was a court's job to decide whether a case was won or lost.

This raised the question of why Zuma had not been charged alongside Shaik. The answer, Brassey suggested, was that the NDPP had been anxious about taking the country's deputy president to court. In other words, he had been swayed by political considerations. So he had considered it wiser to charge Shaik alone – thus using him as a 'dummy run' or 'stalking horse'. If the case against Shaik were successful, the state could then move against Zuma.

A number of judges asked Brassey what difference Zuma could have made, because he obviously would not have said anything implicating himself. Brassey replied that speculation was irrelevant: either Shaik had been 'irregularly' charged and thus given an unfair trial, or he had not. But, pressed harder by the bench, he said: 'Can you imagine if Mr Zuma had been tried alongside Mr Shaik? … Can you imagine the quality of the trial and how different it would have been if Mr Zuma … had entered the box and said 'I want to tell you how it is between me and Shaik. Shaik is a friend of mine. You are asking me to tell you that Shaik tried to influence me in the execution of my decision-making powers. I want to tell you that he helped me, he helped me comrade-to-comrade, he helped me in the way a father helps a son.'

In June, as more legal skirmishing continued over the documents in Mauritius, Kemp made a remark that summarised his and Hulley's approach to the case against Zuma – then and afterwards. Asked why Zuma and Thint were fighting so hard against the Scorpions laying their hands on originals of documents that everyone had seen anyway, he said that his client was viewing the whole issue of the Scorpions' 'ongoing investigation' as similar to the battle of Stalingrad – something that needed to be fought house to house, every inch of the way. 'If I can legally stop the Scorpions from getting originals of the documents, then I am going to do that,' Kemp said.

In August the time had come for both sides to get their affidavits and heads of argument into the Supreme Court of Appeal regarding the NPA's appeals against the High Court findings on the search warrants. Zuma, Mahomed and Hulley had already won their High Court battles to have the Scorpions' August 2005 raids on their homes and offices declared unlawful, but had now to fight the state's efforts in the Supreme Court of Appeal in Bloemfontein to have these rulings overturned.

It had been two years since Zuma and his lawyers were raided by 300 black-suited investigators, but Zuma – Kemp said in his papers – was still upset about the 'breathtaking invasion of his privacy'. Kemp argued that Durban High Court Judge Noel Hurt had been correct to find that the warrants were 'hopelessly overbroad'. He pointed out that the warrants enabled the Scorpions to seize 'every document which may assist in locating and tracing [Zuma's] whereabouts, meetings and engagements during this period (1995 to 2005). Thus, if he met and dined with a friend, or had a romantic liaison, documentation evidencing that fact should be seized and scrutinised. This is a breathtaking invasion of privacy and violation of dignity,' Kemp said.

Kemp also seemed less than impressed with the state's justification of its fraud and tax investigation against his client. 'The alleged crime investigated is this: Zuma took bribes from Shaik during various tax years. If Zuma did not declare these as income, he defrauded the fiscus/contravened the Income Tax Act. Hence the National Prosecuting Authority wants to investigate every single financial deal of his in order to establish this,' he said, adding that 'the artificial nature hereof is obvious. What were the prospects that Zuma would, if the monies received were bribes, have declared them as income?' Kemp asked.

Also in August, in their papers regarding the Mauritian documents, the prosecuting authorities wanted Zuma to be censured for his 'scandalous', 'gratuitous' and 'unwarranted' accusations of dishonesty and political engineering against the state. They asked the Supreme Court of Appeal to order that he foot a multimillion-rand legal bill as punishment. Zuma claimed that the state's investigation into possible corruption charges against him was 'engineered' to tarnish his name ahead of the party's elections in December, painting him as a criminal. The state said such claims were 'scurrilous and unmerited'. The counsel for the state – Guido Penzhorn sc, Billy Downer sc and Anton Steynberg – argued that Zuma and Thint's criticism of the state had 'become a constant feature' of their legal battles with the NPA and would continue 'unless the courts intervene'.

'The National Director of Public Prosecutions accepts that, in an open and democratic society, a state institution such as the NPA may legitimately be criticised where the facts warrant this,' they said. 'However, this does not allow an important instrument of our democracy to be gratuitously and unnecessarily scandalised. Such actions unjustifiably bring into disrepute an important organ of government and role-player in the criminal justice system in the eyes of the public.'

Penzhorn and his colleagues further accused Zuma of launching an 'express and implied attack' on Downer's integrity – an attack they said included suggestions he 'stole' the disputed documents. Arguing that two courts previously found Downer's obtaining copies of the 14 disputed documents was 'entirely lawful', counsel questioned whether Zuma 'can honestly continue to believe that criticisms levelled against the state have any merit whatsoever'.

The state claimed its efforts to secure the Mauritian documents were part of the marshalling of evidence it needed before it could decide whether to recharge Zuma and Thint. Two months before, Durban High Court Judge Jan Hugo had granted the NPA an order allowing it to go ahead with its letter of request for the documents to the Mauritian attorney-general. The documents were to be kept 'sealed and under lock and key' by either the High Commissioner of South Africa in Mauritius or by the registrar of the Durban High Court.

When the time came for the actual hearings on the search warrants and the Mauritian documents, the NPA withdrew its case against Julekha Mahomed, once Zuma's attorney. The state attorney wrote to Mahomed's attorney saying he had been instructed by the NDPP 'to concede the appeal with costs', provided the parties involved agreed to certain conditions.

To recap, the search warrants had been used in search and seizure raids conducted by the Scorpions at the end of 2005, before the NPA's case against Zuma was struck off the roll. In fact, one of the reasons Judge Herbert Msimang gave for striking Zuma's corruption case off the roll in the Pietermaritzburg High Court was that the NPA was obviously not ready to prosecute the case. One reason for this was that the 2005 search raids were the subject of the appeals process and the documents seized during them could therefore not be used by the NPA.

The first raid was conducted on the premises of Mahomed, the second on Zuma's premises and those of Hulley, the third at Thint and at the private home of its chief executive, Pierre Moynot.

Following the raids, Mahomed, Zuma and Hulley, and Thint each took the NPA to their respective high courts – Mahomed in Johannesburg, Zuma and Hulley in Durban, and Thint in Pretoria. Mahomed and Zuma and Hulley were successful, so the NPA took them on appeal. Thint was unsuccessful, so it took the NPA on appeal.

The NPA said it would drop the Mahomed matter, provided she agreed to a 'preservation' order, in terms of which all the things seized relating to Zuma be left in the safekeeping of the Witwatersrand Court Registrar until it had been decided whether Zuma would be re-charged.

Zuma went to the SCA for the search warrant appeals. But, as Karyn Maughan reported in *The Star*, he 'might have entered the Supreme Court of Appeal with a spring in his step yesterday, but he left it legally bruised and no longer certain of stalling the State's relentless digging into his financial affairs'.

Three of the Bloemfontein court's senior judges led the charge against Kemp, slamming him for 'vague submissions' which they said had no basis in law. Kemp faced a marathon grilling from Judges Robert Nugent, Ian Farlam and Tom Cloete, who seemed unimpressed with his suggestions that the state might have taken privileged documents when it raided Hulley's offices, potentially resulting in any future case against Zuma being rendered a mistrial. Pointing out that Hulley was an experienced attorney, the judges questioned his claim to the Durban High Court that he had not known that he could refuse to hand the documents over because they might be privileged.

'I must say that I find that incredible,' Judge Farlam said. However, he added that it was to Hulley's credit that he did not claim privilege when he was not sure exactly what documents were contained in the two boxes seized from his office.

The state claimed the disputed documents were simply Zuma's financial records which were once kept by Schabir Shaik. Zuma's legal team had made much of the state's failure, given the claims of attorney-client privilege, to seal the documents and lodge them with the court's registrar. However, the judges took issue with the fact that no one from Zuma's legal team had asked for copies of the disputed documents so they could ascertain which, if any, were in fact privileged.

Closing the state's argument, Wim Trengove sc dismissed the entire debate over the validity of the warrants as being academic. This was because, despite Zuma and his legal team's claims that the warrants used to search them were 'fatally flawed', they had never said they had not understood their terms. They had also never contended that any of the thousands of documents seized fell outside the terms of the warrants and, further, they still did not claim any of the documents were actually privileged.

Should the state fail in its appeal, it asked the court to consider granting an order 'preserving' the documents until their admissibility could be argued at a possible future trial. After Judge Farlam reserved judgment on the hearing, a tired but smiling Zuma made a quick exit from the court to the cheers of a small, yet vocal crowd of supporters outside.

Meanwhile, in the Pretoria High Court, Zuma applied for the setting aside of the application granted to the Scorpions, allowing them to seek international assistance so they could examine documents at the London solicitors of Kögl. In this application, Zuma stuck to his guns that 'political motives' underpinned the state's efforts to investigate him for fraud and corruption.

According to Kemp, the state's purpose in trying to procure the information in London was 'to try to link Zuma to improper payments for purposes of prosecution'. Zuma had previously described himself as 'disturbed' by the state's renewed efforts to investigate him, just months before the ANC was to decide who its next leader would be. Attacking the state's efforts to gather potential evidence against him from both Mauritian and UK authorities, Zuma claimed that the NPA 'wished to engineer a situation whereby [I] would appear as a criminal/accused/ suspect during the crucial period of the latter part of 2007'.

Confronted by Zuma's refusal to back down from his 'vexatious, fictitious and scandalous' claims, the state demanded that the Pretoria High Court throw his allegations out of court and order him to pay its legal bills as punishment. In an earlier response to Zuma's conspiracy claims, Deputy Director of Public Prosecutions Anton Steynberg stressed that the state 'has no interest in Zuma's political ambitions'.

Meanwhile, in a different kind of legal matter, some leaders and other senior members of the ANC-led tripartite alliance said they feared that prosecutions for apartheid-era crimes could be used to hobble those not in President Thabo Mbeki's camp, and that Jacob Zuma in particular might be one of those targeted. Their concerns flowed from the prosecution of Adriaan Vlok, a former minister of Law and Order, and four former policemen for attempting to murder Frank Chikane, the Director-General of the Presidency, in 1989. All five received suspended sentences in exchange for pleading guilty.

Zuma, they pointed out, was working hard to get himself nominated as president of the ANC at the party's national conference in December and, consequently, as the next president of the country. But if Zuma were to be found guilty of a crime for which the sentence would be more than minor, he would not be able to hold public office.

The anxiety of the tripartite leaders surfaced in the wake of an NEC meeting on 27 and 28 July. Insiders claimed that, towards the end of the two-day meeting, Mbeki spoke passionately of the need for there to be a *quid pro quo* on the part of ANC members in response to the Vlok prosecution. Mbeki is believed to have pointed out that the ANC had not chosen 'group indemnity' at the Truth and Reconciliation Commission and that it was therefore possible that some members of the party could be charged by the NPA, which now had the power to charge and to arrange plea bargains for politically related offences committed before 11 May 1994.

The president reportedly said that the ANC had lawyers standing by and that, if any members of the party were charged by the NPA for 'apartheid-era atrocities', they needed to give serious consideration to choosing the option of a plea bargain. Zuma, who attended the NEC meeting but had to leave early for KwaZulu-Natal before Mbeki 'took control of the discussion', had argued that he would never plead guilty to any action he had taken as part of the struggle.

Zuma adherents said that the incident being talked about 'in ANC circles' as one for which Zuma could be prosecuted related to the death in November 1989 of Thami Zulu within a week of his release from detention by ANC security officials. TZ, as we know, was the *nom de guerre* of Muziwakhe Ngwenya, a Soweto-born man who was the commander of the ANC guerrilla campaign in Natal in the 1980s.

'This is not rocket science,' said a lawyer from the Zuma camp. 'The corruption case against Zuma has snagged for the moment. There are even noises emanating from the NPA that they might not charge Zuma, if at all, until next year. So what happens? The hoax e-mail saga comes up and then the Browse Mole report [both had been faked reports implicating Zuma in all kinds of malfeasance, including receiving money from Muammar Gaddafi of Libya]. Those might all be rubbish, and yet Zuma is still connected with them in one way or another and that has an effect on people's minds.

'And then look at the speed with which the Vlok plea bargain was arranged. Incredibly fast for that kind of matter. And then imagine if Zuma were charged in October with murder or being an accessory to murder while he was head of ANC counter-intelligence in Zambia? It would be the end of him.'

Mac Maharaj said he disagreed strongly with this view: 'Although it sounds like the quintessential Mbeki plot, it would be sheer madness for anyone to charge Zuma with a struggle crime. He would become a national hero immediately and would sweep the country before him. He would not split the party – he would take it,' he said.

Another very senior member of the alliance said he believed a list existed of ANC members who could be charged by the NPA, and that Zuma's name was on it. But a highly placed source at the NPA said that, as far as the list and charging Zuma were concerned, he had 'never heard such bullshit in [his] life'.

Whatever the case, since the end of 2007 the NPA has not laid charges against anyone in the ANC leadership for apartheid-era crimes. Concerns were probably symptomatic of the growing unease among senior alliance members with Mbeki and his motives. And, as it happened, much of Mbeki's dirty washing was hung out in the last quarter of 2007.

Among the claims and statements made by Billy Masetlha, the axed Director-General of Intelligence and a well-known Zuma supporter, during his trial in September were that Mbeki and Ronnie Kasrils had conspired against him in an underhand and malicious way simply because Masetlha did not see things the way they did. Mbeki had gone so far as to lie under oath by signing an affidavit he knew to be untrue. And Kasrils flouted the law and blatantly set up Masetlha by, among other things, arranging that his [Kasrils's] legal adviser, Corenza Millard, was part of a group convened by the Inspector-General of Intelligence (IGI) to interrogate Masetlha, although the IGI was required by the intelligence oversight laws to operate independently of the minister or anyone else.

An emotional Masetlha, who told the court that he had worked as a 'trusted ANC cadre' for 28 years, said the worst part of the 'betrayal' was that he really did not know the reasons for it. Masetlha said he could only surmise that the president and Kasrils had 'conspired' against him because he had differed with them over the submission he made on behalf of the National Intelligence Agency to the Khampepe Commission about the Scorpions. Masetlha thought, unlike the president and Kasrils, that the Scorpions should be responsible to the police and not be a 'law unto themselves'. Masetlha was also of the view – again as a result of intelligence investigations – that Zuma was not involved in any plot against anyone.

The evidence that Masetlha gave as background was remarkable.

He painted a picture of a presidency prone at best to legal bungling and, at worst, to lying and malice. Masetlha said he had struggled to get a top secret report to the president. The report had to be shown to the president alone because it cast Kasrils in a very unfavourable light. Masetlha was vague about exactly what the activities were that Kasrils was implicated in, but said that soon after he gave it to the president, he was summoned to Mbeki's residence, where Kasrils was present – and where Kasrils suspended him. Masetlha said he had pointed out to the president that, in terms of the constitution, only the president could suspend the DG of one of the security cluster ministries. And Masetlha read out to the court the letter in which Kasrils suspended him. Later, however, the president had put in an affidavit to the Pretoria High Court, in which he said he [Mbeki] had suspended Masetlha, in contradiction of the facts.

At no time, said Masetlha, had the president or Kasrils explained why they were suspending (and later firing) him. Masetlha said he could not explain to his family what had happened and had felt at times as though his family thought he was not telling the truth.

'But my truth and honesty are all I have. And so I did not accept the payout that was made into my account later, even though I am broke,' Masetlha stated. Later, he said, when he was summoned to a meeting with the IGI, he was amazed to find that Kasrils's legal adviser, Millard, was present. 'The IGI is supposed, in terms of the Intelligence Oversight Act, to investigate independently and reach the truth about issues. Why was Kasrils's person there?' Masetlha asked.

Later, in October, Masetlha was vindicated by the Constitutional Court. Seven of the 10 justices who heard the case, Chief Justice Pius Langa, Deputy Chief Justice Dikgang Moseneke, who wrote the majority judgment, and justices Navsa, Nkabinde, O'Regan, Skweyiya and Van der Westhuizen, found that Mbeki had the constitutional power to terminate Masetlha's contract. But they ruled that Masetlha was entitled to be placed in the financial and 'status' position he would have enjoyed if his contract had not been terminated early. In other words, though Masetlha had been lawfully fired (lawfully, because the president was 'permitted' to do so), he had not been fired because he had breached his contract by doing something wrong or illegal. Consequently, he was entitled to a full and proper payout.

Then, at the end of September, it emerged that Mbeki was going to suspend Pikoli, the National Director of Public Prosecutions. Pikoli's career apparently came to an end because he had insisted on moving against Jackie Selebi, the National Commissioner of Police, for corrupt activities. Pikoli was the fourth 'security official' to be pushed aside under Mbeki's rule. His predecessor, Bulelani Ngcuka, had resigned; Masetlha was suspended and then fired and was contesting his dismissal in court; and ex-SA National Defence Force chief, Siphiwe 'Gebuza' Nyanda, resigned to join the world of business, though many believe he was pushed. Pikoli, it was announced, would be subjected to a commission of inquiry and his deputy, Mokotedi Mpshe, would take over as NDPP.

These events were significant because Mbeki, who had become Zuma's main rival in the succession race, had done some other strange things, which had weakened his position and made even his own supporters wary and jittery.

He had handled the matter of Dr Manto Tshabalala-Msimang, the Minister of Health, badly – supporting her through thick and thin notwithstanding her bizarre comments and behaviour regarding the HIV-AIDS pandemic; and even though it had emerged that she had been caught thieving while a nurse in exile. He had also summarily, and without real explanation, dumped Nozizwe Madlala-Routledge, the Deputy Minister of Health, for 'not being a team player' but in fact for criticising some hospital staff.

In the matter of Masetlha, it suggested a presidency that was growing increasingly paranoid and was deeply sensitive about anyone connected with Zuma; the Pikoli suspension, which would have far-reaching consequences, seemed to demonstrate that Mbeki was interfering directly in the activities of the NPA – which he (and Pikoli) had denied in 2005.

Then, on 2 October 2007, the Constitutional Court turned down Shaik's application for leave to appeal, ruling that there might be a constitutional issue worth appealing related to the seizure of his assets. But for Shaik, the legal road had finally come to a cul-de-sac. It also meant that one of the obstacles standing in the way of the NPA when it came to re-charging Zuma had been removed.

In November the SCA delivered four judgments in which the court found against Zuma (and Hulley and Thint) on the search and seizure warrants and the Mauritian application. The SCA found that the search warrants were not 'over-broad' – the Scorpions were at last free to use the documents seized from Hulley/Zuma and Thint against Zuma and Thint.

Were the judgments major turning points in the floating opera? Did they signify 'the end' for Zuma, just five weeks before the ANC conference? Was his succession bid all over?

To charge Zuma, just before the ANC conference, might bring the country to the point of eruption, with Zuma going to court and saying that his being charged at that point clearly equalled 'conspiracy' and an 'unfair trial', a claim to which any judge would have to listen hard. In addition, Pikoli had been suspended and the Scorpions were in a state of disarray.

Even if Zuma were charged, most ANC delegates to the Polokwane conference were likely to view the SCA judgments as merely another scene from the floating opera. But, still, the clouds were gathering again and political analyst Adam Habib was doubtless correct: never mind global warming, the judgments were going to ratchet up the temperature in the ANC to boiling point.

CHAPTER 15

2007

Siyaya Limpompo!
(We are going to Limpopo!)

As 2006 turned into 2007, it was time to start preparing for the 52nd ANC conference at Polokwane. And, while Zuma and everyone else involved or potentially involved in the forthcoming elections spent a great deal of time denying that they were interested in standing for the ANC presidency, they were busy with little else.

Zuma was quietly planning a campaign with Blade Nzimande of the SACP, Zwelinzima Vavi of Cosatu, Fikile Mbalula of the ANC Youth League, and countless other allies within the 'leadership structures' of the ANC. But, so as not to put the wind up Mbeki's sails, they were keeping it low key. As far as the presidency of the ANC and the country were concerned Zuma would stick throughout the year to the boilerplate response of all ANC leaders that so frustrated the media and public alike. This is perhaps why, in January, Zuma 'angrily' denied that he had discussed the forthcoming December conference, party elections or candidacy with 'tycoon' Tokyo Sexwale.

Zuma's 'office' – Ranjeni Munusamy – issued a statement reacting to what it termed 'continuing media speculation' about discussions between Zuma and Sexwale. Zuma referred to the 'speculation' as a 'gross misrepresentation of the facts' culled from a 'faceless' source. There had been a newspaper report alleging that he had met Sexwale twice in 2006 to discuss the possibility of a Sexwale 'leadership challenge' at the end of 2007. According to the report, Sexwale had told Zuma that he, Sexwale, had heard that Cyril Ramaphosa, pushed out of the party by the Mbeki/Zuma axis some years before, was planning to make a return to politics and that Sexwale hoped Zuma would support him against Ramaphosa. (If the story was accurate, what was Sexwale thinking?)

The media loved these sorts of stories, not only because any ANC election was exciting grist to the media mill (and Polokwane was not going to be just any conference; Mbeki biographer Mark Gevisser would call it 'the most important moment in the movement's history'), but because Zuma was controversial – the ANC leader that everyone in the media loved to hate.

Was he not after all guilty of corruption? It was pretty much assumed by most members of the media that Zuma was deeply implicated along with Shaik in 2005; that Msimang's judgment was some kind of aberration; and that the rest of the floating opera of 2006 was merely Zuma trying to avoid 'having his day in court' – a phrase first used by Mbeki in the 2005 speech in which he fired Zuma and then repeated *ad nauseam* in newspaper editorials whenever Zuma returned to court for whatever reason.

Was Zuma not after all a seducer of young women? Was he not the ultimate in political incorrectness? I mean, really: imagine thinking that because a young woman walks around your home naked except for a wrap that she has the slightest sexual interest in you! Imagine having a shower to avoid contamination by HIV! Was he not an insulter of gay people? Was he not in thrall to that strange, arrogant family of Indians from Durban? Was he not therefore obviously a huge disappointment to good South Africans and card-carrying ANC members? There were countless newspaper editorials and articles, ranging from the hand-wringing ('Woe are we to be faced with the likes of Zuma as ANC president when we once had Mandela') to the contemptuous.

Above all, the media would salivate throughout 2007 – and this salivation would become a fast-flowing stream in the last quarter of 2007 – when it seemed that someone besides Mbeki and Zuma would contest the ANC presidency – people such as Sexwale or Ramaphosa, the latter being the media and 'white liberal' favourite . As a backdrop to the plethora of articles and analyses that appeared in newspapers, wise and considered political writers[1] argued cogently why Zuma would not or should not be elected ANC president. Quite late in the year, at his public presentation of *Thabo Mbeki: The Dream Deferred* in the great hall of Wits University, Gevisser, while stressing that Zuma was a shrewder and more impressive personality than most people seemed to realise, said (rather unnecessarily, it seemed – he was there to talk about Mbeki) that there were 'good reasons' why Zuma should not be elected president of the ANC.

Some well-known political analysts such as Harald Pakendorf had already made up their minds by April: 'One must never confuse noise with influence and neither the masses nor the senior ANC men and women will elect a leader who is a democratic myth,' he said in a *Sunday Independent* article headlined 'Zuma no longer the great contender in the Eastern Cape'.

Even long before the nominations process, which would be in October– November, 'compromise candidates'– so-called because they would keep both Mbeki and Zuma out of the presidency – had been mooted in the media. Ramaphosa and Sexwale were among those named, alongside Kgalema Motlanthe, the Secretary-General, and Zuma's ex-wife, Minister of Foreign Affairs Nkosazana Dlamini-Zuma. Ramaphosa continued to deny that he was interested in the post.

Motlanthe, previously the general secretary of the powerful National Union of Mineworkers, Cosatu's biggest affiliate, had, however, suffered political damage among Mbeki supporters after he appointed an ANC-led task team to investigate a series of 'hoax' e-mails implicating Zuma in all sorts of skulduggery but which Mbeki supporters considered, or pretended to consider, gospel.

Dlamini-Zuma served under Nelson Mandela as health minister. She was well liked, her popularity soaring in 2002 when she took on pharmaceutical companies over affordable medication for the poor. She also instituted compulsory community service for medical students, partly to remedy the lack of physicians in rural areas. She did, however, have egg on her face over the mismanagement of funds in connection with the musical production *Sarafina II*.

A national coordinating committee led by Gauteng finance minister Paul Mashatile and NEC member Enoch Godongwana, supporting Sexwale, was formed soon after his announcement in May 2007 that he would be available for the ANC presidency. By July, the committee had already drawn up a preliminary list of names for other top posts. Among other prominent names linked to the Sexwale campaign were past Minister of Arts and Culture Pallo Jordan, Minister of Safety and Security Charles Nqakula and Minister of Social Development Zola Skweyiya.

In April, Zuma said at the Cape Town Press Club that he would stand for the ANC presidency 'if asked to'.

Before the ANC conference itself, two major events were scheduled for 2007. The first was the ANC's policy conference at the end of June and the second was the choosing of lists by the regional ANC offices in November.

On 27 June Thabo Mbeki delivered the opening address at the policy conference in a bitterly cold Midrand. Fifteen hundred delegates attended the four-day meeting, called to debate how best, in the ANC-speak of party spokesperson Smuts Ngonyama, to 'take forward the ANC's programme of building a better life for all'. But of course it took place against intense behind-the-scenes jockeying over the leadership of the party and coincided with a bitter public service strike.

Though the conference had no decision-making powers, it would set the tone for the impending succession battle. Mbeki admonished alliance partners (largely Zuma backers) for their public attacks on the ANC and for pushing a socialist agenda within the ANC. In February 2007, a draft South African Communist Party document had been leaked to the media laying out future directions for the organisation, such as abandoning its role in the tripartite alliance. Drafted in 2005, the document reflected the tensions that had emerged within Mbeki's presidency because both the SACP and Cosatu had been sidelined in major economic policy decisions.

Providing a framework for the debate were 13 discussion documents that had been widely circulated since early in the year, including the controversial Strategy and Tactics document, setting out the party's political vision and a broad plan of action. The documents were discussed behind closed doors.

An indication of the importance attached to the Strategy and Tactics document was that most of the first day was devoted to discussion of it. It came under heavy fire by the delegates from Cosatu and the SACP who pushed for more radical economic policies and the 'recognition of the working class as the driving force of the revolution'. *Business Day* reported on the opening day of the conference that job creation in South Africa's formal economy slowed sharply in the first quarter of the year, providing ammunition to those who attacked the party's business-friendly policies.

Addressing a pre-conference media briefing, Ngonyama dismissed suggestions that the ongoing public service strike would affect the tone of the conference. But Ngonyama was ever the man for trying to put a shiny gloss on life in the ANC. He did, however, criticise what he said were the 'insults' that had been levelled at 'the leadership of our country' during the strike. 'We can do better in respecting our President and those that we put in positions of responsibility,' Ngonyama opined.

Also on the agenda were a review of the electoral system, the future of the provinces, the desirability of floor-crossing legislation, a restructuring of the hierarchy of the courts to give overall supremacy to the Constitutional Court, and proposals for a review of the structure of the ANC itself. The organisational review document argued for an increase in the size of the party's 60-member National Executive Committee, and called for 'effective regulatory architecture' to improve accountability and transparency in the funding of political parties.

Decisions taken at the policy conference were not binding. They were formulated as 'draft resolutions' to be fed back to individual branches for further debate before the national conference in Limpopo in December.

Of course the matter that produced the most robust discussion was the so-called 'two centres of power' issue: whether it was desirable for the leader of the party and the leader of the country to be different people. In other words, since Mbeki was precluded by the constitution from a third term as president of South Africa, should he stand in December for a third term as president of the ANC? He was permitted to do so, but was it wise? Would it be intelligent for the president of the ANC to be different from the president of the country? The debate pitted provinces such as Eastern Cape, which had already decided it wanted Mbeki back for a third term, against others including KwaZulu-Natal, Free State and Mpumalanga.

The talk of two centres of power was seen by some party provincial structures and the ANC Youth League as a way for Mbeki to hand-pick his successor if he took a third term as party president. Three proposals were made to change the leadership election. These were made by pro-Zuma provincial delegates – all three seeking to curb the two centres of power that would emerge should Mbeki take a third term at the ANC's helm. The three would have limited Mbeki's chances and required changes to the organisations. In the end, a compromise was reached in a unanimous decision that the ANC president, whoever he or she might be, should ideally be the party's candidate in the national race.

A number of delegates 'advised' Mbeki not to stand in December and officially the ANC as a whole resolved that it would be 'preferable' that its leader also be the country's president – but it did not deny Mbeki the right to stand again for ANC president. And, by the end of the weekend, Mbeki announced that he would make himself available for a third term as ANC leader 'if asked'.

The *Sunday Times* reported that Mbeki, despite overwhelming opposition from delegates, had insisted that he should stand for a third term as ANC president. But the ANC head office responded that the newspaper report was 'wholly and deliberately fabricated'. And then there was a deafening silence.

This report, reaction and ensuing silence were an indication of an interesting phenomenon. It had started becoming apparent that, while a few key ANC members spoke to the media, and that while of course the ANC mandarins read, listened and reacted to the media, 'ordinary' ANC members seemed not to give a damn about newspapers, in particular. An abyss seemed to have opened up between newspapers and ANC delegates – with the effect that newspapers could report what they liked while the 'real action', the true thoughts and views of the ANC man or woman in the street (at delegate level, anyway, and particularly dissident ones – Zuma supporters, for example), remained secret. The result of this was that the public did not really know what was going on in the proverbial hearts and minds of the majority of the ANC delegates. This 'trend' seemed to be the result of a sense among people that the newspapers said what they wanted to say willy-nilly, with little interest in what the people with the ANC vote thought, and also the fact that many ANC people do not in any case trust the newspapers: in the opinion of Ronald Suresh Roberts, 'Selling no more than 600 000 copies to a predominantly privileged readership in a country of 50 million people, most of whom are black and poor and get mainly the radio news, the print media remains resoundingly elitist, as the ANC website pointed out in a multipart-series on the 'Sociology of Public Discourse'.

Ebrahim Fakir of the Centre for Policy Studies said: 'The fact that Mbeki has made himself available is a good thing. He is following Sexwale.' What Fakir seemed to be saying was that at least the succession battle was coming into the open; up till then the only indication that there was such a battle had been Sexwale saying that he had been lobbied by ANC comrades to throw his hat into the ring. According to Adam Habib, then of the Human Sciences Research Council, 'Both sides [the Mbeki and Zuma camps] are not strong enough to impose their will. They are beginning to explore other options.' Susan Booysen of Wits University described the ANC's resolution as a compromise. She said it was what the Mbeki camp had hoped for. 'The alternative was for the guillotine to come down on Mbeki's head,' she said. Cape ANC provincial secretary Mcebisi Skwatsha said: 'If the president avails himself for the third time, it's fine. But we stand by the decision of the general council … that the new ANC president should also be the country's next presidential candidate.'

Meanwhile, Mosiuoa 'Terror' Lekota, the ANC's national chairman, launched an attack on people who sang songs such as *'Awuleth' mashini wami'* (now, who might that be?). First popularised as a struggle song by MK during the apartheid years, it had made a comeback during Zuma's rape trial and had become his trademark song. In the weeks before Polokwane, many walls in Johannesburg's inner city were plastered with posters advertising a recently released CD, 'Zuma for President,' on which *'Umshini'* was a main feature.

Lekota said that only people 'not right in their heads' chanted such a song. Instead of chanting irrelevant struggle songs, 'comrades' should sing songs about the current socio-economic challenges, he said. His comments unleashed a barrage of demands for a retraction and an apology from the Communist Party, Cosatu, the ANC Youth League and the Young Communist League. Lekota refused to apologise, or to say anything at all. Cosatu upped the anti-Mbeki and pro-Zuma ante at a Johannesburg meeting – the inaugural national conference of the Creative Workers' Union – at which Zwelinzima Vavi said: 'The SABC is showing clear signs of returning to its previous role as a broadcaster for the state, not the public. Increasingly, our government and the SABC talk about controlling and limiting what the public broadcaster can or should convey to our people.'

Vavi said it had become clear that one of the biggest threats facing the nation was 'the unwillingness of the state to accept criticism and support independent culture'. He made his remarks a day after it became known that Jacques Pauw had resigned from the SABC. Pauw said he had quit because he had lost confidence in the organisation's leadership. He cited the SABC's withdrawal from the South African National Editors' Forum (Sanef) as 'the last straw'. The brouhaha had followed in the wake of a letter by Dali Mpofu, the SABC's group chief executive officer and editor-in-chief, to Jovial Rantao, Sanef's chairman, in which Mpofu charged that the media had behaved shamefully in their reporting of the theft conviction and alleged propensity for alcoholic beverages of Manto Tshabalala-Msimang, the Minister of Health.

Mpofu's letter to Rantao was revealed by Mpofu on the same day that Mbeki wrote in his weekly online letter that anyone who questioned Tshabalala-Msimang's behaviour showed a singular lack of respect and was lacking in *ubuntu*. Mbeki also said that those who had asked whether the minister had 'jumped the queue' in getting a liver from a donor for her transplant in March clearly had wished death on her.

Vavi also lambasted people who failed to understand that the struggle songs of the people 'do not have a sell-by date'. 'When we sing *Umshini wami*, we express our memories of our past struggles. It gives those of us who still have a reason to struggle an inspiration to struggle on … Perhaps others have arrived in the Promised Land, but the working class and the poor have yet to make it there,' he said.

In October, a memorandum was leaked by someone in the Scorpions to the *Sunday Independent* and the *Sunday Times*. Though not much of a fuss was made of it at the time, it would figure significantly later as an embarrassment to the DSO. It seemed the bosses had discussed how best to 'spin' the ANC. The meeting took place in June and was chaired by Leonard McCarthy, the deputy NDPP. He told those present that they needed to think of ways in which a resolution taken at the ANC's policy conference – that the Scorpions should 'reside' in the South African Police Service and not in the justice department – should be 'dealt with' so that the Scorpions could remain where they had always been.

McCarthy told the 12 top members of the Scorpions that all of them, including himself, had to put on their thinking caps because the 'problem' that the resolution presented needed to be dealt with before the ANC national conference in December. McCarthy said four matters in particular were 'problematic' for the DSO because the public thought of them as examples of its 'targeting and prosecution of high-profile individuals': the

'Zuma matter', the 'Mac Maharaj matter', the 'Ramatlhodi matter' and the 'Bad Guys matter (Agliotti/Kebble)'. And he invited his colleagues to express their opinions on how the four issues could be 'handled' so as to undermine the resolution and to ensure, instead, 'that the status quo [in terms of which the DSO resides within the justice department] remains'. According to a source, the minutes were leaked because the 'team spirit' at the NPA had come under pressure after the suspension of Pikoli by Mbeki. The suggestions debated during the meeting were aimed at influencing the ANC resolution by enhancing the DSO's reputation and thereby weakening perceptions that the DSO was power-arrogant. These included: going back to the so-called 'Hollywood style', to show the public that the DSO was still alive and kicking; exploring other publicity exercises to sell the DSO to the public, government and business; identifying politicians and business executives who were 'favourable' to the DSO and trying to influence them; and possibly mounting a legal challenge to the recommendations of the Khampepe Commission, which had recommended that the Scorpions be disbanded and subsumed by the SA Police Services.

In late October, Norman Mashabane, who had lost his job as a diplomat for being a 'sex pest' and had been killed in a car accident, was buried in the small town of Phalaborwa. The funeral turned out to be a worry for the ANC's old guard. As *Sunday Times* editor Mondli Makhanya wrote, it was bound to be a showdown: 'According to those that were there, it was clear from the start who was in control. It was Ngoako Ramatlhodi, Billy Masetlha, Jacob Zuma, Zwelinzima Vavi and other members of the "coalition of the wounded"… But nobody would have foreseen the unseemly scenes that would break out later on. At no point would anyone have predicted that [Selo] Moloto – premier and ANC provincial chair – would be booed and heckled by the people he leads. Nor that Mbeki supporters would respond in like fashion when ANC Youth League leader Fikile Mbalula got up to speak.[3]

Zuma faced his own share of opposition, but conducted himself as coolly as the proverbial cucumber. Addressing a meeting in Eastern Cape in November, on a hot and dusty Sunday, he was confronted by a fractious crowd of about 800, of whom half were staunch Mbeki supporters and wouldn't let him start his speech until they had finished singing 'Mbeki for President'. After waiting for them to finish, he delivered a 40-minute speech in isiXhosa and English about the celebration of the 63rd anniversary of the ANC Youth League and the ANC in general. 'We carry the future of this country and it will be the responsibility of the people who will meet in Limpopo to exercise their rights as members of the ANC.'

One side of the stadium's bleachers was full of Mbeki supporters, carrying placards that read 'Mbeki for President'. The other side was full of Zuma supporters dressed in T-shirts that read '100 percent' above a picture of Zuma. On the back were the words 'Innocent until proven guilty'. These T-shirts had supposedly been banned at ANC meetings – Lekota had complained about them as well.

When half the crowd started chanting and singing 'Zuma for Limpopo', Zuma responded with *Awuleth' mashini wami.* The President of the Youth League, Fikile Mbalula said: 'The Youth League has made it clear that no one but JZ should be president of the ANC.'

At the end of November, less than a month before Polokwane, I went to visit Zuma at home. *Sunday Independent* photographer TJ Lemon and I went to take – not tea, but *umqombothi*, fermented sorghum beer, and to eat *nyama* (meat) with Jacob Zuma and two of the four official Mrs Zumas.

We had travelled about two-and-a-half hours north and inland of Durban to Zuma's rural retreat in Nxamalala, in the Nkandla district of deep KwaZulu-Natal. Of the Mrs Zumas, we met only Nompumelelo Ntuli Zuma, Zuma's jolly fourth wife, but we managed to spend a few hours with Zuma.

'Let's pretend for a moment,' I said to Zuma, 'completely hypothetically, of course, that by 21 December you are the new president of the ANC: What would be the first thing you would do?'

But it was no use.

Relaxing for a moment in a chair in the sun, in a 'Madiba' shirt, dark trousers and new white running shoes, Zuma was already smiling by the time I reached the word 'hypothetically'. He knew what was coming and was not going to react to my feeble attempt at provoking him into stating clearly that he believed he was going to be the next ANC president.

'I am not going to talk about the December conference or the ANC presidential succession battle,' Zuma said. 'This is not a matter for the media. It's an ANC matter. So it's no use asking me. What is there to say at this point that would be of any use? What will take place will take place, and we will see what we will see.' But as uMsholozi said this he was grinning very broadly indeed, and closely resembled the proverbial cat that ate the cream – or the hungry herd boy who ate the *nyama* and drank the beer.

Zuma knew as well as I, if not better, that SMSS had been coming in all day to the cell phone of one of his five sons, Edward, and that each message signified that yet another grouping or person had indicated that it, he or she would be voting at the ANC December conference in Polokwane for Zuma to be the organisation's next president.

'As far as Zuma is concerned,' one member of his camp had said to me the day before in Durban, 'this is a one-horse race. The numbers coming in show that Zuma's going to take it. And I don't think he's interested in compromises. Some provinces are not going to state that he's their choice outright [they are too fearful] but you'll see what happens on voting day. I believe that about 80 per cent of the voting ANC delegates are Cosatu members. Do you have any more questions?'

Zuma would also not discuss the charges of corruption, money-laundering and tax evasion that are reportedly to be brought against him. But members of his legal team in Durban said that, contrary to newspaper accounts, the National Prosecuting Authority had given no sign that it would lay charges against Zuma before the end of the year. (They were wrong, of course – but let's not get ahead of ourselves.) Zuma was due to leave South Africa to attend a wedding in India and travel to a number of foreign capitals. He would not be back for about 10 days. But no one had suggested to his legal representatives that he should not travel, or specified when he should return.

Zuma would also not say much about the fracas that allegedly took place between him and Lekota at the previous Sunday's meeting of the party's NEC. Lekota was said to have publicly upbraided Zuma for running, contrary to ANC practice, a 'visible' campaign for the presidency. He also criticised him for the '100 percent Jacob Zuma' T-shirts worn by many at ANC rallies.

'What's to say?' Zuma asked rhetorically. 'This fellow's been saying the same thing for months.' He shrugged his shoulders.

'Are you not even a bit nervous?' I asked, trying again to get some indication about where he believed he was positioned for the December vote.

'Nervousness and I are not good friends,' replied Zuma, repeating a favourite line of his and smiling again.

Then, shifting the conversation, he gestured expansively around him – pointing to the group of thatched rondavels and the kraal that are his Nkandla home, and at the mountains, the lush vegetation and the Mome Gorge, which runs through the Nkandla district.

It was in the gorge, in April 1906, that Bhambatha and his followers, who had been hiding in the Nkandla forest, were killed by an English expeditionary force. This put an end to the Bhambatha rebellion but also marked 'the beginning of the armed struggle against apartheid', or so Zuma likes to portray the event.

Zuma said that his political consciousness began when, as a child, he was told stories by his parents, grandparents and other elders about the Bhambatha revolt. 'I've walked all over this area because that's what the old people told me to do. You know, I always did what I was asked to do.'

'Just as you have in the ANC?' I asked. 'That's true, actually,' replied Zuma, laughing. Zuma likes to laugh. 'Like me in the party. But look around you. What a wonderful and beautiful place this is. And the people are so friendly. Can you blame me for liking to come here?'

In the kraal, close to where Zuma was sitting, a cow had been slaughtered and Zuma family members were cutting it up and handing meat to the men of Nkandla village and other guests who had congregated in a corner of the kraal. There was no particular reason for the celebration, Zuma said, other than to give thanks and to propitiate the ancestors.

'This is where I regenerate and reconnect. This is where I come back to myself. This is a particularly Zulu environment and yet this is where I become a South African. If I become too high-flying, this is the place that puts me back on my feet.'

Though Lemon and I arrived at Zuma's Nkandla homestead at about noon, it took about four hours before I could have a private – or, rather, semi-private – chat with Zuma. That was because, in Nkandla, no less than in Johannesburg, there is a seemingly endless river of people waiting to talk to him. They are of all sorts, ranging from clearly down-and-out villagers to foreign business people, and all want to discuss something or other – from a new sanitation scheme to a manufacturing project. Zuma gives them all the time of day, and more.

Watching him move from rondavel to rondavel is like being in a medieval kingdom, watching suppliants appearing before the local lord to ask for favours. Having removed the suppliants' cell phones, Zuma's aides deposit each person or group in a different rondavel for the meeting with the great man.

Zuma is a face-to-face person; he's not that interested in e-mails or documents. He does a fair bit of communicating by telephone but, as far as he is concerned, if you want to talk, you do it seated opposite him. Even when relaxing, which is what he was supposed to be doing at Nkandla, he continued with a punishing schedule of meetings – playing, in between, with Thandisiwe, one of his youngest children. He took time to explain to me what I should say when accepting the meat, a choice bit of the slaughtered animal, proffered on a wooden platter.

'You have to say: "Hau! This is not horse" to indicate that you know that you are being offered the finest meat and that we here are not like some of the highlanders upcountry who are forced to eat horse.'

Some issues can unsettle Zuma's bonhomie. He becomes irritated if he feels he has been misquoted. When I remark in passing that some newspapers have reported that he once said that he 'wanted his day in court', he rounded on me swiftly.

'I never said that. That was someone else. I said: "In my case, let justice takes its course." And that's all. I never said anything about wanting any days in court. That's rubbish.'

He also took issue with me when he thought I was criticising the ANC. 'The party has behaved impeccably throughout my saga,' he said. '[But] the behaviour of the National Prosecuting Authority and the government, since I was investigated regarding the Arms Deal, has been deeply questionable. That is why there is divisiveness in the party at the moment. But the party itself has behaved as it should have behaved.'

In the living room of the rondavel of Sizakele Zuma, Zuma's first wife, there are a number of pictures and other mementos hanging on the wall. One, framed and decorated with roses, reads: 'I wish a long life to my enemies so that they may see all my successes.'

Politically speaking, Zuma was going to Polokwane for the ruling party's national conference in December confident that he had the presidency of the ANC in the bag. Knowing that it is always dangerous to count one's chickens before they have hatched, and that it was frowned upon in the ANC to campaign openly, Zuma was not saying an overt word about the matter, but his broad smile and relaxed attitude were easy to read.

Zuma mentioned a number of issues that he had been discussing with ANC members while criss-crossing the country in recent months to attend meetings and rallies. He was due to leave the country for about 10 days. Was he was not nervous about being away when the outcome of the official nominations from the provinces would be announced?

'All the talking that needs to be done has been done. There is nothing further required now,' he replied.

Around Zuma at Nkandla there was talk of little besides the succession battle. His aides and family members oozed confidence about his support base.

'Whatever the official nominations are going to be,' said Edward Zuma, the son born to Zuma and Minah Shongwe, sister of Judge Jeremiah Shongwe, 'you can be sure that there will be tons of horse trading in Polokwane in December. This is just the beginning of the fun.'

Zuma said that one of the issues troubling him was that 'somehow we in the ANC have messed up when it comes to the rural areas. It's places like this, Nkandla, and others that we have not reached, and we should have.'

Zuma said that one group of the steady flow of people who had come to consult him at Nkandla had presented 'a really exciting sewerage project. Some modern technology is truly amazing – and the river pollution in this area, for example, is a serious problem from many points of view. That's just one of the things we need to take care of in the future.

'Someone needs to ask the National Director of Public Prosecutions how much money has been spent on investigating and prosecuting my father,' chimed in Edward, 'including the cost of my father's defence, which is [being] borne by the state. The cost must be in the millions by now. Then compare that cost to the amount of money my father was alleged to have wanted as a bribe – R500 000 – and consider what could have been done with the wasted money in an area like this. Look at that broken-down school over there on the hill. Some of the money could have gone to fixing it up.'

Zuma said that 'clearly' something also had to be done about the lives, and especially the housing needs, of the urban poor. 'Not everyone can grow up in a rural environment like this. Many of our people are already in the city and have been there for a while. But why does a boy who grows up in Houghton perform so differently from one who grows up in a poor part of Soweto? It's not the city itself that is the problem. It's the immediate environment in which the Soweto boy grows up that's the problem. Those single-storey matchbox houses, with everyone living on top of one another … we have to find viable alternatives. What's wrong with decent buildings of flats?' he asked.

On Monday 26 November, according to *The Star*, 'ANC President Thabo Mbeki and his lobbyists were humiliated on Sunday, as the majority of the ruling party's provinces and branch delegates said no to a third term for Mbeki and an overwhelming yes to Jacob Zuma.'

With the last of the votes for ANC presidential nominations filtering in on Sunday, it was clear that in terms of overall head count and provincial support, Zuma was streets ahead, and that the rank-and-file wanted change. According to unverified results, Zuma had mustered a total of 2 236 votes (842 votes more than Mbeki's 1 394), and his lobbyists were quick to urge the president to throw in the towel.

Still, hurdles for Zuma along the way to the final Polokwane vote included a possible corruption charge; a heightened campaign by Mbeki's lobbyists; fickle voters swayed by patronage; and behind-the-scenes horse-trading.

Mbeki bagged four provinces with relatively modest margins (Eastern Cape, Limpopo, North West and Western Cape), while Zuma comfortably led the pack in the remaining five provinces. The tally excluded figures from the ANC Youth League, earmarked for Zuma, and possible Women's League support for Mbeki, as well as votes from the NEC delegates who would cast secret ballots at Polokwane.

Voting delegates from the NEC, Women's League, Youth League, and so on totalled 400, as opposed to 3 675 branch voters. Among the last votes in on the Sunday were those from Gauteng, with 262 to Zuma and 94 for Mbeki.

Zuma was not at home for his successes; he had gone off to India, Los Angeles and London. Mbeki returned from the Commonwealth Heads of Government Meeting in Kampala, Uganda, and flew into Zuma's heartland, where he was embarrassingly thrashed by 508 votes to nine. He had gone to Durban for the World Cup draw. However, Mbeki's lobbyists, particularly in the party's Eastern Cape stronghold, were not talking compromise or considering calls for their man to withdraw.

Mbeki's allies also appeared to feel the backlash. Former Northern Cape premier Manne Dipico and his successor, Dipuo Peters, were among those axed from the province's NEC nomination list. And in KwaZulu-Natal, another Mbeki ally, Premier S'bu Ndebele, narrowly escaped embarrassment when the provincial ANC leadership moved to block a popular motion to remove him from the NEC list. The big shock in the Free State came when Lekota was defeated in every position for which he was nominated. He was a candidate for deputy president, chairperson and secretary-general, but garnered only five, four and 49 votes for these positions. For the deputy president's position, the province nominated Kgalema Motlanthe with 295 votes. For the party chair, Nkosazana Dlamini-Zuma gained the nomination with 305 votes, and for the position of secretary-general, South African Communist Party national chair Gwede Mantashe was nominated with 292 votes.

Earlier, the KwaZulu-Natal provincial governing council voted overwhelmingly to remove ANC strategist Joel Netshitenzhe and Justice Minister Brigitte Mabandla from the list and replaced them with former deputy health minister Nozizwe Madlala-Routledge and former MP Ruth Bhengu.

Independent political analyst Lawrence Schlemmer said the results were a 'serious indication' of how things would go in Polokwane. 'There's a rough rule that applies: If your branch has decided, by a majority vote, the candidates who should be favoured, people ... are under an obligation to carry that particular preference through to their final vote. It exercises ... considerable leverage on the preferences of individuals. I wouldn't say it's necessarily a good, hard indication [of how ANC delegates will vote in Polokwane], but I'd say it was a serious [one] ... it's a serious indication, is how I would see it,' he said.

But Mbeki decided to fight back. His supporters and strategists held a series of meetings across the country at which they discussed how to respond to his humiliating setback at the provincial conferences at the weekend. It was announced in the *Mail & Guardian* that a campaign to 'set the record straight about Jacob Zuma' was central to a fight-back plan by Mbeki's strategists. The campaign was allegedly set to 'resurrect Zuma's links with fraud convict' Schabir Shaik and Zuma's 'controversial' rape trial.

Lekota told the *Mail & Guardian* that the Mbeki camp had decided the 'truth must come out' about Zuma. In particular, Zuma's claims to be a victim of a conspiracy had to be laid to rest: 'The disinformation that is being spread needs to be stopped and the correct information needs to be put out,' he said.

Lekota said Zuma went 'behind the backs of his comrades' in becoming involved with Shaik's company Nkobi Holdings, after the ANC decided not to buy shares in the firm. 'When Schabir was arrested, it was the first time it came to light that Zuma had a shareholding in Nkobi. Now they say he was sent to Nkobi Holdings to get arrested. We are telling people that he went there on his own.' He said Polokwane delegates would be told the truth about Zuma because 'we are not prepared to sacrifice the ANC for the sake of one man'.

Thus far, the ANC deputy president had been 'protected' by the party, Lekota said. 'We have reached a point where we cannot keep quiet any more. He must face up to what he did. Before now we had to keep to party discipline, but if we don't expose this man, [delegates] will not change their votes.' Delegates would also be reminded of how Mbeki and Zuma were once as close as 'tongue and saliva' and that Zuma had served as 'executioner' when Lekota was fired as Free State premier. 'How can he now claim to be a victim?'

Mbeki supporters would also explain that the suspensions of spy boss Billy Masetlha and prosecutions chief Vusi Pikoli were not an ANC matter and 'are being dealt with'.

Boosted by claims of irregularities at some of the provincial conferences, the Mbeki camp, according to the *Mail & Guardian*, remained confident of a turnaround at Polokwane. According to official figures, more than 300 delegates nationwide did not turn up for the conferences, meaning that these votes were still up for grabs.

'It's like guerrilla warfare now. A lot of comrades are keeping their real vote close to their chests to ensure an ambush at conference,' said an unidentified Mbeki lobbyist, who believed 'substantial' gains would be made in Polokwane. 'The Zuma camp will go to Polokwane lulled into a false sense of security. It is at the conference that some delegates will reveal themselves. A deal will be brokered. It has happened before.'

With a fortnight to go, senior figures from both the Mbeki and Zuma camps lashed out; and the ANC's top brass were set to hear claims of vote-buying and other irregularities. Lekota confirmed that the NEC was preparing to meet to make final plans for the Polokwane conference.

The timing of the meeting was significant, with the ANC's electoral commission due to release the collated leadership nominations lists. There was speculation also that the National Prosecuting Authority might be ready to make a final decision on several high-profile investigations, including reopening corruption charges against Zuma.

However, in the tradition of the ANC, and especially given the decision by the ANC executive that the run-up to the Polokwane conference should not be seen by the public to be nasty, the contenders stepped out of the ring and sent in their seconds to do the punching. In the case of Mbeki, this was Lekota; in Zuma's corner, the fighter was Zweli Mkhize, the MEC for finance in KwaZulu-Natal and Zuma's friend and confidant.

Lekota – whom one of Zuma's aides described as having 'an indecent obsession with Zuma' – was the first into the ring when he accused Zuma of having asked to be fired from the Cabinet in June 2005. Zuma had therefore behaved disingenuously by later claiming that there was a 'conspiracy' against him, he said. Zuma had also effectively lied about Mbeki and the party by claiming there had been such a conspiracy.

Zuma said from London that he was not going to comment on Lekota's 'nonsense' until he returned in the next few days: Mkhize was handling the matter. Mkhize, also a member of the NEC, hit back: it was untrue that Zuma had requested to be relieved of his position as the country's deputy president, and that he had shares in any of Shaik's companies. Lekota had been cautioned during the last NEC meeting to desist from intemperate, public attacks on the ANC deputy president, Mkhize said, yet he persisted in carrying on with them. Mkhize demanded to see or hear what proof Lekota had for any of the claims he had made, and he also believed that 'the leaders of our movement must call the chairperson to order and consider disciplinary action against him'.

In an interview given to SABC on 27 November, Mbeki vowed to continue campaigning for a third term as ANC president. The party's wishes, and not personal ambition, he said, were the paramount factor in his decision; in other words, in the Mbeki camp, no one else could be found whom they believed could defeat Zuma. Sexwale and Ramaphosa, besides not being in the Mbeki camp, had clearly dropped out of the running – not that Ramaphosa had ever truly been in, once he had seen which way the wind was blowing; he was too smart for that.

'Shock' might be too strong a word, but many people were definitely very surprised when they discovered that ANC members had overwhelmingly nominated Zuma as their next president. Remarkably, it was members of the media, both print and electronic, as well some political analysts – the very people who were supposed to know what was going on and to tell society about it – who seemed the most flabbergasted by the 'surprising' turn of events.

But why did these results come as such a surprise to so many analysts, editors and political journalists? Why did they not foresee the depth of Zuma's support – or, depending on how you want to see it, the depth of the desire for Mbeki to move on? According to Anton Harber, professor of journalism at Wits University, the answer was pretty straightforward: 'Too much speculation by journalists, not enough legwork. Reporting, he said, 'was largely reduced to carrying claims and counter-claims from each side, and providing a channel for leaks, instead of trying to find out what was happening at branch level in the ANC. It should have been clear, since the National Executive Council meeting, when Zuma was reinstated as party deputy president, that Mbeki was in trouble. But you also have to keep in mind that this is all new to us – journalists are only now learning how the ANC process works, how we have to understand it and what it will take to cover these things properly.'

Patrick Laurence admitted that he had 'assumed much too readily that Mbeki was the master of the political manoeuvre – remember when he outfoxed Cyril Ramaphosa and Tokyo Sexwale in 2001? So I assumed his political invincibility. And the media clearly did not talk to the people to whom they ought to have been talking – ANC branch-level members. So there was simply insufficient empirical evidence for our prognostications ... I think too few whites have an understanding of grass-roots black people, and black journalists don't seem to bother with them either. So there was no understanding coming out in the media of what the people in the townships were thinking.'

There was another important factor, Laurence added, that played a significant role in the media's misreading of Zuma's support: 'I think this applied especially to white journalists – but, then again, black journalists did not seem to operate differently. It was a kind of shutting of the mind to the possibility of a Zuma presidency. For many whites, and apparently for many black media people as well, the idea of Zuma as president was – to quote John Vorster, unfortunately – just "too ghastly to contemplate".'

Remember that Zuma was badly tainted, initially – in the days when Bulelani Ngcuka was NDPP – by the corruption allegations levelled at him. Also – again, perhaps, in the eyes of whites more than of others – Zuma was perceived to have made a fool of himself by the things he said during his rape trial.

'People forgot, or did not even know,' Laurence said, 'that Zuma might not have an impressive formal education, but he is astute and perceptive. Finally, there was not a full appreciation of the *gatvol* factor among ANC members with regard to Mbeki. Mbeki does appear to be disdainful and aloof – a representative of the patrician classes, if you like – whereas Zuma has made certain that he has remained a man of the people.'

Chris Whitfield, the editor of the *Cape Argus*, said he did not entirely agree that the media had got it wrong. 'Sure, I suppose there was some wishful thinking in the media – they did not want Zuma to win so they couldn't see, in a way, what was happening in the ANC. But our Mbeki sources kept telling us that Mbeki was going to walk it – that he was going to thrash Zuma in the nominations. So it wasn't so much that we, the media, got it wrong, as that the Mbeki camp did.'

Moe Shaik said: 'Journalists never, never understood the enormous fury that swept through ANC members when Mbeki fired JZ. Journalists did not understand how difficult and painful that was for the ANC rank and file. I think the media also missed the depth of JZ's support, because they spent too much time analysing their own fears and prejudices. They were too busy with their own worries about "what will happen if JZ becomes president?" when they ought to have been talking to people in the branches a long time ago. Journalists were talking to themselves.'

Not everyone readily agreed that the media had called the succession battle incorrectly. Adam Habib said he was not at all surprised by the Zuma ascendancy. He maintained, however, that the battle was far from over. He believed there was a strong possibility that a compromise deal would be struck between the party's head honchos, Zuma and Mbeki, in terms of which someone else would take control of the party and the country, 'with the quid pro quo being that the charges against Zuma are going to disappear'.

Mark Gevisser said he had not been taken aback by the result, 'though I must concede that I was gob-smacked by the Women's League coming out in support of Zuma'. He conceded that the Mbeki camp had been 'too confident', and that 'there might also have been a lot of wishful thinking among the commentators. I think many people hoped that there would be two equally balanced forces in the end, and that this would lead to a situation in which there could be a "third way", another candidate. But that isn't what's happened.'

Nkosazana Dlamini-Zuma joined the Mbeki camp after receiving a nomination for deputy president – this came after the Mbeki camp said that gender parity was ANC policy. Vavi dismissed the call for 50–50 gender parity, saying it was merely a ploy by 'womanisers' to further their interests. This was presumably a reference to Mbeki who had been known as quite a swordsman up until the mid-2000s – and Vavi yet again caused a great deal of consternation.

Winnie Madikizela-Mandela made a return to the limelight. She drafted a 'status quo' solution in an effort to save party face and end the rift, proposing Mbeki stay on as ANC president and Zuma as deputy president. She was silent on the issue of the 2009 national presidency for neutrality's sake, she said.

Mbeki kept trying to win back some attention – apparently from the ANC delegates – but it was feeble stuff. In early December, he told the *Sunday Times* that he did not remember Zuma's firing the way Zuma did, and that in 2005 he had proposed a commission into the alleged 'conspiracy' against Zuma after Zuma had brought his concerns to him.

And he asked in an interview with the *Mail & Guardian* whether it looked as though he had horns. But overall Mbeki's reaction to the nominations was strangely muted. He appeared to be someone sleep-walking into a disaster.

Polokwane on a baking Saturday afternoon was waiting for the summer rains – but 15 December brought 4 000 ANC delegates and another 2 000 observers, diplomats, political analysts, and international and local media people flooding into the Limpopo capital.

By 3 pm the line of cars waiting to enter the precinct of Gateway, Polokwane's international airport, where a hangar was being used for registration, was 500 metres long. The precinct was packed with groups of delegates moving around and singing. Many of them wore Jacob Zuma T-shirts even though these were supposedly banned by the NEC.

Around the Turfloop campus of Limpopo University in Mankweng, 30 km east of Polokwane, where the conference was being held, there were numerous roadblocks manned by scores of policemen. In the city centre, delegates mixed with locals doing Christmas shopping, leading to long queues at several stores. But most of the action remained at the registration centre at the airport, where Zuma supporters proudly declared their allegiance to their hero. 'I am 100% Zuma,' said one.

Lekota received only a feeble '*awethu*' to his shout of '*amandla*' as he entered the registration hall. His traditional raised-arm salute was also largely ignored by groups of delegates. Health Minister Manto Tshabalala-Msimang wore a bright orange T-shirt declaring that she was strengthened by vitamins and minerals.

In one Polokwane street there were two signs reading 'ANC registration this way'. But each pointed a different way: one towards Thabo Mbeki Street, the other in the opposite direction.

CHAPTER 16

2007–2008

The Zuma tsunami

Right from the start, on Sunday morning, 16 December 2007, the chairman of the ANC, Mosiuoa 'Terror' Lekota, never stood a chance. He would shout a rousing '*amandla*', clearly expecting an '*awethu*' in response. But the 4 000 delegates, or what seemed like most of them, simply went on singing '*Awuleth' mashini wami*', Jacob Zuma's trademark song, and waving placards with Zuma's picture on them. They were doing it on purpose because it had been only a couple of months before that Lekota had complained bitterly about Zuma singing the struggle song.

Trying to quiet down the crowd and grasp their attention, Lekota shouted '*amandla*' even more loudly and firmly. But the delegates at the ANC's 52nd annual conference weren't having any of that. They sang 'Bring me my machine gun' even more loudly, at least four or five times.

The delegates effectively shut Lekota out of the conference that he was supposed to be chairing and leading. The ANC's leaders, including those at the front table on the stage – Thabo Mbeki, Zuma, Secretary-

General Kgalema Motlanthe, Treasurer-General Mendi Msimang and Deputy Secretary-General Sankie Mthembi-Mahanyele looked sombre and seemed flummoxed. Even Zuma, who appeared extremely tense – his facial muscles were bunched like a fist – did not smile at the singing of 'his' song.

It got worse. When Lekota showed he was irritated and growing angry, the crowd stood up and made the signal of soccer fans when they want one player substituted for another – they bicycled their arms around and around in the air. It was also said to be the sign of 'the Zuma tsunami'. The delegates were telling Lekota in no uncertain terms that they wanted 'change' – that it was time for him and others to go.

Lekota had not even left his starting blocks. He still needed to have the conference programme and rules adopted by the conference. But he was never allowed to move beyond calling for a proposer – when he would be interrupted. The delegates fell silent only when Motlanthe came to the podium.

The stifling heat in the gigantic marquee on the Turfloop campus of the University of Limpopo did not help much. But, whatever the weather, it was clear that an overwhelming number of the delegates had come to the conference unwilling to concede an inch to those perceived as Mbeki supporters or as being against Zuma. Large blocs of delegates, those from the provinces that nominated Zuma for the ANC presidency, behaved truculently. They waited for the 'top table' to walk into the hall, and as the video cameraman focused on individual NEC members and their faces flashed on to the big screen, those leaders aligned to Mbeki were roundly booed. Those allied to Zuma received loud applause.

Foreign Minister Nkosazana Dlamini-Zuma, Minister in the Presidency Essop Pahad, former Speaker of the House Frene Ginwala and Home Affairs Minister Nosiviwe Mapisa-Nqakula were all booed. Blade Nzimande, transport minister Jeff Radebe, former premier of Mpumalanga Mathews Phosa, SACP Deputy General Secretary Jeremy Cronin and Motlanthe were all cheered by the crowd.

In a clearly stage-managed move, Mbeki and Zuma entered the marquee together, so that it was not clear who received the most support.

Delegates, however, burst out, 'Zuma, Zuma, Zuma' and sang *Umshini wami* for a long time despite Lekota's calls for order. Zuma looked straight ahead, or pretended to be studying the papers in front of him, while Mbeki, looking uncomfortable, spoke to Mthembi-Mahanyele and Motlanthe.

Zuma supporters began the conference by fighting to have the counting of votes done manually. They have claimed that computers could be manipulated and bring in a pro-Mbeki result. The ANC Youth League had strongly opposed the notion of electronic vote counting and continued doing so, repeatedly proposing that votes be counted manually so that there could be no gerrymandering, until Motlanthe had to step in and restore calm, as he did a number of times during the morning's proceedings.

ANC electoral commission chair Bertha Gxowa evoked a chorus of boos when she told delegates that the counting of votes would take place electronically. 'Comrades, we should not spend so much time on this. Where disputes crop up, the votes would be counted manually,' she said.

Earlier, Eastern Cape Zuma loyalist Phumulo Musualle of the SACP, addressing delegates from Eastern Cape's OR Tambo region outside the main conference venue, had said: 'Our position is that all votes should be counted manually. We reject any suggestion to have votes counted by a computer as that could easily lead to vote-rigging.'

'What is not transparent about electronic counting?' Lekota asked.

The Youth League's Sihle Zikalala replied that manual counting was preferred because the ANC was a 'transparent organisation'.

Not long after these opening salvoes, veteran photographer Alf Khumalo made his way into the cordoned-off VIP area to show Mbeki and Zuma some pictures from the 1950s. He said he found Mbeki, his wife, Zanele, and Zuma seated together laughing.

'It was a total contrast to inside the hall,' said Khumalo. 'There was no animosity – just warmth and laughter.'

By the end of the first day of the conference, even diehard opponents of

Mbeki were expressing sympathy for him. The hostility shown to him by members of his own party must surely have been one of the most humiliating episodes of his life.

At first it had seemed that the antipathy of most of the delegates was aimed at Lekota. Then Mbeki took the podium and delivered his long political report, summing up the events and achievements of the past few years. He was not interrupted but when he asked at one point, 'What divides us?' members of the Youth League and delegates from KwaZulu-Natal responded: 'You!'

'What should be done?' Mbeki also asked at one point during his speech.

'Step down,' howled a number of delegates.

Mendi Msimang, the ANC treasurer-general, was booed and shouted down as he berated the delegates for misbehaving. He said they should allow Lekota to carry out his duties and that they had misbehaved while the cameras were focused on them and now the whole world 'knew about them'.

The giant white marquee was a place of tension, animosity and, above all, mistrust. Yet, listening the next day to Jeff Radebe and Smuts Ngonyama, both members of the NEC, one might have thought that the 4 000-plus delegates had spent the day having a teddy bear's picnic in a Limpopo meadow. It wasn't until deep into their press conference that Radebe finally conceded that 'Well, yes, the atmosphere yesterday was not what we are used to at ANC conferences. The tension was very visible; you could cut it with a knife.'

Asked about specific behaviour by delegates that he found objectionable, Radebe replied: 'It's very unusual that speaking delegates are booed down.'

Ngonyama's deadpan response was: 'We have a very vibrant, cohesive conference today, unlike yesterday, when we had some challenges.'

Nominations for the position of ANC president and the other top officials in the party were supposed to be dealt with in a session late on Sunday night. But the conference had adjourned early because, Ngonyama said, a hastily formed conference steering committee had to deal with the accreditation of delegates and look at 'the business of conference on many fronts'.

Radebe said that the steering committee had discussed delegates' behaviour. Delegates would no longer be allowed to carry placards 'with the faces of comrades standing for positions' in the conference venue. Asked about 'the deep mistrust' that had been evident in the hall – as characterised by the Youth League's Sunday proposal that electronic vote-counting be disallowed because it lent itself to vote-rigging – Ngonyama appeared a little baffled but said that 'some people in the ANC were quite young and perhaps they don't really understand. They don't really know perhaps that there has never been any vote-rigging during the ANC's history.'

Journalists pressed Radebe and Ngonyama, but both seemed unimpressed by the seriousness of the party's own Youth League suggesting that someone might be cheated by the party's own electoral officers.

'I think it's just that people want things to be precise and exact,' said Ngonyama, still looking a little baffled. At any rate, though the party's electoral commission had decided that manual vote-counting could be used for both the top six leadership positions and the 60 National Executive Committee (NEC) positions, the steering committee would still decide on the rest of the elections because it would affect logistics.

The conference was still scheduled to end on the Thursday, said Ngonyama, as many delegates had responsibilities elsewhere and, Radebe added, the cost of extending the event would be a concern. Then all the hacks shuffled off to wait for what everyone was really interested in: the outcome of the clash for the top post between Mbeki and Zuma, the only two people whose names had emerged in provincial pre-conference nomination conferences.

Meanwhile, it was reported that Democratic Alliance leader Helen Zille had slammed the singing of Zuma's anthem. 'What will the world conclude about delegates who sing "Bring me my machine gun" – and that on the official Day of Reconciliation?' she demanded. No one in Polokwane – neither officials nor journalists – seemed to care either way.

Zuma was chosen as the ANC party president on 18 December 2007. He received 2 329 votes to Mbeki's 1 505 votes.

During the hours before Zuma was proclaimed president, his close friends suggested that he prepare for a party and draft a press statement. He responded with a Zulu proverb: 'The *makhoti* [bride] should not prepare the bridal bed until the groom actually arrives.' And, while it seemed that many of Zuma's supporters had already started celebrating well before the election results were announced, and while many hundreds certainly spent most of the night carousing, Zuma returned from the conference to the place where he was staying in Polokwane, 30 km away.

'Yes, and he spent the rest of the evening quietly, with some family members,' said his son Saady.

Zuma continued as softly-softly the day after the results, cancelling a media conference until he had had time 'to talk to the delegates themselves first – after all, they're the ones who voted me in'. He spent most of the day after in discussions with the other five new members of the ANC leadership: Deputy President Kgalema Motlanthe, Chairman Baleka Mbete, Secretary-General Gwede Mantashe, Deputy SG Thandi Modise and Treasurer-General Mathews Phosa.

'JZ is remarkable … He's just quiet, calm … he's like a man at peace with himself,' said Ranjeni Munusamy.

I visited Zuma late on Wednesday night and he was indeed quiet and composed, though tired and a little tense. He was working on his speech with Lakela Kaunda, who had been his spokesperson in the days when he was deputy president of the country. We talked a little about 'inflation targeting' – journalists were always nagging him about his 'economic plans', which was slightly annoying for him because his plans for the economy were going to be those set out by the ANC.

Meanwhile, Zuma's allies in Cosatu and the SACP held a joint press conference at which Blade Nzimande, Jeremy Cronin and Zwelinzima Vavi made it clear that they did not consider Zuma indebted to them, and that claims that he was so irritated them deeply. Asked about his earlier comment, in connection with Cosatu support for Zuma, that 'there are no free lunches', Vavi said that this did not mean Zuma would have in some way to toe the Cosatu economic line.

'The ANC has a policy, and we are mostly with that policy,' said Vavi. 'The point about comrade Zuma is that we will now be free to engage openly with the National Executive Committee and the party on our economic views.'

As the new president of the ANC, Zuma closed the Polokwane conference. There was nothing triumphant about his speech; instead he delivered a straightforward, brief and apparently heartfelt reconciliatory statement – 'reaching out', as the Americans say, to his comrade, friend and 'leader', Thabo Mbeki, preaching unity and calming the fears of investors.

Zuma's theme was that the unity of the party was paramount and that all divisions had to be healed. He stressed that the party's leaders – the 80 members of the ANC's NEC – would honour their mandate from the members or face being replaced. This was a clear reference to the virtual sacking of four of the former top six NEC officials: former ANC president Thabo Mbeki, former party chair Mosiuoa Lekota, former Deputy Secretary-General Sankie Mthembi-Mahanyele and former Treasurer-General Mendi Msimang. Kgalema Motlanthe, the former Secretary-General, and Zuma were the only survivors from the top six.

Zuma paid tribute to Mbeki, calling him 'a friend and brother'. 'I have known and worked with comrade Mbeki for over 30 years. I never thought that the two of us would one day compete for the same position in the ANC. However, contesting positions does not make us enemies. We belong to the same family, the ANC, and we will work together to unite and build a stronger ANC,' Zuma said to loud applause.

Delegates remained spellbound once Zuma began speaking, yelling and applauding only at points where they were clearly supposed to do so, in marked contrast to the unruly catcalling and hand signals that characterised the first day of the conference. But though Zuma kept fiery rhetoric to a minimum, he left the delegates rocking and rolling when he ended his speech by singing two well-known struggle songs.

He then stepped away from the lectern, but when the crowd started singing 'Bring me my machine gun', Zuma returned to give a heartfelt rendition of his trademark song, replete with dancing.

Zuma's speech was not the sort that Mbeki would have delivered. It was much shorter, and there were no quotations from poems, but Zuma's audience didn't care. Afterwards, a newspaper editor, who I'm sure would like to remain anonymous, said: 'I have never been able to understand any of Mbeki's speeches, but I understood this speech easily.'

Zuma said: 'Let me reiterate that decisions with regards to policies in the ANC are taken by conference and not by one individual. There is therefore no reason why the domestic or international business community or any other sector should be uneasy. I tried to calm these fears before the conference during my meetings with various business groupings at home and abroad. Our resolutions [taken at the conference] on economic matters will bring about closure and certainty on these matters.

'All structures … should actively participate in the fight against HIV and AIDS in all facets of the national strategy – prevention, treatment and providing support to families affected and infected. We must live up to our slogan and build a caring society that does not discriminate against those living with HIV … This cannot be left to the government and the NGO sector alone.'

Zuma offered a pointed thank you to the ANC's tripartite allies, Cosatu and the SACP, saying that without them the alliance would not be as strong. He also mentioned the conference's decision to increase the quota of women in ANC structures from 30 to 50 per cent and reminded delegates that anti-racism and anti-tribalism were pillars of ANC policy.

Zuma said that, as far as rampant crime was concerned, ANC branches were to lead in the fight for safety; on AIDS that support for victims and families affected was called for; on the economy that a need for foreign investment remained; on the land issue that 30 per cent needed to be redistributed by 2014; on gender issues that the ANC needed to deal with patriarchal oppression. Regarding the 'two centres of power', Zuma pledged to work with Mbeki – demonstrating once more than not even the president of the ANC ever knows what the future will hold.

So all the king's horses and all the king's men had not been able to make Thabo Mbeki the president of the ANC again. Not even the SABC, a number of highly influential newspapers, the bogeyman of 'international disinvestment', or a supposedly imminent corruption trial for Zuma could bring Mbeki back into the chief's seat and keep Zuma out. Two days before the election in Polokwane, Mbeki told a journalist that 'it would never happen' that ANC members would elect Zuma as president.

An hour before the results of the election for the ANC's top six officials were announced, Trevor Manuel, the Minister of Finance, told a well-known foreign correspondent that it looked as if the race were 'neck and neck' and that Mbeki would scrape in as president.[1] Manuel, who came in first in the NEC elections at the previous ANC conference, was placed 57th on the general NEC list. The same sentiments – that it looked as though Mbeki would win – were expressed just before the results came out by Ronnie Kasrils and Karl Niehaus, a member of the NEC and former ambassador. Kasrils did not make it on to the NEC on Thursday night, and nor did Niehaus.

In fact, Mbeki – and all the former top six NEC members – except Zuma and Kgalema Motlanthe – were sacked by the ANC delegates. Mbeki was replaced by Zuma; Mosiuoa 'Terror' Lekota was replaced by Baleka Mbete, the Speaker of the House and a long-time Zuma follower; Sankie Mthembi-Mahanyele was replaced by Thandi Modise, a well-known ANC 'woman soldier'; and Mendi Msimang was replaced by Mathews Phosa. Motlanthe was elected deputy president and replaced by well-known trade unionist Gwede Mantashe as secretary-general.

'Jeez, so what happened?' – as the proverbial drunk man mugged on his way home from the pub asked the next morning from his hospital bed.

In a way, nothing odd happened. Before the results for the top six were announced, a colleague of mine, who was not in Polokwane, sent me by SMS his best guesstimate for the final tally. All he did was send the amounts extrapolated from the provincial nominations – and though he was out by a couple of hundred votes, he was pretty much on the money.

The members of the ANC provincial regions had given their delegates a mandate – bring in Zuma and his ilk and dump Mbeki and his kind – and the delegates fulfilled the mandate, as they were obliged to do. It's called democracy.

The ANC delegates to Polokwane were a fraction of those registered at the country's branches nationwide and also just a fraction of those men and women who voted in the ANC in the national and provincial elections of 1994, 1999 and 2004. They acted as representatives of those branches and carried a mandate from them. According to political journalist Patrick Laurence, in all probability less than two per cent of the ANC's membership was directly responsible for voting Zuma into power. The national president, like the ANC president, is also indirectly elected, voted into office by the National Assembly at its first sitting after a national election. Thus at Polokwane, with 9 out of every 10 voting delegates being branch representatives, it was clear that the decision regarding the ANC's – and in all likelihood South Africa's – next leader would rest in the branches, and it did. Mbeki's spin doctors' conviction that the branch delegates would renege on their mandates and be convinced to change their minds when they reached Polokwane was wishful thinking.

Ironically, although the literal meaning of *Umshini wami*, the struggle song adopted by Zuma and his supporters, is 'machine [of war]', not actually 'machine GUN', the Youth League made certain that there would be no machines involved in the counting of votes. The league rammed through a motion on the first day of the conference ensuring that computers would not be used, but that all votes had to be counted manually. The league was not, as we have said, going to allow for the possibility that someone might inadvertently press a button twice, or six times, in Mbeki's favour.

But what really happened? Why did Zuma and his list do so surprisingly well, despite the spin to the contrary? Obviously, the Mbeki machine was completely and frighteningly out of touch with ANC delegates and, presumably, 'the people'. There was clearly – and obviously had been for a long time – a serious 'disconnect' between ordinary ANC members and the party's ruling coterie.

'There are many kinds of denialism, you know. AIDS denialism is only just one sort,' said Jeremy Cronin, who did well in the NEC election.

But, besides denialism, four other issues emerged at the conference.

The first was that, while analysts and the media had made much for months and years about the 'imminent split-up of the tripartite alliance', the leaders of Cosatu, notably Zwelinzima Vavi, and of the SACP, notably Blade Nzimande, had not been fussing about divorce, but had been focusing on making the marriage work – their way, and via the ballot box. It became clear at the conference that Cosatu and the SACP had played a decisive role in influencing ANC members, many of whom are members of Cosatu, during the provincial nominations process and in the prior months.

Second, there were many people, though clearly not among the ANC membership, who tended to write off the Youth League as a noisy irritant and its leader Fikile Mbalula as a demagogue. Such people needed to think again. At Polokwane the Youth League was far more influential than had previously been realised. The league was in fact very influential and it fought hard, long and noisily on behalf of Zuma.

Third, what became rapidly evident – within an hour of the conference starting – was that a huge abyss had been opening up over the last years between ordinary ANC members and Mbeki over the president's high-handed behaviour: firing Nozizwe Madlala-Routledge, the Deputy Minister of Health (voted on to the new NEC), firing Billy Masetlha, the former chief spook (also voted on to the new NEC), protecting Minister of Health Tshabalala-Msimang and Jackie Selebi, the National Police Commissioner, and suspending Vusi Pikoli, the National Director of Public Prosecutions.

Above all, Mbeki was perceived as inaccessible by all except his closest *handlangers*, such as Essop Pahad, Minister in the Presidency, who did not make it on to the NEC either. More importantly, there was at the conference an obvious abyss between rank-and-file ANC members and the party's old guard, the former NEC members. The members wanted change and they made this abundantly clear.

Fourth, the palpable irritation of delegates with the old guard was not just about personalities. Speaking to delegates, I sensed a deep anger over the fact that they had not cashed in on the new South Africa, as had others; that, despite fine-sounding words, ordinary people still remained mired in unemployment, poverty, and generally sucking the hind one.

In addition, there was a general irritation at the apparent national obsession with Zuma's alleged corruption – the delegates knew what it was like to need money and help – and with the fuss over his rape trial. They felt that they knew what happened at his house with Khwezi – that it was a story as old as time – and they were tired of righteous words about morality and ethics.

So we saw at Polokwane a proverbial seminal moment in South African history. The people of the ANC, whether by themselves or spurred on by the Youth League and the Left, or both, had taken back the party and warned their leadership that they wanted to see a bit more action and less talk.

One wit remarked that – given their previous misdemeanours, crimes or alleged crimes – the new NEC looked like a Who's Who from the television programme *Crime Watch* – Zuma himself, Winnie Madikizela-Mandela, Tony Yengeni, Baleka Mbete, Manto Tshabalala-Msimang, and a few others.

Maybe. But the people had spoken.

'In the deserted harbour there is yet water that laps against the quays. In the dark and silent forest there is a leaf that falls. Behind the polished panelling the white ant eats away the wood. Nothing is ever quiet, except for fools.'[2]

Michael Hulley is no fool and nor is anyone else on Zuma's legal team. And, given that the conference at Polokwane was about to start, and then started, without a peep from the NPA, they felt in November and December that the NPA was not likely to re-charge Zuma in 2007. This was despite the various vague rumblings from the NPA (these were actually 'raised' at Polokwane by the Youth League), despite the leaked memorandum of October (in which the NPA's leaders stressed that something had to be done about the 'Zuma case'), and despite the November decision by the Supreme Court of Appeal that the notorious search warrants had been valid.

After all, Pikoli had been suspended, which was a surely a major blow to the case against Zuma. And at the end of November, Hulley filed papers at the Constitutional Court arguing that the August 2005 warrants, previously found unlawful by the Durban High Court, but lawful by the Supreme Court of Appeal, were riddled with imprecision and vagueness and violated attorney-client privilege, and therefore infringed Zuma's constitutional rights to privacy and dignity.

But there had been media reports that the Scorpions had been drafting recommendations to acting National Director of Public Prosecutions Mokotedi Mpshe that Zuma be charged with corruption, tax evasion and money laundering. This would cover not only the R1,3-million Zuma received from Schabir Shaik, and the R500 000 bribe he allegedly received from Thint, but also subsequent payments from Schabir and other business people from the mid-1990s to mid-2005. The payments were said to be several times more than those previously said to be from Shaik.

Just 10 days after he was elected ANC president, Zuma was charged again. This time the National Prosecuting Authority had added three new charges – money laundering, racketeering and tax evasion – to the original corruption and fraud charges, and he was being put in the dock for actions right up until June 2005.

Zuma was irate that the indictment had been served on his Forest Town home while he was handing out Christmas gifts to children and the indigent at Nkandla during his annual Christmas party. In a statement through Hulley, he said that, according to the indictment, his trial was set for 14 August 2008. He said he found the timing of the indictment 'most peculiar', coming so soon after his election to the ANC presidency and so long before the scheduled date of the trial. 'In light of the NPA proposing a trial date in August 2008, one cannot imagine the need for such haste and the service of the indictment over this Christmas period, when much of the world, commercial, legal and otherwise, is at rest.'

The serving of the indictment, the statement claimed, had been timed to 'redress the popular support and call to leadership by the ANC', giving rise to the belief on his part 'that the Scorpions are influenced and their prosecution informed by political considerations'. Zuma said he would vigorously defend himself against the charges 'in the context of the belief' that the Scorpions had acted improperly to discredit him and ensure he could play 'no leadership role in the political future of our country'.

Zuma was charged – along with Thint Holdings and Thint (Pty) Ltd, represented by Pierre Moynot, the chief executive of both – on 18 different counts, mainly of fraud and corruption, but also racketeering and money laundering. Many of the charges related to the dealings between Zuma and the Nkobi Group, the companies formerly controlled by Shaik.

At the Polokwane conference, Kgalema Motlanthe advised the NPA to think very carefully about recharging Zuma, because the length of time they had been investigating him was 'suspect'. Gwede Mantashe said: 'They couldn't wait for the holidays to be over to create sensation. This story is an old story that is just kept alive in the media. [The NPA] threatened to do it on the last day of our conference in Polokwane. There was even an article in a newspaper which outlined the charges. The ANC NEC will meet on January 7 so that we can work out a structured manner to deal with this matter.' Earlier Mantashe warned that any 'state or political manipulation' behind recharging Zuma could spark 'a mass resistance movement'. He added that the NPA should be mindful of the fate of its investigative arm, the Scorpions, whose demise was provisionally endorsed at Polokwane. 'If [the NPA] is misreading the environment, and the mood, it will actually have to go back and analyse why that resolution [on the Scorpions] was brought,' Mantashe said.

So the country met Jacob Zuma the racketeer, the Al Capone of South Africa, who was consciously involved in an 'enterprise' that aimed to win contracts or score business deals by using his 'political connectivity'. The 66-page indictment seemed at first glance to be pretty similar to the charge sheet that was used to prosecute Shaik. The only major difference appeared at first to be that the amount of money allegedly paid by Shaik to Zuma had jumped from a total of roughly R1,2 million to a total of R4 072 499.85. This was because the Scorpions had, in Shaik's case, looked at payments to Zuma from October 1995 to roughly 2003. The time period had now been extended to July 2005.

It was stated in the indictment, even more baldly than in the papers at Shaik's trial, that the payments to Zuma during that decade made no legitimate business sense because Nkobi Investments, Shaik's group of companies, was far from financially healthy. The new indictment read that, 'whatever their description', all of Shaik's payments to Zuma were intended as bribes, because no attempt was ever made by Shaik to recoup any of the money.

Although the two indictments seemed similar, there were two vital differences between them. The first was that, while encompassing charges of corruption and fraud, the new indictment was focused on charges of racketeering. Racketeering, read in conjunction with the Prevention of Organised Crime Act, is defined as being guilty of carrying out illegal activities 'while associated with any enterprise ... [and participating] in conduct of the enterprise's affairs through a pattern of racketeering activities'. In other words, Zuma was no longer being accused of merely being in a corrupt relationship. The business relationship between him, Shaik and Thint, and the companies through which they operated, is portrayed as an ongoing, tripartite enterprise that existed in many (though not all) cases for the sake of conducting illegitimate business. The 'illegal activities' were the use of Zuma's influence during the periods that he was the MEC for economic affairs and tourism for KwaZulu-Natal (from May 1994 to June 1999), deputy president of the ANC (from December 1997), and deputy president of South Africa and leader of government business (from June 1999 to June 2005).

The joint ventures in which Nkobi and Thint were involved were not limited to the Arms Deal but also included sectors such as transport, tourism, justice, finance, prisons, hospitals, water, Durban airport, the government ID card contract, the third cellular network contract, and the N1, N3, and N4 road projects.

The second difference in the new indictment was that Thint was portrayed as a major player in the conspiracy to commit crime, whereas previously it was characterised as a kind of adjunct to what went on between Shaik and Zuma.

The main count, of racketeering, was aimed at both Zuma and Thint, as was the count of money laundering, while many of the counts of fraud and corruption were aimed at Zuma alone. The basic charge against Zuma was that, although as a provincial or government official he was not allowed 'to undertake other paid work, expose himself to situations involving risk of conflict between official and private interests', he clearly benefited by being paid by Shaik, Nkobi and Thint for using his influence. 'Shaik and Thint,' the indictment read, 'set out to bribe Zuma from October 1995 onwards for their own interests', and from October 1995 to July 2005 he received payments totalling R4 072 499.85.

The ways in which Zuma allegedly assisted Nkobi and Thint were similar to the ways set out in the case against Shaik: helping in negotiations with African Defence Systems and various other matters related to the strategic defence package acquisition, or Arms Deal. When investigations began into aspects of the Arms Deal, following the September 1999 statement made in Parliament by Patricia de Lille, Shaik and Thint resolved that they needed Zuma to protect them from these investigations, especially into the corvette deal in which Thint and Shaik were involved. It was then that Shaik negotiated a R1-million bribe – broken into four R250 000 instalments over two years – for Zuma with Thint. According to the indictment, Zuma needed the money to build his 'residential village estate' at Nkandla.

The indictment also read that Zuma was responsible for writing the letter that went to Parliament's standing committee for public accounts, saying that it was unnecessary for the Heath special investigating unit to be involved in investigating the Arms Deal. This was odd because it became clear during the Shaik trial that, although Zuma had signed the letter, it was actually written by Thabo Mbeki. The trial, at which Zuma would be asked to answer the charges in the indictment, was set down for 14 August in the Pietermaritzburg High Court.

A 16-page KPMG report – reproduced in the *Sunday Times* early in January – formed the cornerstone of the state's case against Zuma for fraud and racketeering. It painted a picture of the complete 'financial hold' Shaik allegedly had over Zuma. One of Zuma's aides remarked: 'It's funny that no one ever thinks that maybe it was Zuma who had the hold over Schabir. They always paint Zuma as the puppet, not the other way round.'

The document shows that Shaik allegedly funnelled a total of R4 072 499 to Zuma in 783 separate payments between 25 October 1995 and 1 July 2005. The Durban businessman continued to pay Zuma during his own fraud and corruption trial, with the last payment going through in July 2005, two months after Shaik's conviction.

Shaik's companies allegedly gave money to Zuma's ex-wives, paid his rent, supplied his children with pocket money and forked out for his many debts. They even paid R10 to cover the cost of a 'wash and vacuum' of his car. Within days of Zuma being fired as deputy president of South Africa, the last payment was made on his behalf – R393.80 to Absa on 1 July 2005 for insurance on a Toyota Tazz vehicle.

Shaik also paid doctors, pathologists and hospitals, traffic fines, electricity and water accounts, car repayments, insurance and phone bills. Even housekeeping costs were covered while Zuma was deputy president.

Zuma's 'traditional home' was bankrolled with help from Shaik, his 'financial adviser'. Cash was also paid to Zuma's ex-wives. The Minister of Foreign Affairs, Nkosazana Dlamini-Zuma, who divorced Zuma in 1997, received R22 000. Kate Zuma, who committed suicide on 8 December 2000, received R23 400. One of the payments to her was for R400 on 24 July 1998. She received two payments in a single day on 31 August 1998 – R1 500 from the account of Pro Con Africa and R7 000 from the account of Schabir Shaik. The payments to Zuma and his family ranged from the 'wash and vacuum' R10 to a R300 000 cash deposit directly into his personal bank account just three months before Mbeki fired him.

Shaik paid Zuma's family travel and accommodation costs, including aircraft charter (R14 200), a tab from the exclusive Twelve Apostles Hotel in Cape Town, Avis car rental costs and tickets to fly on South African Airways, according to a spreadsheet in the KPMG report.

He also paid R44 100 for 'Zuma family travel costs' for a trip to Cuba (tickets and allowance) on 13 December 2002. During Shaik's trial it emerged that, as an MEC in KwaZulu-Natal between May 1994 and June 1999, Zuma earned about R20 000 a month. As deputy president of South Africa he earned a salary, including allowances, of around R870 000 a year.

Yet, even after becoming deputy president, the schedule lists one payment of R140.01 (21 April 2000) from Shaik's firm Kobitech, under the heading 'petrol for Zuma's car'. Five months later R25 in cash was doled out for a 'mini-valet for Zuma car' followed days later by R10 in cash for 'wash and vacuum Zuma car'. More valet and petrol costs followed, including R150 paid for a traffic fine. Shaik even paid panel beaters in Durban for work done on a Mercedes-Benz listed as a Zuma vehicle.

Zuma wore designer clothes thanks to his benefactor, who dished out tens of thousands of rands to the exclusive Casanova boutique in Durban. In just two weeks in August 2001, one of Shaik's companies paid the store R18 000 for Zuma's purchases. A month later the store was paid another R18 000 – and further payments followed.

A large portion of the payments received by Zuma was made in cash. Vast sums were also spent on educating his numerous children. Shaik's Nkobi Group forked out money for school books and paid regular fees for Zuma's children to attend Holy Family College, Sacred Heart College, Empangeni High School, the University of Zululand, Westerford High, Pretoria Boys, Herschel School, St Catherine's, Cape Technikon and the International School of Cape Town. The payments are listed under the heading 'Zuma children education'. There were also numerous payments for 'Zuma children allowance', separate amounts to different children ranging from a few hundred rands to R5 340. One child received R12 160 in just two months. Regular monthly payments were made for a Hyundai Sonata and Mazda Etude listed as 'Zuma children vehicle costs'.

According to the schedule, Shaik also paid R21 000 to the ANC to settle Zuma's outstanding party levies. Members of Parliament are expected to pay a percentage of their salaries on top of their membership fees to the party.

The indictment showed that Shaik was supposed to handle Zuma's tax returns and his declaration to Parliament and the Cabinet's registers of interests. Zuma now faced tax evasion charges for allegedly not declaring to the taxman the income he received from Shaik and his other funders. He was also being rapped for failing to fully declare his interests as the law requires of serving MPs and members of the Cabinet.

The report omitted to mention, however, that Shaik had been responsible for the disbursement of all of Zuma's money, so that some of the money about which the *Sunday Times* reported so breathlessly had presumably in fact been part of Zuma's salary, and not a gift or loan or bribe.

The decision of the NPA to recharge Jacob Zuma only days before New Year was widely interpreted as a direct response from the Union Buildings to Mbeki's unceremonious ousting by Zuma from the ANC presidency. The ANC Youth League, Cosatu, senior ANC members, political analysts and legal experts all blamed Mbeki. They claimed Mbeki had forced Moketedi Mpshe to cut short his leave to oversee the serving of the charges on Zuma, and warned that the decision could plunge the country into crisis, given Zuma's massive support among the rank and file of the ruling party. But Mpshe vehemently denied he or his agency had been improperly influenced. Mpshe, who had been on leave since before the ANC conference, said Mbeki had not been briefed by his investigators. He said members of the ANC had been aware that charges against Zuma were imminent. 'That is what they were expecting, but it never happened because we are not moved by what is happening, be it a conference or any political issues. We just do our job.'

One legal source said the timing of the charges was largely irrelevant; the real reason for Zuma being charged now was strategic. Mbeki, he said, wanted to prove to Zuma that, though he had won the political battle for the soul of the party, Mbeki remained president of the country.

Cosatu called the indictment of Zuma a continued violation of his rights. The timing of the indictment had the 'hallmarks of vengeance, deep-seated anger and frustration by the NPA, and whoever else is behind this', it said.

Zuma had received better Christmas presents in his time. But he was soldiering on, seemingly unfazed, with his life – and he had a pleasant surprise planned for his fourth 'wife', Nompumelelo Ntuli.

CHAPTER 17

2008

'Let's kill all the lawyers'

As a celebration of his victory at Polokwane, or perhaps because the time had simply come, on 8 January 2008 the 65-year-old Zuma officially married 33-year-old Nompumelelo Ntuli, with whom he has two children, in a lavish traditional ceremony at Nkandla.

Zuma delivered the bride price of 11 cattle for Nompumelelo and had another four cattle slaughtered for 500 guests, many of whom (like Zuma himself) were traditionally dressed and carried traditional Zulu paraphernalia. After an exchange of wedding gifts, Zuma, attired in a leopard skin, led a group of warriors in singing a Zulu war song, *Wawuyaphi ungapethete isibhamu?* – 'Where are you going without a gun'?

We have already encountered Sizakele Khumalo, Zuma's first wife, who lives at Nkandla; Foreign Affairs Minister Nkosazana Dlamini-Zuma, with whom he had four children, but from whom he is divorced; and Kate Mantsho Zuma, with whom he had five children and who committed suicide in December 2000.

Now that he was ANC president, 'new' information about Zuma was suddenly emerging, and it was also strongly rumoured that in 2002 he had married a woman called Mantuli, a 'housewife' who lived in Durban ('the city wife') and with whom Zuma has a five-year old daughter and a ten-month-old son. Mantuli is said to have been the woman referred to in Kate's suicide note as 'the new *makhoti*' (bride).

Spicing up the rumours even further was the story that Zuma had paid lobola to the clan of Thobeka Stacy Mabhija, 35, with whom he was alleged to have two children as well; that he had paid 10 cattle as lobola for Swazi Princess Sebentile Dlamini, 38, and had also paid lobola for Bongi Ngema, with whom he is alleged to have a three-year-old son.

Zuma reportedly has 18 children, including his son Edward, the result of his liaison with Minah Shongwe. I am uncertain where the count of 18 comes from; I calculate 17. But for this book Zuma refused to discuss the details of his private life or the number of children he has fathered. It will be interesting to see, when (and if) Zuma is inaugurated as president, who will accompany him. At Thabo Mbeki's inauguration in 2004, he was accompanied by Sizakele.

Turning from the joys of polygamy to the business of January 2008, the fired and shamed former deputy president of the country had been elected president of the ruling party. Although Zuma dislikes the office and prefers to work from his Forest Town home, he was doubtless greatly relieved to have a high-powered official infrastructure back in place. And the Union Buildings beckoned again.

Although it is not written into the ANC rules, and although one can hardly refer to a practice of only 13 years' duration as a 'tradition' (as Thabo Mbeki pointedly told an interviewer towards the end of 2007), since 1994 the incumbent ANC president had always become South Africa's president following the national general elections. These are held every five years, with the next due in April 2009. But, although there is no legal limit on the number of terms that an ANC president can serve, the president of the country cannot serve more than two terms.

In short, prior to Polokwane it looked very much as though Zuma, if he won the ANC presidency, would become the next president of South Africa. This was anathema to Mbeki and his circle, but there was no other Mbeki candidate who was strong enough to beat Zuma at Polokwane. This was why Mbeki had indicated at the July 2007 conference that he would stand for a third term as ANC president – and had gone ahead and done so, with disastrous results for himself. As for the ANC branch and provincial delegates, they did not want 'two centres of power' – Mbeki issuing orders from Luthuli House, and whoever the national president would be issuing orders at the Union Buildings. Many of them did not want Mbeki anyway.

So Zuma looked more certain than ever to be president. Yet, 10 days after his election at Polokwane, he had been (re-)charged with corruption and fraud and the NPA had added in racketeering, money-laundering and tax evasion for good measure.

The political biographer Isaac Deutscher wrote that he had not used the conventional term 'rise and fall' in connection with Leon Trotsky 'because I do not think that a man's rise to power is necessarily the climax of his life or that his loss of office should be equated with his fall.'[1] In my view, the contrary applies in Zuma's case. He considered his sacking from the deputy presidency as a serious fall; and, though he did not say so, his election to the ANC presidency was for him, if not the climax of his life, then one of them; and he certainly viewed the possibility that he might not become the president of South Africa as potentially a very serious fall.

And so he immediately moved vigorously into 2008 as 'the President of the ANC' – going to engagements, delivering speeches, visiting different communities, and playing an active role in the NEC. His life became extremely busy, even feverish. At the same time, he agreed again with his legal team that they needed to employ Stalingrad tactics: the charges had to be fought every inch of the way; every uncrossed t and every i without a dot, and even those that were crossed or dotted, had to be challenged.

At the beginning of the year, Zuma called on people to remain calm and disciplined in the wake of the NPA's charging him with corruption and racketeering. He needed to do this because supporters were angry about the timing of the indictment and remained adamant that the planned prosecution was a plot to quash his presidential aspirations. They also argued that the manner in which the case had been handled since 2004 had robbed Zuma of his right to a fair trial.

In a strange foreshadowing of what would be said later in the year by Julius Malema, new president of the Youth League, Zet Luzipho, the Cosatu leader in KwaZulu-Natal, said that blood would be spilled and the country thrown into chaos if Zuma were forced to appear in court. His statement was 'withdrawn' by Patrick Craven, Cosatu's national spokesman, who said union members would not resort to violence.

Zuma was firm: 'On no account should there be any violence or burning of property or anything like that because of these charges against me. I know why people are so angry on my behalf. But there are other ways, legal ways, with which to deal with such matters.'

'We don't want to have here the kind of thing we are seeing in Kenya,' he added, soon after meeting the ANC's five other senior officials in preparation for the first meeting of the party's new NEC. He said he had discussed the indictment with Kgalema Motlanthe, Baleka Mbete, Gwede Mantashe, Thandi Modise and Mathews Phosa, and had every intention of delivering the ANC president's special message at the ANC's birthday celebrations in Atteridgeville in Tshwane.

In an unusual step, Arthur Chaskalson, the former Chief Justice, and George Bizos SC, an eminent advocate, jointly called on the public to respect the country's judiciary and not to criticise the courts in connection with Zuma. They issued a signed statement saying: 'We are concerned at the tone of the debate around the contemplated trial of Mr Jacob Zuma', emphasising that they did not want to say anything about whether he should have been charged, or the substance or lack of substance of the charges against him. They were concerned with only one issue, 'and that is the implication from some of the statements that have been made that our judiciary as a whole lacks the independence and integrity to ensure that Mr Zuma will receive a fair trial'. This was harmful to the judicial process, constitutional democracy and the country's reputation, they said, appealing to all political leaders and their supporters, opinion-makers, commentators and the media to let the courts decide on these issues.

According to Chaskalson and Bizos, an example of the integrity of the judiciary being called into question was when a Cosatu member reportedly said: 'It does not matter who the judge is, we do not believe the judiciary will be able to be objective. The trial against Zuma is a politically motivated exercise ... and he has been subjected to trial by public opinion for the past seven years. We have been convinced for some time that he will not get a fair trial ... workers will not allow the NPA and whoever is handling them, to abuse its power in this matter.'

Cosatu spokesman Craven denied the union federation was questioning the independence of the judiciary. 'On the contrary, we are defending the independence of the judiciary against what we perceive are attempts to manipulate them by people outside for political ends,' he said.

Bizos and Chaskalson rejoined: 'Guilt or innocence cannot be established by rhetorical statements. The question of whether Mr Zuma is guilty or innocent must be decided by the courts, not by his detractors or his supporters; so too, the question of whether he gets a fair trial is a matter for the judiciary.'

In short, alliance pressure was starting to build on the prosecuting authority and the courts. (Though, of course, the NPA had been caught between the devil and the deep blue sea: if it had re-charged Zuma before Polokwane, it would have been accused of damaging his chances of being elected ANC president. But, then again, why do it over the Christmas period?)

The situation was further exacerbated when National Police Commissioner Jackie Selebi was sent on extended leave of absence and prosecutors said they would charge him with corruption. On the day of the ANC's birthday, Mbeki announced that Selebi had been replaced by Tim Williams, one of four deputy national police commissioners, who would be the country's acting national commissioner. But Mbeki, who said that he had decided that the national police commissioner should go on leave, said it was business as usual and appeared deliberately to downplay his decision to suspend Selebi.

Selebi was the fourth administration or government official connected with national safety and security to get the chop on Thabo Mbeki's watch. The other three were Zuma, Billy Masetlha, the former head of the national intelligence agency, who was suspended and then fired by Mbeki after falling out with him, and Vusi Pikoli, the national director of public prosecutions, who was suspended apparently for getting a warrant for Selebi's arrest without telling Mbeki or the Minister of Justice, Brigitte Mabandla.

Zuma's life intersected with Selebi's because it seemed clear, from Mbeki's behaviour regarding Pikoli, that the president was interfering with the NDPP and that he afforded certain people (Selebi) special protection. At the press conference at which he announced Selebi's leave, Mbeki became palpably flustered when he was asked why he had treated Zuma and Selebi differently. 'If you look at the statement I made after Deputy President Zuma was relieved of his duties in 2005,' he said, 'and at the statement that Zuma made at the time, you will see that there is a world of difference between the two matters.'

In February, Zuma went to Mauritius over the Thint documents – the contents of which everyone knew – because the island's law requires that anyone bringing a legal action be present in court. 'Judge Hilary Squires, who convicted Shaik, found the documents admissible,' said Hulley, 'so everyone's seen them – there's nothing secret or shocking or anything like that. But the state knows that we would argue strenuously that they were unlawfully obtained – this is how we read the deal struck all those years ago by the Scorpions and the Mauritian authorities. The state, wanting to have this aspect of the case against Zuma and Thint cleaned up, applied covertly to the Mauritian attorney-general for the official transmission of the documents to the NPA. It's simply this that we are opposing,' said Hulley.

In May, a remarkable *faux pas* came to light. It turned out that the NPA had not properly arranged for Zuma's trial with the office of Vuka

Tshabalala, the Judge President of KwaZulu-Natal. The NPA had not discussed with Tshabalala whether there existed a suitable time slot for the trial on the court roll and whether there was a judge available. Although Tshabalala said nothing publicly about there having been a 'mess up' on the part of the NPA, I learnt reliably that he had made it abundantly clear at a meeting with all the parties that he found it 'unacceptable' that the NPA had made a public statement about the proposed date for Zuma's trial, copied all documents to the registrar of the High Court in Pietermaritzburg – and then expected that everything would happen like clockwork.

'A high-profile case such as Mr Zuma's requires many court days and therefore careful arrangements are required by me. The registrar's office is not my office, and I cannot run the courts according to what I read in the newspapers. It is the correct protocol to consult me directly,' Tshabalala said to the legal representatives of the NPA, Zuma and Thint.

Present at the meeting were Tshabalala, Billy Downer, SC, and Anton Steynberg of the NPA. Also present were Kemp J Kemp SC and Hulley, Zuma's legal team, and Ajay Sooklal, the attorney for Thint.

Besides – Zuma's representatives told the meeting – they would be applying for a review of the case on the basis that neither Zuma nor Thint had been asked for a response to the charges laid against them and because the charges were not reviewed by the NPA – not in 2005 when they were charged following the guilty verdict in the trial of Shaik, and not in December 2007, when they were re-charged because the 2005 trial was struck off the roll in September 2006. The defence teams said they would argue that an accused person's right to a review if re-charged is protected by the constitution and also that, if re-charged, an accused person should be allowed to respond to the charges before going to court. If the court were to find in Zuma and Thint's favour, then the NPA's decision to re-charge could be declared unlawful.

It was agreed by those present at the meeting that Zuma's legal team would put in papers on the 'review application' in the next few months, that the state would respond to these, and that the matter would start being heard on 4 August by whichever trial judge Tshabalala nominated.

The criminal trial would be adjourned on 4 August to 8 December, at which point a criminal trial date would be set – possibly for late in 2009, but this would depend on what had happened in the 'review application'.

Further complicating matters was that the defence legal teams intended filing an application in September arguing that Zuma's and Thint's right to a fair trial had been jeopardised by the state's flouting of such tenets as being presumed innocent until found guilty. This would be an application for the case against Zuma and Thint to be permanently stayed – struck off the roll for ever.

This application would also be heard by the 'Zuma judge' nominated by the Judge President and would also be subject to appeal by both sides. In addition, all parties were waiting for the Constitutional Court finding on the constitutionality of the search and seizure warrants that allowed the state to seize documents from Hulley's office in August 2005. There was also the matter before the Mauritian courts related to the legality of documents that the state planned to use against Zuma.

In short, Hulley was able to announce at the end of May that it looked very much as though Zuma was not going to face a trial for corruption, fraud and other criminal charges until he was president of the country – and it might even be deep into his first term before he had to take a seat in the dock.

'Given the agreements reached at our meeting with Vuka Tshabalala, the Judge President of KwaZulu-Natal, I can't see a criminal trial taking place before 2010,' Hulley said. He was able to say this because it had been agreed that the criminal trial would not start until 8 December, on which date it would in any case be adjourned until some unspecified date in 2009. Secondly, the two applications set to take place before December – the application for the setting aside of the 'prosecutorial decisions' due to lack of 'representations' and the application for a permanent stay – would doubtless be appealed (before the SCA and then probably the Constitutional Court) by whichever side 'lost' them.

In the meantime, although Zuma was putting himself about, the new president of the ANC remained, in the view of veteran political journalist Patrick Laurence,[2] 'an enigma to many South Africans …

Zuma's inclination to make contradictory statements [this year] and his related tendency to appease his immediate audience and interlocutors compounds the contentiousness of his candidacy for the national presidency, as they create not one public image of Zuma but many, conflicting images.

[Some people] take heart from Zuma's defence at the September 2006 conference of the Congress of South African Trade Unions of existing ANC economic policy, with its emphasis on fiscal discipline, inflation targeting, and maintaining a (relatively) open market …

The trouble with the scenario that foresees a modest, practical Zuma is that it does not address the possibility of Zuma being surrounded by several advisers offering conflicting advice. His track record so far portrays him as a politician who is wont to flip-flop ideologically, depending on which adviser or interlocutor has his ear. He tends to take on the ideological colouring of his immediate interlocutors. It is for these reasons that Barney Mthombothi, the editor of the *Financial Mail*, describes him as the 'ultimate chameleon'.

To illustrate the point concretely, Zuma has in recent months:

- Endorsed the ANC's commitment to the constitutional court's outlawing of the death penalty as contrary to the declaration of human rights in the constitution, while simultaneously expressing support for holding a referendum on whether to reinstate the death penalty if the demand for it is strong enough – without explaining what he could do in the likely event of overwhelming support for restoration of capital punishment.
- Expressed willingness to consider relaxation of the present rigid laws to encourage entrepreneurs to offer employment to the 'poorest of the poor', only to retreat into denial by claiming he was quoted out of context when confronted by Cosatu.
- Exhibited willingness to reappraise affirmative action policies in an exchange of views with members of the conservative trade union

Solidarity, merely to backtrack at the first sign of opposition from within the ANC-led tripartite alliance.

Extrapolation from these observations leads to another scenario: that of a Zuma presidency distinguished by vacillation and attempts by Zuma to placate a variety of contesting interests, a *modus operandi* that more often than not ends by pleasing no one and alienating everyone.

A modification of the above scenario is one where Zuma appears to be reasonable and willing to lend a sympathetic ear to a disparate array of voices but is actually the ideological captive of militant neo-communists – the species that pays obeisance to the need for multi-party democracy – without sacrificing its quest for control of the means of production by the state, or, more specifically, for control of the levers of state power on behalf of the poor and down-trodden …

Though not flattering to Zuma, in that it assumes that he is a man without independence of mind, it should not be dismissed lightly, bearing in mind (1) the resurgence of Cosatu and the SACP in the two-and-a-half last years of President Mbeki's second term of office, as well as (2) Zuma's political indebtedness to dedicated leftists in Cosatu, the SACP in general, and in particular to Zwelinzima Vavi and Blade Nzimande, the general secretaries of Cosatu and the SACP …

Following his election to the ANC presidency, Zuma's 'story' became everyone else's as well; he became the epicentre of South African politics. From January 2008, the country had started living through a tussle between the 'two centres of power': the national, provincial and municipal governments, big business, and even perhaps ordinary citizens, were caught between the government, headed by Mbeki, which by half-way through the year had only nine months left to govern, and the party, headed by Zuma.

This uncomfortable situation was exacerbated by most of 2008 not being a happy or prosperous time. The economy slowed down, a deceleration that included, as in much of the rest of the world, high inflation and exorbitant food prices (and it would grow even worse when the world markets crashed in October and the rand slumped). People and major industry struggled through an (electricity) energy crisis during which there were blackouts throughout the country; it did not help that this, as it turned out, was mainly the result of incompetence and was redeemable.

In May there was an eruption of murderous and frightening pogroms against African foreigners – living mainly in so-called informal settlements – during which 62 of them were brutally murdered. At about the same time, the equally murderous farce of the Zimbabwean election was taking place, a clear suggestion that the rule of law could not be taken for granted in southern Africa.

What seemed politically significant about the outbreak of xenophobia was that – just as the ruling coterie had no idea about the support for Zuma among ANC delegates – no one at Luthuli House, not even those supposedly in touch with the working class, had the faintest inkling that it was going to take place, or why it had. Suddenly even the Zumas, Nzimandes and Vavis of the world looked as out of touch as the old guard had on the stage at Polokwane. Zuma was one of the few ANC leaders who went out into the informal settlement communities to talk it out – but it was too little, too late.

However, according to one experienced researcher, it was local 'political uncertainty' – at the centre of which was Zuma – that frightened South Africans the most.[3]

On the second-last day of May 2008, the 11 judges of the Constitutional Court issued a very unusual statement. The judges – who were busy writing judgments on a number of Zuma appeals that were serving to delay his main trial date – publicly accused Judge John Hlophe, the Judge President of the Cape, of having tried to sway two or three of their number into making Zuma-friendly judgments.

The man tipped as a future chief justice under a Zuma government was alleged to have lobbied at least two Constitutional Court judges for a pro-Zuma ruling and faced possible impeachment. The Constitutional Court's unprecedented complaint that one of the country's most senior black judges tried to influence it improperly over the Scorpions' raids on Zuma and Thint plunged the judiciary into its biggest crisis yet. With the judiciary jealously guarding its constitutional independence, news that a senior judge, rather than a politician or the government, might be guilty of interference, shocked the legal community.

Hlophe had previously escaped an impeachment inquiry related to other complaints against him, including his alleged moonlighting on the bench and his relationship with the Oasis group of companies. However, the complaint by judges of the highest court in the land provoked renewed calls for him to step down pending an investigation by the Judicial Service Commission (jsc) and a possible impeachment inquiry for gross misconduct.

The media established that the two judges who were allegedly lobbied were Justice Bess Nkabinde and Judge Chris Jafta of the Supreme Court of Appeal, who had been appointed an acting judge in the Constitutional Court earlier in the year. Speculation had been rife that Hlophe had an eye on a Constitutional Court appointment. With Chief Justice Pius Langa expected to retire in 2009, the post of top judge was alleged to be the prize, especially if a new president, and not Mbeki, was going to appoint the successor. Dikgang Moseneke, Langa's deputy, had burnt his bridges with the Zuma camp and it was rumoured that Hlophe could fill the breach.

Hlophe's allies dismissed the statement as yet another smear by those who believed that because the Judge President is an isiZulu-speaker, he must be aligned to Zuma. Hlophe said he was convinced the attack was another 'anti-Hlophe' campaign: 'I'm in Cape Town. How do I influence 11 judges, including the Chief Justice, in matters they are handling? This is an irritation, but I would be very happy to hear the complaint, although I am of the view that even if this matter is resolved, they will bounce back with more allegations.'

The statement by the Constitutional Court stressed that the judges were not suggesting that Zuma had had anything to do with Hlophe's alleged behaviour. Nevertheless, some leaders of the tripartite alliance, and other commentators and analysts as well, accused the Court of having issued a public statement (instead of quietly informing the jsc) because it had a pro-Mbeki bias (in the shape of Moseneke, the influential

Deputy Chief Justice, known to be favoured by Mbeki).

The fact that the Court found some seven weeks later against Zuma on the search warrants, and said in its judgment that it looked askance at people who indulged in litigation aimed at delaying their main trial, propelled the alliance leaders into launching a well-coordinated attack on the judiciary and prosecutorial authorities at the end of July 2008.

This was just before Zuma applied, on 4 August 2008, in the Pietermaritzburg High Court, for the decision to prosecute him to be declared invalid on constitutional grounds – another case of unnecessary 'pre-litigation' activity, or so the Constitutional Court judges might have said.

Gwede Mantashe said that Constitutional Court judges were 'counter-revolutionaries'; Blade Nzimande said that everyone had known that the Constitutional Court would find against Zuma; and Mathews Phosa, an attorney, said that the judges could find as they wished, but they needed to understand that there existed another constituency in the country that didn't necessarily see things the way they did.

In the interim period, on 16 June, Julius Malema, president of the Youth League, a group often used by party leadership as a stalking horse, had said, while on the same podium as Zuma, that he, Malema – and, by extension, every other loyal ANC member – was 'prepared to kill for Zuma', sentiments echoed not long afterwards by Vavi. This did not go down well with South Africans, it seemed, and would have far-reaching consequences.

Both were summoned to apologise for 'hate speech' by the Human Rights Commission, one of the constitution's guardian organisations. But their apologies were not apologies at all, but mealy-mouthed chop-logic. The essence of the attack on prosecutors and the judiciary, and the 'hate speech' from Malema and Vavi, seemed to be that the alliance be-lieved that Zuma had been 'persecuted' by the prosecutorial authorities (driven by Mbeki and his people). Zuma was the elected leader of the ruling party, the man it had chosen to be king – this being the case, just who exactly did the judiciary think it was, standing in the way of that decision? Who, after all, had fought the war of liberation – the ANC or the judiciary? And, of course, the attack was aimed at putting good, old political pressure – trade union-style – on the judges.

This onslaught was launched not long after Robert Mugabe had stuffed down the toilet such meagre vestiges of the rule of law as remained in South Africa's northern neighbour so that he could remain president of Zimbabwe. It also happened at about the same time that, in accordance with a resolution taken at Polokwane, Parliament, which is controlled by the ANC, held public hearings about what was in fact a *fait accompli*: the dismantling of the Scorpions – who had, of course, been at the forefront of all Zuma investigations.

At about this time, as well, newspapers started mentioning the possibility that Zuma, once he was in power, might come up with legislation that would allow for a moratorium on the case against him while he was a sitting president. There were also discussions in the press about a general amnesty for those who had benefited illegally from the Arms Deal. This was somewhat off the point as far as Zuma was concerned, because the bribe he allegedly sought from Thint was one of his minor alleged crimes. At any rate, the 'idea' of a moratorium, amnesty or any mechanism that would shield Zuma from a trial presumably emanated from ANC sources.

In July, the NPA responded to Zuma's attempt to have the decisions to prosecute him in June 2005 and December 2007 set aside. The application was to be heard on 4 August in the Pietermaritzburg High Court, but the NPA and Zuma starting trading arguments and insults in their preparatory court papers. Replying to Zuma's application, the NPA put in a 140-page affidavit by Johan du Plooy, a senior special investigator in the Scorpions.

The nub of the NPA submission was that the ANC president should stop posturing by introducing 'political propaganda' and extraneous issues into his legal submissions. Instead, he should settle down and face the charges of racketeering, money-laundering and corruption that had been levelled against him. The NPA denied strenuously that there was 'any improper leitmotif to convict Zuma at all costs'.

'It is denied that the NPA is on an improper frolic of its own. It is acting in accordance with its constitutional and legislative mandate to prosecute without fear, favour or prejudice.'

The NPA said that the decision to prosecute Zuma, following the conviction of Schabir Shaik, had been based on hard new evidence and was not part of a political plot. The same applied to the decision to indict Zuma in December 2007, even though the 2005 case against him had been thrown out of court in 2006 because the state had not been ready to proceed.

The NPA said Zuma's surmise that Vusi Pikoli, the suspended NPA head, had discussed his decision to prosecute Zuma with President Thabo Mbeki in about June 2005 (supposedly while they were both on a government trip to Chile) was 'nothing more than unsupported and self-serving conjecture' and did not even 'begin to cast doubt on Pikoli's sworn denial of any such briefing'.

In his application for his prosecution to be set aside, Zuma had argued that Pikoli and Mokotedi Mpshe, Pikoli's successor, had infringed his constitutional rights by not giving him an opportunity to make representations before he was charged with corruption, fraud, racketeering and money laundering. Du Plooy rejected Zuma's argument and most of his affidavit in a highly detailed summary of the litigation between Zuma and the NPA, intended to refute Zuma's reading of history and especially his claim that he had been the victim of a political conspiracy in which the NPA heads had been complicit.

'A substantial portion [of what appears in the Zuma papers],' wrote Du Plooy, 'is devoted to the allegations [made by Zuma] of political motives ... [allegations that] glibly accuse three successive national directors of public prosecutions [Ngcuka, Pikoli and Mpshe] of serious unlawful conduct and gross abuse of power, without putting up a shred of evidence other than innuendo, speculation and dark hints at further details in subsequent applications. [The allegations] also tend to bring the NPA, and hence the administration of justice, into disrepute. [These allegations] are scandalous and vexatious, and serve no purpose other than to slander gratuitously the NPA ... and to generate self-serving political propaganda.'

Du Plooy said there appeared to be a perception taking root that Zuma could not have a fair trial because he was the victim of a political conspiracy: 'This perception is both founded upon and perpetuated by unsubstantiated allegations such as the ones contained in the present [Zuma] papers.'

The new evidence against Zuma, uncovered after 2003, said Du Plooy, consisted of, among other things, Shaik's admission during his trial of numerous matters about which the NPA had known nothing, including that payments to Zuma had continued after 2004; the existence of a 'revolving loan agreement' between Zuma and Shaik, which the Shaik trial judge had found to be a sham; and testimony during the Shaik trial by certain witnesses that Zuma made 'blatant attempts' to coerce them into accepting Shaik as a business partner.

Regarding Zuma's claim that he was not allowed to make representations about his case in 2005, Du Plooy said that Pikoli had testified that he had discussed his decision to prosecute Zuma with Zuma, but 'it is noteworthy that [Zuma] never suggested that the announcement of this decision should be postponed until he had an opportunity to make representations'.

Meanwhile, in the middle of July, the (Frene) Ginwala inquiry into whether Vusi Pikoli was fit to be the country's NDPP drew to a close. The Ginwala inquiry had been Kafkaesque: it pitted Pikoli (who said he had in fact been suspended by Mbeki for going after Selebi) against the Minister of Justice, who said her relationship with Pikoli had broken down, but never gave evidence, and nor did Mbeki. But it had also been fascinating because Pikoli, having been the NDPP (well, he still was – though suspended) was of course at the nexus of almost all the major court cases, legal matters and investigations that had gripped the country's imagination, including Zuma's. One of the red herrings of which Pikoli was 'accused' by the state advocates at the inquiry – one of his alleged misdemeanours – was not 'exercising proper oversight' and control over the notorious search and seizure raids on Zuma's former office at the Union Buildings. These raids were in turn the subject of the pending judgments in the Constitutional Court and therefore at the nub of the battle between the judges of that court and Hlophe. Finally, besides the strangeness of the inquiry into Pikoli, there was at its heart a mystery that resonated, as the academics say, with Zuma- and Mbeki-watchers: Why had Mbeki gone so far to protect Selebi? Was it simply loyalty to an old comrade that caused the president to suspend Pikoli? Was it the proximity in time to the Polokwane conference at which Mbeki wanted to be returned to the ANC presidency? Or was there something else that made the president want to avoid at all costs having Selebi in court?

A reliable person who was close to Zuma – though not Zuma himself, I must stress – told me that Pikoli had made contact with Zuma after he was suspended, and again once Zuma was elected ANC president, and that Pikoli had asked whether Zuma was willing to listen to what he had to say. Zuma's response had apparently been that he listened to whatever anyone had to say. But nothing had come of this '*toenadering*'.

I knew, like everyone else, about the 'two centres of power' – the government on the one hand and the ANC on the other. But there also seemed to be a 'parallel universe' – two separate realities coexisting next to one another – operating in the country. That, at any rate, is what it felt like in Pietermaritzburg on 4 and 5 August observing Zuma's application in the High Court and the events surrounding it.

On the one hand, there were the actual legal events in the court and what they seemed to signify. On the other, there was what was going on around the court and what was said by the tripartite alliance leaders. Both sets of reality coexisted, yet they often seemed to have little connection with one another. They seemed to be happening in parallel worlds that didn't touch at any point, like a set of railway lines – or like two people talking at – and not to – one another.

Starting with the events outside the court: the leaders of the tripartite alliance swept into a dusty and warm Pietermaritzburg to make a general statement that went something like this: The prosecuting authorities and the courts can do and say what they like, but the ruling alliance believes in Jacob Zuma's innocence; it feels he has been unfairly prosecuted (if not persecuted); and the alliance is going to see to it, come the proverbial hell or high water, that he becomes the next president of South Africa.

It was a well-organised show of support for the ANC president. Supporters were bused in and there was an overnight vigil. Jesse Duarte, the ANC spokesperson, was present with her support staff and other staff from Luthuli House, working hard to ensure that the much-maligned 'media' interviewed alliance leaders as much as the usual talking heads.

Of course, with the exception of Kgalema Motlanthe, all the bigwigs were there. Motlanthe's absence was notable, because if Zuma did get knocked out of the race for the national presidency because of his legal problems, it was presumably Motlanthe who would become the front runner. Yet there were strong rumours of a growing rift between the two men.

The important people included Baleka Mbete, Gwede Mantashe, Mathews Phosa, Lindiwe Sisulu, the Minister of Housing, Siphiwe 'Gebuza' Nyanda, the former chief of the SANDF, a full array of KwaZulu-Natal ANC officials, Julius Malema of the Youth League, Zwelinzima Vavi and Blade Nzimande.

At the end of both days of court proceedings, Zuma was escorted to the stage in the taxi rank outside the court by his phalanx of bodyguards. An honour guard of MK veterans stood to attention in front of the stage, saluted, and then fell out (militarily speaking) – once with so much vim and vigour that Debra Patta of eTV almost got up-ended.

Once they had done this, and Vavi had breathed fire and brimstone about the attitude of the prosecutorial authorities and Nzimande had done much the same, Zuma came to centre-stage to thank the crowd for coming to support him – and, at the end of the second day, to explain to them what had happened in court (as best he could – it was highly technical stuff). He also delivered on both occasions a resounding version, replete with vigorous dancing, of *Umshini wami*, which brought the house down each time.

With the exception of Nzimande, who is not especially interested in matters sartorial, and Malema, who was dressed for battle in a Zuma T-shirt, all the ANC officials and members were beautifully turned out, as though attending a wedding. Vavi's fine suit and tie, for example, looked as though they cost a great deal more than the average worker's salary, as did Mbete's various get-ups.

There was a joke doing the rounds that 'if you want to be in the next Cabinet, you had better be seated in the front row at this trial', and inside crowded courtroom A, there was much jostling among the important people to win bum space in the front row of the hard wooden public benches. There was also much hugging and kissing exchanged by those in the front and other rows, behaviour which seems to be *de rigueur* for those who were involved in the struggle and presumably still are.

The event that everyone had come to attend was not at all the big one about which everyone had been talking, merely a preliminary skirmish. Zuma had brought an application asking that the charges of racketeering, corruption, fraud and tax evasion against him be declared invalid because he had not been afforded an opportunity to have them reviewed when he was charged in mid-2005 and again in 2007.

According to Kemp J Kemp sc, Zuma's counsel, both the constitution and the National Prosecuting Authority Act ordered 'unambiguously' that Zuma was entitled to such a review, and therefore the charges against him were unlawful. But, according to Wim Trengove sc, the state's lead prosecutor in the matter, this was not so – and, in any case, Zuma's application was effectively side-stepping the main issue by dealing with the decision to prosecute him as an 'administrative' matter and not with whether he was innocent or guilty.

'[Zuma's] attack does not say you cannot prosecute me because I am innocent, or that I am being unfairly tried,' said Trengove. 'It says that I should not be put on trial because the decision to prosecute me was unlawful. It is quite divorced from innocence or guilt.' And it was, therefore, Trengove argued, beside the point: the trial needed to continue.

The difficulty, however, was that, besides the arguments being very technical and descending at times to basic linguistic analysis – what did the constitution and Act actually mean? – the acoustics in courtroom A were poor; Kemp was clearly suffering from the after-effects of a cold or flu and, despite being asked by Judge Chris Nicholson to speak up, he was mostly inaudible. So there was a minimum of 'juicy material' available, which meant there was little for the analysts and the main Zuma spokespersons to get their teeth into.

Besides, the real legal action was taking place behind the scenes and not in the courtroom. Apparently buoyed by the Constitutional Court's criticism of Zuma's strategy of pre-trial challenges, delivered 10 days earlier when it turned down his appeal against the validity of search and seizure warrants, and given that the state was 'trial-ready', State Prosecutors Billy Downer SC and Anton Steynberg started pushing for a main trial date of April 2009, arguing that any unfinished business should be dealt with at the trial and before Nicholson, the trial judge.

Zuma's legal team was not happy at all with this suggestion. Obviously, Zuma wanted to be president before he went to real trial. He might, for example, be able to introduce legislation, once he was president, which would make it illegal for a sitting president to stand trial. And it was reliably understood that there were 'resource' problems in the Zuma legal camp. Both Kemp and Michael Hulley, Zuma's attorney, had other commitments. They were not as free as state prosecutors to give 100 per cent attention to the Zuma matter.

Nicholson was apparently unable to get the various sides to agree on anything. He accordingly ordered them to sort out their 'squabble' and to set dates for the interchange of papers for the permanent stay application, which would be heard on 25 November. He apparently did not have any objections to the state prosecutors pushing to set a date for the main trial, one that could be finalised on 8 December.

Nicholson told all parties to be back in court on Friday, 15 August, to give him these dates. And he said he would give judgment on the present application on 12 September.

Outside the High Court, though Vavi, Nzimande, Malema and Duarte tried their best not to show disrespect to the courts and the rule of law, they could not help doing so. Duarte said Zuma had been 'maliciously persecuted' by the NPA over the years. Vavi said that 'we' would not allow Zuma to go to any 'kangaroo court' (it was not clear to which court he was referring) and Nzimande said that justice wasn't just about 'a day in court' but about the 'whole process'.

But that was just one line of a set of railway lines. The other line – the legal process – seemed to be continuing inexorably in its parallel world. And yet it felt as though there was about to be a serious collision – perhaps in the days following 12 September when Nicholson was due to give judgment on the application that the NPA's prosecutorial decisions had been invalid.

CHAPTER 18

September 2008

Let's fire Mbeki instead

Did anyone have a suspicion about the bomb that Judge Chris Nicholson was going to detonate in the life of Jacob Zuma and modern South African political history?

Some people said that 'the ANC' did have a clue; that there had been some kind of leak. This was why, they claimed, at the height of the alliance attacks on the judiciary, Zuma, two days before his 12 September judgment, had made a speech at the University of Johannesburg praising the rule of law. Why else – they asked – notwithstanding the damp squib that the court hearing had been on 4 August, had the tripartite alliance leadership, accoutred like peacocks, returned *en masse* to Pietermaritzburg to hear a judgment that everyone said was going to knock Zuma for a six?

The closest I came to what Nicholson's judgment might be was a story told to me by a lawyer. He said that a close friend of his, an advocate, had gone into Nicholson's chambers where he saw the State vs JG Zuma and Thint file on the judge's table. 'Well,' he asked Nicholson, 'have you reached a verdict?'

'Yes,' Nicholson allegedly replied, sombrely, to my friend's friend, 'and there are going to be many unhappy people.'

I took this story as an omen that Nicholson would indeed find against Zuma, which seemed to be everyone's view. And I don't believe that Zuma or the ANC or anyone else knew beforehand what Nicholson would say. One need only look at video footage of the judgment — Zuma looking exhausted, tense and at times puzzled, Kemp often with his head in his hands — to realise that they were simply waiting for the axe to fall.

On 12 September 2008, in the Pietermaritzburg High Court, Judge Chris Nicholson held that the charges of corruption against Zuma were unlawful on procedural grounds: the NDPP had not, he said, given Zuma a chance to make representations before deciding to charge him, as is required by the constitution read in conjunction with the NPA Act. And Nicholson directed the state to pay legal costs.

In paragraph 47 of the judgment, Nicholson wrote: 'The obligation to hear representations forms part of the *audi alteram partem* [hear the other side] principle. What is required is that a person who may be adversely affected by a decision be given an opportunity to make representations with a view to procuring a favourable result. The affected person should usually be informed of the gist or the substance of the case, which he is to answer.' He held that the NDPP's failure to follow the procedure outlined in Section 179(5)(d) of the constitution rendered the decision by the NDPP to re-charge Zuma unlawful.

But it was Nicholson's other comments that the nation found so riveting. He made these in response to the state's request that Zuma's 'scandalous, vexatious and irrelevant' allegations of how badly he had been treated by the NPA be struck off the record.

Zuma's court papers said, among many things, that he had been badly treated by the NPA; by Bulelani Ngcuka, the NDPP in 2003, who had maligned Zuma by announcing publicly that there was a *prima facie* case of corruption against him but that he would not be charged; by Penuell Maduna, the Minister of Justice before Brigitte Mabandla; and by Mbeki, because of his alleged interaction with Pikoli and his apparent influence on Mpshe. Though these were 'serious allegations', the NPA could probably have reacted to them by stating that they were incorrect and rejecting them, and then have focused solely on matters of law. But the NPA's lawyers over-reacted. They lost their cool, especially as regards Zuma's allegations about the NDPPs, which he had been making for a long time, and decided to punish him.

On 4 September, Nicholson had asked both sets of lawyers in his chambers whether they wanted him to pursue the request from the NPA that Zuma's allegations be struck. The state said it wanted the issue to be dealt with.

Nicholson found that various inferences could be drawn from the timing of the charges levelled against Zuma (such as the fact that he was charged soon after he was elected president of the ANC). These warranted a conclusion that there had been a degree of political interference by the executive arm of government. In paragraph 210 of his judgment, he wrote: 'The timing of the indictment [of Zuma] by Mr Mpshe on 28 December 2007, after the President suffered a political defeat at Polokwane was most unfortunate. This factor, together with the suspension of Mr Pikoli, who was supposed to be independent and immune from executive interference, persuade me that the most plausible inference is that the baleful political influence [on the prosecutorial process] was continuing.'

In paragraph 220 of the judgment, Judge Nicholson went on to write: 'There is a distressing pattern in the behaviour which I have set out above indicative of political interference, pressure or influence. It commences with the "political leadership" given by Minister Maduna to Mr Ngcuka, when he declined to prosecute [Zuma], to his communications and meetings with Thint representatives and the other matters to which I have alluded … It is a matter of grave concern that this process [of executive interference in the prosecutorial process] has taken place in the new South Africa, given the ravages it caused under the Apartheid order.'

Nicholson said clearly that his belief that there had existed political interference was not the reason why he held that the charges brought against Zuma were unlawful; his 'belief' was merely a response to the state's desire to have Zuma's allegations struck off; it was an adjunct to the issues of law. Nicholson also stressed that his ruling did not relate to Zuma's guilt or innocence in the main criminal case against him. But no one really focused on his qualifying statements.

Nicholson had said three remarkable things. First, in declaring the decisions to charge Zuma invalid, although he was not saying anything about Zuma's guilt or otherwise, he was saying that the whole process of charging Zuma had been flawed. This effectively kiboshed the 2007 charges; and the NPA would have to appeal Nicholson's judgment and start from the beginning (yet) again.

Second, in the process of declaring the decisions to charge Zuma invalid, Nicholson delivered a stinging slap in the face to the NPA and the three NDPPs who had been involved with Zuma over the years (Bulelani Ngcuka, Vusi Pikoli and Mokotedi Mpshe) for their cooperation with the executive arm of government.

Third, and most significantly, Nicholson backed Zuma's claims that there had been a political conspiracy against him and said Mbeki and his Cabinet had to take responsibility for abusing the prosecuting authority by using it to try to eliminate Zuma from the 'titanic' political struggle for the ANC presidency. Nicholson drew a comparison between the behaviour of Mbeki and his Cabinet and that of the apartheid governments, though he did not labour it, and inferred that the NDPPs had behaved improperly by allowing Mbeki and some of his ministers to influence them. Nicholson concluded, for example, that it was improbable that Maduna, the Minister of Justice during Ngcuka's time, could have been involved in the action related to Zuma without Mbeki knowing, and that 'in terms of the law, more especially emanating from the constitution, there [was] responsibility attributable to the president' for the actions of Maduna and of Maduna's successor, Brigitte Mabandla.

Regarding the Arms Deal, Nicholson called for a commission of inquiry. He was not handing down judgment on an Arms Deal matter but, because some of the charges laid against Zuma were connected with the

Arms Deal and with his relationship with Thint – in fact the December 2007 racketeering charge alleged that Zuma had been involved in a money-making conspiracy with Thint and Shaik – Zuma's application had touched in part on the Arms Deal.

The judge said it was high time that the Arms Deal saga was sorted out one way or another. However, he knew perfectly well that the only person empowered by the constitution to convene such a commission was the president. This being the case, the judge said he did not want to indulge in what is known as a *brutum fulmen* ('inert thunder' or, as Nicholson translated the Latin, 'a useless thunderbolt') – the legal term for a 'powerless order'. In other words, Nicholson knew he could make a suggestion only.

It is not an exaggeration to say that the whole country was aghast at Nicholson's judgment. People talked of little else. Prior to the hearing there had been, as we know, a spate of criticism of the judiciary by Zuma supporters; the delicious irony now was that this was the third time (including the rape case) that the judiciary had found in Zuma's favour. And it is remarkable to realise that, although it was not Nicholson's intention or his job to find a political solution for the Zuma saga, his finding was probably the best thing – or, at any rate, the most elegant possible outcome – this country could have wished for.

Not far from the judge's mind was clearly what is known as the 'fruit of the poisonous tree', an American legal metaphor for evidence that is tainted because it was gathered illegally or in an unacceptable way – the logic being that if the source of the evidence (the 'tree') is poisoned, then anything gained from it (the 'fruit') must be likewise. It's a reference to Matthew (7.17): 'Every good tree bringeth forth good fruit; but the corrupt tree bringeth forth evil fruit.'

The main consequence of his judgment was, or could have been, to put it bluntly, this: game over for the NPA. In ruling that the decisions to prosecute Zuma were invalid, and in a number of other comments, Nicholson had upheld – in a court of law – the claims that Zuma had been making. He had reached his verdict by applying his (and his two assessors') legal intellect and experience to the history of the matter, the precedents, the claims and counter-claims, and, above all, the law. The verdict was reached, in other words, not by politicians from any camp, United Nations' facilitators, journalists, or a life coach, but by a respected high court judge.

For one thing, Nicholson was the nominated trial judge for all Zuma matters. What would be the legal sense in trying to prosecute Zuma in front of a judge who had just ruled that the decisions to prosecute him were the fruit of a distasteful, dismaying, and perhaps even illegal political frolic involving the most powerful people in the land?

The NPA could ask for leave to appeal (and, as we will see in a minute, did), and then, having allowed Zuma his representations, re-charge him. But, though this was a possibility and might be the 'right thing to do' legally, it would be unwise in another way.

There was another, bigger game in town: political power, governing the country, call it what you like. And part of the main consequence of Nicholson's judgment was this: game over for the Zuma legal saga. No more wailing and gnashing of teeth, no more insults, from the leaders and members of the alliance about the perceived intransigence and bias of the judiciary relative to their president. No more threats to the rule of law. No need any more for dark mutterings about fiddling with the constitution or the law so that a sitting president cannot be charged. In other words, no more unrest; and businesspeople, the drivers of the economy, dislike instability above all.

Everyone, including especially Zuma, could have got on with the national elections and with attending to the issues to which everyone ought to be paying attention: combating poverty and HIV-AIDS, eradicating crime, doing something about skills shortages, educating the educators, and any number of other 'challenges'. The country could have moved on instead of chasing its own political tail in ever-decreasing circles. It might not have been a perfect solution, but in the real world, or the world of *realpolitik*, there are few perfect solutions.

This is not to claim that Nicholson's judgment was without flaws. There were some questionable elements – at least in the view of many – in his ruling. For one thing, another consequence of Nicholson's ruling (if it were not appealed) was this: Zuma would be let off the charges for which he had been indicted twice.

Did the flawed prosecutorial decisions of the past five years make Zuma innocent of corruption and racketeering? The answer to those questions was the same. No one could know until the evidence was tested and weighed by a judge. But everyone who had followed the state's case against Schabir Shaik, which was the basis of the case against Zuma, and had read the December 2007 indictment against Zuma, knew perfectly well that *prima facie* (at first look), the state had a strong and well-documented case against Zuma. This did not mean he was guilty. But it certainly seemed, based merely on common sense, that he would have a tough time explaining why he, a very influential politician and later the deputy president, was given about R4-million by Shaik, a businessman who needed certain favours but was short of money. The law is unequivocal about this kind of thing.

Nicholson's response would probably have been: if the tree is poisonous, one simply can't eat the fruit. It is enough now; Zuma has been pursued too long, it has been too messy, there has been too much questionable behaviour – it's time to let it go; in fact it would be a travesty of justice to continue with it. In fact Nicholson said there was a 'ring of the works of Kafka' about Zuma having been under threat of prosecution for years and yet never brought to trial.

There were other 'problems' about Judge Nicholson's ruling. He said that, because a decision had been made to prosecute Shaik in 2003, and given that bribery was a 'bilateral crime' (it takes two to tango), and given too that there existed a *prima facie* case against Zuma, the decision by Ngcuka not to prosecute him 'had been bizarre to say the least'.

One understands what Judge Nicholson was saying: this was yet another example of the NDPP not acting independently but in fact reacting to pressure from higher places and thereby tainting the whole process. But hadn't Nicholson lost the plot here? The reason Ngcuka made such a 'bizarre' decision, and the reason his superiors, Maduna and Mbeki, concurred with the decision, was because Ngcuka and the rest were in those days protecting Zuma – this was in 2003 – because he was the deputy president of the country and the ANC and their comrade. This only really changed, at least for Mbeki, when, in June 2005, Zuma refused to go gently into oblivion following Shaik's conviction; this, as we know, was when Mbeki really turned against Zuma.

Similarly, Judge Nicholson said he found it difficult to believe that Maduna was on 'a frolic' of his own; the president must have known what his Minister of Justice was up to. This is not necessarily correct. Maduna was a well-known maverick, inclined to go on frolics of his own; he was one of the ministers who had served under Nelson Mandela and were in fact 'independent' of Mbeki. They tended, for better or worse, to do things without checking every two seconds with the 'chief'.

Nicholson also found it unacceptable that Maduna had been involved with Ngcuka in setting up a plea bargain with Thint in return for an affidavit from Alain Thétard. In fact, he found the overall plea bargain distasteful, a sprat used to catch the big mackerel, Shaik.

Two points need to be made here. First, Zuma was the second most senior politician in the land. Of course Ngcuka wanted his boss, a full minister and an attorney, involved. He was dealing with seriously explosive material. Can you imagine what would have happened if he had sat on the evidence and not told Maduna or Mbeki? Second, the encrypted fax was a very vital piece of evidence – without it, the Arms Deal charge against Shaik would never have stood up – but Ngcuka had no real proof that it was what it was claimed to be. It had come into the NPA's hands circuitously and from a questionable source.

So Ngcuka had to make a choice: to go to court against Thint and Shaik without real proof as to the authenticity of the encrypted fax, or let Thint off the hook but at last have proof, from the author himself, that the fax was genuine.

In short, one learned yet again from the Nicholson judgment that, when it came to the Zuma saga, it was very difficult to locate the truth, especially because one was dealing with poisoned fruit. But then, as Pontius Pilate, the Roman prefect in Judea, once allegedly asked: 'What is truth?'

The state prosecutors were not interested in fruit or peace in our time; they were appalled by the judgment. Nicholson had said there was a 'ring of the works of Kafka' about Zuma having been under threat of prosecution for years and yet never being brought to trial. They said there was something equally Kafkaesque about Zuma not having to stand trial despite the strength of the case against him. Within four days, they had indicated that they would seek leave to appeal Nicholson's judgment at the Supreme Court of Appeal. (Nicholson later granted them this permission, as he was bound to do.)

The leaders of the tripartite alliance were not concerned about fruit or truth either. Nicholson's judgment sent them into a paroxysm of joy and feelings of vindication. By Sunday, two days after the judgment, every newspaper in the country was reporting that the leaders of the tripartite alliance were looking for a way to move Mbeki out of the presidency early and to install Zuma, or to hold early elections.

By the following day, this seemed an unlikely scenario, especially as Zuma declared publicly on the Sunday afternoon that it was a waste of energy to continue beating a 'dead snake'; the present administration should be allowed to finish its term; it was time for ANC 'unity' and election preparations. But this, as we shall see, was either a ploy on Zuma's part (he was playing for time and not alerting Mbeki to the Zuma Express that was about to come thundering down the line); or he was simply treading water and seeing what would happen. If everyone let bygones be bygones, so to speak, well then, the status quo could continue. But if not, it was time for war …

On 20 September, a week after Nicholson delivered his judgment, the 86-strong NEC decided that Thabo Mbeki would be 'recalled' – as it was quaintly phrased – 'from the presidency' of South Africa. He, realising that he had little choice, agreed.

What had happened?

Zuma's main supporters – Mantashe, Nzimande, Vavi, and Malema – had been ecstatic after the judgment. They said that it vindicated Zuma and demonstrated that everything he had been saying for years was true. They were especially pleased that their arch-enemy, the Machiavellian Mbeki, had been outed by a court as a manipulator of the state apparatus.

Zuma had been more circumspect. He knew from his lawyers that the application and judgment had nothing to do with the main charges against him, that the NPA could re-charge him, and that it was only one judgment (he had lived through many). When everyone screamed for Mbeki's head on the Friday and Saturday following the judgment, Zuma called for calm and said it was a waste of energy to keep stamping on a dead snake.

Zuma, his closest and more measured confidants, and his lawyers, wanted to see what the NPA would do. They all hoped that it would at that point let things go – both for the sake of the country and because Zuma did not want to face a long trial, especially one for which it seemed that the state had a strong case. But the NPA quickly indicated that it would seek leave to appeal. Not only that; the Cabinet, under Mbeki's steward-ship, said it rejected Nicholson's inferences and was 'taking legal advice' on how to have them 'struck' from the record. (A week later, Mbeki ap-plied to the Constitutional Court in his personal and official capacities to have Nicholson's judgment declared unconstitutional and set aside.) It had seemed that both Zuma's legal saga and the ANC's political prob-lem were over; that Nicholson had indeed provided an elegant outcome. But clearly some people weren't prepared to let sleeping dogs lie.

On the evening of 17 September, Zuma and Mantashe had a meeting late into the night with a number of lawyers, including Kemp J Kemp SC and Hulley. The constitution was pored over and discussed in detail, with the aim of establishing the best way to remove Mbeki from the presi-dency and replace him with a caretaker president until the April 2009 elections. (Zuma, having been fired, was no longer an MP and could not take up any parliamentary position.) This would take some juggling in Parliament, but it could be achieved.

A decision was taken. The NEC would be presented with the situation on Friday, 19 September. It would be recommended that Mbeki's resig-nation be asked for. And then the NEC's decision would be taken to the parliamentary caucus. The difficulty was that Zuma and his inner circle did not want Deputy President Phumzile Mlambo-Ngcuka – Ngcuka's wife and, above all, an Mbeki person – to take over the reins. So it was decided that she would be asked to go quietly.

At this point, we might ask what was driving Zuma, who is above all an ANC man. He makes decisions according to a consensus reached by party leaders, especially the four other people who manage the ANC at the moment. He is also a shrewd operator; he would not push for anything that was politically dangerous. But we must remember, at the risk of stating the obvious, that Zuma is also a human being, and that in June 2005 Mbeki had fired him. Mbeki had initially sent emissaries to ask Zuma to resign, a foolish thing to have done; he ought to have gone to see Zuma himself. Zuma had told the emissaries that he was innocent of wrongdoing and would not resign. Mbeki sent the emissaries back to ask Zuma to reconsider, at which point Zuma told both them and Mbeki to get lost. This episode was not something that Zuma had forgotten. Neither had he forgotten that, immediately following that humiliation, he was charged for the first time, by Pikoli. And, though Pikoli had denied that he discussed Zuma's case with the president, Zuma did not believe him – and neither, apparently, did Nicholson. So, though Zuma might not say much, though his expression might give away little, and though desire for revenge does not seem to be part of his make-up, no one should underestimate the depth of his bitterness and humiliation.

In short, history replayed itself. As a result of a verdict by a grey-haired KwaZulu-Natal judge, Mbeki fired Zuma. As the result of a decision by a grey-haired KwaZulu-Natal judge, Zuma resolved to fire Mbeki. Another irony is that it was the decision by Charin de Beer, the prosecutor in Zuma's rape case, to ask questions about Khwezi's sexual history that opened the door for Kemp to apply formally (in terms of section 227 of the Criminal Procedures Act) to do the same. Similarly, it was the NPA's decision to punish Zuma by asking for the striking out of his allegations of scandalous, vexatious and irrelevant prosecution that opened the door for Nicholson to make the comments he did.

By Friday morning, Mbeki had an idea of the size and velocity of the train that was heading his way and he took legal opinion. It is said that he seriously considered the possibility of applying for an interdict against the NEC.

Unbeknown to nearly everybody, Zuma also did not make the mistake of sending an emissary to Mbeki. Early on Friday 19 September – before or while the NEC deliberated – he met Mbeki in the Denel buildings adjacent to OR Tambo airport, and told him that, in the light of Nicholson's judgment, the reaction of the Cabinet to the judgment, and the feelings in the ANC, the NEC was going to talk about asking him to quit. Mbeki replied that he would respect any decision by the NEC and resign if he had to do so.

On Friday night, while the NEC was still meeting, Mbeki talked to Mlambo-Ngcuka at his home. Some say he tried to persuade her to stay on, though he knew that the Zuma camp did not want her.

Meanwhile, the nation waited. A press conference was scheduled for 7.30 pm on Friday. Everyone knew what was going to happen and what had to be done. But nothing could be said before the NEC had reached consensus. Zuma spoke little, leaving it to Mantashe and others to present the case. So Mantashe stalled the nation by saying that discussions were 'in the middle of nowhere'. They were not, of course; it was merely that a few recalcitrant arms had to be gently twisted. But there were not that many. Mbeki had accused Cyril Ramaphosa, Tokyo Sexwale, and Mathews Phosa of being in a coup plot against him; he had suspended Billy Masetlha; he had 'pushed' Siphiwe Nyanda; he had fired Nozizwe Madlala-Routledge; he was not happy about Malema of the Youth League and his assertion that loyal ANC members should 'kill for Zuma' (despite having come to the ANC presidency in 1997 on the back of Peter Mokaba's 'Kill the boer, kill the farmer' chant).

Early on Saturday morning, Mantashe – but not Zuma, for obvious reasons – went to Pretoria to tell Mbeki what had happened. Mbeki had been fired – just as Zuma had been fired three years previously.

What was it that Judge Hefer had said in his report?

Months have elapsed since Mr Maharaj had been questioned by members of the directorate [but] no charges have yet been preferred against

Mr Maharaj or against his wife. In the meantime, press reports about allegations against them kept appearing … one cannot be assured that the Prosecuting Authority is being used for purposes for which it was intended.

It seemed that Nicholson had been thinking along the same lines. And who and what was it that Mbeki had quoted in 2005, a few days before firing Zuma, at the swearing-in of Chief Justice Pius Langa? It had been Canadian Appeal Court Justice Rosalie Silberman Abella:

> The occasional judgment will collide with some public expectations, which will, inevitably, create controversy. But judgments that are controversial are not thereby illegitimate or undemocratic; they are, in fact, democracy at work.

Mbeki applied to the Constitutional Court to appeal Judge Chris Nicholson's ruling: 'It was improper for the court to make such far-reaching "vexatious, scandalous and prejudicial" findings concerning me. The interests of justice, in my respectful submission would demand that the matter be rectified. These adverse findings have led to my being re-called by my political party, the ANC – a request I have acceded to as a committed and loyal member of the ANC for the past 52 years. I fear that if not rectified, I might suffer further prejudice.'

The NPA then withdrew its charges against Thint. Anton Steynberg, the Deputy Public Prosecutor who helped Billy Downer SC successfully to prosecute Shaik, and who had been working on the Zuma prosecution since June 2005, said that, in the wake of Judge Nicholson's judgment, the NPA had no choice but to withdraw its case. 'The judge said that we erred by not allowing Mr Zuma representations. Well, if that was so, then presumably the same would apply to Thint. So we must withdraw the charges against Thint and then see where we are after our appeal against Judge Nicholson's judgment is heard by the Supreme Court of Appeal.'

Steynberg conceded that, if the appeal were successful, and if Thint were re-charged, it would be the fourth time that the arms dealer had been charged. The first time was in the Shaik trial of 2004 (withdrawn in terms of a plea bargain), the second as a co-accused with Zuma in 2005 and the third, also as a co-accused with Zuma, in December 2007. This succession of indictments is likely to be looked at askance by a judge.

'But,' said Steynberg, 'it wasn't our choice to have the charges against Zuma declared invalid – and, presumably, if there is a re-charging and a trial, the presiding judge will bear that in mind.'

One legal commentator suggested that another reason for the NPA dropping charges against Thint now was that, if it were to re-charge Thint and Zuma, the matter would start from the beginning and come before a new judge.

The NPA was then forced to oppose Mbeki's Constitutional Court bid to have Nicholson's findings against him declared unconstitutional and set aside. Mbeki had said that Nicholson, in the Zuma matter, 'ought not to have made findings of and concerning [Mbeki] in his personal capacity, or in his capacity as president and head of the national executive, without having afforded him a hearing'. Mbeki asked the Constitutional Court to rule that the findings concerning him of the High Court in the Zuma matter, made without affording him a hearing, constituted a violation of his constitutional rights. But, in an 11-page affidavit opposing Mbeki's urgent application, Johan du Plooy, the Scorpions' special senior investigator, asked the Constitutional Court not to hear the application for the moment. He said Mokotedi Mpshe, the acting NDPP, believed that there were 'good reasons not to consider and determine Mr Mbeki's application at this juncture'. One of these was that the NPA intended to appeal against the findings against Mbeki, among others, in the Supreme Court of Appeal.

'This means that the very issues that Mr Mbeki seeks to contest in this court will, or might also be, before the Supreme Court of Appeal if the [NDPP] is given leave to appeal to that court. [Mpshe] respectfully submits that it is inappropriate, while this case is on appeal to the Supreme Court, for some of the issues arising in the appeal to be determined by this court at the behest of someone else. It would be an insult to the Supreme Court and unfairly expose the director to a risk of prejudice in his case.'

Du Plooy said that allowing Mbeki's application to be heard now 'might result in this court dealing prematurely and unnecessarily, and without the benefit of the views of other courts, with aspects of [Nicholson's] judgment'.

Zuma, who was named, along with the NPA, as one of the respondents in the Mbeki matter, said he would contest Mbeki's application. A number of senior counsel, not connected with the Zuma matter, said they found Mbeki's application astounding.

'I would hate to be accused of overstating my point of view but I must say that the former President's application to the Constitutional Court is insane. The law is clear that only the parties involved in litigation have a right to appeal against a finding,' said one. If there were utterly exceptional circumstances then this rule might be waived, but not if one of the parties involved was appealing in any event. 'As we know,' he said, 'the NPA is appealing against the Nicholson judgment.' An appeal must be against an order – 'such as "go to jail", "pay a fine", or whatever. You can't appeal against a judge's opinions. If a judge says "I say you're a liar, therefore go to jail", you appeal against the order that you must go to jail. That he made his decision because he thinks you're a liar is neither here nor there. Judges have thousands of opinions. If people could appeal against a judge's opinions, there'd be no end to appeals.'

The bottom line, however, was that Mbeki, Zuma's long-time comrade and friend, was gone; he had resigned and Kgalema Motlanthe – speedily co-opted to Parliament and to Cabinet to provide a 'bridge' between the ANC (the incoming government) and the outgoing government – became the caretaker president of South Africa until next year's elections. Not even if the NPA successfully appealed Nicholson's judgment could Mbeki return. It was yet another astounding outcome of Zuma's odyssey.

And there would be others. There was much newspaper coverage about who might leave the government with Mbeki and who would stay.

Finance Minister Trevor Manuel was an especially 'big issue' because it was mistakenly reported that he had resigned (causing jitters on the markets) and because in October, the world plummeted into a financial crisis; and the rand sank too. In the end, one of the few who did resign from the government was Mosiuoa Lekota, the Minister of Defence and Zuma's old bugbear. Lekota then, along with Mbhazima Shilowa, the Premier of Gauteng, who resigned from the ANC, set up a splinter party that decided to form a coalition with opposition parties and to contest the elections against the ANC. They said that Zuma's ANC had behaved in a dastardly fashion by firing Mbeki and that it was a party that threatened the values of the constitution.

So, although the end of October was too early to tell whether the new party was of any real significance, yet another outcome of Zuma's story was that he presided over the first split in the ANC since the breakaway of the PAC in 1959. Zuma did not seem enormously perturbed about this.

CHAPTER 19

November 2008

President-in-waiting

Zuma's election to the ANC presidency was not the preordained outcome of another ho-hum party conference. It was the highly dramatic result of a painstaking behind-the-scenes campaign on the part of Zuma and his allies. The unceremonious ousting of Mbeki from the ANC presidency hit the country in general, as well as Mbeki and his coterie in particular, like a punch on the bridge of the nose. At Polokwane, in the hours following Zuma's election, one encountered politicians, political analysts and veteran local and international journalists who looked, and who said they felt, literally stunned.

No one had seemed to grasp that major elements of the ANC, Cosatu, and the Communist Party did not view Zuma as an untouchable at all. Nor, clearly, did a majority of ANC members. They were unfazed that he had been charged with corruption and rape. They believed they had good reasons for giving Mbeki and his people the bum's rush and they were intent on doing so, using Zuma as their spearhead. They were saying that a veteran ANC leader, who had given his life to the struggle, whom they had voted into position, and who told them he was innocent of any wrongdoing, was good enough for them. Never mind the NPA. They also seemed to be saying: the good times have not happened fast enough for the majority of the people; free enterprise may be good for some but has not lifted most out of poverty; and we don't want a person at home on the international stage, a kind of a schoolmaster, to be our president. We want one of us in charge. And to have been desperately short of money (as it emerged during Shaik's trial that Zuma was), to have been in trouble with the law, and to be perhaps a little *laissez-faire*, or at any rate not holier-than-thou, on matters of morality, *is* to be one of us.

But outside the ANC, and even in pockets inside it, some people said that the real source of the anger of 60 per cent of the delegates at Polokwane was the result of serious anti-Mbeki campaigning by the Communist Party, Cosatu, and the Youth League; that the delegates had been bullied into dumping Mbeki and most of his NEC. Others argued that most of the delegates were annoyed with Mbeki because, to put it bluntly, they had for years been denied a place at the trough.

Zuma's victory was not acclaimed by all for one main reason – the opprobrium attached to him because of the evidence that emerged at the Shaik trial and the other controversy that flowed from that trial and from the rape one.

'Post-apartheid political biography,' Anthony Butler has written, 'has mostly presented a procession of saints. Nelson Mandela, Oliver Tambo and Walter Sisulu, great and tough-minded political leaders, have been rendered as cuddly as teddy bears.'[1]

There might be some people who consider Zuma cuddly, but, following his court cases, few can be seeing him as a saint. And his reputation was not helped by what was said in October 2008 by Mosiuoa Lekota and Mbhazima Shilowa when they broke away from the ANC. They splintered from the ANC because they were loyal to Mbeki and had lost their places in the expensive seats; but what they said was that Zuma's ANC did not respect the Constitution, allowed the Youth League's Julius Malema to run riot, and contained people 'who had stolen money'.

What emerged about Zuma from the Shaik trial was, on the face of it, deeply damning. The state was trying to take the country's president-in-waiting to court to face a raft of charges which raised serious questions about his probity. Some of the charges involved the Arms Deal, one of the most enduring thorns in the flesh of the body politic. And then there was Zuma's relationship with Shaik, added to things he said at his rape trial, and things that happened outside the rape trial.

Some people – admittedly most of them white – are offended by Zuma's polygamy. *Awuleth' umshini wami*, 'Bring me my machine gun', an ANC struggle song, raises the hackles of many, again most of them white. An example of this, and of the kind of irrational bias and fear (and gratuitous nastiness) that Zuma engenders in people, was the comment made in September 2008 by, of all people, Nadine Gordimer, the Nobel literature laureate. When she heard Zuma 'ranting' (one thing Zuma does *not* do is 'rant') and calling for his machine gun, Gordimer 'thought of Hitler in the Munich beer hall', she said. Gordimer was born in Springs on the East Rand in 1923 – the year of the Munich *putsch* – so why did Hitler spring into her mind? She could have chosen PW Botha, the former President, Eugene Terre'Blanche of the Afrikaner Weerstandsbeweging, Zimbabwe's Robert Mugabe, or any of the other demagogues that have been so much closer to home and to our time.

Zuma has been accused of being a greedy careerist; a chameleon; a puppet of leftist forces (VI Lenin's classic 'useful idiot') or of other evil and venal people who have no use for the rule of law or morality; and of marking a decline in the standard of ANC leadership. Zuma has repeatedly been portrayed by the media, or some of the media, as a marauding Zulu warrior of yore; a Luddite and illiterate; a bit of a *klutz*; an inveterate and veteran womaniser; and an amoral populist.

On 19 December 2007, the day after Zuma won the presidency at Polokwane, the English newspaper, the *Daily Mail*, ran a story under the headline 'Machine-gun man takes over ANC – God help the Rainbow Nation'.[2] Among the choice paragraphs in the story were ones such as this: 'Zuma had made pre-[Polokwane] sacrifices of chickens and goats to his ancestors, as well as holding a session with a witch doctor, before ousting Thabo Mbeki as ANC leader.' And: 'Attracted by the low cost of living … [South Africa] has become the fastest-growing destination for British people. Now all this is under threat. A committed communist, Zuma has signalled his intent to "Africanise" the country.'

Zuma is also frightening to some people, especially whites, because he comes from a world of which they are not part. Mandela might also have come from 'another world', but some of his closest colleagues and friends were white, and, above all, he made 'reconciliation' a priority; on his watch, whites were never allowed to feel unwelcome in the country. Mbeki was – or came to be portrayed as – aloof and cold, and he often played the race card and got into childish tiffs over perceived racial slights. But he had a master's degree in economics from an English university, he was the son of a venerable ANC leader, he spoke and practised capitalism and he seemed at home hobnobbing with world leaders.

Zuma, on the other hand, was often seen at political rallies in the company of 'hotheads' and 'lefties' – Vavi and Nzimande, not to mention the 'big mouths' from the Youth League – all of whom are not much interested in being ingratiating to whites and are not cuddly either. Zuma is also more 'working class' (for want of a better term) than Mandela or Mbeki. He comes from a humble black family. Economics is not his favourite topic of conversation. He does not, like Mbeki, quote Yeats. He has been photographed wearing animal skins, the traditional garb of a Zulu male.

Yet, in almost every historical account in which Jacob Zuma had featured, even peripherally, he is portrayed as intelligent, brave, committed and exceptionally pleasant. These range from the memoir by Albie Sachs of how apartheid regime operatives blew off his arm and destroyed his eye (*The Soft Vengeance of a Freedom Fighter*, 1990); veteran journalist Allister Sparks's 'inside story' of South Africa's 'negotiated revolution' (*Tomorrow Is Another Country*, 1994); Patti Waldmeir's tale of the end of apartheid and the birth of the new South Africa (*Anatomy of a Miracle*, 1997); Luli Callinicos's biography of Oliver Tambo (*Beyond the Engeli Mountains*, 2004); Mark Gevisser's biography of Thabo Mbeki (*The*

Dream Deferred, 2007); and lawyer Peter Harris's remarkable story of the Delmas Four (*In a Different Time*, 2008).

Why, then, even after Zuma won at Polokwane, even though his constituency (ANC loyalists) clearly revered him, was he encountering such a high level of irrational hostility – from whites (those who had not met him), the media, the chattering classes, and from some black people? Why did the man perceived by clever observers to be intelligent, brave, committed and so on, suddenly have horns (as well as a shower head, courtesy of Zapiro, the cartoonist) growing out of his skull?

It was not the economy, stupid. Besides his 'otherness', it was essentially seven issues: that, in return for helping Shaik with his business endeavours, Zuma took money from him; that he had unprotected sex with an HIV-positive woman and said foolish things during the rape trial; that, despite claiming to want 'his day in court', he did his damnedest to stay away from being tried in connection with Shaik and French arms company Thint; that he was implicated in Arms Deal venality; that his main supporters were bright-red lefties who would do appalling things to the economy; that 'Zuma's ANC' had viciously attacked the judiciary and the principle of 'equality before the law'; and that, in a dastardly move, 'his' ANC had recalled former president Thabo Mbeki, the philosopher king.

What have I learned about Zuma by talking to him and others about him; by observing him; and 'reviewing' the past 66 years of his life?

Zuma is slightly above average in height. He wears thick spectacles. In his youth, he grew his hair and sported a black beard; he now clean shaves his head and face. He puts on and sheds small amounts of weight, apparently quite easily. He sweats easily, which is said to be a sign of fitness. He does not smoke and he does not drink alcohol; he favours tea with honey. I earlier omitted to tell the story of why, when he was a youngster of 10 or 11, Zuma resolved never to drink: it was because one Sunday he saw a pillar of the community, a teacher, dressed in his Sunday finery, suit, white shirt and tie, drunk as a lord, but not behaving like a lord – vomiting uncontrollably as he lay spread-eagled at the side of the road.

Zuma is physically strong and his energy and endurance levels are high; one of the few advantages, perhaps, of having graduated from Robben Island. Despite his age, he goes to bed at about midnight yet rises early.

Zuma enjoys good clothing but has been known to fall into a quandary about which is the best tie for court on a particular day. Like many of his generation, he sometimes struggles with modern technology. One evening Ranjeni Munusamy received an urgent phone call from Zuma. 'I need to make bullets,' he said, 'I need to make bullets. How do you make bullets?' 'What in heaven's name is the man raving about?' Munusamy wondered in a slight panic. But Zuma was not referring to the projectiles that are fired from a weapon. He was having trouble making the little black blobs known as 'bullets' on his computer screen.

Zuma loves his wives and his children, provided the children observe a basic modicum of discipline, and he is very proud of all of them. He suffers no qualms about polygamy – and nor, apparently, do his wives.

Zuma also apparently loves the sexual act – and he has, of course, been accused of being a 'womaniser'. It is difficult to know how to respond to this accusation other than to say 'yes, and your point is?', and to recall the remark by Constantine Fitzgibbon, one of the early biographers of Welsh poet Dylan Thomas, who was accused of alcoholism. Fitzgibbon said that, as far as he could tell, an alcoholic was someone else who drank as much as you did, but whom you disliked. I assume this comment also applies, *mutatis mutandis*, to the appellation 'womaniser' and to those who make the accusation.

Because of the rape charge brought against Zuma by Khwezi, there remain people, mainly women, whose lips curl contemptuously when the name Zuma is mentioned. When the first edition of this book was already almost complete, however, I was put into contact with a woman named Marion Zeeman, who lives in Holland and sent me an e-mail, part of which reads as follows:

Firstly, my name is Marion Zeeman, and in Durban I attended Natal University for some years. Subsequently, I worked at the Trade Unions'

Bolton Hall for a year. Eventually, after being arrested a few times and security police harassment, I left South Africa in November 1977. I joined the ANC in Lusaka and moved to Mozambique around January 1978. The next 3–4 months I spent living at the ANC flat which was near the sea front, and also near the ice-cream shop where all the Zanu cadres used to hang out. Comrade Jacob Zuma was the deputy ANC representative at the time …

Secondly, having been in contact with Comrade Zuma in those days on a regular basis, I can only voice the opinion that he was always very correct in his dealings with people and approachable. He had well developed social skills. In fact he got on with just about everybody: the Mozambicans, the foreign comrades, and other cadres in the movement. He kept my money for me, and, as I was a vegetarian, he gave me extra money to buy greens.

Comrade Zuma was also street wise yet emphatic in his dealings with young comrades coming from South Africa. The ANC flat consisted of several stories with a large open-roof top. The girls were not allowed to spend time with the men on their floor. Separate sleeping facilities: as no liberation movement is in need of pregnant, uneducated young girls. Thus, contrary to some negative popular opinion about Comrade Zuma's attitude to women, he was quite straight really. I can wholeheartedly endorse the fact that he really tried to keep some moral discipline going under trying circumstances.

Zuma obviously has little time for recreation. For him, true relaxation, even though he is often pursued there by hordes of people who want to talk to him, is spending time at Nkandla, with his wives and his family – and of course his beloved cows. Zuma also seems to enjoy attending church services and, like many South Africans, he is punctilious about attending funerals.

Though someone allegedly 'not properly educated', Zuma not only speaks a number of African languages fluently and well, his English is fluent and his vocabulary and command of the language are certainly far superior to the average SABC radio reporter or, for that matter, the average politician. This is not to claim that he is *au fait* with every aspect of the language. My favourite JZ anecdote is as follows. (Zuma will not like me telling this story, nor will the other people who were involved – I wasn't one of them – but so be it.)

In May 2006, in the middle of Zuma's rape trial, the editor of *Business Day*, Peter Bruce, wrote in his weekly column of 2 May, 'The thick end of the wedge', as follows: 'ANC deputy president Jacob Zuma will know on May 8 whether he is guilty of rape. He seems not to think so and, quite frankly, I think he may be right.'

Bruce continued two paragraphs later: 'So what I think is that Zuma, whom we already know to be a man of limited moral, financial or even political judgment, has a pretty young girl over to stay, goes a bit gaga at the sight of some flesh normally hidden, and proceeds to make a prick (literally) of himself.'

Members of Zuma's 'kitchen cabinet', who were meeting – not in Zuma's kitchen but in his TV room – were irate. The indignation at Bruce's effrontery, at his having dared to refer to Zuma as a prick, was massive. The general sentiment (and this is putting it gently) was: 'We'll sue Bruce here, we'll sue Bruce there, we'll sue Bruce everywhere.'

Then it was time to go. As the group was leaving, Zuma called one of them aside.

'But tell me,' Zuma asked him, 'what is a prick?'

Zuma prefers talking to people and watching television to reading. This should not be assumed to mean that he is uninformed; on the contrary, I have found him to be pretty well informed on subjects that I would not have expected him even to have thought about (example: the rise of anti-black violence on the streets of modern urban Russia). This is because Zuma has the rare ability to listen properly. And his recall is unfailing; in respect of some subjects, such as happenings in the ANC or political events, he is much like one of the computers that he finds so daunting. He also loves telling stories and he is a wonderful raconteur.

Zuma is, as must be apparent from this book and from other things written and said about him, one of the most genial people one could ever met. He is simply a man of great charm – and he is innately respectful of others. All of these qualities are why so many people, including of course the leaders of the Left, like him and find him approachable. This is why he is considered a consensus-builder, not a dictator – he lets people have their say, he listens carefully, and then he binds together different views. One NEC member who was present for the debate on whether Mbeki should be recalled or not has told me that Zuma said hardly anything during the hours of discussion. 'He listened – and really listened hard, you could tell, unlike some others – and he watched and he left the "process" to reach the conclusion it had pretty much had to reach.'

It is also one of the reasons why some people have called Zuma 'a chameleon'. His response to a debate or a question is to agree with his interlocutor, to draw him or her out, and to see where they get to. But this does not work very well on the public platform, especially when one day's utterance is contradicted by another's and when people want hard and fast opinions. But Zuma's geniality should not be misread. For, though he is doubtless a jovial person, it is also sometimes a mask and a defence – as is his obliquity.

When I was in high school, there was a very South African saying that did the rounds. Obviously I didn't go to a 'good' school, so heaven knows why such a startlingly metaphysical saying did the rounds there. It went something like this: 'That guy is so skinny that if he held up both his arms together above his head, he would disappear straight down his own arsehole.' Zuma can often be so oblique (*Webster's Ninth New Collegiate Dictionary:* 'not straightforward; indirect; deliberately obscure'), that sometimes he seems almost to disappear before one's eyes – metaphysically speaking, of course.

When Zuma first stepped into the witness box during his rape trial, feeling perhaps a little nervous, he began by 'making speeches'. But on all the subsequent long days, clearly having been put back on the straight and narrow by his legal team, he confined himself for the most part – except when asked to amplify a statement – to being a master of obliquity. 'Yes, your lordship' and 'No, your lordship' were the only responses he offered to most of the questions put to him.

I am also told that there is a certain management technique, the main element of which is the strict avoidance of 'taking on' other people's problems. It's the opposite of being a mother hen. It is also, I suppose, the (healthy) opposite of the adolescent fantasy that you control the world. At any rate, Zuma is the master of a technique that, so to speak, allows the executives to fight it out in the boardroom while he calmly eats a sandwich in his office.

Zuma is patient – he waits for the game to be played out before he strikes – a major character trait of any intelligence chief. Rugby fans will know that one hallmark of the so-called modern game – rugby as it has been played since it became professional – is what the sports writers describe as 'taking the ball through the phases'. This means that the ball is carried forward, and then, when the ball carrier is halted, usually by being tackled, mostly a ruck (or informal scum) is formed. This is called the 'breakdown' point. The idea then is that the ball carrier and his fellow team members feed the ball back from the breakdown point to the members of his or their own team – and the process starts all over again, until one of them reaches the other side's try line, or until the ball is lost, either to the other team, by being kicked away, or whatever. The skill lies, in the first place, in not having the ball 'turned over' – lost to the other side during the ruck, or at any point, or through one's own actions – and, secondly, in patiently waiting for the ball to come back from the breakdown and re-cycling it – and thus launching the next phase. Some teams can go through nine or ten phases of re-cycling. Given that rugby is such a fast and very unsubtle game, watching a skilful team taking the ball through the phases can be remarkable to watch; it can, at the best of times, look like a piece of choice choreography. The point is that it requires enormous patience and poise. Impatient and anxious teams lose the ball very quickly.

Zuma's way of dealing with information – his manner of dealing with much of his life – is to have the kind of poise and patience that the best rugby teams have when they take the ball through the phases. Zuma is poised, canny, polite, wily and, above all, patient. Perhaps this is not an innate characteristic, but one learnt in prison. Richard Stengel, who ghost-wrote Mandela's famous autobiography, said that he learnt from

Mandela that one of the most important lessons learnt on the Island was 'rigorous control of passions and emotions'[3] and discipline.

Zuma also seems to be an expert on the so-called 'need to know', the term used by military or espionage organisations to describe the restriction from certain people of data considered very sensitive. As I got to know him and his circle a little better, I was often surprised to find that a certain member of his circle knew one piece of information while an equally loyal one knew nothing about it. Zuma does not necessarily play off one person against the other – not if they are his friends – but he knows all about keeping people and information in separate compartments. As we know from countless thrillers, it's an old intelligence practice: don't let operative x know what operative y is doing because such information might only end up comprising x anyway. Zuma, in other words, plays his cards very close to his chest.

Another example of behaviour that seems to have been learnt rather than innate came to light at the Hefer Commission of 2003. Moe Shaik told the commission that Zuma had instructed him – in 2001 when he was the deputy president – not to give information or documents related to the Ngcuka 'spy allegations' to Penuell Maduna, the Minister of Justice and therefore Ngcuka's boss. Much water has flown under the bridge since the Hefer Commission, and it has since come to light that, in certain matters not unrelated to the Zuma story, Maduna played an odd role – so, even in 2001, presumably, Zuma might have been wary of him. Besides, it seemed clear that Maduna was close to Ngcuka. Yet to keep a Cabinet colleague in the dark about suspicions that the country's attorney-general was an apartheid spy was, to put it mildly, a little strange – unless, of course, you are Zuma. If you are Zuma, you keep silent about a range of things and only ever use them if you really need to do so.

Perhaps this decision by Zuma was not only about being Zuma. It emerged, when I started research into this book, that Peter 'Kill the boer, kill the farmer' Mokaba, the belligerent former president of the Youth League, had been investigated by Zuma's department in 1989 on suspicion that he was a security police informant.[4] Journalist Gavin Evans, a

former member of the SACP underground, outed Mokaba in the *Mail &*
Guardian in 2002 when Mokaba died.[5] According to Evans, he had been
asked in 1989 to compile a dossier on Mokaba and Zuma had wanted to
detain him. But Oliver Tambo had intervened, saying Mokaba should
be 'rehabilitated'. Mokaba vehemently denied the allegations and threatened to sue anyone who made them, though he never did.

Mac Maharaj's biographer, Padraig O'Malley, who conducted exhaus-
tive interviews about the Hefer Commission, has argued that one of the
things that Judge Hefer did not understand about the ANC was that it
did not always act against known spies, at least ones who were senior.
O'Malley said he raised the issue with Zuma 'with regard to an individual uncovered as probably a spy who was a member of the NEC', but
about whom nothing was done, and 'Zuma smiled and said, "That's not
the way we operated."' [6] This perhaps was the case with the Ngcuka information and Maduna. But Judge Hefer was not privy to the ways of
ANC intelligence and Moe was left dangling in the wind.

Zuma, as has been stressed throughout this book, is a party man.
'There was a helluva fight at some point during Hefer between Moe and
Mac,' said Yunis. 'Mac said we needed to go for the throat and pull the
ANC in – blame the whole party, the whole government, for Ngcuka's
abuse of power. Mac said it wasn't sufficient to zero in on Ngcuka alone.
So he and Moe conferred with Zuma. And his response was: "Don't
throw your spear at the flag. Throw it at the man holding the flag, but
not at the flag".'

Zuma can also be shrewd, perhaps even Machiavellian in his own way,
though that sobriquet seems to have become Mbeki's personal property.
Zuma pretended that he played no major role in the recalling of Mbeki.
But, once his 'magnanimity' immediately after the Nicholson judgment
('let's not stamp on dead snakes; let's get on with the elections') was
snubbed by Mbeki, Zuma moved fast and hard, playing a central role in
ousting Mbeki.

'Oh, Zuma is someone who leads from the front, make no mistake,'
said someone who knows him well. 'But more and more he'll take a back
seat now and leave the dirty work to Gwede Mantashe.'

Finally, although Zuma is measured and generally careful, and has become more so as he has grown older, one has to say that it is in his character to live dangerously. What the reason is for this risk-taking – whether Zuma is a chance-taker by nature, plain arrogant (he does what he feels like doing), or whether there is in him the obliquity that I have mentioned – a kind of vagueness about his own motivations (and other people's) – that leads him into living dangerously, or whether the reason is a mixture of all three, I do not know.

But he disobeyed Mbeki in Swaziland at the end of 1975 and sneaked back into Natal despite the danger to himself and to the struggle. And in the middle of preparing for a very serious corruption trial, he hopped into bed with a woman who was not only the daughter of an old friend and some 30 years younger, but was also, according to herself, HIV-positive, even though no condoms were readily available. There is nothing wrong with sexual intercourse between consenting adults and, as far as Zuma was concerned, the woman had signalled interest and consent. But given that the nation's eyes were on him at the time (and the gaze was none too kind), given the obvious emotional precariousness of the other person in question (though it is an element of Zuma's character that he probably never noticed), and given her physical condition – it's not difficult to conclude that Zuma often lives dangerously.

Zuma, then, is genial and a smiling man. But he is equally canny, guarded, experienced, sometimes impetuous, and politically sophisticated, especially in the world of *realpolitik*. People would be making a serious mistake if they thought his decision, for example, to speak only isiZulu at his rape trial, or his penchant for wearing leopard skins on ceremonial occasions, bespeak a bumbling backwoodsman.

There is a part of him that can set like steel, as Mbeki found out when he expected Zuma to resign in June 2005. It was not so much, I believe, that Zuma had designs on the presidency; the issue was that his dignity had been affronted. And, having said that, it *was* also that he had designs on the presidency – there is a part of Zuma that believes he is owed

ZUMA — A BIOGRAPHY

something; he has put in the hard yards ... so why not? Why Mbeki and not him? Young herd boys, who have started with nothing and climbed their way to the top, also have something to prove, even if they smile beautifully.

And, allied with the steel in his soul, Zuma has little interest in remorse, guilt, or any similar sentiments. Those are for people who have the emotional time for such sentiments; and men who have spent 10 years in jail and 15 in exile have been busy surviving and striving.

Still, though Zuma does have a self that is private and well defended by joviality, he is an open man. And there is presumably very little in his life that has not been uncovered. On Robben Island, he and other prisoners had to undergo the 'tausa' ritual: the full body inspection during which naked prisoners had to jump up and down to shake loose anything that might be hidden in their private parts. Zuma's legal travails and the attendant media spotlight have been a species of 'tausa'. 'Hell, there can't be anything left to discover that we don't know about,' said one of his friends. 'I certainly hope that's the case. I couldn't stand any more revelations.'

Perhaps the most important lesson one gleans about Zuma by talking to himself and others about him, by observing him, and by having 'reviewed' the past 66 years of his life, is that Zuma's legal travails, and the issues from which they have come – his 'relationship' with Shaik, the Arms Deal – represent only a small percentage of what Zuma has done and achieved in his life.

Despite Zuma's stoical attitude to things in general, he has lived his life with a fair share of heartbreak and difficulty. He does not talk about Kate Mantsho, his wife who committed suicide, but one does not have to try too hard to imagine what his feelings, defended as they might be, were and are about her death.

Zuma does, however, talk about Mbeki. I once said, in passing, something along the lines of 'that was a strange thing for him to have done, you were good friends.'

Zuma looked and me, then said quietly: 'We were more than friends.

We were great friends and we were brothers.' Then he turned away.

Some of us also sometimes forget, perhaps, now that we are years 'into democracy', about the bravery of people such as Zuma as well as many of the other people who appear in this book. Most of us have encountered them – usually through what we have read, heard on the radio, or seen on television, but in some cases personally. And at certain times and in certain situations, their conduct has no doubt been 'lacking in majesty and decorum', to use a phrase of Richard Ellmann's. So we censure Zuma and the rest of them heavily, in whatever way we choose to do this. Journalists and political commentators write opinion pieces; private citizens tell their children, write letters to newspapers, complain to their friends loudly in coffee shops, or have their say on talk radio; some people maybe change their vote; and so on. Because Zuma and many of the others have been, or are, state officials or political party office-bearers, this is as it should be. But, more than a decade after apartheid has gone, and having discovered that such people have feet of clay, what we perhaps sometimes forget is that each in his or her own way fought hard in the bitter struggle against the apartheid system, the appalling horror of which we seem to have forgotten astonishingly fast.

I am not suggesting that Zuma and others are beyond censure because of their role in the struggle. What I am saying is that such people did not choose the easy road; they made a choice to fight apartheid actively and nearly always at huge personal cost – a choice that maybe you, and certainly I, did *not* make; and that it might be worthwhile, from time to time, to take a minute to remember that.

Though I have eschewed psychologising, I think the discomfort engendered in some people by Zuma goes deeper than a dislike of his alleged corruption or a dislike or fear of his populism or alleged male chauvinism. It occurred to me, especially during his rape trial, that Zuma and the events around him served to rub people's noses, so to speak, in the reality of South Africa.

We have one of the most civilised constitutions in the world and like to believe that we have in a very short time become one of the most civilised societies in the world. And we were mostly right until the May 2008 xenophobia erupted. But there is a great deal going on under the surface about which we would prefer not to be reminded; there is a great deal to which we aspire but do not always reach. Zuma has caused us to look under the surface.

We like to think we are ruled by thoughtful people who care about us and are taking care of business. Then Zuma's supporters hit the streets with the message that it is not the people in Pretoria whom they trust. It is Zuma, and it does not matter if he got a bit of money here or there, or if he has fathered children here, there and everywhere. We like to say that we are not racists any more; we are a rainbow nation whose members are not torn apart by ethnic sectarianism. Then Zuma's supporters come out wearing T-shirts saying, '100 percent Zulu boy'. We like to say that we are moving towards a greater respect for women and that we have '16 days of activism' to prove it. Then Zuma comes to the Johannesburg High Court on a rape charge and his supporters rail at the women who are there supporting Khwezi and throw stones at a member of the crowd whom they mistake for her. In those moments, 16 days of activism and our attempts to allow women the respect and care they are due were set back 16 years.

In short, Zuma is continually setting our national agenda on its head, continually showing us our own ugly visages.

According to the script of Oliver Stone's movie, *Nixon*, Richard Nixon, the disgraced American president, stood during his last days in the White House, musing in front of a portrait of John F Kennedy, in those days everyone's golden boy.

Nixon muttered to himself: 'When people look at you, they see what they want to be. When they look at me, they see what they are.'

CHAPTER 20

January–April 2009

Off the hook

The year 2009 started with stories of romance. It was reported that Zuma planned to marry a fifth wife – Thobeka Madiba or Mabhija, for whom he had already paid *ilobolo* and who was scheduled to present pre-nuptial gifts known as *umbondo* to Zuma's family in Nkandla. Traditional bridal gifts include items such as food, including pumpkins, and traditional liquor. One newspaper reported that the two families – the Zumas and the Mabhijas – were 'racing against time' to hold the gift-giving ceremony because Zuma needed to get to the Eastern Cape for the ANC's traditional 8 January statement and the launch of its election manifesto in East London.

It was exactly a year after Zuma's wedding to Nompumelelo Ntuli of KwaMaphumulo (Zuma's mother's home town) and it seemed like a nice idea to the media. But the hacks had it wrong by a year; it would not be until January 2010 that Zuma would marry Thobeka.

After the Nicholson judgment, Zuma had hit the campaign trail for the April 2009 national elections as hard and fast as he could. Though outwardly disdainful of the new-fledged Cope, privately there was a surprising amount of concern in ANC circles about how it might do at an election – and this feeling grew as 2008 drew to a close. Perhaps another reason for not getting married just then was that Zuma also had his mind, as did many others, on what would happen in the Supreme Court of Appeal (SCA) deliberations on the Nicholson judgment.

It turned out not to be good news for him. On 12 January 2009, the NPA's appeal against Judge Chris Nicholson's 12 September 2008 ruling was upheld by a full (five-judge) bench of the Supreme Court of Appeal.

The court ruled that Nicholson had been (a) wrong in law to have claimed that Zuma had been entitled to make new representations about the charges against him and (b) that Nicholson had overstepped the judicial mark in commenting that the case against Zuma had been sullied by political interference. In short, the SCA bench effectively gave the NPA the go-ahead to bring Zuma to trial for corruption, fraud, money-laundering, and the rest.

But my last two paragraphs do not communicate the drama surrounding the court's judgment – delivered by Louis Harms, acting deputy president of the SCA, with judges Ian Farlam, Azar Cachalia, Nathan Ponnan, and Mandisa Maya concurring – nor the derisive curl of the lip that the court managed to direct at Nicholson for having found that former President Thabo Mbeki (and others) had meddled in the bailiwicks of the various national directors of public prosecution.

Beeld's headline, 'Appèlhof braai Zuma-regter', 'Appeal court braais Zuma judge', was spot-on, even though Harms was careful to stress that the judgment, where it dealt with the Mbeki and the NDPPs, was 'not about whether there was political meddling in the decision making process. It is about whether the findings [made by Nicholson] relating to political meddling were appropriate or could be justified on the papers [put before Nicholson].'

Harms wrote that Nicholson had failed 'to confine [his, Nicholson's] judgment to the issues before the court', had decided 'matters that were not germane or relevant', had created 'new factual issues', had made 'gratuitous findings against persons who were not called upon to defend themselves', and had failed to distinguish 'between allegation, fact, and suspicion'.

Nicholson's findings against Mbeki and the Cabinet, said Harms, 'were not based on any evidence or allegation. They were instead part of the judge's own conspiracy theory and not one advanced by Mr Zuma. Furthermore, the finding, by implication or otherwise, that a non-party [to a particular case, i.e. Mbeki] may have committed a criminal act where this was not alleged, where it was not in issue, and without hearing that party, is incomprehensible.'

The SCA described Nicholson's straying from usual judicial norms as 'impossible to fathom'. 'Political meddling was not an issue that had to be determined. Nevertheless a substantial part of his judgment dealt with this question,' Harms said. 'He [Judge Nicholson] overstepped the mark ... He changed the rules of the game, he took his eyes off the ball,' Harms said, adding that Nicholson's failure to confine his judgment to the legal dispute before him set a 'dangerous precedent'. Nicholson's finding of political meddling in the Zuma graft case was 'erroneous' and 'unwarranted'. Harms also said Nicholson's support for a commission of inquiry into the Arms Deal and criticism of Mbeki's decisions to fire Zuma and to stand for ANC president in 2007 clearly demonstrated how Nicholson had gone beyond what he had been required to decide.

Zuma and his legal team did not come to court for the ruling. After witnessing the mauling that Kemp J Kemp SC, Zuma's advocate, had taken at the pre-trial hearing in late November 2008, they knew what was coming. But was Harms justified? Had Nicholson's judgment really been so way off the mark?

I didn't think so and I wrote a piece that appeared in *Rapport*. (The then editor, Tim du Plessis, kindly translated it into Afrikaans.) In English, it went like this:

As often happens in life, especially on playgrounds and in pubs, quite a few people this week joined Acting Deputy Supreme Court of Appeal

President Louis Harms in kicking Judge Chris Nicholson when he was down.

There will doubtless be a reaction to this. An equal number of journalists, so-called 'legal experts', and analysts will write about how gratuitously nasty and 'personal' Harms and his fellow four SCA judges were to Nicholson this week when they overturned Nicholson's September 2008 high court judgment on the application by Jacob Zuma to have the charges against him declared unlawful.

But analysing Harms' judgment on an *ad hominem* basis – that is, to focus on the men involved rather than the ball – is a bad idea because it misses the real issue. And this is that Harms might well have thrown out the baby with the bath water.

Last year Nicholson was required to judge whether in terms of section 179 of the Constitution, Zuma had a right to make 'representations' about his case to the National Director of Public Prosecutions (NDPP), and whether Zuma had a legitimate expectation of being thus heard, before being charged in December 2007.

Nicholson found in favour of Zuma on both these legal issues. But he also commented – at the insistence of the state, let us not forget – on whether some of the accusations made by Zuma against the various NDPPs were 'vexatious, scandalous and irrelevant'.

Nicholson found, on his reading of the papers before him, that Zuma's allegations were not unreasonable. In fact, there seemed to Nicholson to be proof that there had been a political conspiracy against Zuma; that in fact there was a 'distressing pattern' of political interference in the actions of the NDPPs, interference that stretched all the way up to the then president, Thabo Mbeki.

However, the SCA this week found that Nicholson was wrong on the legal issues: Zuma did not have an inalienable right to be heard nor should he have had a 'legitimate expectation' to be heard.

But even worse, said Harms and his brothers, Nicholson had strayed way beyond the borders of his judicial authority by commenting on issues not even argued by Zuma and had impugned people (cabinet members, Mbeki) who had not been able to defend themselves.

The SCA bench was, strictly speaking, correct. In terms of the way in which the law operates, it was not up to Nicholson to comment on non-legal issues. He should have made a finding on the two legal issues and called it a day.

But this immediately raises three questions.

The first is that, as I have noted, it was the state that asked Nicholson to judge whether some of Zuma's ancillary allegations were vexatious and scandalous. It is common cause, as the lawyers say, that Nicholson asked the state's counsel in chambers whether they really wanted to proceed with the issue of the ancillary accusations, and they said yes. Why then should Nicholson not have commented?

Second, if Nicholson's comments were strictly speaking irrelevant to the legal issues before him – which they were – why did the SCA make a finding on them? After all, the SCA found – also correctly in terms of the law – that Mbeki had no right to enter into the proceedings. So why let Mbeki off the hook, why 'find' that Nicholson was wrong about him – through the back door, so to speak?

Harms might reply that Mbeki was not absolved; that the SCA merely found that Nicholson's comments had been irrelevant and unfair. But this reply would be ingénue in the extreme. There was a good reason why Mbeki's counsel, Marumo Moerane SC, left the court with a spring in his step.

Most important, however, is this question: Were Nicholson's comments on Zuma's allegations so far off the mark and irrelevant, or was his judgment actually, albeit unorthodox, a progressive and intelligent one?

It seems clear that not far from Nicholson's mind was clearly what is known as the 'fruit of the poisonous tree', an American legal metaphor for evidence or a prosecutorial process that is tainted because it was gathered illegally or in an unacceptable way – the logic being that if the source of the evidence or the process (the 'tree') is poisoned, then anything gained from it (the 'fruit') must be likewise.

It's a reference to Matthew (7.17): 'Every good tree bringeth forth good fruit; but the corrupt tree bringeth forth evil fruit.'

And anyone involved with Zuma's legal travails – anyone with the slightest knowledge of real life as opposed to life as presented in legal papers and arguments – knows that the steps to Zuma's prosecution over the past seven years have not taken place in a pristine vacuum, that all kinds of people were involved on all sorts of levels, and that there is very little that Nicholson said that could be faulted.

All that Nicholson was saying was that the tree of the prosecutorial process against Zuma was obviously irretrievably tainted and that therefore it should be dumped. He does not seem to have been so far off the mark.

But, my brave and clever words notwithstanding, the bottom line was that Zuma would have to fight an election campaign later in the year with corruption charges hanging over him; he would have to face yet another long court battle in his bid for the highest office. Zuma's legal saga had, as Daniel Howden of the London *Independent* wrote on 13 January 2009,

reshaped the political landscape in Africa's biggest economy, forced Thabo Mbeki to resign the presidency, split the ANC and shaken many South Africans' faith in their legal system. And yet the Zulu elder remains on course to take over from stand-in Kgalema Motlanthe who is widely believed to be keeping the seat warm for him. ... [The resignation of Mbeki] caused a major rift inside the ANC and a splinter group emerged, the Congress of the People (Cope), led by a close ally of Mr Mbeki's, Mosiuoa Lekota. With Cope making a good showing in local elections last month the stage is set for the ANC's first ever serious electoral challenge. Yesterday's blow came just as the ANC was seeking to promote its election manifesto. It also spooked markets with investors concerned that Cope and the ANC will veer to the left in a battle for grassroots support.

Jeremy Gordin, Mr Zuma's biographer, said that while 'no one is impervious' to pressure, the ruling is unlikely to worry the veteran politician. 'After five or six years of battle it's just another step in court.' He said the real question was whether the ANC leadership would 'stay strong' in its backing for the party leader. 'It depends whether there are voices in the

ANC leadership asking if he is the right man, or if it might be better for everyone if someone else [came in],' he said.

So what was the next step for Zuma and his legal team, especially if they didn't want support for Zuma to flag? In terms of the 'Stalingrad' legal strategy ('fight them every inch of the way, with whatever you have') that Zuma, Kemp and the others had put together since December 2007, the Zuma legal team were going to continue with an application for a permanent stay of the charges against Zuma. This had been their next step in September 2008 when Nicholson's remarkable judgment intervened, so to speak.

Michael Hulley, Zuma's attorney, told the media that the team was considering whether to approach the Constitutional Court. Hulley also mentioned – without anyone, except Karyn Maughan of *The Star*, paying too much attention (but it was, as we shall see, a very significant remark) – that the team was arranging to continue making representations to the NDPP – those very representations that Zuma and the NPA had been fighting about in court and that had lost Mbeki his job, gotten Nicholson into trouble, and stoked the SCA's ire.

James Myburgh, the editor of Politicsweb.co.za, wrote (15 January 2009):

The question now is where to for Jacob Zuma's supporters in the ruling party? There are two obvious options for the ANC to pursue, given that the ruling party is determined not to let the case come to trial. The one is for Jacob Zuma to continue to pursue his legal strategy of endlessly appealing on every conceivable point, no matter how contrived. This is only possible given the unlimited (taxpayer) funds at his disposal. This may buy time, but it does not make the problem go away.

The other is to make the case quietly disappear through a behind-the-scenes subversion of the judicial process. This is what has been euphemistically termed the 'legal solution'. Here, a centralised but currently headless National Prosecution Authority is the obvious target of the 'baleful political influence' that needs to be exerted.

Then it happened. Three months later, the mother of all bombshells fell. On Monday, 6 April 2009, just a few weeks before the general elections, the acting NDPP, Mokotedi Mpshe, announced that he had decided to withdraw all the charges against Zuma (as well as co-accused French arms company Thint).

It was the most remarkable *deus ex machina:* 'a god, or an event, introduced into a play to resolve the plot'; an artificial or surprising intervention. I use the Latin term – which literally means 'god out of a machine', from the Greek *theos ek mékhanés* – not to be a smart-ass, but because it seems so apt. The decision by Mpshe to drop the charges – notwithstanding everything that had gone before, including the successful conviction of Schabir Shaik, Zuma's financial backer – did put one in mind of a staged event. It felt like a play during which, at the critical moment, some sort of giant, puppet-like golem descends from 'the gods' (the topmost part of the stage) and intervenes to change completely the expected outcome of the proceedings. The charges that had been dogging Zuma for so long, like the hound in NP Van Wyk Louw's chilling 'Ballade van die bose',[1] really did appear, finally, to be gone.

Mpshe made his decision due to a number of revelations which showed that the legal process had been 'tainted'. The revelations related to a number of intercepted phone calls. Apparently, the former head of the Scorpions, Leonard McCarthy, and Bulelani Ngcuka, the former NDPP, had conspired over the timing of the charges laid against Zuma, their aim apparently being to help Mbeki politically.

Mpshe stressed that the withdrawal of the charges was due to abuse of the process and did not amount to an acquittal. But no one cared about that; the point was that Zuma was off the hook.

Mpshe said the telephone conversations between McCarthy and Ngcuka, as well as a few others, demonstrated that there had indeed been a conspiracy against Zuma – that a person or people in the NPA, instead of behaving without fear or favour, had been involved with others in late 2007 in planning how best to bring Zuma down. And there was a reference during one of the calls to 'the big man at Luthuli House' (presumably Mbeki).

What had been going on, and had in fact been going on 'from way before Polokwane', almost entirely away from the public eye, was that Hulley had been involved in making those 'representations' to the NPA – and, after Nicholson's judgment, the NPA had started focusing a little harder, and then by April, the 'representations' had finally borne fruit. For, remember, Zuma, formerly head of ANC intelligence in exile, formerly the deputy president, and now the ANC president, had a lot of friends in important places, including of course the state intelligence and security fraternity. And they had been talking to Zuma *prior* to Polokwane, telling him certain things and 'sharing' certain documents and transcripts with him …

Mpshe began by saying that he had to announce the most difficult decision he 'ever made in his life'. He then read from the transcripts of the tapes that were made of McCarthy and Ngcuka talking to one another.

> '**BN**: If this thing comes out the way we discussed it yesterday, those key issues, right, it will be a devastating one for them, and it will cause people to wake up to know what they are actually doing without being dramatic, without you making arrests, it will say, this is what we have, and we are forced to state it now and people will wake up [and] think [about] what we are doing. **LM**: Friday, [but by] by Friday people are packing bags, they won't even read the fucking newspapers.'

This purported to be a discussion held by McCarthy and Ngcuka on 12 December 2007 (while the Polokwane conference was in session), about when to file the NPA's reply to Zuma's application to the Constitutional Court in the search warrant matter.

Mpshe said that in light of such recordings and what they implied, he had come 'to the difficult conclusion that it [was] neither possible nor desirable for the NPA to continue with the prosecution of Mr Zuma'. And that was that.

The tapes were made available to the NPA by Zuma's legal team in a bid to prove that the charges against JZ should be stayed because they came about through a top-level political conspiracy. Mpshe revealed that the recordings were made by the NIA as part of an investigation into the 2007 Browse Mole Report that was drawn up by the Scorpions, in a bid to discredit Zuma.

The country was in an uproar. Mpshe's decision was not universally acclaimed. There were biting and uncomplimentary questions about the reasons behind Mpshe's decision and about the provenance and legality of the transcripts that he read in public. Why had Billy Downer sc, the lead state prosecutor against Zuma, and the man who had 'led' the legal charge against Zuma for so long, accepted Mpshe's decision with such apparent equanimity? Why had the decision been accepted, also with such apparent ease, by the man who led the NPA delegation in final discussions with Hulley – Willie Hofmeyr, head of the Special Investigating Unit, and a man generally considered to be of the highest probity?

The matter became even more vexed when, on 14 April, James Myburgh wrote and demonstrated very clearly on politicsweb.co.za that Mpshe had apparently plagiarised an obscure judgment handed down by Justice Conrad Seagroatt of the Hong Kong High Court on 13 December 2002 ('Did Mpshe plagiarise a Hong Kong judge?'); and 'plagiarism' is not an unfair word to use, because Mpshe made no reference to Seagroatt in his own judgment or later, nor did he ever concede that he had made use in any way of the Seagroatt judgment.[2]

Was it the end of democracy and the rule of law? Had Zuma simply taken over and poisoned all that was valuable in the new South Africa?

The Democratic Alliance filed an application for a judicial review of the NPA's decision, arguing that Mpshe's decision was 'not reasonable' and ought to be set aside. Helen Zille said at the time that Mpshe had 'not taken a decision based in law, but [instead had] buckled to political pressure'. The case is due to be heard on 7–9 June 2010.

It might be a difficult case for the DA to win, for a number of reasons. Above all, there is one issue (in my view) that is close to legally sacrosanct, and it's the one that Nicholson had stressed. If the 'prosecutorial process' is tainted, if a police officer searches a home without a warrant and finds a key to a gym locker, in which he finds illegal drugs, the introduction of the drugs as evidence would in all likelihood be found to be inadmissible – because the key was found illegally (without a warrant). As I mentioned, the Americans use the term the 'fruit of the poisonous tree' as a legal metaphor to describe evidence that has been 'illegally' gathered or a tainted prosecutorial process. Go before a judge and tell him that your client was the subject of unfair treatment because some members of the prosecution were trying 'to catch him out' – and the judge is going to look very unfavourably on the prosecution. It is an absolute no-no to tamper with evidence or the process. Once Mpshe had been presented with evidence that the process had been tainted because of the 'conspiracy' of McCarthy and Ngcuka, there was no way that he, Mpshe, could continue with the process. This was how it had to be – no matter how strong the case, how affronted the members of other political parties or the world's media, or whether Mpshe's decision was just or not.

Of course the $64 000 questions were: To what extent was Zuma involved in getting the tapes? Who handed them over to Zuma? Why was someone handing secret intelligence tapes, the property of the NIA, to Zuma? Mpshe was in a certain sense a *deus ex machina*, but who was the real *deus ex machina*, the person introduced to resolve the plot – and save the day for Zuma?

'So far no one has come close to working out where we got that information,' said Hulley. And, according to him, the emphasis on a couple of audio tapes alone is also mistaken. He says the 'representations' were a process that continued over a few months and that it was not just a matter of telephone intercepts but other documents, including for example e-mails. 'We had a clear case proving that the prosecutorial process had been compromised,' Hulley said. 'That's what making representations was all about.'

On the evening of 6 April, Zuma held a party for about 600 of his closest friends at his Forest Town home to celebrate the charges against him having been dropped. He said he was relieved to have the whole saga of the previous nine years behind him. At last the Union Buildings were in sight and finally all the legal issues – all the conferences with his 'learned friends', as he called his lawyers – were to be a thing of the past.

But he was tense too – he would not feel really comfortable until the next morning, when the charges were formally dropped at the Durban High Court, and also the election was close and needed to be fought. I had not seen him since December the previous year and he told me had enjoyed reading his biography, though it had some mistakes that needed rectifying, and he wrote me a kind personal note on the title page of my copy.

The next day, after the charges were dropped, Zuma held a press conference where he made the following speech:

Today the Durban High Court withdrew the indictment against me following the decision of the National Prosecuting Authority not to prosecute. This marks the end of a long and painful period. The investigation has brought untold pressure on the entire Zuma family especially my children and relatives. We have been sustained throughout this by the unwavering support of comrades, friends and scores of well wishers nationally and internationally. We thank all of them for believing in my innocence, my assertions of a political conspiracy and of being a victim of a systematic abuse of power.

I do not regard myself as being above the law and I believe that no public representative should be beyond scrutiny. That is why throughout the eight-year period, I did not use my position to interfere with the due process of the law. I have always been ready to co-operate with the NPA and have presented myself in courts whenever needed.

My quarrel with the NPA was on the methods and the motives of the investigation. The probe was supported by a vicious media campaign designed to find me guilty in the court of public opinion. In addition to routine media leaks, the infamous off-the-record briefing by the then National Director of Public Prosecutions Bulelani Ngcuka contravened the fundamental principle that individuals are innocent until or unless found guilty.

It was in this briefing where he showed his real motives and said he wanted to try me in the court of public opinion and asked the editors present to help him. This was the beginning of the abuse of power.

The actions of the NPA, which fuelled my view that there was more to the investigation than pure legal matters included the following amongst others:

a) The decision by Bulelani Ngcuka not to prosecute in 2003, saying the case was not winnable in court, but choosing to announce this publicly in order to leave a cloud of guilt, further confirmed what he had said in the off-the-record briefing. There was a clear agenda so that I should remain guilty forever. There never was a case against me. We have now discovered that Ngcuka continued to manipulate and abuse the investigation process long after he resigned as head of the NPA. The agenda was clearly to improve the chances of his preferred candidate for leadership of the ANC, assisted by the head of the Directorate of Special Operations, Leonard McCarthy.

b) The subsequent decisions to prosecute by Vusi Pikoli and Mokotedi Mpshe. No reasons have ever been given as to why the decision of Ngcuka was reversed. We are pleased that it is now finally clear why these decisions were taken. The reasons were political and manipulative.

c) I was alarmed by the failure by the then Minister of Justice and Constitutional Affairs and that of the Head of the NPA to co-operate with the Public Protector in his investigations arising out of my complaint in 2003, that my rights had been violated by the NPA. My assertion was confirmed by the Public Protector, but his report was subjected to ridicule by Bulelani Ngcuka and Penuell Maduna, and its recommendations were never acted upon. Nobody defended the Public Protector.

… We were also suspicious of the excessive use of monetary resources to drive the investigation both locally and abroad. Also alarming was the political nature of the meetings held by the NPA to discuss the ANC's resolutions taken at its policy conference regarding its future and initiatives to counter such. We were also startled by the fact that in 2005, the NPA instituted charges first, and then later raided my properties, former offices and those of my lawyers, an indication that they charged first and looked for evidence later. This was a sign of desperation and I had to seek relief from the courts to protect my rights.

All said and done, let me emphasise that my conscience is clear. I have not committed any crime against the State or the people of South Africa. I had no difficulty with responding to the charges as I knew they were baseless. I sought legal remedies in the courts simply because I felt my rights were being violated for reasons that appeared very suspicious. And I have clearly been vindicated. Our country has gone through a very painful and divisive period, and it is a time for healing and unity. I would not wish for any South African to go through what I went through over the last eight years. Retribution will not take us anywhere. Now is the time for us to focus on improving people's lives.

And it was also time for Zuma to get on to the election trail in earnest.

CHAPTER 21

April–December 2009

Siyanqoba!
(We are victorious)

Luthuli House was concerned about Election 2009,[1] and rightly so. Not that there was any chance that the ANC would lose, or even come close to losing, but because this election was different. It did generate an unusual amount of excitement – mainly because of a man named Jacob G Zuma, and also because his rise to the ANC presidency had resulted in the formation of Cope. As Roger Southall wrote:

> For some of [Mbeki's] supporters … his ejection from office was an indication that, having lost control of the ANC, they should continue the struggle with Zuma from outside the tent. Zuma's ANC, it was said in such quarters, was no longer the ANC of Albert Luthuli, Oliver Tambo and Nelson Mandela. It had lost its purity in power, and had increasingly become a vehicle of corruption and personal ambition.[2]

This was painful and anger-provoking stuff for Zuma to hear. Grown-ups might know that what had been going on in the ANC had precious little to do with 'purity' – but Luthuli, Tambo and Mandela were among Zuma's heroes and it hurt him to hear himself held up as one of those who had led the ANC away from what they had created.

There were also questions – among political pundits and analysts, if not among ordinary people – about the extent to which the 2009 election would 'shake' the country's democratic ethos. The DA seemed well-organised and had moved away or tried to move away from its historical positioning as a 'white' party, and Cope was apparently throwing down a large gauntlet. How would the ANC deal with a serious challenge at the polls?

The three previous elections for the National Assembly had given the ANC successively larger majorities: 62,6 per cent in 1994; 66,4 per cent in 1999; and 69,7 per cent (under Mbeki) in 2004. In many ways, ANC dominance had been valuable: unity in diversity, national reconciliation, non-racialism and black advancement, with an emphasis on equality and democracy – and economic stability and growth – was clearly 'good' for the country.[3] Still, there were serious criticisms from many people about the politicisation of the public service through the 'deployment' of party functionaries to state offices; the subordination of Parliament to the Executive; the destruction of the independence of supposedly 'neutral' public institutions (the SABC); the collapse of key government services (health, education, the courts and the police) – collapses that it was claimed were related *inter alia* to the ANC emphasis on racial 'representivity' and the favouring of political loyalty over ability. Above all, the spread of corruption through the body politic – something with which Zuma was stained, and would be for ever – alienated and angered many.

Besides these 'problems', which made the electoral terrain more uncertain than it had been since 1994, there were other 'difficulties'.[4] First, there were demographic changes among the electorate. A constantly increasing proportion of those aged 18 and over had little direct memory of apartheid; they'd grown up, for better and worse, under an ANC government. In addition, population growth had been uneven. Although the fertility rate had fallen (3,3 in 1991 to 2,8 in 2004) and life expectancy at birth had declined (from 66 in 1994 to 50,5 in 2007), the population had grown from 40,6 million in 1994 to 48,7 million in 2008. Then, an increasing proportion of the population was non-South African (up from 0,1 per cent in 2001 to 5 per cent of the total population in 2008).

Second, in 2009 South Africa still remained one of the most unequal countries in the world. According to a measurement utilised by the United Nations Development Programme – the Gini coefficient – SA was the eighth most unequal out of 177 countries in the world. And in 2005 it was estimated that more than 22 million people out of the population of 44 million were living under the poverty line (R322 per person per month). What these depressing numbers meant was that, while there were many citizens dependent on 'ANC grants', there were just as many who were (or so the pundits said) deeply disappointed with their living conditions and enraged at the highly visible inequalities they saw around themselves every day.

Third, there was the matter of service delivery – of basic services. A look at the actual numbers – for electricity, running water, expenditure on education, health spending, and proportion of households living in formal dwellings – shows that since 1994 the ANC governments had in fact not done too badly at all. But – *but* – in the years preceding 2009, there was undoubtedly 'a sense of relative deprivation amongst the poor … fed by resentment at inconsistencies of provision, a sense that the government had had time enough to do better, and particularly by perceptions of corruption amongst politicians and officials, especially at local government level'.[5] In 2005 there were an officially recorded 881 'unrest incidents' – all about so-called service delivery.

Fourth, there was in the air a feeling that the glue that had held the country together as a political society since 1994 – the ANC – might be losing its adhesion. There had been a spate of service delivery protests in 2005-6 and then a horrific eruption early in 2007 of xenophobia that had resulted in the murder of 70 people. With these as a backdrop, and with the glue seeming to weaken, pessimists said the 2009 election might be very ugly in parts, with clashes between the ANC and Cope members in, say, the Cape. Optimists said; no, never, we are a strong constitutional democracy – no violence and political intolerance. Which was it going to be?

The country was going to the polls with more than its own troubles looming: by early 2009 the global economic boom of the previous 20 years had bellyflopped – it was back, almost, to the recession days of the 1930s. Locally, there was high unemployment and low levels of savings and investment, though the banking sector did not crumble, as in other places – the Reserve Bank and the monetary authorities had kept it on the straight and narrow.

As for good ol' democracy, it was not only having a bad time in Kenya and Zimbabwe, but some people (especially white liberals, like me) were asking, for five main reasons,[6] about the ANC's commitment to the big D.

First, there was the 'deployment' of party personnel to civil service and supposedly independent institutions. Second, there was the way the ANC diverted government monies into the party's pockets. Third, the ANC had dealt with corruption in a pretty *laissez-faire* manner – and that Zuma was number one on its election list and that there were convicted folk on the list as well, did not help much. Fourth, 'democrats' feared for the independence of the judiciary, especially in the wake of the behaviour and words of Zuma 'supporters' and others (such as ANC secretary-general Gwede Mantashe) at the time of the Nicholson judgment. Mantashe had said the judges of the constitutional court were 'counter-revolutionary'. If the ANC were badly hurt at the polls, was democracy going to hold in South Africa?

So Zuma and the ANC planners went into the 2009 campaign – which, in the finest ANC tradition, JZ was going to spearhead – thinking about the decline in registered voters, the party's 'disconnection' from young people, and the general alienation of the voters due to perceived bad service delivery, rampant corruption, joblessness, soaring HIV infections and AIDS deaths (running at about 350 000 a year in 2009), the Eskom 'load shedding' debacle (would water and health services also crash?), and the xenophobic pogroms.[7]

National candidate selection was presided over by the ANC Deputy President, Kgalema Motlanthe. Provincially, Gauteng and KwaZulu-Natal were well-organised, the Western Cape was a shambles, and in the Northern Cape and Free State, Zuma coat-tailers John Block and Ace Magashule took control.[8] When the national list came out, Zuma and the leadership decided to tread very, very carefully: they were not going to throw out the baby of some of the ANC's major former leaders with the bath water of Mbeki. They were also guarding very carefully against any further defections to Cope. Trevor Manuel, whom Zuma's leftist supporters allegedly loved to hate, was there at number four; Jeff Radebe, who'd kept a low profile in Mbeki's time, was at number seven; and even Naledi Pandor, a poor Minister of Education, and Joel Netshitenzhe, Mbeki's prince of planners, were at 12 and 41, respectively. Interestingly, given later wails from commentators and pundits that the ANC was shifting 'leftwards', not many SACP and Cosatu members achieved top-of-the-list status.

In keeping with the way it started electioneering in 1994, the ANC manifesto was a worthy, wide-ranging, detailed, and boring policy programme (a bit like talking to Zuma about ANC politics!) that focused on unemployment (particularly of young people in rural areas); health (a national health insurance scheme was promised); education; rural development; and crime and corruption.

There seemed to be lots of the folding green stuff available; Luthuli House spoke of an 'initial budget' of R100 million and in the view of Professor Anthony Butler – quoting *The Times* – a realistic estimate of the campaign was in the region of R500-million. The ANC really wanted a victory in the election, and they wanted it with a gold star!

The manifesto launch was held on 10 January 2009 in East London – a direct challenge to Cope, which wanted to take over the province of Mbeki, Mandela and the ANC. Zuma's ANC hired 300 buses, 100 minibus taxis, and three trains to bring 75 000 supporters to the launch, as well as many popular entertainers. There was a turnout of at least 60 000 people at the Absa Stadium and at an overflow stadium close by.

Luthuli House had set up a team in late 2008, headed by NEC elections head Ngoako Ramatlhodi and campaign head Fikile Mbalula. Cosatu and the SACP contributed organisers, some full-time, as did the Youth League and the MK veterans. It was all shoulders to the wheel. Door-to-door canvassing was the order of the day, as well as conventional community hall meetings. The ANC consciously targeted religious leaders, professionals, traditional leaders, black business people, young people, and Afrikaners.

Zuma went down especially well with church leaders – even though he had clashed with Desmond Tutu, Archbishop Emeritus of the Anglican Church, and the presidential candidate of Cope was Mvume Dandala, a former Methodist bishop. As Butler put it: 'Zuma's achievement here required a genuine and intuitive grasp of the character of religious practice in these churches. He also managed to appear humble before God, and thereafter the people, a thespian accomplishment that was beyond the capacity of Thabo Mbeki'.[9] Zuma also did well in his meetings with traditional leaders – this 'key social formation' always having been a strong point and preference of his. Zuma would much rather pass the time of day with the king of the amaXhosa or the amaRharhabe than a room full of foreign journalists. Who can blame him?

Since love of the bottom line seems to be as blind as true love is said to be, there was an unexpected conversion of certain business leaders to the Zuma camp, and of course Zuma made certain during the early months of 2009 that he was on hand to offer a sympathetic ear to business people stricken with anxiety over what the new order might bring.[10]

The focus on bringing younger people into the ANC fold was probably responsible for the projection of Youth League president Julius Malema. He was disrespectful, rude to older political leaders, and inclined to rhetorical excess. In fact he was clearly the ANC's attack dog, and bore the brunt of criticism for this kind of 'negative campaigning' (as Butler calls it, in a classic English understatement) – and he was therefore an effective campaigner.[11] The ANC also targeted the youth by holding 'Ride 'n braai parties' at which the message was 'It's really funky in the ANC'.

Another Zuma master-stroke was to ask Nelson Mandela to endorse the ANC campaign. He appeared next to Zuma on 16 February in the

Eastern Cape. There were not too many better endorsements for Zuma than that.

'Words, words, words,' as the famous (fictional) Danish prince said. I am referring to the 2 000 or so of them preceding this sentence – for in the end, despite all the 'complicating' factors listed and briefly analysed above, the ANC easily won a famous victory. It secured 65,9 per cent of the votes cast and a total of 264 seats in the 400-member National Assembly.

This, relative to the 2004 election, represented a loss of 15 seats and 3,8 per cent of the vote, and of course the DA triumphed in the Western Cape and the ANC lost ground in urban areas. But as far as the major provinces were concerned, the Eastern Cape was a huge victory for the ANC – one for which it had worked very hard – and KwaZulu-Natal was another locus of victory, mainly because of one JG Zuma.

Everyone in the ANC was well pleased. An apparently impromptu party was held at Luthuli House on the evening of 24 April and Zuma looked relaxed for the first time since 6 April.

Zuma – heavily criticised after Polokwane for having been brought to power by a minuscule number of the country's population – was clear that he had now been given a mandate to rule by almost everyone, three months after Judge Louis Harms had told the NPA to go and get him and 16 months after he had been charged with corruption and fraud. He was also President of South Africa four years after having been fired as Thabo Mbeki's deputy.

Five thousand people were invited to the 'formal' part of Zuma's in-auguration, in the amphitheatre of the Union Buildings, on Saturday, 9 May. There was a fuss in the media about the cost of the proceedings – R75-million (paid for by the Departments of Foreign Affairs and Public Works). But there was no way the ANC was not going to have the finest inauguration that money could buy.

It was a wet morning – and among the guests wrapped in blankets and sitting under umbrellas were Finance Minister Trevor Manuel and his wife Maria Ramos, former Transport Minister Mac Maharaj, ANC Youth League president Julius Malema, the new speaker of the National

Assembly, Max Sisulu, Zuma's lawyers Michael Hulley and Kemp J Kemp, and former ANC spokesperson Carl Niehaus.

The rain drenched the seats in the VIP area, and some of the guests sought shelter in the media area. The Shaik brothers, Yunis and Moe, arrived just after 9 am. Former Speaker of Parliament Frene Ginwala and Unisa Vice-chancellor Professor Barney Pityana were also there. Heads of state, MPs, newly-elected premiers, presiding officers of Parliament, diplomats, bodies such as the UN, African Union and Southern African Development Community, as well as local and international business and community leaders, were invited. No one minded the rain too much because, as the newspapers explained later, 'In Africa it is considered a blessing when it pours during a ceremony.'

For the less formal part of the proceedings, thousands braved the rain and flocked on to the south lawn of the Union Buildings. When the formal inauguration ceremony ended at midday, while the dignitaries and VIPs ate lunch in a giant marquee at the presidential guest house, the '30 000' onlookers on the lawns were treated to a concert.

But, before that, as rays of sunshine broke through the downpour, the people in the amphitheatre leapt to their feet, danced, cheered and ululated as the country's chief justice, Pius Langa, administered the oath of office and Zuma was sworn in as the President of South Africa. At the top of their lungs, they sang the ANC's new favourite, 'My President'. When Mbeki arrived, some of Zuma's supporters booed.

There was a 21-gun salute after Zuma took the oath of office. Having made a short speech, the new President then broke with protocol by moving down and singing to the crowds.

Zuma moved uncharacteristically fast in announcing his new Cabinet – in fact he did so the day after his inauguration. It was clear that he and his closest advisers wanted to play, as the Americans might say, a completely new ball game – and Zuma announced an 'extended' Cabinet with 34 ministers and 28 deputy ministers.

First, economy and finance. Trevor Manuel, it seemed, would not fly as Finance Minister; the Communist Party and the trade unions would presumably not have him, though the tension between Manuel and the unions/left is always exaggerated by the media, which loves to have a 'ANC left' versus 'ANC centre' battle raging. So Zuma and his advisers re-organised that cluster of ministries. In something of a master stroke, they brought in the former boss of the Revenue Service, Pravin Gordhan, as the new Finance Minister; made Ebrahim Patel, a former trade unionist with impeccable union credentials, the new Minister of Economic Planning; and appointed Rob Davies, a former member of the Communist Party, as the Minister of Trade and Industry. All would be autonomous, yet each would report – or work with – a new National Planning Commission, under Manuel, and which would in turn work with a department of 'performance monitoring and evaluation' under Collins Chabane. (Both Manuel and Chabane, whose sections fell under the presidency, had the status of ministers.)

What was smart about the new 'economics/finance cluster' was that it kept Manuel in the heart of the government – he was too experienced, and too beloved in international financial circles, to let go – but moving him out of the finance portfolio, thus assuaging, as we have said, the Left; while Gordhan, who had been a key player in the famous Operation Vula and had been so manifestly successful as head of the Revenue Service, could not be so easily criticised by the Left.

Clearly, education was in trouble, so Zuma split it into two new entities, Higher Education and Basic Education, with Blade Nzimande at the helm of Higher Education. Defence went to Lindiwe Sisulu, senior carrier of the Sisulu baton in the ANC, and a former aide of Zuma's. A ministry of Police was created – the rather feeble name 'Safety and Security' having been dropped – with Nathi Mthetwa in the hot seat and Fikilie Mbalula, former head of the Youth League, and architect of the successful election, as deputy. As a return 'gift' for his 'cooperation' at Polokwane (he didn't make any waves), Tokyo Sexwale was given the oddly-named ministry of 'Human Settlements', formerly Sisulu's ministry of Housing. Justice went to Jeff Radebe, who had pretty much laid low and said nuffin' during Mbeki's time but had suddenly come out of the closet as a Zuma man. And Communications went to Siphiwe

Nyanda, a Zuma stalwart and former chief of the Defence Force, who had clashed with Mbeki.

It looked a promising and creative Cabinet and one that might achieve something if it could get going. There was criticism from various quarters that it was an excessively leftist Cabinet and was going to – horror of horrors – move away from Mbeki's macro-economic GEAR to something more beneficial for the majority of South Africans.

But local opposition politicians and analysts were mostly prepared to give Zuma the benefit of their doubts about him and to see what his new government might be able to achieve. Without wishing to overstate the case, they were also, it seemed, slightly shell-shocked by the ANC election victory, by the efficient and speedy way in which Zuma had announced his Cabinet, and by the potential it suggested.

On Wednesday 3 June Zuma made his first State of the Nation address. It was not substantially different from the ANC election manifesto and it was not a detailed speech. But it was reasonably solid, straightforward fare. And, by Thursday mid-morning, when the leaders of the opposition parties stood up in Parliament to reply officially, they had some reasonably interesting things to say.

DA parliamentary leader Athol Trollip warned that Zuma needed to beware of an overly socialist agenda. Patricia de Lille, leader of the Independent Democrats, pointed out that 'without implementation and monitoring, the best plans will come to nothing'. Freedom Front Plus leader Pieter Mulder seemed the most cogent and focused when he pointed out that one of the largest problems bedevilling the body politic was the civil service and he argued that in its present form, and given the way it operated, it wouldn't be able to deliver on Zuma's many promises.

But what was most striking was the immediate response – on the Wednesday, immediately after Zuma spoke – of various opposition politicians, television and radio reporters, talking heads and others. It was remarkably underwhelming. Straight after the address, when radio and television microphones were shoved under their noses, most said something along the lines of: 'Er, nice enough speech, addressed many issues, probably too many. But there was no detail, no detail at all ...'

This was countered by ANC Secretary-General Gwede Mantashe, who appeared to be wandering around the parliamentary precinct like a hyperactive spin doctor, ensuring that the ANC reaction got an airing on every conceivable radio and TV channel. Mantashe pointed out that detail was not the President's business, not in a State of the Nation address anyway; and that, in any case, as pointed out by Zuma, ministers were going to be working out the finer print of the important strategies between then and July.

Even by Wednesday evening, to judge by the statements published in Thursday morning's newspapers, the reactions to Zuma's speech were pretty lacklustre. The Congress of the People said: 'There are parts of the statement no South African can disagree with ... But [the speech] was a missed opportunity to outline a programme of action that can inspire South Africa and mobilise the South African people behind a uniting program to deal with the challenges of the day.' Vacuous stuff, really, and pretty short on detail too.

Athol Trollip was a little better: 'Within this broad agenda, there were positive initiatives and policy proposals. However, while President Zuma did well to cover most areas of concern in general terms, his speech lacked detail and specificity ...' (We have already – or, rather, Mantashe had – dealt with the matter of 'specificity'.)

DA leader Helen Zille's reaction immediately after the address was perhaps the most interesting of all. Even though she expressed concern about the ANC's Orwellian (in her view) move towards a centralised civil service, she was, by her usual standards, almost stunned. She seemed to be struggling to find something to say, and struggling too with having to say that, well, actually she didn't think it too bad a speech at all. Why was this? Why were the opposition politicians and analysts in a state of apparent perplexity about Zuma's speech? Why was damning him with faint praise the best they could do?

There is a two-part answer to my questions. The first part is that Zuma's speech was pretty smart – and this took everyone aback. Zuma covered all the bases for which he would have been lambasted if he had not covered them. He made certain to connect his administration to Nelson Mandela's. He moved seamlessly between the requisite Olympian overview and the personal touch that we mere mortals love – telling school kids to do their homework and teachers to come to class on time. By trying to speak Afrikaans, by not speaking isiZulu (and choosing instead Sesotho and isiXhosa), and via his comments on national unity, he stayed well away from Mbeki's petty-minded, divisive carping. Most importantly – and only the Freedom Front Plus's Pieter Mulder seemed to have picked this up rapidly – he firmly closed the door on the Mbeki-type denialism that South Africans had had their noses rubbed in for a decade. Zuma might have been short on detail. But at least, and at last, HIV/AIDS, crime, the Zimbabwean situation and a host of other ills, from the global recession to unemployment and the state of health care, were dealt with in an adult fashion as realities, and not defensively either.

Why were people apparently unable to recognise these qualities? Why did they not know what to say? The second part of the answer to these questions is that the media and the opposition still did not trust Zuma. There was still a strange air of begrudging disbelief – almost as if they expected Zuma suddenly to stop making a measured and careful presidential speech and to rip off his suit and tie, revealing leopard skins beneath, frothing at the mouth and calling for his machine gun.

He was not likely to do any of those things. He had apparently moved on and was taking his job very seriously.

Monday 17 August marked the man from Nkandla's first 100 days in the proverbial hot seat. Of course the concept is an American thing – in particular, it's an American media thing; as the DA's Trollip said, although the first 100 days in office of a new leader might be a useful tool for identifying some broader patterns, it is not of much help in measuring particulars of leadership or governance.

Thinking on that day of JZ's first 100 days, two disparate and not entirely uplifting images came to my mind. The first was from 20 years previously and it was of the Exxon Valdez, a gigantic oil tanker that spilled about 40 million litres of crude oil into the pristine Prince William

Sound off Alaska. As a result of that spill, a large number of people knew about the huge amount of time and space required to stop and/or turn a supertanker. The second image was of boys at high school opining that 'trying to find out anything from x is like punching a plastic bag full of water'.

Zuma's prospects of success were obviously 'compromised', as Trollip put it, by 15 years of bad management, not to mention the global economic meltdown. That, it seemed to me, was one hell of a supertanker to turn around in 100 days. And then, trying to find a direction for the country, and/or trying to get society 'to retain its shape' (a phrase beloved of today's soccer coaches), was like punching a plastic bag full of water. Economically, these were fluid and shapeless times.

What then was there to say about Zuma's first 100 days? For one thing, he had not been passive. He had created a new Cabinet, set to make big changes. He had also made a number of other appointments. Not all had been welcomed, but at least he had moved ahead. Even a cursory visit to any website dealing with Zuma showed how busy he had been: 'Tutu and Zuma bury hatchet'; 'Zuma's choice of top judge queried'; 'I will make time to visit communities'; and so on.

For another thing, Zuma was big enough to take responsibility and to apologise, on behalf of the ANC, for a variety of shortcomings. So it seemed that at least the Mbeki era of denialism and defensiveness was past.

In brief, Zuma's first 100 days were not looking too bad; it felt as though the supertanker was in the turning circle. The trouble was that what most people on the third-class decks could see was still the same. Clearly, the ship needed to come round a lot faster.

I attended Zuma's inauguration. Given what had happened in the previous 67 years of Zuma's life, this was a remarkable event. Yet I saw my favourite image on television and not at his inauguration.

On 3 June 2009 Zuma was about to make his first State of the Nation address at Parliament. All those important enough to drive into the parliamentary precinct arrived in what is euphemistically referred to as 'a luxury German sedan'. Then a pudgy-looking white bus – presumably a special bullet-proof one, but looking for all the world like one of the 'new' taxis of Russian make – pulled up to the beginning of the red carpet and out stepped President JG Zuma and the three Mrs Zumas: Nompumelelo, Thobeka, and Sizakele. All the wives were gorgeously dressed in bright colours – and, after all the years of innuendo and confusion about Zuma's wives, there was something special about seeing them all out of the closet and accompanying their husband.

Zuma had really arrived and was looking confident and resolute – and one could almost feel the country relax and, as it were, look collectively forward to the future.

CHAPTER 22

January–March 2010

The honeymoon ends

As 2009 wound down, the political opposition, analysts, media, and people in general cut Zuma a lot of slack. The 'marks' given to him and his Cabinet by some newspapers and by the Democratic Alliance (the traditional end-of-year 'report card') were mediocre. Still, there seemed to be a large dollop of goodwill mixed in with the criticism.

Towards the end of November, a highly regarded and unashamedly left-leaning senior foreign correspondent of the *Guardian*, Jonathan Steele, visited South Africa – which he had covered on and off for decades, mostly championing the ANC cause. On 30 December, he published a piece in the *Guardian*,[1] in which he wrote:

With the World Cup nearing, 2010 will be South Africa's year. The self-proclaimed Rainbow Nation will receive a rainbow crowd of visitors, the largest and most diverse group of tourists in its history. The spotlight on the country's progress since apartheid will be more intense than ever. The

World Cup host, President Jacob Zuma, will bring Britain his message of success with a state visit here in March. Eight months in office, he has surprised his critics.

Steele then mentioned some of Zuma's attributes – an ability to listen to others, his recent speech on HIV/AIDS, a 'sharp correction' to Mbeki's 'denialist line'. But, he asked, could Zuma make a difference to the country's social and economic problems? Or – posing the dreaded question – would '2010 be an own goal for the Rainbow Nation?'

Economic growth, Steele pointed out, was projected to fall in 2010; unemployment was 'massive'; and service delivery riots a few months before had demonstrated that black South Africans were increasingly angry. In his view, they had good cause.

Steele did not only read reports: a journalist of the old school, he eschewed the internet and drove off to a township school not far from Johannesburg. There he found that 'each day dozens of pupils have to walk over two hours from the shacks where they live. Class sizes average 50, and the cramped school has no assembly hall or gym. At least the pupils get a meal … but even this vital help is not financed by the government. It comes from private donors.'

The good news, Steele wrote, was that at least jobless people's rage was no longer directed at immigrants, but at officials of the ruling party. The bad news …

The bad news is that the government and the media seem unwilling to engage in serious debate, let alone action [in the case of the government, presumably], on how to supply people with what they need. South Africa's press and blog sites are dominated by rightwing thinking. They regularly headline claims that the government is 'lurching to the left' … South Africa's simplistic economic debate does not even recognise Keynesianism as a legitimate alternative to the failed ANC strategy of the last decade and a half.

'South Africa has made huge strides since its first democratic government in 1994,' Steele concluded. 'But slippage is accelerating and Zuma needs to reverse it soon.'

So, what was going on with the government of the country.? According to Anthony Butler, Professor of Political Studies at Wits University,[2] there had in fact not been much of a honeymoon period from April-May 2009 onwards. Rather, 'the country's problems closed in around [Zuma's] administration almost immediately' in the form of strikes and community protests.

Nonetheless, Zuma's ministerial appointments, especially in the economic sector, were initially greeted as adroit; the Treasury – *the* heart of governance – seemed to maintain its status; and planning and monitoring capabilities under ministers Manuel and Chabane were in any case 'the realization of Mbeki-era plans'. Furthermore, Zuma changed the tone of national politics by allowing free-flowing debate by ministers on corruption, HIV/AIDS, crime and the crisis in the educational system.

But, Butler observed, though the new president might have proclaimed education as a priority and said he wanted to meet every school principal in the land, he showed 'no stomach' for bringing the obstructive teacher unions into line; though he supposedly championed fiscal prudence, he facilitated certain public sector pay settlements that placed government budgets under pressure; and though he encouraged debate over elite enrichment and corruption, no one seemed to believe he would actually allow action against his own allies.[3]

Besides the mainstays of ANC policy – health care, education, crime, rural development, and land reform – Butler looked at the Zuma government through three prisms – 'three key issues [that] have dominated analysis of Zuma's ANC in government'. These were: the supposed shift to the left in ANC economic policy; the touchy issue of corruption and patronage; and whether the new government had made any meaningful 'institutional reforms'.

The great shift to the left. 'Such a shift has simply not occurred and nor does it seem likely to do so,' wrote Butler. Finance Minister Pravin Gordhan's first speech (in 2009) 'explained the constraints on fiscal policy … [and that] the economic environment will no longer allow scope for leftist experimentation or the pouring of national resources into supposedly "strategic" parastatals.' (And Butler wrote his essay *before* Gordhan's February 2010 budget speech, which was an even more constraining one.) In fact, under Zuma there had been a reassertion of economic orthodoxy and a 'significant shift towards social authoritarianism', rather than a shift to the left.[4] 'There is every prospect,' wrote Butler, 'that Zuma will drift right under the influence of his own prejudices [regarding pregnant children, gays, capital punishment, etc] and the need to court the country's socially conservative electorate.' Anyway, it was *'time to accept that the one direction the society is not moving is left.'*[5]

Corruption and patronage. Many people had observed that Zuma's rise had merely changed the composition, not the (ugly) character, of a venal and predatory elite. The SACP, Cosatu and others had argued for a variety of controls: the banning of external directorships, the closing of the revolving doors between public and private sectors, the banning of gifts from companies doing business with the government; and later on, for 'lifestyle audits'. But Zuma had responded, in a Zuma-like fashion, with a series of non-decisions.[6] (And, again, Butler was writing before reports about Siphiwe Nyanda's companies, or the explosion caused in late February 2010 by media revelations of the wealth that seemed to have come the way of Julius Malema via political clout.)

The issue of institutional reform. Zuma's set piece speech for the first three months of his presidency concerned his supposed motivation for increasing government departments and reconfiguring the Cabinet sub-committee (or 'cluster') system — that is, what would be the roles of the new Planning Commission and the new Department of Economic Development relative to the Department of Finance or the Treasury? And the big question was: what was the role of the Finance Minister? In Butler's view, the relationship between the head of government and the Finance Minister is the most important one in any administration. And of course it is one that foreign investors watch with the proverbial eagle's eye — and they wanted above all to know what was happening to Trevor Manuel and what shackles, if any, Pravin Gordhan had on his wrists.

Yet, as far as Butler could tell, 'Zuma has been playing political poker at the expense of Treasury credibility in the middle of a global economic crisis'. If public finances were to be kept on a sustainable path, unpopular decisions must be taken by a government about financial priorities. Government departments cannot help but generate poorly considered and opportunistic expenditure proposals. The private interests of politicians and officials make matters infinitely worse. And ideological arrogance – 'strategic investment', 'industrial policy' – can be used to justify the relaxation of Treasury controls even when a fleecing of the state is a predictable outcome. It is the Treasury that must be the thin line holding off an explosion of wasteful spending – by demanding justification for expenditures.

But, wrote Butler, 'Zuma's team has peddled the idea that the Treasury was becoming a [just another] "normal" department' and, worse, had also brought into the heart of the government a disdain for the 'culture of justification [of expenditures]'. The announcement by the presidency that the Finance Minister would no longer sit on all ministerial cluster committees was, for Butler, ominous. Previously, '[n]o policy proposal was reached without an agreed statement of anticipated financial implications signed off by the Treasury'. This was how it should be. Every ministry and department should be obliged to justify their proposals in the same way. Gordhan 'has set out a balanced plan to bring public expenditure trends under control'.

With regard to institutional reform, 'when resources are scarce and constituencies are hungry ... no Treasury head has the personal power to face down packs of ministers and directors-general in pursuit of public money. Only a president can protect the precious culture of justification ...' However, Butler concluded, there was 'no reason to believe that Zuma respects or even understands this [financial justification] imperative'.[7]

By the end of 2009, Zuma and the ANC were running into other troubles. One was with the ANC's policy of non-racialism. Zuma's Cabinet appointments seemed to make amends for the historical under-representation of leaders from Limpopo, KwaZulu-Natal and Mpumalanga. But when he appointed Gill Marcus as Governor of the Reserve Bank, there was a wail from Duma Gqubule, a writer and commentator on black empowerment. He complained about there being so many 'minority' appointments in the economic/financial portfolios – Manuel, Planning Commission; Gordhan, Finance; Patel, Economic Development; Rob Davies, Trade and Industry; and Barbara Hogan, Public Enterprises. He said it demonstrated a lack of confidence in blacks of African descent. His plaint was picked up by Julius Malema, who complained loudly that non-Africans had been shunned for the top jobs in the finance cluster.[8]

Racial conflicts of this sort continued late into 2009 in extended sagas over the appointment and resignation of Transnet and Eskom senior managers. And when Zuma appointed the KZN MEC for Safety and Security, Bheki Cele, as the new National Police Commissioner, there were denunciations of the 'Zulufication' of the security, intelligence and judicial organs. Nathi Mthethwa had been appointed Police Minister; Siyabonga Cwele, Minister of State Security; Jeff Radebe, Minister of Justice; Vusi Mavimbela, DG of the Presidency; Nkosazana Dlamini-Zuma, Home Affairs; and Siphiwe Nyanda, Communications. Of course most of those appointed by Zuma were those he had worked with in the underground or in ANC intelligence and so were of Zulu or Indian descent.[9] But the concern about Zuma having appointed those closest to him to the justice and security sectors was that a small group of closely associated politicians and officials could manipulate the Police, the Directorate of Priority Crime Investigation, the prosecuting authority, and even the courts.[10]

So, notwithstanding the political bonhomie that seemed to be floating around on the surface[11] towards the end of 2009 and at the start of 2010, observations such as Steele's, or a sober analysis of the ANC under Zuma such as Butler's, reveal that there was – to put it mildly – a lot of work for Zuma to do.

However, 'Jacob Zuma, the polygamous president of South Africa', as one foreign newspaper called him, would not be deflected from matters of the heart and he married his third first lady, Thobeka Madiba, in a traditional Zulu wedding on Monday 4 January 2010.

Overcast skies in Nkandla did not dampen the spirits of guests – dressed in animal skins and African prints – who walked along muddy trails to the Zulu ceremony, known as *udwendwe*. The media were mostly kept away from the proceedings, but buses transporting the guests were seen outside Zuma's house, where three big tents were erected. Several sheep, goats and cows were slaughtered for the wedding feast. During the ceremony, Zuma and Thobeka were presented to society as husband and wife for the first time. With his entourage of men dressed in leopard skins, Zuma sang and danced (a sudden fall did not seem to be part of a traditional Zulu ceremony, though bystanders rushed to assure the media that this had been an 'intentional' part of the dance). Madiba was then presented with her own entourage of young Zulu men and women. The Madiba family presented Zuma with a chest of drawers as a wedding gift.

Zuma had paid *ilobolo* (bride price) to the family of Madiba, described as a socialite from Durban, and she had accompanied him to official events for some time. Unknown to most people, she had insisted on living at his Forest Town home from the beginning of 2009, which neither Nompumelelo nor Sizakele had had the temerity to do, but the wedding had been postponed until January 2010 because of Zuma's work commitments.

Zuma spent Christmas at his homestead in Nkandla. According to newspaper reports, he relaxed by shooting birds with a slingshot, drinking *umqombothi* (traditional beer) – though Zuma does not drink, so one wondered about the newspaper reports – and taking part in a chess tournament. It was also reported in the *Mail & Guardian* that a R65-million expansion of the Nkandla residence was under way, with new houses being built to accommodate the three first ladies.

At the end of January, Zuma went to snow-covered Davos, Switzerland, where the world's financial and economic movers and shakers (the World Economic Forum) get together every year to impress one another with their erudition, charm, and so forth. Zuma entertained and charmed many of the attendees, especially the press, by defending polygamy. But, not surprisingly, he had his mind on football, the upcoming soccer World

Cup to be precise, and on some of the other matters that had raised their heads at home. As he told the gathered dignitaries:

[Besides the soccer tournament] 2010 is also an important year for us, because we will be marking the 20th anniversary of the release of Nelson Mandela from prison, which kick-started dramatic political change. We have achieved a lot since that dramatic day of February 11, 1990. South Africa has performed admirably in the economic, political and social spheres. This includes the political transition to a democratic State, the subsequent strengthening of South Africa's democratic institutions, as well as economic growth. We have built a resilient economy which has been able to survive the global economic crisis, and which is actually beginning to show signs of recovery.

We have not been spared job losses, but we have put plans in place, working together as business, labour and government to ensure that the recovery becomes faster and inclusive. We are making significant improvements in key areas of domestic policy, such as health, education, as well as visible, vigorous and effective crime prevention. The country's transport, energy, telecommunications and social infrastructure are being up graded and expanded. This is contributing to economic development in the midst of a global recession, while improving conditions for investment. This investment has been made possible by the judicious management of the country's finances. It is thanks to this approach that we have been able to respond to the first recession of the democratic era without placing undue strain on our public borrowing requirements.

On 22 January 2010, the cover of Johannesburg's *Financial Mail* read as follows: 'Nine months into the Jacob Zuma administration and we're drowning in policies and statements of intent … it's time for the president to take charge and deliver.' But Zuma didn't have much of a chance to oblige – for he took an unexpected tumble that made his slip at Nkandla seem positively balletic.

I might have anticipated something of the kind, since back in April 2009 – on the evening of the day on which acting NDPP Mokotedi

Mpshe had dropped charges against him – I had been at Zuma's Forest Town home, chatting to him and Ranjeni Munusamy, when Zuma had excused himself to take a phone call on his mobile. But he had not moved very far from us and we were able to hear him whispering – well, he was hardly whispering – proverbial sweet nothings to someone on the other end. I *assumed* it was Thobeka to whom Zuma was speaking, which in retrospect was foolish of me, since if I think back now, she was in the house that evening. But, as I say, the focus that night was on the dropping of the charges against Zuma, not on romance or related matters …

And on a beautiful Sunday morning, 31 January 2010, when Zuma was still away on his Davos trip, the *Sunday Times* announced that he had 'fathered a child with the daughter of powerful soccer administrator and long-time friend Irvin Khoza'. It turned out that the child, a girl, Thandekile Matina Zuma, born on 8 October 2009, had been begotten in about January 2009.

The beloved country went a little bit gaga. At first I thought it was the usual national song-and-dance about Zuma being a polygamist and about him not having used a condom for extra-marital activities (shades of the 2006 rape trial). And it was indeed partially about both. The *Sowetan* newspaper wrote on 1 February 2010:

In a different democracy, the latest scandal to hit President Jacob Zuma would have been enough for him to stand down as head of state. In such democracies, the head of state is an embodiment of the values and aspiration of that nation. Going by that principle, what does it say about our national value system and aspirations when the head of state blatantly preaches one message and practices [sic] a different one?

It is now clear that none of the lofty statements made on Aids Day, a mere two months ago, came from the heart. None of his exhortation that 'be responsible and do not expose yourself to risks' or telling the youth that 'each individual must take responsibility for protection against HIV. The future belongs to you' was mere mouthing of a speech prepared by aides.

But beyond HIV and AIDS, there are unspoken and unwritten

expectations we have of leaders. We cannot therefore honestly say that there is nothing to be concerned about with the latest revelations that he is a father of a four-month old child born to neither a woman he married a few weeks ago nor to the woman he is engaged to be married to.

There is certainly nothing illegal that Zuma is guilty of. We would however be failing in our civic duty if we did not ask if this is the kind of behaviour that is commensurate with our expectations of our head of state.

On 3 February Zuma confirmed that the child was his, and that he had paid *inhlawulo*, acknowledging paternity. He protested against the publishing of the child's name, saying it was illegal exploitation of the child. He denied that the incident had relevance to the government's AIDS programme, and appealed for privacy. Then on 6 February, he announced that he 'deeply regretted the pain that he caused to his family, the ANC, the alliance and South Africans in general'.

Zuma might have been a little chilled by the relative silence of his allies and supporters. Previously, when he had been criticised by the public or by any person or 'formations' outside the alliance, the voices raised in his defence had been cacophonous, sometimes even threatening. But during the first 10 days of February, the response from the ANC and Cosatu was at best lukewarm. On 5 February, the ANC acknowledged the widespread disapproval by saying that the experience had 'taught us many valuable lessons', and that they had listened to the people. Cosatu passed no judgement but hoped that 'it' would be 'a matter on Zuma's conscience'.

Some sources said that Zuma had promised 'the elders' of the alliance that, following his 2006 rape trial, there would be no further embarrassment of a sexual nature. Members of the government and the alliance were clearly deeply annoyed and embarrassed. In private, senior party members said the latest in a long line of sexual scandals was the 'last straw'. It suddenly became obvious that Zuma had become politically vulnerable (ironically, it was just before this time that Jeff Radebe had told me during an informal meeting that 'Zuma is starting, I think, to enjoy himself as president').

No matter what the politicians said publicly, it was not – among them – about 'ethical' issues, it was not about infidelity or polygamy or women's rights, it was not even about using condoms. (Of course the media had to take a 'moral' line.) The nub of the matter seemed to be that the tripartite alliance was coming unstuck. It seemed suddenly clear that Zuma had been trying to appease everyone – all the various factions vying for power at the top of the ANC and squabbling with one another.

But the trouble with trying to appease everyone is that you please no one. You can't keep all your promises to everyone; and 'everyone' tends to grow irritated if, when they are at each other's throats, or in some cases just trying to do a good job, it turns out that Zuma has mostly been focused on having a good time – that he has been cavorting in his PJs when he ought to have been working.[12] JZ's relationship with Ms K, and their baby, were not going to go away in a hurry. Leaving the morality and righteousness to one side (for the media), it could prove to be one of the most expensive *political* gaffes Zuma had ever made.

The exposure of his relationship with Sonono Khoza and child out of wedlock was a 'watershed' moment for Zuma. He had been speared by the fickle finger of his own brand of conciliatory politics; the response to his peccadillo served to demonstrate just how exasperated all his 'supporters' were feeling because no one had in hand yet what he or she really wanted.

Who were these groups? There was the venal group: those playing the political game for the sake of the meat and gravy in the top trough and who wanted *inter alia* to plunder the SA Reserve Bank and the mines. Then there were the lefties, including Cosatu, and the SACP (whose chairman is Gwede Mantashe, the ANC Secretary-General), who were annoyed that some vaguely sensible people, e.g., Manuel, Gordhan, had been left in charge of the economy and that the attack dog Julius Malema had been allowed to continue running up and down the yard without a leash. Others included the young *nudniks* from the ANC Youth League, who had gone to war with lefties such as Jeremy Cronin, and also with Barbara Hogan and Mantashe; the economic apparatchiks, e.g. Manuel and Chabane, who seemed frozen in some kind of no-man's land because Zuma was not allowing them the scope they wanted; and the politicians who were out for themselves and to further 'capitalism', e.g. Tokyo Sexwale and Cyril Ramaphosa. And don't forget the group from KwaZulu-Natal, with Zweli Mkhize at the helm, which had decided that the day of the Zulu had clearly come to pass and that the other groups needed to stand back. But the four main pit bulls – a term coined by veteran journalist Stanley Uys – fighting to control the power of the presidency and therefore Zuma, were certainly the ANC, Cosatu, SACP and the Youth League.

It was a chastened man who presented his second State of the Nation address on 14 February. Zuma was visibly not himself; he presented badly, and it was not a particularly good speech. He was clearly feeling as besieged and vulnerable as he had in the days before April 2009 when he had corruption charges hanging over his head. It was only the Finance Minister's efficient, no-nonsense speech – not enjoyed by the Left – that averted a parliamentary debacle.

In the view of politics writer Karima Brown of *Business Day* (22 February), what was driving the ANC apart was principally 'economic policy fissures' – which, with 'the public-relations nightmare caused by the messy private life of SA's first citizen, threaten[ed] to unravel the brittle coalition that brought President Jacob Zuma to power, setting the scene for a very fluid political landscape…. [Zuma's] leadership is being tested, and it remains to be seen if he can hold the centre.'

In Brown's view, trade union leaders were very angry with Gordhan's Budget speech (which came later but was nonetheless close in time to the *Sunday Times* story about Zuma's love child). They raged that the road to job creation and to doing things differently on the economic front had been hammered out in the Polokwane resolutions of December 2007, and that post-Polokwane they had been included in running the country. But then pro-business interests in the ANC, fearful of losing their patronage networks, had come out against the Left and warned Zuma to beware of the 'communist influence' – especially after Cosatu and the SACP launched their anti-corruption drive aimed at 'tenderpreneurs', politically connected businessmen who live off government tenders.

Hence the anti-Mantashe campaign, with the Youth League arguing that as SACP chairman, he was 'conflicted' and had to be removed from his Secretary-Generalship to restore the ANC 'back to basics'.

Zuma's world *was* cracking up all around him, as one headline writer put it. But was it really a 'crisis', as some commentators wrote?

No, it was not a crisis (yet); but it was certainly a serious state of affairs – and, alas, the seeds of what happened had always been there. They were foreshadowed in nearly every chapter of this biography. It is clear from the first 67 years of his life that Zuma might fail to grasp the nettle of good behaviour and discipline – that he would not, to use an old cliché, keep his eye on the ball at all times.

And of course the 'crisis' had been on the cards ever since the motley crew that swept Zuma to power started jeering at the old fogeys on the podium in Polokwane in December 2007. Some people hoped such a situation wouldn't come to pass. But it had been, it seems, only a matter of time before the squabbling started between various factions (the 'businessmen' vs. the Lefties, those represented by Malema vs. Mantashe, the Zulus vs. the rest, and so on), with JZ doing mostly nothing about it. It was only a matter of time before he was nabbed making babies with someone who was not his wife (though the making of the love child predated his inauguration) when he ought to have been busy giving the various factions stripes on their collective behinds. It was only a matter of time before a big mouth such as Malema, or a facsimile thereof, started frightening foreign investors with his shrill squeaks about nationalisation. How long would it take before a Zuma government started looking rickety? Things went along pretty well until the love child – which was when everyone realised that they were irritated with JZ because few of them were getting what they thought was their due.

By the beginning of March, there was gossip that at the ANC general council meeting in September, a motion of no confidence will be tabled against Zuma. This, it seemed clear, was idle prattle. There was no way that the ANC would 'recall' the President and throw themselves and the country into turmoil – if only because there is no candidate just now who would be accepted by all the factions and could discipline them. Besides, the soccer World Cup, due to start in June, and for which the ANC and the whole of South Africa were going to present a united front, was doubtless going to help save Zuma's bacon. (Constitutionally, Zuma's five-year term as President only expires in 2012.)

Still, Butler was doubtless correct[13] in his prediction that the months immediately following the tournament are destined to be filled with power struggles. In Butler's view, 'the ANC in KwaZulu-Natal has its own plans for the succession and cannot afford to see Zuma depart early. … The president will stagger onwards to the ANC's National General Council in Durban in September, where KwaZulu-Natal provincial barons will presumably arrange a regional and ethnic show of force.'

At the beginning of March, Zuma went to see Queen Elizabeth II. It was a visit that had of course been pre-arranged a long time before and it was in fact about trading between the two countries as much as about the British government recognising the new president of England's long-time consort, trading partner and home from home for many of its people at the tip of Africa.

Zuma stayed at Buckingham Palace for two nights – his companion was wife number three, Thobeka Madiba – and he joined, as the phrase goes, an illustrious group of heads of state from across the world by becoming an honorary Knight Grand Cross of the Order of the Bath. The name of this order of chivalry is derived from the medieval ceremony for creating a knight, which involved bathing as a symbol of purification. So of course a number of jokes did the rounds about Zuma's notorious advocacy of a shower for cleansing purposes. US presidents Ronald Reagan and George Bush, as well as France's Nicolas Sarkozy, were made knights, but Zimbabwe's Robert Mugabe was stripped of his knighthood in 2008.

Zuma responded to his knighthood by bestowing the Order of the Companion of OR Tambo on the Queen, the highest South African honour for a foreign national. It was quite something to see the one-time herd boy from Nkandla dressed up in his finery, reviewing the Queen's Life Guards and hobnobbing at the palace, and there were some glorious photographs on show. Zuma was quite funny about the experience, remarking that staying at the palace did make it quite difficult, for example, to pop out to buy some sweets from the corner shop.

However, despite the achievements of the trade discussions and meetings between Zuma and his English counterpart, Gordon Brown, it seemed, at least from a South African point of view, that the limelight had been stolen by the plethora of media attacks. The leading one came on 2 March from the *Daily Mail* (which specialises – and, as far as Zuma is concerned – has always specialised in such scurrilous attacks). The headline ran: 'Jacob Zuma is a sex-obsessed bigot with four wives and 35 children. So why is Britain fawning over this vile buffoon?'

Zuma responded publicly – some argued that, diplomatically, this was a mistake on his part – by suggesting that the English were somewhat barbaric to criticise him for his polygamy, number of children, and so on, but the damage was done – or, at any rate, a slew of moralising articles appeared in the South African press. And of course the Brits, as well as most of the local press, had (as was usually the case with Zuma) missed the point. They were playing the man and not the ball – the severe strains in the tripartite alliance, unemployment, the lack of service delivery, dysfunctional legal, medical and educational systems, and the distasteful behaviour of Julius Malema.

Some journalists did not miss the point, however. On 1 March the *Financial Times*'s world news editor, Alec Russell (author of the very fine *After Mandela: the Battle for the Soul of South Africa* and a former FT correspondent in South Africa), noted that it was a mistake to be diverted by 'cartoonish caricature' and that it was always too easy to underestimate Zuma.

When [Zuma] came to London just over two years ago, at the height of his battle for the ANC leadership, only a few bankers would see him. He roamed central London one evening all but barred even from the South African high commission in Trafalgar Square. Now he returns as the most powerful man in sub-Saharan Africa to all the pomp that Britain can offer.

But, Russell argued in a thoughtful article, after a year's honeymoon, western investors were starting to fret. They wanted Zuma to go beyond equivocating and mollifying various factions, as well as ANC bigwigs with a 'voracity for business deals', and to be a tough leader. 'The country needs him to face down the [anti-free enterprise] radicals by recapturing the resolve that brought him into the anti-apartheid struggle. Or, when his presidency ends, he risks being remembered only in parody – as a part-time populist with a roving eye.'

It is indeed always a mistake to underestimate Jacob G Zuma's resilience and the depth of his support, as many have discovered. On 12 March he delivered a 'political overview' to the NEC of the ANC covering the past and future months – and the top members of the NEC had met with the SACP leadership the day before. It looked very much as though Zuma, Mantashe *et al* had called for calm and also told everyone to behave themselves. Suddenly it seemed as though the press and the commentators had been growing over-excited and exaggerating Zuma's woes, as usual.

But the events of February and March did underline that Zuma's honeymoon period in the presidency was indeed over and that life as an up-and-down rollercoaster ride continues for the man from Nkandla. It seems clear that he needs to grasp the rudder of state firmly and to start leading from the front; and that he needs to do his best to change a lifetime of living on the edge. Or are such ideas merely wishful thinking? We shall see.

APPENDIX I

The Pedro Document

As I noted in the new preface, David Beresford and Paul Trewhela criticised the first edition of this biography for the way in which I had failed to deal with Zuma's membership of the SA Communist Party and my failure to 'finger' Zuma sufficiently for alleged complicity in the death of Thami Zulu.

On 22 February 2009, Beresford wrote in the (Johannesburg) *Sunday Times* that the book failed to mention 'that Zuma was a life-long [sic] communist'. Beresford said that the omission was curious because Zuma had himself mentioned his party membership in an autobiographical piece he wrote for the ANC on 2 May 1985 under the alias 'Pedro'. Beresford continued: 'Zuma seems to have been anxious not to have this detail widely known. Nor is membership of the SA Communist Party mentioned in Zuma's government and ANC biographies.'

Firstly, I did mention (on page 56 of the first edition) that Zuma had quit the Communist party in 1990 – ergo, that he had obviously been a member. But let me not be defensively punctilious. Beresford's point is that I did not make much, if anything, of Zuma's membership of the party – an issue requiring examination – and that this was a failing.

Second, Beresford's assertion that I somehow connived with Zuma (or the ANC or whomever) to downplay Zuma's membership of the SACP – hence my avoidance of the 'Pedro' document – was incorrect for a simple reason. When a woman asked Dr Samuel Johnson how he came, in his famous dictionary, to define 'pastern' wrongly as 'the knee of a horse', he replied, 'Ignorance, madam, pure ignorance.' In short, I did not know of the Pedro autobiography.

As for Trewhela, he wrote on 15 February 2009 on Politicsweb that 'Zuma has never, to my knowledge, accounted publicly in any way for his role – whatever that might have been – in the arrest, imprisonment, interrogation, release and subsequent murder by poisoning while in close confinement of Thami Zulu.' (Actually, according to Trewhela's own version, TZ was not in 'close confinement' when he was poisoned, but be that as it may.)

Trewhela also wrote that: '[Gordin] makes no further inquiry … into the nature or duration of Zuma's membership of the SACP, surely a significant matter concerning a probable future President of the Republic ….' In addition, Trewhela also complained, in another article, that I had not used the 'Pedro' document.

Let me deal first with Zuma's membership of the SA Communist Party. Beresford and Trewhela were correct. I ought to have dealt in greater detail with Zuma's membership of the SACP and there is no excuse, as the saying goes, for my not having 'found' the 'Pedro' document and interviewed Zuma about it.

However, having said that, although Trewhela and Beresford find some sort of frightening or at least large significance in Zuma having joined the SACP, in having trained in the former Soviet Union, and having remained in the party till 1990, I do not.[1]

I think that Zuma joined the SACP because that was what young revolutionaries did then, the SACP being the one party that had remained resolutely opposed to any kind of compromise with apartheid and because the major source of assistance for the ANC stemmed from communist-aligned countries. Help or aid for the ANC was not exactly forthcoming from the CIA or MI5. It was almost *de rigueur* for people such as Zuma to join the party then.

To be sure, Zuma wrote in his 'Pedro' document that he '[h]ad political ed. [sic] at the beginning of 1960's [sic]. Began with Labour Theory and General politics with emphasis on our struggle, and late[r] I was put in study group where we were taught M/L [Marxist-Leninist] theory.'

So what? I mean no disrespect to Zuma when I say that, from what I know of him, he is as about as familiar with Marxist-Leninist theory as I am with quantum mechanics. Of course Zuma was *for* the working class – he came from the working class – he was the prototypical 'peasant'! – and the SACP undoubtedly provided a home from home for him in many ways.[2] But when Zuma and Blade Nzimande (the General Secretary of the SACP and the Minister of Higher Education) meet of an evening, I do not think they discuss Marxism and/or plot revolution. As Chris McGreal, the *Guardian*'s former Africa correspondent, succinctly put it in April last year: 'Although once a member of South Africa's Communist party, [Zuma] comes across today as almost shorn of ideology'.[3]

I do not mean, let me stress, to diminish Zuma's commitment to the Struggle, including an engagement with its ideology, part of which would presumably have been a version or versions of Marxist-Leninism. Clearly, if he had not been committed, he would not have chosen the life he did. But I do think his membership of the SACP should be kept in perspective and I think, if you will pardon the cliché, that times change and people with them. If anything, exposure to communism would, in my opinion, have benefited Zuma by broadening his outlook and moving him away from the African nationalism of some of his contemporaries.

I also do not mean, let me also stress, to demean Trewhela's anguish; I believe I understand what he is trying to convey when he quotes Leszek Kolakowski's words that Marxism was 'the greatest fantasy of our century ... [which] began in a Promethean humanism and culminated in the monstrous tyranny of Stalin'.[4] However, I am not certain of the connection he makes 'between the men of power who led Russia onto the rocks', on the one hand, and Zuma and present and past members of the SACP on the other. Certainly, we don't yet have a 'monstrous tyranny' holding sway in South Africa. To suggest that we do, as Trewhela does in his homage to Kolakowski, is just irresponsible hyperbole.

After Zuma's return to South Africa in the early 1990s, I think that the most apposite words applicable to Zuma's life and concerns are not to be found in the works of Karl Marx or Herbert Marcuse. They are, rather, ones attributed to Woody Guthrie, the legendary American folk-singer. 'I ain't a communist necessarily, but I been in the red all my life.'

Let me deal, secondly, with Zuma's alleged role in the death of TZ.

The murder of TZ was appalling and horrifying. Equally appalling was the manner in which his parents were dealt with and that there was no 'closure' for them – that no one appears to know who killed their son and why. But that is unfortunately, tragically, the point. Trewhela and others can bang on till the cows come home to Nkandla about Zuma's alleged complicity in the murder of Thami Zulu (and they probably will) – *but no one really knows*. Or, if anyone does, he or she is not saying anything. Zuma, of course, might know something about it – so Trewhela and Beresford would suggest. But, if he does, he is not saying either.

In short, all I could do in this biography was to set down the known facts, so ably provided by Trewhela and the other reports, and let those facts speak for themselves.

Finally, the Pedro document. I have taken the text from Trewhela's article of 21 April 2009 on Politicsweb. Trewhela in turn took the Pedro document from the magazine *Molotov Cocktail*, edited by James Sanders and RS Roberts, which is now defunct. As far as I know, the document is a legitimate one. Zuma has not commented on it; but he has not denied its legitimacy or that he wrote it.

On 2 May 1985 (with a further addition in 1989), Jacob Zuma, alias 'Pedro', sat down to write his story for the SACP. This Zuma 'autobiography' says he joined the party (or 'the family' as it is euphemistically referred to) at the age of 21, in 1963.

There are some gaps in the document: there is no reference, for example, to any training he might have received as head of intelligence in *iMbokodo* ('the grindstone', the nickname among ANC members for Zuma's department).

Terms such as 'labour theory' (the labour theory of value) and 'M/L theory' (Marxist-Leninist theory) refer to standard training in the Marxist thought structure of the SACP. 'PMC' refers to the Political Military Committee in the command structures of Umkhonto we-Sizwe.

The text as it appears here, taken from *Molotov Cocktail*,[5] is published as Zuma wrote it in English, not his first language.

THE AUTOBIOGRAPHY OF JACOB ZUMA, AS WRITTEN FOR THE SACP

(1) Family name: Pedro.

(2) Age: 46.

(3) Sex: Male.

(4) Race: African.

(5) Level of Education: Self educated up to Junior Certificate.

(6) Class background: worker.

(7) Political or special education:

Had political ed. at the beginning of 1960's. Began with Labour Theory and General politics with emphasis on our struggle, and later I was put in study group where we were taught M/L theory. In 1978 I received military training in the Soviet Union.

(8) Date of joining the family: 1963.

Deployment in the fraternal org.: NAT (Head of Int.).

QUESTIONNAIRE (1989, Apr.)

Name: Pedro.

Age: 46 years.

Sex: Male.

Educational Level: Form III.

Political or Military Education: yes.

Past Occupation: Clerk/ordinary worker.

Present Occupation: NAT full-time functionary.

When did you join the Party: 1962.

Pedro's biography – 2/5/85

I was born in 1942 at Nkandla area. This is the area where my father (Gcinamazwi Zuma) comes from. It is situated at the centre of Zululand.

I'm the first born from my father's second wife. My father's first wife had 7 children. Of these, 3 were boys and 4 were girls. From my mother we are 5. Of these, 3 are boys and 2 are girls.

My mother (Nokubhekisisa, Betty Zuma) comes from Maphumulo area. This area is situated between Stenger and Kranskop.

Our father died whilst we were still very young, particularly we from the second wife. I in fact never saw him. The death of my father resulted in my mother leaving the Nkandla area for Maphumulo area. At Maphumulo she started working as a domestic worker.

Shortly after this she went to Durban where she continued to work as a domestic worker. Her going to Durban from after us. But she of course did not get a better pay.

The death of my father and the fact that my mother was not in control of the situation in many ways, led to my being not in a position to go to school. Though she wanted me to receive education, but it became impossible. During this time I was not staying in one place; I was moving from one area to another, but spent more time with her in Durban.

Because of the situation I started working at my early age at this time. Not yet registered, but as a small boy working in tea-rooms, shops and doing domestic work. This was an attempt to help my mother who was pulling hard in life.

It was at my early age that I started to feel the problems of life. They manifested themselves through the family situation. During mid 50's I started to see public meeting organized by the ANC. At the same time my brother was is the first from my father's first wife was an active member of the ANC. He used to talk a lot at home about the ANC and the struggle. At this time I got influenced politically.

In 1958 I joined the ANC and the ANC Youth League. But at this time my activities consisted mainly of my attending public meetings of the organizations. In 1959 I joined SACTU. Again here I was not very active at the beginning. I was mainly attending public meeting.

However, between 1958 & 59 together with my brother who was in the ANC long before me we organized and influenced an anti-pass campaign in the Noxamalala district falling under the Nkandla area. We took advantage of the fact that the chief of the Noxamalala area was our clan brother (Chief Vusumbango Zuma). As a result of the trust and confidence this chief had my brother and myself, I ended up attending many meetings called by him to receive and discuss his reports on what the government was saying on the Bantustan policy. In these meeting was specifically able to influence the chief and his people.

In 1961 became involved in the discussions organized by SACTU in the Durban area. In the heart of these discussions was the labour theory. And other generalized political discussions. These discussions were one of the most important developments in the Durban area.

In 1962 I was introduced to a political study group in the area where I stayed, i.e. Cato Manor (Mkhumbane). During the same year (1962) I was recruited into MK. In 1963 I was recruited into the SACP. But this time the MK activities took up a lot of time, as a result there was very little done regarding the party work. It was not long after this that I got arrested in June 1963. I was arrested in the Transvaal on my way out of the country for military training. I was then detained under 90 days detention law. And later sentenced to 10 years, which I spent on Robben Island prison.

Whilst on the Island prison I served in a number of responsible positions in the ANC structures. These include being a group leader at different times and in different cells (places where we were staying), being PRO (Public Relations Officer), cell leader and being the chairman of the political committee, which was one of the responsibilities I had towards the end of my sentence, until I left the Island.

Soon after the arrival on the Island, I was among the few Cdes from Natal who initiated some political study groups. With time these study groups became a serious bone of contention; and resulted in a serious ideological battle.

Regarding the party situation whilst I was on the Island there was nothing much that happened. I approached one party Cde (H.T. Gwala) with an aim to find as to what was supposed to be the position. I explained my position to him which I assumed he knew on the basis that he also came from the same province. His response was that he was going to consult.

Indeed after some time he came back and said that the whole question of how the party was going to function was being considered. And that at that time he was still observing the developments around the political study group which has been mentioned above.

When the ideological problem arose of which I was also deeply involved, I was told that the situation had become even more difficult. And that it had become more necessary that some of us should not be exposed. I appreciated this position because the problem had indeed affected to some degree the party Cdes in terms of the approach to some questions relating to our struggle in general.

In 1974 shortly after my release from prison I was among the few cdes who took the initiative of reviving the ANC underground in the Natal area. In this process again cde H.T. Gwala played an important role. He was one of the most experienced leader in the area, and one of the most politically clear and ready to work at any level of the movement. In the Durban area I was the main person coordinating our underground activities.

During this time cde Gwala's idea was that after establishing a firm ANC underground throughout Natal, the process of further re-organising the party will have to be vigorously worked on. This was again interrupted by the fact that an arrest which included cde Gwala took place. This very arrest led to my leaving the country in December 1975 to Swaziland.

When I came to Swaziland I immediately joint the collective that was in charge of the internal work. Early in 1976 I secretly entered into the country to re-establish contact with some cdes in the Durban area and its surroundings. This was done without problems. Few months thereafter I was detained by the Swazi police with two other cdes. This arrest was precipitated by the arrest and murder of cde Joseph (Mkhuzi) Mdluli in Durban Lamontville. We were then deported to Mocambique where I immediately started working until now at the time of writing this biography.

In the year 1977 I was co-opted into the national executive committee (NEC) of the ANC. And since then I have been given various responsibilities by the ANC. But all have been mainly related to the internal work. These included serving in the Natal military machinery, ordinance department, deputy chief representative in Maputo, member of the political committee responsible for T.Q., secretary of the senior organ, and later member of the PMC & P.H.Q.

In 1978 I received my training in the Soviet Union. The training took a period of 3 months. It was called leadership course. In 1977 I was also incorporated in the party. Before my incorporation I was asked to give an account of my participation in the party which I did. And part of what I said is reflected herein above. And I have participated in the work of the other party in this area since then up to now.

by Pedro.

The Jacob Zuma Family: Wives, Fiancées, Friends and Children

Jacob Zuma's first wife was **Gertrude Sizakele Khumalo** (MaKhumalo), whom he met in 1959 and married shortly after his release from prison in 1973. She lives at his home at Nkandla, KwaZulu-Natal. They have no children.

JZ's second wife was **Kate Mantsho** (or Mantsholo), a Mozambican. They married in 1976; she committed suicide on 8 December 2000. Their five children are: Mxolisi Saady (b. 1980); twins Duduzile and Duduzane (b. 1984); Phumzile (b. 1988); and Vusi (b. 1993).

JZ had a relationship with **Minah Shongwe**, probably in 1976. They have a son, Edward Mziwoxolo Zuma (b. 1977).

JZ's third wife was **Nkosazana Dlamini-Zuma** (presently the Minister of Home Affairs; formerly Minister of Foreign Affairs and of Health. They married in 1984 (though this date is not certain) and divorced in June 1998. Their four children are: Gugulethu Zuma (Gugu) (b. 1984);

Msholozi Zuma (b. 1985); Nokuthula (Thuli) (b. 1988); and Thutukile (Thuti) (b.1990).

JZ's fourth wife is **Nompumelelo Ntuli** (MaNtuli), who was born in 1975 and comes from KwaMaphumulo near Stanger. They married in January 2008. They have two children: Thandisiwe (b. 2002) and Nqobile (b. 2006).

JZ's fifth wife is **Thobeka Stacey Madiba** (born Mabhija, her mother's name) from Umlazi. They married in January 2010. They have one child: Sinqobile (b. 2007). She has another of Zuma's out-of-wedlock children, Bridget, living with her.

There are thus three first ladies: Sizakele Khumalo, Nompumelelo Ntuli, and Thobeka Madiba.

JZ has two daughters, born 18 January 1998 and 19 September 2002 respectively, with Pietermaritzburg businesswoman **Priscilla Nonkululeko Mhlongo**.

JZ is affianced to – he has apparently paid *ilobolo* or 'a bride price' for – **Gloria Bongekile Ngema**, with whom he allegedly has a three-year-old son, Sinqumo, and whose family is understood to have presented *umbondo* (marriage gifts in response to *ilobolo*) to the Zuma family.

JZ also apparently became affianced to Swazi **Princess Sebentile Dlamini** in 2002, though it is unclear whether this match is still on.

On 31 January 2010 it was revealed in the *Sunday Times* – and eventually confirmed by Zuma – that some time at the end of September 2009, he had a child – a daughter, Thandekile Matina Zuma – with **Sonono Khoza**, daughter of well-known soccer administrator, Irvin Khoza.

This is a total of 18 children, though a number of 20 has been bandied about. There are unverified reports that Zuma has a daughter named Jabulile with a woman from Richard's Bay; and a son named Jabu, as well as twins, with a woman from Johannesburg. This would bring the total to 22. But neither Zuma nor the presidency has said a word about the last four children. It is possible that the four unnamed children have been confused by Zuma children-counters with Gloria Ngema's child and/or with the two children of Priscilla Nonkululeko Mhlongo.

On 17 March 2010, the Minister in the Presidency for Performance Monitoring and Evaluation, Collins Chabane, replied to a DA parliamentary question that the cost of the spousal support office would increase by more than R7,5-million under President Jacob Zuma. Since 2005, there has been a near-fourfold increase in the cost associated with the President's spousal support office. The figure stood at R4,5-million in 2005/06, at R8-million in 2008/09, and would now stand at R15,6-million.[1]

Operation Vula

Jacob Zuma might charm many people and smile at most, but this does not necessarily mean that he trusts many. The reasons for his attitude seem obvious. Zuma comes from the ANC underground, from the smoke-and-mirrors and often murderous world of intelligence and counter-intelligence (he was appointed the ANC's chief of intelligence and counter-intelligence in about 1988 in Lusaka); and the causes and conduct of his legal saga during the last nine years have often been, to put it mildly, Byzantine.

Who then does Zuma trust? In an article titled 'Operation Vula gurus return' – on 24 May 2009, in the *Sunday Independent* – senior journalist Janet Smith wrote: 'The appointments of Siphiwe Nyanda and Pravin Gordhan as ministers in President Jacob Zuma's cabinet have resuscitated memories of one of the ANC's most secret plans. And the possible revival of Operation Vula in the political imagination may be further inspired by the rumoured return to centre stage of one of the party's most controversial and colourful figures: Moe Shaik.'

Smith was largely correct in pointing out – as one of the Vula members recently said to me – 'Hey, it looks like the boys and girls from Vula are back!'

Yet Zuma's relationship with Operation Vula and its members was not always as clear-cut as is thought – not, at any rate, in the view of Vula's commander, Mac Maharaj. More importantly, a look at the backgrounds of those whom Zuma trusts – those whom he has, to put it another way, placed in key positions – reveals that in addition to his old intelligence contacts, he also favours some old friends in the Natal underground and on Robben Island.

Operation Vula was, as Padraig O'Malley puts it in his biography of Mac Maharaj, 'an ambitious project aiming to locate senior leaders, including members of the NEC and the PMC [politico-military council of the ANC], within South Africa to take overall charge of the struggle. Vula was under the direct command of Oliver Tambo (OR), assisted by Joe Slovo (JS). ... It was [also] to set up the infrastructure for the people's war ...'[1]

Aware of the porousness of the ANC underground structures, Maharaj's primary goal was to keep Vula ultra-secret. No one besides Tambo, Slovo and (initially) Zuma knew about Vula, or was supposed to know about it. Maharaj was the commander, 'Gebuza' Nyanda was his deputy, and the operation was set in motion in 1986.

As Maharaj tells the story, or has O'Malley tell the story, when Vula was first mooted, none of the top ANC leadership besides him was too keen on going into South Africa. O'Malley suggests that, when push came to shove, most, more or less comfortably ensconced in Lusaka, preferred 'an armchair revolution'. According to O'Malley, however, Zuma was initially asked by Tambo to go into South Africa as part of Vula and was keen to do so. But at just that time he was appointed ANC chief of intelligence, so he couldn't. Unfortunately, O'Malley's interview with Zuma on which this information is based is embargoed till 2030.

Vula, which really only got going in mid-1988, did not manage to organise a 'people's war'. By then the people's war was, in any case, more in the hands of the internal Mass Democratic Movement than the ANC. But Vula did succeed in setting up an excellent and vital communications conduit from inside South Africa to ANC headquarters, a channel which included Nelson Mandela in Pollsmoor Prison. Vula's operatives also successfully brought a great deal of arms and war matériel into South Africa.

Among those who were actually part of Operation Vula were Nyanda, now Minister of Communications in Zuma's government; Gordhan, formerly Commissioner of SARS and now Minister of Finance; Charles Nqakula, formerly Minister of Safety and Security in Thabo Mbeki's government and now one of Zuma's emissaries to Zimbabwe (as is Maharaj); Ivan Pillay, who went to SARS with Gordhan and is still apparently there; Raymond Lala, who became head of SAPS intelligence and is still a top cop; Solly Shoke, who is chief of the army; and Ronnie Kasrils, who ended his political career as Minister for Intelligence in the Mbeki government.

Another member of Vula and the underground struggle in KZN (a 'Natalian'), although he is not mentioned by Maharaj and was clearly a lower-level cadre, was Nathi Mthethwa, now the Minister of Police.

The Shaik brothers — Moe, Yunis, and Schabir — were not strictly speaking part of Vula. And yet in a sense they were. Moe and Yunis (along with Jayendra Naidoo) ran their own operation, the MJK unit. Their baby was Operation Bible, their successful infiltration of the security police data bases, communications and some personnel; and they reported directly (though often via Pillay) to Zuma. Maharaj reported to Tambo and Slovo.

But, as Moe Shaik explains, 'Though we were structurally not integrated — as much for everyone's protection as for any other reason — we provided all kinds of support, not the least of which was intelligence support, to Vula high command. And Zuma knew about this and supported it. There was definitely a symbiotic relationship between Vula and MJK.'

Schabir Shaik handled a number of financial arrangements for Vula — getting foreign currency into South Africa and having it changed on the black market – but for his own protection was never told on precisely whose behalf he was doing this work.

Vula unravelled completely in July 1990 with the arrests by the security police of Nyanda and then Maharaj. The ANC was then in negotiations with the government of FW de Klerk, and the uncovering of Vula was, to put it mildly, highly embarrassing for the ANC leadership.

Ironically, in the end the main repercussion was positive. The uncovering of Vula resulted in the ANC agreeing on a unilateral cessation of the armed struggle ('The Pretoria Minute'). Mandela was also able to finesse the situation with De Klerk and the charges against those involved were ultimately dropped.

But Maharaj was furious – and remained so. He felt that he and his people had been betrayed by the attitude of the leaders – Mbeki, Slovo, and Zuma – because, when Vula was publicly uncovered, they looked down their noses at the operation, as though the cat had brought in something particularly unsavoury. Worse, they left him and others languishing in custody for weeks. Maharaj was especially angry with Zuma – who, Maharaj has said in O'Malley's book, 'was fully attuned to [Vula's] operations'.

Moe Shaik, it must be said, disagrees with Maharaj: 'Let's face it, the leadership was in the middle of difficult negotiations. The discovery of Vula could have derailed those negotiations. In fact it was pretty close. …Yes, Zuma was "in the Mbeki camp" then, but, besides that, he had to play it very smart. How could he, one of the main negotiators, run around saying, "Well, yeah, gee, we've been running this successful underground operation for two or three years and have successfully penetrated your security police and have imported arms into the country – and, what's more, we've continued doing it while talking peace and love to you"?'

Shaik also argues that on Mbeki's watch those from Vula, and those connected with the operation, were indeed 'punished' – with the exceptions of Kasrils, who had his 'own' relationship with Mbeki, and Nqakula, who was not from the Natal sphere of operations anyway. (Nqakula was the Cape commander.)

'Gordhan was never made a minister,' says Shaik. 'Nyanda had to leave his job as SANDF chief. But Zuma has brought them to the fore. So, notwithstanding views to the contrary, Zuma was appreciative of Vula.'

Zuma was indeed appreciative of Vula, but there are others, who were not part of Vula, whom the new President has placed in key positions. They are mostly former MK operatives – and either took part in the 'Natal' sphere of operations or were involved in intelligence and counter-intelligence.

The new Minister of Justice and Constitutional Development is Jeff Radebe, who has of course been in government for a while. Interestingly, although not much is made of it in his official CVs, Radebe applied for amnesty from the TRC, whose report reads as follows:

During the period 1991 to 1994 [Radebe was among three] senior members of the ANC who held office in the Southern Natal region of the ANC. The 1st Applicant [Jeff Radebe] was, during 1991, the deputy chairman and thereafter the chairman of the ANC Regional Executive Committee...

The ANC at its Consultative Conference which was held towards the end of 1990 resolved, *inter alia*, to assist communities which were subjected to political violence in the setting up of SDUs [ANC self-defence units in the townships, involved in combating mainly the IFP]. The 1st Applicant, in his capacity as deputy chairperson and later as chairperson of the ANC in Southern Natal received instructions from the late Chris Hani, who was the Chief of Staff and Deputy Commander of MK, to facilitate the implementation of the ANC national decision to set up SDUs in the Southern Natal region. He was thereafter contacted by MK headquarters personnel, including Mr Ronnie Kasrils, and arrangements were made for the distribution of weapons for use by SDUs in the region. ... He was, however, throughout the period under consideration, fully aware of and involved in the illegal procurement and distribution of arms to SDUs in the region.

The new Minister of Defence and Military Veterans is Lindiwe Sisulu, who has also been in the government for some time – Deputy Minister of Home Affairs, Minister of Housing – and comes from a famous struggle family. It also so happens that in 1990, after the unbanning of the ANC and other political organisations, Sisulu returned to South Africa and resumed work as personal assistant to one Jacob Zuma, and was thereafter an administrator in the ANC's Department of Intelligence and Security.

The Minister of State Security is Dr Siyabonga Cwele. The KwaZulu-Natal-born medical doctor has been a passionate Zuma supporter and was formerly the chairman of the Joint Standing Committee on Intelligence. In this position, he chastised the Scorpions about the controversial Browse Mole Report that damned Zuma for various things. Not especially highlighted in his CV is that from 1984 to 1990 he operated in 'ANC underground structures' – in KZN.

Minister in the Presidency (Performance Monitoring and Evaluation and Administration) Collins Chabane joined the ANC in 1980, did his military training in Angola and went underground from 1981. He was arrested in 1984 and served a term on Robben Island. He was singled out in a speech given by Zuma at the funeral of Peter Mokaba: 'In the Northern Transvaal among comrades identified to do this specific work was the late Comrade James "Mawelawela". It was he who identified Peter Mokaba and others for recruitment. These included among others Collins Chabane. This is the group that I have called the "warriors".'

Zuma went on to say that he was well-acquainted with this group of young men who had returned to South Africa.

The new Director-General of the President's Office – replacing the Reverend Frank Chikane – is Vusi Mavimbela. He left South Africa to join the ANC in 1976, became DG of the National Intelligence Agency until 2004 and was political adviser to Mbeki when the latter was Deputy President between 1994 and 1998. Mavimbela also served as Mbeki's special adviser on intelligence and security. From 1993 to 1994, Mavimbela was chief of ANC intelligence and security in KZN and prior to that worked in intelligence circles in Lusaka – under the command of guess-who?

Zuma's new parliamentary counsellor is Ayanda Dlodlo, an MP, member of the NEC, and – this was a key post in the run-up to Polokwane – secretary-general of the Umkhonto weSizwe Military Veterans' Association. And, after Polokwane, she led meetings with the head of the NPA, Mokotedi Mpshe, on behalf of the veterans, to convince Mpshe to drop the corruption charges against Zuma. In the middle of her matric exams in 1980, Dlodlo heard the police were looking for her, so she fled into exile. There she did military training in Angola and intelligence training in the Soviet Union – under the aegis of the ANC's intelligence and counter-intelligence department.

One other alumnus of Zuma's long career in the ANC is his old Robben Island cell-mate, Ebrahim Ismail 'Ibi' Ebrahim. He is now one of the two deputy ministers in the new Ministry of International Relations and Cooperation.

In conclusion, the 'Vula boys and girls' are indeed back in town. But Zuma's people – those to whom the key jobs of finance, justice, defence, police, monitoring government performance, and presidency positions, have gone – are not only from Vula. To have been active in the underground struggle in KZN, Zuma's stamping ground, and secondly, to have been connected with ANC intelligence and counter-intelligence, are also important qualifications.

Notes and Sources

PREFACE TO THE SECOND EDITION

1 See Allister Sparks's eloquent article, 'Obama, Zuma and a question of leadership,' *Business Day*, 31 March 2010.

PREFACE AND ACKNOWLEDGEMENTS

1 Eric Hobsbawm, *Interesting Times: A Twentieth-Century Life* (London: Abacus, 2003, p xiii).
2 Ian Kershaw, *Hitler: 1889-1936: Hubris* (London: Penguin, 1998, p xxi).
3 Bernard Crick, *George Orwell: A Life* (Harmondsworth: Penguin, 1982, p 30).
4 Letter to Arnold Zweig from S Freud, 31 May 1936, in *Freud: A Life for Our Time* by Peter Gay (New York: WW Norton, 1988, pp xv–xvi).
5 Isaac Deutscher, *The Prophet Armed: Trotsky: 1879-1921* (Oxford: Oxford University Press, 1970 (1954), p vii).
6 Samuel Johnson, *Lives of the English Poets*, selected and edited by Robert Montagu (London: The Folio Society, 1965, p 7).
7 'Out in Chicago Humboldt became one of my significant dead', Saul Bellow, *Humboldt's Gift* (Martin Secker & Warburg, 1975, p 9).

CHAPTER 1

1 As historian John Laband describes it in *Rope of Sand* (Johannesburg: Jonathan Ball Publishers, 1995).
2 Leonard Thompson, *A History of South Africa* (Johannesburg: Jonathan Ball Publishers, 2007 (2001), pp 82-83).
3 Dan Wylie, *Myth of Iron: Shaka in History* (Pietermaritzburg: University of KwaZulu-Natal Press, 2006, p xiii).
4 Leonard Thompson, 'The Subjection of the African Chiefdoms, 1870–1898',

pp 245-85, in *The Oxford History of South Africa*, Vol. 2, ed. Monica Wilson and Leonard Thompson (London: Oxford University Press, 1971, p 266).

5 Jeff Guy, *The Maphumulo Uprising* (Pietermaritzburg: University of KwaZulu-Natal Press, 2005, p 1).

6 Interviewed by Bongani Mthethwa of the *Sunday Times*, 19 June 2005. http://www.sundaytimes.co.za/articles/article.aspx?ID=ST6A126104

7 In the Helen Suzman Foundation magazine. www.hsf.org.za/publications/kwazb/issue-11/interview-with-jacob-zuma

8 Chief Albert Luthuli: 'Who will deny that 30 years of my life have been spent knocking in vain, patiently, moderately and modestly at a closed and barred door? What have been the fruits of my many years of moderation? Has there been any reciprocal tolerance or moderation from the government be it Nationalist or United Party? No! On the contrary, the past 30 years have seen the greatest number of laws restricting our rights and progress until today we have reached a stage where we have almost no rights at all.'

9 Since the days of Willem Adriaan van der Stel, the 'naughty' governor of the Cape, the control of liquor supply has been a major issue in South Africa – and no less so in the early conurbations and townships. *Cf.* 'Randlords and Rotgut 1886–1903', pp 44–102, in *Studies in the Social and Economic History of the Witwatersrand 1886–1914, Vol 1: New Babylon*, by Charles van Onselen (Johannesburg: Ravan, 1982); *Rooiyard: A Sociological Survey of an Urban Native Slum Yard* by Ellen Hellmann (Cape Town: Oxford University Press, 1948); and 'The Illicit Sector', pp 267-98, by Jeremy Gordin, in *Conspiracy of Giants: The South African Liquor Industry* by Michael Fridjhon and Andy Murray (Johannesburg: Divaris Stein Publishers, 1986).

CHAPTER 2

1 The name given by Luli Callinicos (based on a Langston Hughes poem) to that period during which numbers of people fled the country, mainly to undergo military training: in *Oliver Tambo: Beyond the Engeli Mountains* (Cape Town: David Philip, 2004, pp 303-20).

2 Greg Arde interviewed Ngcobo and Mzimela in *The Mercury* of 28 November 2007.

3 Luli Callinicos, *Oliver Tambo: Beyond the Engeli Mountains* (Cape Town: David Philip, p 249).

4 *Ibid*, p 290.

5 *Ibid*, p 305.

CHAPTER 3

1 For information on life in jail on Robben Island, I have also consulted Tom Lodge, *Mandela: A Critical Life* (Oxford: Oxford University Press, 2006); Mac Maharaj and Ahmed Kathrada, *Mandela: The Authorised Portrait* (Johannnesburg: Wild Dog Press, 2006); Nelson Mandela, *Long Walk to Freedom: The Autobiography of Nelson Mandela* (London: Abacus, 1994); and Padraig O'Malley, *Shades of Difference: Mac*

Maharaj and the Struggle for South Africa (New York: Viking, 2007).

2 Chuck Korr and Marvin Close, *More than Just a Game: Soccer v Apartheid* (London: Collins, 2008, pp 97-98).

3 Padraig O'Malley, *Shades of Difference: Mac Maharaj and the Struggle for South Africa* (New York: Viking, 2007, p155).

CHAPTER 4

1 James Joyce, *A Portrait of the Artist as a Young Man*: 'I will not serve that in which I no longer believe, whether it call itself my home, my fatherland or my church: and I will try to express myself in some mode of life or art as freely as I can, and as wholly as I can, using for my defence the only arms I allow myself to use ... silence, exile, and cunning.'

2 Mark Gevisser, *Thabo Mbeki: The Dream Deferred* (Johannesburg: Jonathan Ball Publishers, 2007, p 343).

3 *Ibid*, pp 314-17.

4 *Ibid*, p 316.

5 *Ibid*, p 345.

6 *Ibid*, pp 341-2.

7 *Ibid*.

8 *Ibid*, p 351.

9 There is of course the other side of the coin to be considered. 'The record is not all negative. By establishing an external network and a guerrilla army, the ANC reaped a number of significant advantages. The bases abroad established the movement and a core of its leadership to survive the onslaught and to provide a continuity of principle. It was able to establish a central organization that [had] gathered about it new leaders who [cleaved] to the principles of a colour-blind democracy.' Allister Sparks, *The Mind of South Africa: The Story of the Rise and Fall of Apartheid* (Cape Town and Johannesburg: Jonathan Ball Publishers, 2003 (1990), p 279).

10 See Volume 2, chapters 2 and 3, of the *Truth and Reconciliation Commission of South Africa Report* (1998); Vlakplaas commander Eugene de Kock's autobiography (as told to Jeremy Gordin), *A Long Night's Damage: Working for the Apartheid State* (Johannesburg: Contra Press, 1998); and chapter 8 of Stephen Ellis's and Tsepo Sechaba's *Comrades Against Apartheid: The ANC & the South African Communist Party in Exile* (London: James Currey, 1992).

11 Padraig O'Malley, *Shades of Difference: Mac Maharaj and the Struggle for South Africa* (New York: Viking, 2007, pp 218-9).

12 Mark Gevisser, *Thabo Mbeki: The Dream Deferred* (Johannesburg: Jonathan Ball Publishers, 2007, pp 348-9).

13 Padraig O'Malley, *Shades of Difference: Mac Maharaj and the Struggle for South Africa* (New York: Viking, 2007, pp 250 and 250n).

14 Stephen Ellis & Tsepo Sechaba, *Comrades Against Apartheid: The ANC & the South African Communist Party in Exile* (London: James Currey, 1992, p 168).

15 TRC Report, Volume 2, p 366. See also 'Appendices to the African National Congress Policy Statement to the Truth & Reconciliation Commission, August 1996', produced by the ANC for the TRC hearings; and 'The Dilemma of Albie Sachs: ANC constitutionalism and the death of Thami Zulu', pp 34–53, by Paul Trewhela, in *Searchlight South Africa: A Marxist Journal of Southern African Studies*, Vol 3, No 3 (no 11), October 1993, eds Baruch Hirson, Paul Trewhela, London.

16 See 'Commission Report on Death of Thami Zulu, 1989', no page numbers, in 'Appendices to the African National Congress Policy Statement to the Truth & Reconciliation Commission, August 1996', produced by the ANC for the TRC hearings.

17 Padraig O'Malley, *Shades of Difference: Mac Maharaj and the Struggle for South Africa* (New York: Viking, 2007, pp 427-8).

18 See Eugene de Kock (with Jeremy Gordin), *A Long Night's Damage: Working for the Apartheid State* (Johannesburg: Contra Press, 1998); Peter Harris, *In a Different Time: The Inside Story of the Delmas Four* (Cape Town: Umuzi, 2008); Jacques Pauw, *Dances with Devils: A Journalist's Search for Truth* (Cape Town: Zebra Press, 2006), and author's interview with Katzew.

19 Eugene de Kock, *A Long Night's Damage: Working for the Apartheid State*, (Johannesburg: Contra Press, 1998, p 20).

20 Peter Harris, *In a Different Time: The Inside Story of the Delmas Four* (Cape Town: Umuzi, 2008, pp 234-5).

21 *Ibid*, pp 252-60.

22 *Ibid*.

23 Luli Callinicos, *Oliver Tambo: Beyond the Engeli Mountains* (Cape Town: David Philip, 2004, pp 572-610).

24 Allister Sparks, *Tomorrow is Another Country: The Inside Story of South Africa's Negotiated Revolution* (Johannesburg: Struik, 1994, pp 81-86).

CHAPTER 5

1 Patti Waldmeir, *Anatomy of a Miracle: The End of Apartheid and the Birth of the New South Africa* (New York: Norton & Co, 1997, p 159).

2 Allister Sparks, *Tomorrow is Another Country: The Inside Story of South Africa's Negotiated Revolution* (Johannesburg: Struik, 1994, p 122).

3 Padraig O'Malley, *Shades of Difference: Mac Maharaj and the Struggle for South Africa* (New York: Viking, 2007, p 387n).

4 Such as Allister Sparks' *Tomorrow is Another Country*; Patti Waldmeir's *Anatomy of a Miracle*; Jacques Pauw's *Into the Heart of Darkness*; Vlakplaas commander Eugene de Kock's *A Long Night's Damage: Working for the Apartheid State*.

5 Interview with the author, 1998.

6 Nicholas Haysom, *Mabangalala: The Rise of Right-Wing Vigilantes in South Africa*. Occasional Paper No 10, Centre for Applied Legal Studies (CALS), University of the Witwatersrand (Johannesburg: CALS, 1986, pp 80-84).

7 Patti Waldmeir, *Anatomy of a Miracle: The End of Apartheid and the Birth of the New*

South Africa (New York: Norton & Co, 1997, p 171).

8 *Ibid*, p 172.

9 William Mervin Gumede, *Thabo Mbeki and the Battle for the Soul of the ANC* (Cape Town: Zebra, 2007).

10 Mark Gevisser, *Thabo Mbeki: The Dream Deferred* (Johannesburg: Jonathan Ball Publishers, 2007, p 600).

11 *Ibid*, p 605.

CHAPTER 6

1 Mark Gevisser, *Thabo Mbeki: The Dream Deferred* (Johannesburg: Jonathan Ball Publishers, 2007, pp 632-33).

2 Interview with the author on the day of the ANC election victory.

3 Anthony Butler, *Cyril Ramaphosa* (Johannesburg: Jacana Media p 319).

4 *Ibid*, pp 315-16.

5 Padraig O'Malley, *Shades of Difference: Mac Maharaj and the Struggle for South Africa* (New York: Viking, 2007, p 264).

6 William Mervin Gumede, *Thabo Mbeki and the Battle for the Soul of the ANC* (Cape Town: Zebra, 2007, p 312).

7 Mark Gevisser, *Thabo Mbeki: The Dream Deferred* (Johannesburg: Jonathan Ball Publishers, 2007, p xxxvii).

8 *Ibid.*

9 *Ibid*, p 648.

CHAPTER 7

1 Paul Holden, *The Arms Deal in Your Pocket*. (Johannesburg: Jonathan Ball Publishers, 2008, pp 283-315).

CHAPTER 8

1 Padraig O'Malley, *Shades of Difference: Mac Maharaj and the Struggle for South Africa* (New York: Viking, 2007, p 414-423).

2 *Ibid.*

CHAPTER 9

1 Paul Holden, *The Arms Deal in Your Pocket* (Johannesburg: Jonathan Ball Publishers, 2008).

2 *Ibid*, pp 147-48.

3 *Ibid*, pp 159-60.

4 *Ibid*, p 108.

5 *Ibid,* p 163.

6 *Ibid*, p 164.

CHAPTER 12

1 http://amadlandawonye.wikispaces.com/2007
2 *Ibid.*

CHAPTER 14

1 John Barth, *The Floating Opera* (Harmondsworth: Penguin, (1956) 1970).

CHAPTER 15

1 Richard Calland in his *Anatomy of South Africa,* William Mervin Gumede in a
   new chapter, 'The Battle for Succession', of his book, *Thabo Mbeki and the Battle for
   The Soul of the ANC,* and Anthony Butler in *Cyril Ramaphosa* argued cogently why
   Zuma would or should not be elected ANC president.
2 Ronald Suresh Roberts, *Fit To Govern: The Native Intelligence of Thabo Mbeki*
   (Johannesburg: STE Publishers, 2007, p 23).
3 Mondli Makhanya, 'When a funeral is desecrated by fisticuffs, you know it's war out
   there', *Sunday Times*, 28 October 2007.

CHAPTER 16

1 I have not named the correspondent, who does not live in South Africa, because
   Manuel has told his biographer Pippa Green that he was 'not surprised' Zuma won
   at Polokwane. See excerpt from *Choice not Fate, the Life and Times of Trevor Manuel*
   in *The Star*, 2nd edition, 31 October 2008, p 11.
2 Alan Paton, *Cry, the Beloved Country* (London: Jonathan Cape, 1948, p 175).

CHAPTER 17

1 Isaac Deutscher, *The Prophet Armed: Trotsky, 1879-1921* (London: Oxford University
   Press, (1954) 1970, p v).
2 Patrick Laurence, in *Focus, Journal of the Helen Suzman Foundation*, September 2008.
3 Veteran media researcher Jos Kuper on the Jenny Crwys-Williams programme,
   Radio 702, 22 July 2008.

CHAPTER 19

1 Anthony Butler, *Cyril Ramaphosa* (Johannesburg: Jacana Media, p xi).
2 http://www.dailymail.co.uk/news/article-503311.
3 Mac Maharaj and Ahmed Kathrada, *Mandela: The Authorised Portrait* (Johannesburg:
   Wild Dog Press, 2006, pp 172-73).
4 Mark Gevisser, *Thabo Mbeki: The Dream Deferred* (Johannesburg: Jonathan Ball
   Publishers, 2007, p 635); see also Gavin Evans, *Dancing Shoes is Dead: A Tale of
   Fighting Men in South Africa* (London: Doubleday, 2002).

5 Gavin Evans, 'The two faces of Mokaba', *Mail & Guardian*, 14 June 2002.
6 Padraig O'Malley, *Shades of Difference: Mac Maharaj and the Struggle for South Africa* (New York: Viking, 2007, p 427n).

CHAPTER 20

1 '… ek trap in jou spoor/ soos 'n goeie hond', 'Ballade van die Bose', in *Oh wide and sad land: Afrikaans poetry of NP van Wyk Louw*, translated by Adam Small (Cape Town: Maskew Miller, 1975, p 60).
2 And the 'full' story about this matter has apparently not been told: it is Myburgh's belief that the plagiarism was committed not by Mpshe but by someone else (in fact the whole judgment was put together by someone else), a legal person working in the government, who has since become fairly notorious, but whose name cannot be published here because his involvement has not yet been proven.

CHAPTER 21

1 The first half of this chapter is built on 'Zunami! The Context of the 2009 Election' by Roger Southall (Professor of Sociology at Wits University), pp 1-22, and 'The ANC's National Election Campaign of 2009: Siyanqoba!' by Anthony Butler (Professor of Political Studies at Wits), pp 65-83, both from *Zunami!: The 2009 South African Elections*, edited by Roger Southall and John Daniel (Johannesburg: Jacana Media and the Konrad Adenauer Foundation, 2009).
2 Southall, pp 4-5.
3 *Ibid*, p 7.
4 *Ibid*, pp 9-22.
5 *Ibid*, pp 11-12.
6 *Ibid*, pp 20-1.
7 Butler, p 67.
8 *Ibid*, pp 71-2.
9 *Ibid*, pp 77-8.
10 *Ibid*, p 79.
11 *Ibid*, pp 79-80.

CHAPTER 22

1 Jonathan Steele, 'Why 2010 could be an own goal for the Rainbow Nation', http://www.guardian.co.uk/commentisfree/2009/dec/30/zuma-failing-black-south-africa. Accessed 4 January 2010.
2 Anthony Butler, 'The ANC under Jacob Zuma', p 11, (first) draft, unpublished paper intended for publication in *New South African Review* (NSAR), edited by Roger Southall and John Daniel, in mid-2010; dated 18 November 2009.
3 *Ibid*, p 12.
4 *Ibid*.

5 My emphasis. So much, by the way, for the cries of some commentators that the ANC is descending into a Marxist/Communist pit of iniquity. But perhaps I give them too little credit. Perhaps they mean a Stalinist pit ('social authoritarianism') – about which they might unfortunately be more accurate than one would like them to be.

6 Butler, p 12.

7 *Ibid*, pp 13-14.

8 *Ibid*, p 15.

9 *See* Appendix on Operation Vula.

10 Butler, p 16.

11 There was, however, not much bonhomie among a number of political commentators. From the middle of 2009, James Myburgh and veteran journalist Stanley Uys (in the UK) were writing very trenchant and concerned analyses and criticism of the new government on Politicsweb.co.za, as was Butler in *Business Day*.

12 It emerged on 15 March, courtesy of Sapa, that diplomatic gifts bestowed on the president included blue pyjamas from Italian Prime Minister Silvio Berlusconi, who also gave Zuma two bathrobes, two sets of bed sheets, two jackets, two pairs of sunglasses, two leather bags and a tie in July 2009 when Italy hosted the G8 summit.

13 *Business Day*, 1 March 2010.

APPENDIX ONE: THE PEDRO DOCUMENT

1 I have read Trewhela's book, *Inside Quatro: Uncovering the exile history of the ANC and Swapo* (Johannesburg: Jacana, 2009), especially the essay, 'The problem of Communism in Southern Africa'. And I have also read of Rian Malan's qualms about communism: 'Report from Planet Mbeki', in *Resident Alien* (Johannesburg: Jonathan Ball Publishers, 2009). I think these books, along with Anthea Jeffery's *People's War: New Light on the Struggle for South Africa* (Johannesburg: Jonathan Ball Publishers, 2009), form an important part of our history precisely because they do *not* take an ANC line.

2 Ebrahim 'Ibi' Ebrahim, Zuma's comrade on Robben Island, and now the Deputy Minister for Foreign Affairs, actually said (not unkindly, but descriptively) when we were discussing JZ's level of literacy on the Island: 'The man was a peasant, after all, a real peasant from a village.'

3 Chris McGreal, 'The Rainbow nation brought low,' reviewing *inter alia* Alec Russell's very fine book, *After Mandela: The Battle for the Soul of South Africa* (London: Hutchinson, 2009), Guardian website, 19 April 2009.

4 Trewhela, 'The ANC: Fifteen Wasted Years,' *Inside Quatro*, pp.132-4.

5 *Molotov Cocktail*, issue number 2, July 2007, pp 27-8.

APPENDIX 2: THE JACOB ZUMA FAMILY: WIVES, FIANCÉES, FRIENDS AND CHILDREN

1 The question on presidential spousal support was submitted by the DA on 11 February 2010 (question no. 17) and the reply given on 16 March 2010. Source: Politicsweb.co.za.

APPENDIX 3: OPERATION VULA

1 Padraig O'Malley, 2007, *Shades of Difference: Mac Maharaj and the Struggle for South Africa* (Penguin, London, p 244).

Index